SAMURAI WIDOW

CARROLL & GRAF

JUDITH JACKLIN BELUSHI

SAMURAI WIDOW

Carroll & Graf Publishers, Inc.
New York

B - BEL

First Carroll & Graf edition 1990

Carroll & Graf Publishers, Inc
260 Fifth Avenue
New York, NY 10001

Library of Congress Cataloging-in-Publication Data

Belushi, Judith Jacklin.
    Samurai widow / Judith Jacklin Belushi.—1st Carroll & Graf ed.
        p.   cm.
    ISBN 0-88184-575-2 : $21.95
    1. Belushi, John. 2. Belushi, Judith Jacklin. 3. Comedians—
—United States—Biography. 4. Wives—United States—Biography.
5. Artists—United States—Biography. I. Title.
PN2287.B423B44   1990
792.7'028'092—dc20
[B]   90-33998
                                                               CIP

Photo section designed by Judith Jacklin.

All photos are from the Belushi photo collection. In the event of any
question arising as to the use of any material, the author, while expressing regret for any inadvertent error, will be happy to make the necessary
correction.

Manufactured in the United States of America

DEDICATION

To Victor, for awakening my heart and offering a second chance.

AUTHOR'S NOTE

Many people have helped with this book: with much needed encouragement, understanding and patience; with research, typing and endless copying; with editing and business advice; with heartfelt praises and loving criticism; with help on the home front. My family has been especially important, without their support, I would not have pursued this goal. I resist listing individuals, as many (but not all!) would be a repetition of those whose names fill my book. But each contributor's part was gratefully accepted and sincerely appreciated.

I take one exception to make a personal thanks, in loving memory, to Agnes Belushi, "Mom." Her unswerving belief in me, her pride in my work, her happiness for my good fortune in life, will forever be an inspiration.

What we call the beginning is often the end.
And to make our end is to make a beginning.
The end is where we start from.

T.S. Eliot

SAMURAI WIDOW

CARROLL & GRAF

INTRODUCTION

In 1978 John Belushi was at the height of his profession. He was the star of the country's top money-making movie, *Animal House,* on its way to becoming the top money-making comedy of all time. He was a cast member of "Saturday Night Live," the number one late-night television show, and he had released his first music album with his band, the Blues Brothers. On January 24, 1979, John's thirtieth birthday, the album became number one on the charts. No other performer has ever held all three top positions simultaneously.

John was an easily recognizable star. It wasn't just his face; people seemed to recognize his body, gestures, and walk. His grace defied his portly build and he seemed much taller than five feet nine. People reacted to John. Heads turned, people pointed, smiled, yelled hello, came up to him. He was a larger-than-life kind of personality, yet one felt he was approachable. He had an amazing variety of fans. Walking down the street with John you felt you were with an old-style people's politician. His boundless energy and infectious enthusiasm seemed to draw people to him. They wanted an autograph, a moment of his time, some contact, a slap on the back, a handshake, a kiss for the ladies. I think John typified the American Dream to people: the son of an immigrant risen to fame and fortune on guts, talent, and hard work. But his work looked like fun, and everyone was included in his fun. His was the gift of laughter and people loved him for it.

I loved John Belushi, too, but long before he was a star. John was my first love from the time we met in high school. John was my husband.

This is not a book about John, however—although he is an integral part of it—but a book about healing, my healing.

1

John's death in 1982 is its catalyst, and who he was explains some of the situations I found myself in at the time of his death.

People often talk about the "overnight fame" which came to John after *Animal House*. It didn't feel all that fast. By the time he graduated high school, John was committed to his dream to be a movie actor and worked in the business for ten years before his first movie role. This transition was a period of growth, filled with struggles, disappointments, and successes. During the fifteen years we shared our lives, I helped John pursue his dream, letting it become our dream. I wanted to be an artist, and I pursued that as well, but John's work quickly became the first priority. His struggles, his disappointments, his successes—these too became mine.

I didn't realize how intertwined our lives had grown until long after John's death. I was a teen of the sixties and thought I had maintained an independence that my mother's generation had not. John and I lived together for five years before we were married, I used my maiden name professionally, I made certain my name was on credit cards and contracts. But these external acts did not stop the internal integration. Maybe this happened because we were so young when we became involved that we didn't have a full sense of ourselves as individuals before we merged our lives, and therefore developed a common ego of sorts, an intense interdependency. I suppose this happens to some extent in any long relationship. At any rate, John's death meant not only the loss of my loved one, but also the death of a part of me. The grieving that followed, although perhaps more complicated due to our history, I believe is basically universal; or at least it was that notion which inspired me to write about this overwhelming transition.

What I've attempted to capture on these pages is my emotional progression and subsequent evolution during the first seven years after my husband's death. I wrote in stages, sometimes setting the book aside for up to a year to allow more time to pass. I would like to stress that my stories are based on my memory and my viewpoint and interpretation of incidents. I have tried to stay in the time frame of which I write and not allow hindsight to interfere with what I'm describing. Sometimes this was difficult to do, as there are many issues I see differently now than when they occurred. But that progression, that chronicling of events and reactions, is the heart of my story.

After John's death I began keeping extensive journals, accumulating twenty-four in as many months. The excerpts in the book are about eighty-five percent as originally written. There were times when something was in such shorthand as to be unclear to anyone but me, and so I rewrote it. And occasionally I rewrote something to make it less awkward, or to fill a gap. There are also a few inclusions which are actually from an audio tape. My objective, however, was to remain as true to the original diaries as I could.

I began this process because I felt it would be helpful to me and I hoped that, ultimately, it would be helpful to others. The result is a memoir of my journey through a troubled time, toward . . . well, toward now. It was a journey I didn't want to take, down a road I didn't want to travel, with a destination I could not have imagined.

Chapter 1

OUT OF CONTROL

FRIDAY, MARCH 5, 1982

I'd been thirty for over a year. That was how I liked to think of it. After all, turning thirty was a milestone, so why not hold on to it? I was lamenting that I had tonsillitis, a kid's ailment, not respectable for a woman my age. The fever had broken, but the doctor said I should take it easy over the weekend. God, I hated having tonsils. I'd had a lot of throat problems in my mid-twenties, and asked the doctor if I should have them removed. He said it was a "stage," I'd get over it. I thought I had, so why was it back now? Stress, no doubt. I expected my husband, John, to return from California that night and we had some serious issues to discuss. My mind began to race. He was abusing cocaine again and that interfered with everything in our life, it threatened everything. . . . Relax, relax, no need to go over that now, I told myself. I turned on the TV and stretched out on the couch to rest. It was late afternoon.

I heard the door open downstairs and wondered who it was, as a number of friends could let themselves in with the combination lock. "Judy!" It was John's partner, Dan Aykroyd. There was an unfamiliar urgency in his voice.

"I'm upstairs in the living room!"

Danny took the stairs several at a time and lunged into the room. He looked startled; or was it stunned? He started to say something, but stopped and just stood there, running his hand over the top of his head, not so much to push the hair off his face as to grab hold of his thoughts. He breathed deeply. "I . . . I don't know how to tell you this," he stammered. "I don't know what to say . . ."

4

Something awful had happened to John. It was there in the way Danny stood, the expression on his face, the way he struggled with his words. My mind flooded with images that drew me to my feet. I saw a car crash. A plane crash. John unconscious and fighting for his life. "Danny, what is it?" I moved to grab him and shake it out. "Has John been hurt?"

"No, honey." His voice was soft. He slowly shook his head in disbelief. "He's dead."

There was an unexpected force in those words. They hit my chest like water from a fire hose, pushing me back several steps. "No!" I cried out, grabbing my head and shutting my eyes, squeezing my eyes, as if I could shut Danny out and make what he said go away.

"We always knew something like this would happen." Danny talked through his tears now, but his voice seemed deep and mechanical. He was pacing. I couldn't catch everything he was saying. "When Bill went to get John at noon he found him—he was already dead."

I was in a deep haze. Motionless. Weightless. Bill? Bill? . . . Oh yes, John's physical trainer, Bill Wallace . . . I heard something about a syringe and heroin being found in the room. No, I could not believe this. This is not real. I mustn't listen to this. I felt myself moving through space and realized I was running across the room. What am I doing? I thought. What is going on? I don't feel anything. Shouldn't I be crying?

I threw myself on the couch to cry, but the tears didn't flow. Unable to stop my motion, I rolled off the couch and onto the floor. Danny was still talking, still pacing, and he sounded so far away. I stood up, went over and hugged him for grounding. He felt cold and stiff, I felt cold and stiff; nothing was normal. I backed away and sat in a large chair at the far end of the room, waiting. Just waiting for a feeling I could recognize.

Within moments, there was a loud knock on the upstairs door. I looked up to see Michael Klenfner, a six-foot, three-hundred-pound man, enter with the look of a little boy who'd just run out to the parking lot after his mother, only to see her drive off without him. He surveyed the room, saw me, and charged. I felt as if I were outside my body, observing the room from above. He's going to plow right into me, I observed from my position on the ceiling. But Michael dropped to his knees and collapsed in my lap, hugging my legs and sobbing. Suddenly I was in my body again. Oh, my God, this was real! I cradled his head in my arms and began to tremble and weep. Locked in this embrace we rocked back and forth. There was only one thought, one reality pounding in my chest: John is dead. John is dead. John is dead . . .

I sat on the couch, a box of Kleenex on my lap, and dialed my parents: 668-9418, the same number we had when I was a kid. Damn it. Area Code. Try again. I never debated who to call, I dialed automatically, moving on instinct. I was a little girl, running down the alley behind our Oak Park house, running home, running to Mommy. *Mom!!* Please be home. There was no answer. Maybe I'd misdialed. Again. Still no answer. Then I did a curious—perhaps natural—thing. I phoned my siblings in order of age. First my brother Rob. Not home. Then my oldest sister, Pam. No answer. Finally I rang Pat, the only family member who lived nearby. My mind was blank, I had no thought as to what I'd say. She answered.

"Pat, it's Judy," I cried into the phone. "John's dead!" I blurted and began sobbing. She gasped.

"You're kidding!" she said in shock. "What! How?"

How? I could barely stand to say it, was barely able to. What would my New Jersey-housewife sister think? She didn't even smoke grass. She'd probably think John was a junkie. She'd be appalled, disgusted! I drew a big breath and exhaled, "An overdose."

"I'll be right there," she said and was gone.

I hung up and tried to pull myself together. I felt better having made contact with my sister. There was no judgment in her voice, only concern. I must have been crazy to think anything otherwise. When we were kids she took care of me a lot, helping with homework, teaching me about clothes and makeup. She always called things the way she saw them—and we often saw things differently—but she was always there when I needed her. Just like now. Patsy would be right here.

LATE 1981

Sitting across from Dr. Cyborn for our first session, I took in his dark, paneled, basically brown office, and then him. He was a balding, middle-aged man of medium build, wearing a cardigan sweater, solid-color shirt, and dark pants. He observed me with a pleasant expression from behind dark-framed glasses. I was terribly uncomfortable. He'd be perfectly cast as a shrink, I thought.

Dr. Cyborn asked why I'd decided to see a psychiatrist. I explained that my husband had a cocaine problem, but for the past year and a half it had seemed to be under control. Yes, there had been two periods when he used it, once for a day and once for two weeks. But in general things had been good. In fact things had been, overall, wonderful—until last month. While we were on a publicity tour for *Continental Divide,* he began to use cocaine moderately. This quickly became a binge, and by the time we got to Los Angeles things were really bad. I found myself rapidly plunging emotionally. I was angry, frustrated; I felt I could barely hold on to my sanity. Anger was justified, but something more was happening. I was reacting to past frustration, from that period of a few years ago when we'd last battled the cocaine demons. I realized there must still be old, buried anger, which had made my reaction so intense. This was getting in the way of my being able to help John now.

I explained that after we returned home from L.A. the drugging stopped and so did my acute anxieties. John seemed fine on the surface, but I sensed a renewed struggle in him, and, perhaps more disturbing, I sensed he was frightened. The idea that he might get heavily into cocaine again was exhausting and depressing. I thought he should see a psychiatrist, but he insisted he was all right. I wanted us to make it, and decided *I* needed help.

Dr. Cyborn asked questions about our relationship and about my own family. Then he paused briefly, looking me in the eye. "I think it's important for you to begin to focus on yourself, Judy. You need to slow down and take a look at

your life, at how *you* feel about things." He pointed out that
John and I had become involved very young: I was fifteen
and John seventeen. "You've been living together for ten
years and your life centers around his work, his ambitions,
his problems. You need a better sense of yourself to be a
stronger person, and ultimately, a stronger partner. I think
you should commit to two therapy sessions a week for three
months, either with me or someone else. At the end of that
time, you can decide if it's worth continuing." I was surprised
to have the emphasis placed on me, expecting the counseling
to deal with the drug problem, or what to do about John. All
the same, I agreed.

A month later, I debated accompanying John to L.A. in
January. He had some work to do on a new script called
Noble Rot, and would be there about ten days. Things had
been up and down that month, with John again dabbling in
cocaine. I didn't believe he was capable of moderate use for
long and said so. He insisted the use was very light, he was
in control. I felt that if I went with John to L.A., he would be
less likely to escalate his use. But I couldn't be John's policeman or conscience. What I needed was to focus on my needs,
stick to my therapy, do some work on my current book
Titters: 101, and wean six kittens. John would be working
with his friend Don Novello, a sweet guy I liked very much. I
never knew him to indulge in coke. They'd be together,
working, most of the time. But still, I had a gnawing feeling
that I should go with him.

"What are you afraid of?" Dr. Cyborn asked when I told
him my dilemma. I thought a moment, trying to pinpoint my
fear. I was surprised by my thoughts. I hesitated, reluctant
to share my response. Finally I answered.

"I'm afraid that he'll die."

MARCH 5, 1982, CONTINUED

I'd just finished talking to Pat when the phone rang. I
hoped it would be family.

"Mrs. Belushi?" a man asked.

"Yes," I answered, something about his voice making me uncomfortable.

"This is NBC news. We've had reports that your husband is dead. Would you like to confirm or comment?"

I hung up and began to cry. I pictured an excited reporter, saying "It must be true!" One person's tragedy, another's fascination.

While I was on the phone our business manager, Mark Lipsky, had quietly entered the house. Mark, about thirty-four, was mild-mannered, personable, and straight-ahead. Over the years I had seen him at all hours, under all kinds of circumstances, but I'd never seen him look so lost. Mark was not just our manager but our friend. That made his responsibilities even heavier to bear; he knew how much I would turn to him now.

We talked briefly. I remember thinking it was funny that he'd brought along his briefcase. I don't recall our exact words, but I remember how softly Mark spoke. He said he had reached some Belushi family members, and that someone was on the way to tell John's mother. Bernie Brillstein (John's personal manager) was making arrangements between the Los Angeles Police Department, the coroner's office, and the morgue. As of yet, no cause of death had been given. There were no drugs found in the room, and no signs of violence. This change in information was unsettling. What about the heroin? Mark assured me his information was official. We would have to wait for the autopsy. I realized John must have had a heart attack. Oh, God! I hoped he didn't suffer.

Mitchell Glazer, a close friend, arrived next. We'd met back in 1978, when he wrote John's first magazine cover story for *Crawdaddy,* the now defunct rock 'n roll magazine. After that, Mitch and John began to pal around, and soon we were all close. Besides admiring Mitch's writing, John respected his instincts about music and had recorded more than one song Mitch suggested. He was currently writing a movie for John, and had been working at his apartment around the corner from us when he heard the news. I don't think he talked to me at first, but wandered the room with an incredulous stare. Watching him talking with Danny,

I thought Mitch looked as though his entire body were in pain. And Danny was crying. I'd never seen Danny cry before.

The image of Danny lunging into the room earlier assaulted me and I experienced again the fear, the panic of that moment. The thought made me tense every muscle in my face and I realized I must look disturbingly bad. That's how I felt, so why should I look any different? I recalled my doctor's counsel to "take it easy." Right, that seemed like a suggestion from another life. I suddenly feared I wouldn't make it through the week without a relapse. But there was so much to do! So many arrangements to make! I couldn't possibly be sick.

Deanne Stillman called. She and Anne Beatts were my writing partners. Our first book together was *Titters: The First Collection of Humor by Women,* in 1976. It was Anne and Deanne's project and they'd hired me to do the design and art direction. It was with them that I began writing professionally. Now we were co-authors. We liked working together; we respected each other, got on well, and laughed a lot. We were great friends.

"How ya doin'?" Deanne asked gently. It was clear that she knew.

"Oh, okay I guess."

"Do you want me to come over?"

I couldn't imagine anyone wanting to come over. It seemed too much to ask. "No, I'm fine."

Deanne hesitated. "Are you sure?" She sounded concerned.

"Yeah."

There was an awkward pause. "Well, I just thought you might be there with a lot of guys and that it might be comforting to have a woman friend." I looked around the room and saw that Deanne was right. How funny she would realize that only men were here. My responses were absurd. I wasn't okay and I needed my friends. And maybe others needed to be with friends, too.

"You're right, that would be good," I told her. "Come on over as soon as you can." I hung up and the phone rang.

"Hello, Mrs. Belushi?" I recognized the NBC newsman's voice.

"Please don't call my home again, you're tying up the line," I said and hung up.

I began to think through what would have to be done and a conversation John and I had had the previous summer came to mind. We were out for a drive on Martha's Vineyard, where we had a summer home. I was enjoying the beauty of the island, the peacefulness of the moment, when I thought, I could spend eternity here! Passing the Chilmark cemetery, I suddenly said, "When I die, I'd like to be buried here."

John put his hand on mine and shot me a quick grin. "I think I'd like a Viking funeral," he said and we both laughed at the idea.

A Viking funeral! That was it! I asked Mark to look into the legal problems of having a funeral at sea.

The phones were relentless. Both lines were continually busy. Michael Klenfner and Mitch fielded calls, passing along messages and turning over the phone when appropriate. More sad faces arrived. Whenever someone entered, we would hug and cry. I was startled when my sister Pat appeared, since the drive should have taken longer. But there she was, her arms outstretched, tears streaking her face. We hugged and cried and I truly felt better in my sister's arms. My big sister. Always there for me at times that mattered. She would help make it better, but no one could make it right.

Pat took on the task of tracking down our family. She would find Rob and Pam through their offices. It hadn't even occurred to me that since they both lived out West they would still be at work. My parents, who lived in the Chicago area, had gone to dinner.

John's mother was on the phone. I picked it up and we spoke, weeping. "I can't believe it," she kept saying. Many of the Chicago relatives had gathered at her house, including John's only sister, Marian, and her son, Adam. "It's all up to you, honey. What should we do? What do you want us to do?"

John's body would not be released over the weekend, so it would be a few days before the funeral. "We'll all be together as soon as possible," I told her. "We're going to Martha's Vineyard for a Viking funeral."

"Viking funeral?" she asked suspiciously. "What do you mean? What's that?"

"Well, we'll have a boat, a pyre built, and we put John on that and it's pulled out to sea and set on fire . . ."

"Nooooo!" she wailed, long and loud. "You can't burn him! He'll go to hell!"

Her conviction was clear. Had I promised John a Viking funeral, I would have done whatever it took to give him one. As it was, he was as likely kidding as not. The only other time we talked about it, he said he'd like to be buried in a tomb like Lenin. "Okay," I assured her. "Don't worry, we'll bury him. On the Vineyard."

I was anxious for Kathryn Walker to arrive. She was the only one who really knew what I was going through. About a year and a half before, Kathryn's fiance, Doug, had died. Memories flashed of the many nights we'd spent in her apartment, mourning Doug—sitting up late, listening to music, drinking, talking about life and death and loss and living. "Doug Kenney, founder of *National Lampoon* magazine, co-author of *Animal House,* boy wunderkind of the humor biz, died in a fall from a cliff in Hawaii . . ." That was how the obits read. To me he was sweet Doug, my good friend and confidant, and his death left a hole in my heart. Of course, to Kathryn he was her love, her future. It seemed as if Kathryn cried for a year.

Soon she arrived. I remember her face, how angry she looked. Angry and concerned and sad all at once. We embraced for a long while, then she held me at arms length and looked at me searchingly. "Oh, boy, Jude . . ." she said with the weight of experience, her concerned stare never wavering. "You're going to go through amazing changes."

People continued to arrive. My secretary, Karen Krenitsky, entered quietly, her sad eyes avoiding mine. Rhonda Coullet (actress, singer, and a close friend since *National Lampoon* days) burst through the door as if she were being chased by a ghost. Our cleaning ladies, Alba and Terry, came over. Alba started to clean, seeing it as a way she could help. Terry, on the other hand, became quite hysterical. She began shaking so intensely that I stood and held her for some time before she calmed down. This is getting surreal, I thought. Aren't I the one who's supposed to be hysterical?

Throughout the day friends suggested I have a drink to

calm my nerves. Frankly, I would have liked a drink, but I hadn't eaten all day. There were also several offers of Valium and Percodan and various other tranquilizers. At one point it occurred to me that had I taken everything I'd been offered, I'd be dead.

My youngest brother-in-law, Billy, was on the phone. "What was he doing there alone?" he cried. "Why weren't you with him?" He didn't say it accusingly, it was just that he knew how much John needed me. The words cut like a knife. I burst out crying, trying to talk at the same time.

"I know," I sobbed. "I should have been with him, Billy!" I had felt it all day, a jabbing pain, the guilt of knowing I should have been there. I knew he couldn't handle himself in Los Angeles. He never could. Several people had said, "It's not your fault." Well, if it was "not my fault," then why did so many people assume I might think it was? It was the grand lie everyone was telling to make me feel better. Only a grieving brother would let the truth slip out.

Dr. Cyborn phoned and offered to come over. He received a respectful welcome from my friends, who seemed to find comfort in a doctor's presence, as if he could make me all better. We went down to my bedroom and two friends awkwardly carried in a very large chair, then left us quickly and quietly. It felt like a royal sitting, with subjects backing out of the room, bowing.

We talked about how I felt and Dr. Cyborn wanted to know if my family would be supportive, if I would need help with arrangements, etc. He asked if I knew what had happened and I repeated what I'd been told. "You know there was a woman in John's hotel room?" Dr. Cyborn announced this and asked it at the same time.

That asshole. He really did the whole number. Mysterious death, a woman in the room . . . We had once joked about the idea of dying in the act of an indiscretion. I said if he died that way, I'd kill him. Real funny.

I realized I was slouching, sat up, and pushed my hair off my face. "No. No one's told me," I replied.

"Well," said Dr. Cyborn shifting his weight, "I think it's good to get everything out. It was on the TV news. They led her out of the hotel in handcuffs to a police car."

In handcuffs? My image of a lover was shattered. Why would they handcuff someone who'd been in John's Chateau bungalow? Danny's reference to heroin and a needle came back. It made no sense when he said it because I knew John would never be able to inject himself. He was afraid of needles. Why would they arrest someone if there was no sign of foul play or drug use?

I took a deep breath and tried to sound calm. "Well, doc, don't you think you should give me something for my nerves?" The words sounded funny in the controlled tone.

"I'll tell you what, Judy. This is one of the most significant times of your life and I think it's important for you to go through it with a clear head. It's important for you to experience and remember your feelings. I could give you something to help you sleep, but in general, I'd like to see you try to go through this without any drugs. Now, I'm not going to give you anything tonight, but if you find you can't sleep, you can call me and I'll give you some sleeping pills."

The night dragged on. Plans were falling into place, however. Arrangements were made for my family and some close friends to be in New York the next day. We would meet up with the Belushis Monday on the Vineyard. I was especially relieved when we reached Smokey Wendell and he agreed to come help.

Smokey had worked for us the better part of two years and I really needed him now. His expertise was security; he got us in and out of places quickly and pleasantly, but he'd become more of a live-in personal assistant. He had come to his profession by way of the Secret Service, so his thinking, in terms of security, was precautionary. In a problem situation, Smokey was levelheaded and sharp-witted. And his authoritative posture could be very persuasive. He was a good man to have around. I was going to need him.

It seemed I was on the phone most of the night. At one point, I talked to an L.A. police officer. "What was your husband's full name?" "John Adam Belushi." "Date and place of birth?' "January 24, 1949. Chicago, Illinois." "Nationality?" "American." Oh my God. They would write this on a card, pin it to his body, and roll him away. I cried softly as I spoke. The officer was quick and to the point. Polite. I didn't know John's social security number, but the officer said that was okay. What do you mean It's okay? I thought. If it's necessary to bother me tonight it had better be important! We were finished in a few minutes. That was it! Well, when it comes down to it, I guess there isn't much one needs to know. John Adam Belushi, age thirty-three, is dead and gone. What was it Jimmy, John's brother, had said in one of his Second City scenes? "Sheet over the head, dead, gone, dead . . ." My heart ached for Jimmy. He had called from his dressing room at *Pirates of Penzance* in Chicago. He was going on with the show. He thought that's what John would want.

I was anxious to talk with Bill Wallace, the man who'd found John at the Chateau Marmot, and Nelson Lyon, a friend who had been with John the night before. Finally Bill was on the line. I grabbed the phone. "What happened, Bill?" I cried.

"I was supposed to get him at noon to run. . . ." Bill was crying, too. Big, strong, tough Bill Wallace. "I ran by the Chateau this morning at eight and I thought to myself, I'm gonna go and get his ass movin' early this mornin'. But then I thought, no, John said to come at noon, and that's what I should do."

"It's okay, Bill, you didn't know."

Bill was sobbing. "If only I'd just stopped . . ."

I could feel Bill struggling with guilt. I could feel it because it was in me, too. "It's too late, Bill. It's over. If it hadn't happened now, it might have happened at another time. It's nobody's fault. It's just the way it is."

"Is there anything you want me to do?"

"Just stay with him, Bill," I cried. "Don't let them put him in a drawer."

I was exhausted but not sleepy. Most of the visitors had left and I began to think about sleep. The idea was terrifying. To be in the dark with my thoughts . . . I just couldn't do that. I remembered what Dr. Cyborn had said about keeping a clear head; I knew it was good advice, but I couldn't face sleep, not tonight, not without a sleeping pill. Someone got me one and I asked Rhonda to come to my bedroom with me.

I wanted to talk until I fell asleep. I didn't want to be alone for a minute.

As we talked my mind wandered. It was beyond comprehension that John would not come home again. We had everything going for us, and yet, because of those damn drugs, everything just got out of control. Out of control. That was what I had said to him the last Saturday he was here, in this very room. John woke up and began coughing so hard I thought he might die, right then, just cough to death. I stood there watching him, helpless, wondering how he could do something to himself that affected him so badly. He felt my eyes on him.

"What? What is it?" he said angrily. "What is that look?"

"It's a look of concern, John. I don't know how you can do this to yourself."

"Oh, so I do it to myself?" he said, coughing.

"Yes, you do it to yourself. You know it's the coke. It's this last week in L.A. Your body can't take the abuse!"

"Oh, is that so?" he yelled, taking his pajama top off and throwing it on the bed. "What are you saying? I'm out of control?"

"Yes!" I yelled back.

"I'm out of control?!" His voice boomed with a ridiculousness verging on parody as he stormed into the bathroom and slammed the door.

Kathryn came in and sat with Rhonda and me on the bed, bringing me back to the present. I began to talk about some of the arrangements that had to be made. I wanted the funeral to be Albanian Orthodox, I explained, because as a little boy in Chicago John had been involved with the church. He always spoke fondly of his involvement and seemed to have missed the connection when his family moved to the suburbs. When his grandmother, Nena, died the funeral was at the Albanian Church in Chicago. I liked the service and that's what I wanted for John.

APRIL 1980

Nena suffered a heart attack at home in Julian, California, and John's brother Billy pounded her chest until her heart was going again. During the two-hour drive to the hospital, she had three more attacks. Mr. Belushi phoned looking for John. Nena wanted everyone at the hospital.

John had gone to Chicago for the weekend to see Jimmy in a play. When he phoned later and I told him the news, he became upset. "I know why she wants me to come," he insisted. "I won't go see her die."

"John, she needs you. Let her have it her way."

"No! If I don't go, she won't die."

I went to Chicago and talked to John. He was doing drugs, drinking, whatever he could to block what was happening. The next day I said I was going to see Nena, with or without him. He stormed off, only to return. The entire trip I kept worrying that we'd be too late. At the hospital a nurse recognized John and took us directly to the intensive care unit.

I was surprised at how tiny Nena looked in the hospital bed, so small and fragile with all the tubes and medical hookups around her. John's aunt, Teta Dina, sat at her side. She made a sad gesture, as if to say, "She's not going to make it."

When Nena saw John, she just lit up. John, the consummate actor, put on a happy face and kidded her about being sick and upsetting everyone. He made her laugh. Her eyes sparkled. Dina gave John her chair and he sat holding Nena's hand as they talked. Not having much strength, Nena soon closed her eyes. John put his head next to hers and together they napped.

Later that afternoon I fed Nena and we "talked." Nena did not speak much English, and I only knew a few Albanian words, but I could understand her expressions and attitude. If a nurse came by her bed, she'd introduce me proudly, saying, "Johnny's *nusa*," then she'd pat my hand and say, "*Nusa*, nice!" My heart ached that she was so weak, but her spirits were up, her smile so radiant that I began to believe she would pull through. Soon she was tired again and said she must rest. John should rest, too, she ordered us both. "Too much work!" Nena announced, shaking her head disapprovingly. We said we'd come by early the next day. She told us to sleep late.

The next morning Billy Belushi and I talked in the living room of our suite while John slept. Billy was the little brother I never had and I loved spending time with him. He had grown a lot since the family had moved to California a few years before. He was twenty, tall, thin, and tan. And so cute and sweet. We were laughing when the phone rang. It was Uncle Chris. Nena was gone. There would be no more visits to the hospital. We sat on the couch, hugged each other, and cried. Finally I went into the bedroom to tell John. I shook him gently. "Time to get up, honey," I said and went into the bathroom, rinsed my face, and took some deep breaths. I came back out and sat on the bed. John was not one to wake up easily.

"John." I shook him more firmly. My voice was strained. "Honey . . ."

Suddenly his eyes popped open and he looked at me suspiciously. "Something's wrong," he said, sitting up. I started to speak, but I couldn't. I nodded. "Nena's dead," he said. I nodded again. "Where is everyone?" I told him what I knew and he grabbed the phone and started calling. He told his mother and father he would take care of everything, pay for everything. Nena would have the finest funeral the church had ever seen. He phoned our office and told our secretary to work on travel arrangements, limos for the service, whatever was needed. Nothing was too good. He was up, dressing, complaining about the hotel service, the travel . . . Suddenly he stood still, his back to me, and stated, "I'm not going to cry."

"John," I said, "if you can't cry for Nena, then who can you cry for?"

John crumbled. We sat on the bed, holding onto one another, sobbing. Where is it written that men aren't supposed to cry, I wondered. How does such a notion get passed along?

We returned to Chicago for the funeral at St. Nicholas

Albanian Orthodox Church. I found the service comforting. Men in regal gowns rhythmically chanting in an unfamiliar tongue, swinging incense lanterns as they performed their pageantry on the stagelike pulpit. The swirling smoke reflected subtle colors filtering through the Byzantine stained-glass windows. I liked the fact that the service was in a language I didn't understand. It gave me the freedom to let my mind wander—I didn't have to agree or disagree with what was being said. The ritual was very soothing. Very peaceful.

Nena's six grandsons were her pallbearers. I remember looking at them all in a line at the front of the church. The Belushi brothers were handsome. They each stood in the same manner, hands folded in front, heads cocked to one side or the other, eyes focused on the floor. John, the oldest, the famous son who took care of his family. Jimmy, the young father-to-be. He had shared that secret with Nena before she died. And Billy, the baby. When had he become taller than John?

From John to Jimmy to Billy there was a strong family resemblance. While Billy might not look much like John, with Jimmy standing between them the brotherly ties were evident. I longed to see them somewhere else, smiling. But here we were, to lay to rest their beloved grandmother. We would miss her terribly, but all was not so sad. Nena had a long and decent life, after all. And she had most gracefully waited for Death, facing her last days with calm and dignity. She'd done the ultimate, really—she recognized her time, said her good-byes, and moved on. I knew I would never forget my last image of Nena. It was her smile I would always remember, that radiant, fearless smile.

MARCH 5 CONTINUED

Rhonda and Kathryn let me drift in my memories. When I came out of my haze I realized my face was tense and my eyes dry. I had to blink a few times to be fully in the room again. I felt disoriented, then remembered we were making funeral arrangements. How many pallbearers could there be? We decided eight at most. Five were "givens": John's two natural brothers, his "soul" brother, Danny, and his old buddies Tino Insana and Steve Beshekas.

Tino, Steve, and John had been inseparable for many years after high school. Their friendship had remained strong, spanning three decades and lots of changes. At the College of DuPage, under John's direction, they began a comedy group called the West Compass Players. From that springboard, John became a member of the main cast at Chicago's Second City theater and Tino was hired for their touring company. Steve moved on to a new career as a bartender. I never doubted John's love or respect for both. Throughout his career he valued their opinions, often phoning to discuss new projects.

Steve was Greek, and Tino Italian, so they all shared a sense of growing up ethnic in the predominately WASP suburbs. They quickly established a friendship, based largely, I think, on a common sense of humor. They enjoyed hanging out and staying up late, inspiring each other with a funnier joke than the last one. It was during this time that they first began working out comedy scenes together.

Steve was a lady's man, tall and dark with classic features. He tended to get himself into jams, usually more dramatic than serious. John appreciated Steve's style, and, I think, felt protective of him. During "SNL" John would work Steve's name into a scene, then gleefully call and tell him to watch the show. "What else would I be doing on a Saturday?" Steve would respond. When we returned to Chicago to film *The Blues Brothers* we hired Steve to manage an old bar we rented with Danny as a kind of private club, a place where Dan and John could entertain or hang out without the problems of public places. This was known amongst our friends as the Blues Bar, and we had one in NYC as well. When we left town, we helped Steve set up his own business.

Tino is a big guy, about six foot four, with sandy brown hair. His father, a musician trained in his native Italy, played piano for the West Compass Players. I don't think

Tino realized the power of his size until he played the role of a big bully in John's last film. Not that he became more aggressive, he just seemed to be more comfortable with his stature. During one of our last days together on the Vineyard, John spoke of Tino.

"You know who my favorite person is, other than you?"

"No," I said with interest. "Who?"

"Tino," he stated. "You know why? Because he's smart, and he likes to learn new things, and he does things well, and he's the *funniest* person I know. And he's soooo nice, isn't he, isn't he the sweetest guy?" With his whole body John emphasized the awe he felt, first clutching his hands to his chest as if he might burst out in song, then throwing them up in the air to compliment his raised eyebrows for a nonverbal, "What more can I say?"

Pleasant memories dissolved as tears filled my eyes. I saw the sad faces of John's friends as they carried his body to its final resting place. In terms of John's friendships, I knew who else I should choose, but I could only select three. It was impossible, there were at least seven more men friends who were all very close to John. I couldn't decide right away. I would have to think about it some more.

While scenes of my past filled my memory, another part of my mind worked on the week's agenda. Shortly after the funeral I wanted a memorial service. I was afraid we wouldn't be able to use a church because we were not members, but the others didn't think that was necessarily the case. Kathryn suggested St. John the Divine, and Rhonda said it was a beautiful church. Kathryn was a friend of the Episcopal Bishop of New York, Paul Moore, whom John and I had met. She offered to talk to him.

I was beginning to feel sleepy and rested my head on my pillow. Still, I struggled to stay awake. I couldn't explain my fear of going to sleep; I was like a child, afraid of the unknown. Finally the sleeping pill began to take effect and I let my eyes close. I heard the click of the light switch and was engulfed in an uncomfortable darkness. "Don't turn off the light. Please . . ." Within seconds I was out.

MARCH 6, 1982

I awoke in a void, as if I were rushing through deep, black water toward the surface for air. I expected a rush of relief as I broke through, but instead found large block letters floating before me: J O H N I S D E A D. There was no refreshing breath of life, only this startling image. These three-dimensional letters, surrounded by darkness, bobbed up and down like boats anchored at sea, and took up all the space in my mind. I was overcome by the enormity of this reality; it was suffocating. Must get up, I suddenly realized. Can't be left alone with my thoughts.

My sister Pam was there when I woke. An attorney, she had already instinctively taken on various tasks, and had a list of things she offered to handle. Her eyes were red from crying and her voice was soft. I knew she would feel better if she were busy, and I felt better knowing she would deal with the police and coroners. Pam is bright and thorough and a natural protector. I think she always had a special watch out for me, her baby sister, taking my side in arguments, writing with advice after she went away to college. Thinking back, she always gave good, loving advice. Now, more than ever, I would need just that.

I don't really remember when my brother, Rob, appeared with his girlfriend Liz. They flew in from Aspen. Rob, nearly ten years my senior, was very distant when I was a kid. A teen of the late fifties, he had that restless, young rebel attitude, only he was funny, too. I guess I had a little sister crush on him. But I was just a kid—and a girl; I could never get his attention for long. Finally, when I was in college, Rob invited John and me to stay at his apartment in Chicago, in Old Town. It was a dream come true. We were finally on equal ground and our friendship quickly grew strong. I could see Rob was wrestling hard with John's death. He, too, felt a loss, but at the same time my big brother was really mad at John for hurting me.

Others from out of town arrived. Jimmy's wife, Sandi Belushi, surprised me by showing up at the apartment. I didn't think I would see her until we went to Martha's Vineyard, but Jimmy, knowing we shared a sisterly friendship, wanted her with me. Tino and his wife Dana came from L.A., and Steve Beshekes from Chicago. My friend Laila traveled from Aspen with my brother. For several years she was my constant companion, confidant, my "Blues Sister." Although she'd moved a few years back, we kept in contact and still managed to see each other surprisingly often. It was comforting to be surrounded by so much love.

There were endless tasks and people pitched in willingly. New York friends continued to come over, so the apartment was very active. Pat orchestrated rounding up food on Friday, and now it took some effort to deal with it all. The Shopsins, proprietors of a nearby deli, had sent over what seemed to be a ton. I remember seeing Billy Murray carrying in a large pot of something from his wife Mickey. Cases of liquor and other beverages arrived. Everyone was extremely thoughtful. Flowers filled the rooms. One friend alone brought dozens of yellow tulips.

Every so often I'd go upstairs and say hello to whomever was there and accept condolences. It was an exhausting exchange, so I'd soon retreat to my bedroom. My family and inner circle of friends were always welcomed—needed. At one point, there were about eight women with me, all of us lounging on the king-sized bed, intertwined together. The physical contact was comforting, and we took on a slumber party mood for a while, giggling and joking, as if we'd forgotten what drew us together. Only we couldn't. It was all around us—it was in us—just waiting to burst.

The use of St. John's for the memorial was approved and Bishop Moore came over to talk about the arrangements. Having no church background I left the decisions about songs and passages to him and Kathryn. I knew from the first who should address the crowd at the memorial, however. Danny, of course, John's celebrated best friend and partner. And Jimmy. Jimmy because he was John's brother, yes, and because I knew he could handle it. But more important, because his energy is so much like John's, and I felt there was some comfort in seeing, in knowing that this energy lived on.

Various decisions, like who would speak, came as if I had always known them. Another choice was similarly evident: I knew immediately that I wanted a friend to sing at each service, and I knew what they should sing. I wanted James Taylor to sing "That Lonesome Road" at the gravesite, and Rhonda Coullet to sing a Jackson Browne song, "For a Dancer," at the memorial. James was on tour, however, so it would be difficult for him to come. Since Kathryn now lived with James (a romance John and I had been happy to see growing strong), I spoke to her. She knew James would want to, but didn't know his schedule offhand. She would ask.

I approached Rhonda. I knew she was pretty shaken, and maybe not up to the task, but Rhonda has a voice like an angel—how could I pass up at least asking? "You know I'll do anything you want," she replied unhesitatingly in her Arkansas drawl. I told her I planned to ask Paul Shaffer (the original bandleader for the Blues Brothers Band and current leader of the David Letterman Band) to play piano.

Paul came by the house that afternoon and I presented my request. He agreed immediately, pleased to be asked. He wasn't familiar with the song, so I led him into the sound room, pulled the record, and played it. He suggested we change a part for fiddle to a sax, an idea that I loved immediately, since sax was more appropriate for John—more bluesy. I wanted to ask one of the Blues Brothers' horn players, but which one? The decision was difficult. I thought about it and decided to ask Tom Scott. John and Tom had had a falling out during the scoring of *Neighbors* (John's last film), but they had taken steps toward a reconciliation. I hoped this gesture would complete that.

Tom, it turned out, was working, but his producer rescheduled so he could attend the memorial. "I wouldn't miss it," he kept repeating.

I was anxiously awaiting my parents, and suddenly I turned to see them standing across the room, still in their overcoats, as if they'd been magically transported. My father looked stern as he fought his emotions and my mother reached out, offering a welcoming embrace. "How has this awful thing happened?" she wondered aloud as I fell into her arms and began crying. I felt as if I'd come home.

Arrangements seemed to be coming together. John's body would be released Monday and Michael Klenfner arranged the use of the Atlantic Records (the Blues Brothers' label) plane for transport. Bernie Brillstein would travel with John. I was relieved that his body wasn't going to be shipped; I didn't like the idea of strangers being in charge of John's body.

James's schedule was a problem and it looked as if he wouldn't be able to make it. Then he phoned to say he had chartered a plane and would be there. I was really pleased. I suggested he sing "That Lonesome Road," but he said it was complicated because of the several part harmony. "James, whatever you sing will be fine. I'm just happy you'll be with us."

I saw my dad sitting alone in the kitchen and decided to take advantage of a quiet moment for a hug. "You know, Judy," he began, his voice unsteady, "I haven't said much to you, what with so many people around. I don't want you to think I'm avoiding you, it's just that I feel like such a goof seeing you so sad and there's nothing I can do about it. But I want you to know, if there's anything you need, I'm here." I kissed him on the cheek and we sat together for a while in silence.

When Smokey Wendell arrived, he and I spoke alone. He expressed his sorrow and talked briefly of John, then our relationship returned to its normal "Let's get it done" attitude. Only there was no joy or excitement, or even fear, in our new plans. That felt very different. I had known Smokey would work for us again, but never imagined it would be for this.

Nelson Lyon was the last person I knew to have seen John alive. They had been together Thursday night, in fact I had called John at Nelson's and just missed him. Now I really wanted to speak to Nelson. Maybe he could give me some clue as to what had happened? Maybe he could tell me what no one seemed to know.

It felt like an eternity before Nelson and I finally talked. I wanted to know everything he could tell me. He said John had come by in the late afternoon with a woman, he wasn't sure of her name, but she was the woman he had seen on the news in handcuffs. He assumed she worked for John because of the way they related. Later, they all went to On the Rox, a private after-hours club located over the rock 'n roll venue, The Roxy Theater, on Sunset Boulevard. They returned to the Chateau Marmont a little before two in the morning.

John invited some people from the club to his bungalow, but shortly after they returned, John told Nelson to wait there while he and the woman went "to get some wood." I asked Nelson what that meant, was there a fireplace? Nelson said no, he thought it was a password for cocaine. While they were gone, Robert DeNiro, an old friend of Nelson's, knocked. They talked briefly, then DeNiro went back to his own room. A little while later, Robin Williams arrived and waited for John to return. Shortly before three in the morning Robin left, and Nelson grabbed a cab soon after that.

I asked Nelson if John had seemed depressed. He said John looked tired, but seemed fine. Had John been drinking? Nelson didn't think so. Did they return with cocaine? No. Was John doing cocaine that night? Yes, he was, Nelson admitted. But not a lot. He described him as carrying a small amount. Was John doing downers? No, Nelson saw no other drugs. Lastly I asked if it seemed that John might have been shooting up. His exact response is one I clearly remember: an immediate, emphatic, deep "No!"

Things quieted down by early evening. Someone gave me a catalogue of coffins and my brother and I went through it. It was weird and there were too many choices. I wanted a simple wooden coffin and asked Rob to select one. I just couldn't. He narrowed it down to three, and we chose one together.

Shortly after I got into bed, Bill Wallace arrived from Los Angeles. He sat on the edge of the bed and took my hands in his. "I want to say something to you and I want you to listen. That girl didn't mean a thing to John. Now, I want you to look me in the eye." Bill's face was earnest and his gaze unwavering. "John loved you and that girl was just there for drugs. You know that, don't you?" He was eager for me to believe him, as if this were the duty he owed his friend, making sure I didn't misunderstand. My eyes filled with tears and I nodded. "I know that, Bill. I know that."

Before I went to sleep Bill insisted on giving me a back rub to help me relax. Bill "Superfoot" Wallace had been a world champion in full-contact karate for six undefeated years. He was solidly built and extremely strong, and the way he gently massaged my back reminded me of Lenny in *Of Mice and Men*. I imagined that he might unintentionally crush me. Bill stayed with me for a long while, quietly slipping out of my room moments before I dozed off.

SUNDAY, MARCH 7

In the shower, the rush of water mingled with my tears. It was the first time I'd been really alone since John died. I had cried with people on and off, but now, left to myself, I was in agony. It was a physical attack; I'd felt it coming as I undressed, like a blackness slowly surrounding me, wrapping itself around my body, embracing me with a pressure I could not bear, forcing out tears and leaving me short of breath. I crouched in the tub and hugged my knees, rocking back and forth, silently sobbing. There was an intense energy within me, ripping, clawing its way out. It occurred to me that I might pass out and drown, and I welcomed the idea. I wanted so much to be strong, to handle John's passing with dignity. But it was so hard!

I felt a tremendous responsibility, as if everything were being judged. How the family reacted, how the press covered things, how John died; all seemed to become a part of John's life. How did John die, anyway? Damn him! He thought he was indestructible. I guess I thought so, too.

The attack passed and I stood, gasping. As I dressed, I studied myself in the mirror. My face was the saddest I'd ever seen. I looked so tired! No, I looked plain awful. Gravity pulled inordinately hard on my body. And I was too thin. I realized I hadn't eaten much all week. I decided to go up to the kitchen and force something down.

In the kitchen I spoke to Smokey about the funeral and memorial. I was upset because a friend had been told by Bernie's office that the funeral was private. "Well, I don't know about that, but you know everyone is worried about a crowd problem. I think Bernie feels it's best to say the funeral is private."

I didn't really like that idea, but I figured most friends were in contact and knew they were welcome. I definitely wanted to make an announcement about the memorial. As far as I was concerned, we couldn't have too many people. All the same, I deferred to the opinions of Bernie, Mark, and others, to wait on that.

There had been an interesting mingling of people at my Greenwich Village apartment in the past few days. We were all lost souls, and the place on Morton Street seemed to offer comfort. There was an odd mixture of activity and idleness. Most of my family and those involved with planning were busy taking care of chores delegated to them, listed on the yellow pads they clung to for direction. Travel organization included a fleet of cars and limos, ferry and plane reservations, as well as accommodations for nearly fifty relatives and close friends. Then there were church and funeral home arrangements, which varied from ordering flowers to buying a cemetery plot. We were also planning a reception after each service.

There were a few times when having guests was uncomfortable. At one point, I saw a woman who had worked at "SNL" talking with another woman I didn't know. I was surprised to see her, since we'd never spoken beyond an occasional hello. I sat down to welcome her, but she and the other woman continued talking, ignoring my arrival. I must look so bad she doesn't know it's me, I thought. It seemed awkward to introduce myself. I felt small and vulnerable. I quickly returned to my bedroom sanctuary.

Rob came into my room, and for an unusual moment we were alone. "I've debated telling you this now, I mean, I don't know if it's the time, but I really want to share this with you," he said softly. "I asked Liz to marry me today and she's said yes."

My brother was forty and had been married and divorced in his twenties and decidedly antimarriage since. I knew he and Liz were madly in love and had talked about having kids. I gave Rob a hug and offered congratulations. It was clear that John's death had impressed upon him how fleeting life is. It was good news and I was happy for him, glad he'd told me.

Sunday evening, Laila, Sandi, and Kathryn sat with me as I selected the clothes in which John would be buried. Inspired by the phrase "All dressed up with nowhere to go" I decided to dress him casually. A pair of engineer boots he fondly referred to as his "slam boots" were a must, as were his green army pants. He had worn them to L.A., so I asked Bernie to bring them. No one would see them, anyway. I chose a shirt with a nice cut, a sport jacket and tie, and left them on a hanger for Danny to take with him to the Vineyard, since he was leaving earlier than we were. The clothes took on an eerie persona, hanging sadly on the door, awaiting their final use.

My own clothes would have to be bought on Monday before we headed out. I wanted a tailored black suit and a hat with a veil. The veil was very important because it would hide my face. I didn't feel capable of shopping so I asked Laila and Sandi if they would go. They agreed, but we hadn't thought to get cash for shopping and neither of them had a credit card. I suggested they take mine, which seemed like a good solution, then it struck us as silly as we imagined one of them pretending to be me. Sales clerk: "Oh, Mrs. Belushi, I just want to say how sorry I am about your husband."

"Thank you. I'd like to see something in black."

Kathryn offered her credit card, and as I got into my pajamas Laila sat on the floor practicing Kathryn's signature. Pages with "Kathryn Walker" scrawled across it were soon scattered about the room. I took a sleeping pill and got into bed. The last argument John and I had had kept running through my mind: "Out of control!" he'd yell.

"Yes!!" I replied, louder each time. Now my life was out of control. I tried to think of something else. Control, what can you control? As I drifted off, a thought occurred to me: Art you can control. Life you can't.

Chapter 2

THAT LONESOME ROAD

MONDAY, MARCH 8

It was early afternoon when Sandi and Laila returned, laden with packages, and for a moment there was the gaiety of women home from a shopping spree. Pulling items from the bags, we laughed as the two of them vividly described their outing, including a furious sweep at Bendel's where Laila broke down and cried when told they couldn't return items. "There, there, Miss Walker," the saleslady comforted her.

I was very pleased with one of the suits and put it on. I had a pair of narrow, wraparound black sunglasses which I was determined to wear, although I knew the style was more punk than my parents or in-laws might like. No matter, I wouldn't be comfortable in any other. I stood in front of the mirror. I was happy enough with the outfit, given that I was not happy with its role. I looked terrible in general, and the clothing worked well enough at hiding me—like a uniform it took on more importance than the person it surrounded. My hair was quite long and blah. I had been wearing a ponytail of late, debating whether or not to cut it. I would have to do something with it. Laila said she could make a twist in the back, and that seemed the best idea. They couldn't find a hat with a veil, but bought some veiling. I put on a hat, stuffed my hair under it, and stood still while Laila attached the veil.

So there I was in full widow garb. I was reminded of Jacqueline Kennedy. How had she dealt with it? Just like me, I guessed. You do what you've done all your life. You make each decision and move on. Keep moving, I thought. Don't let anyone or anything stop your motion.

An image of John on the night we'd first met suddenly came to me. It startled me—he was only a boy! I didn't think that at the time, of course. Seventeen and a senior in high school seemed pretty grown-up to a fifteen-year-old sophomore. He was leaning against a car, hands stuffed in his front pockets, thumbs out, James Dean style, talking to some guys. He looked cool in blue jeans, V-neck sweater, and button-down shirt. I drifted back to that night. I had gone to the Little League field to hang out with my girlfriends, and, of course, we hoped some guys would be there. Some of my girlfriends were dating seniors, and I wanted a senior boyfriend. I didn't know John, but recognized him from a school variety show. He was my favorite in the show, because he was funny and cute. He seemed a bit shy that night, not talking much, but that only made me notice his eyes more. I fell in love with his eyes; they were brown and clear and so expressive! We locked glances for a moment and were both embarrassed by the contact.

Smokey cautiously stuck his head into the room. "Time to get moving. We've got a ferry to catch." The island of Martha's Vineyard is seven miles off Cape Cod. We would have to drive four to five hours to Woods Hole where we could catch a ferry. Smokey was right, we were on a tight schedule. Yes, keep moving, I told myself. I went into the bathroom to change and in the privacy of the moment, cried.

I asked Kathryn, Laila, Sandi, and my mother to ride up with Smokey and me in the limousine. I decided I was healthy enough to drink; wasn't that what everyone was supposed to do, drink to the dearly departed? I told Smokey to be sure there was Jack Daniels in the car.

The drive was slow. Smokey rode up front and the rest of us sat in back. I broke open the Jack early, taking a slug from the bottle every so often, passing it around and encouraging the others to partake. Misery loves company.

My mother tried her best to be one of the gang, which is contrary to her style of mothering. She wouldn't drink from the bottle, but accepted a glass of bourbon and water. Not wanting my thoughts to take me over, I kept up a conversation. Still I couldn't shake the image of myself in my black suit. I'm a widow now, I repeated to myself. Never thought I'd be a widow! God, I remember when I thought I'd be a virgin all my life.

I looked at my mother who sat facing me. My mom is pretty cool, the kind your friends tend to like and admire, want to know better. Not because she's "hip," that wouldn't describe her. She's just a really nice, interesting person. She's not athletic, but has a vigor about her which has always made her look younger than she is. She looked cute sitting there, balancing her drink in one hand, maneuvering her book and cigarette in the other. My mother could read through anything! That was her escape, she'd just lose herself in a book. I recognized an uneasy feeling. Was it anger? Yes, a subconscious thought surfaced. My mother was supposed to be a widow before me. Then a rush of guilt. What a horrible thought! But I reasoned that it was a natural reaction. Statistically it was true. This was something *she* was supposed to go through first, so she could offer advice, understand how I felt. It wasn't fair! My mother didn't understand! Only Kathryn really knew. The others could imagine, even fear what I was going through. But only Kathryn knew a part of me was dying before them, that I was in physical pain. I threw back another hit of Jack Daniels. It seemed I'd drunk an awful lot of this stuff, and still I didn't feel it. But I liked the rush of each shot. For that instant when it first hit and felt like fire, for those few seconds, the burn in my throat was the only pain I could feel.

We arrived at the ferry an hour early. Anxious to get out of the car, we headed to the only place open, a bar that drew most of its business from people waiting to go to the island.

When we entered, the room was filled with smoke, or at least I saw it through a haze. Smokey seated us at a table in the back, ordered drinks, then went to the phone. I was extremely unhappy in the bar. I felt both that everyone knew who I was and that no one knew. Both thoughts made me angry. How could they *not* know? I was oozing sadness. I must look like a widow, my vibe must be overwhelming. People were looking at me strangely. No, they were probably just checking out a tableful of women. Why would they put together who I was? I was not a famous face. Just a name in the news, someone to feel for when you heard about the tragedy of the day. A lot of these people are probably talking about John, now, I thought. There must be rumors that he's being buried on the Vineyard. After all, *nothing* goes on there in the winter. The whole island probably knows. *There!* I heard someone say Belushi. What are they saying? I can't hear in here. Maybe I'm hearing things.

The crossing was uneventful. In the darkness of night, we slipped onto the shore of Martha's Vineyard. My brother and Liz met us, as did a small group of reporters. There was a moment of confusion, people in the way, trying to see who was in the limo. The car took a few quick turns and stole away.

We wound down a side street I never knew existed, up to a large old house—the funeral home—where Rob, Smokey, and I got out and Liz led the others off to their lodgings. This is it, I'm going to see John dead. My body was cold and tense as we entered the building. Pam was in the hallway going over some papers with a stranger. I clung to my brother's arm.

I was reminded of my grandmother's wake. Everyone talking in low voices, people with serious faces. I'd stood alone in front of her open casket, studying her. She was very pretty. Though almost ninety-two her skin looked so soft. I didn't like that she wasn't wearing her glasses. Put on your glasses, Granny, and let's play cards. Don't just lie there! She had been so important to me. Letting me see, showing us all, that it was okay to grow old. And to die. "I'm ninety, ya know!" she would announce, sharing her surprise. "Can't last much longer, dear. Oh, and when I go, I want you to have my TV."

"Come on, grandma. I don't want your TV. I want you."

"I'm too old." She would shoo it away with a wave of her hand and a gentle laugh. "I'll be gone soon. It's okay, honey. I'm tired." She wasn't morbid or even resigned, she was accepting and at peace with her life. Now, in her coffin, she looked like she was sleeping. Get up, Grandma. Don't leave us now, Sophie Keller Buchanan. I love you. I reached out and touched her hand. *This was not my grandma!* This hand was as cold as stone. I stepped back, frightened, then quickly left the room.

Now I was going to see John. Not the John I had known for half my life, not the man who loved me, who held me and protected me. He would never return. All that was left now was his body. And it was somewhere in this house—probably the next room. I realized Pam was talking to me. ". . . sorry but I have to send this out by Federal Express tonight. You just need to sign right here." I looked at the papers, but was unable to focus, unable to distinguish words. Everything was a blur. I signed where she pointed. That accomplished, the funeral director asked if I would like to "view the body." Feeling shaky, I held Rob's arm even tighter. I asked Pam to come with us.

I trembled as we entered, Rob on one side and Pam on the other. The casket was across the room, and it seemed I didn't control my motion toward it, I just moved forward. That's not him, I thought for an instant and then I was standing in front of the casket. It was John, all right, and sure enough, he was dead. Right there in front of me. I began crying, sobbing deeply, as did Pam and Rob. John looked uncomfortable to me. His shoulders seemed too large for the coffin, and his hair was wrong. It was combed straight back, not at all how he'd wear it. I can't let him be buried with his hair like that!

We had pretty much cried ourselves out when Smokey came in. I asked the others to let us have a word alone.

"Smokey, he just doesn't look right. He's too crunched looking. Maybe moving his hands would help . . . cross them on his stomach or something? And his hair is wrong. It should be combed down more. You know how he wore it." I couldn't watch Smokey try to remedy the problems, so I left the room.

"How ya doing, kid?" My big brother hugged me. I buried my head in his chest. How could John do this to me? How could he die?

On the drive to where we were staying, Pam, sensing I probably didn't know what I had signed, explained the legal papers again. They gave power of attorney to both her and Rob to deal with the L.A. coroner's office; I had the right to receive autopsy information before a general release, and now they could represent me in those communications.

The Belushis were at our place in Chilmark. I thought it would be comforting to them to stay in John's house, whereas the idea of staying there myself was not. I rented the Flanders House, a large, rambling, bed-and-breakfast place nearby, where I stayed with my family and some friends.

When we arrived, Danny, Michael Klenfner, and Mitch Glazer were there with the local and state police, who wanted to go over travel routes and security with Smokey. There was a lot of shuffling and clearing of throats as the policemen offered condolences. I thanked them, excused myself, and went upstairs.

The little bedroom was quiet, except for the sound of the March wind rattling the windows, and the pounding of my heart. Tired, but unable to sleep, I lay down for an hour before accepting that this wasn't restful. Oh, well, I should go over to my house and see the Belushis. This was a fearful thought. Although a part of me wanted to run to John's family, embrace them, cry, I was also afraid. I wasn't sure I could stand the pain it would bring. It was a hard moment to face.

On the way over I thought about John's parents, Adam and Agnes. What could they be thinking? Feeling? Their oldest son ... I recalled the story of how Adam reacted when his first child was a girl. An Albanian man should have a son! Two years later, John was the first Belushi boy born in America. Adam had worked hard and traveled a long way for this dream. In 1979 John gave his father one of his other dreams: a small ranch in the mountains outside San Diego. It wasn't the Ponderosa, but it was nice and the area offered endless riding. Adam had come to America with hopes of being a cowboy, and he loved horses more than anything. Except maybe the mountains.

So Adam, Agnes, Nena, and Billy had moved to Julian, California. We'd visited at Christmas and had a great time. Everyone seemed happy and healthy, the move seemed to be good. The following spring Nena died, and Billy, who attended a nearby college, moved into a place of his own. Adam spent most of his time with the horses and Agnes was lonely.

The ranch was isolated, and Julian didn't offer much social life. She missed Chicago and the family there. Her dream was that John would buy a place in Chicago so she could pop in for visits. In 1981, when a condo near relatives became available, John bought it and Agnes went to Chicago to decorate. Shortly after returning to the ranch, Agnes decided she would be happier in Chicago. There was never any talk of divorce, just a parting of the ways.

Adam and Agnes did seem remarkably different. Agnes has an infectious enthusiasm and youthful energy; she is inherently funny and makes friends easily. There is a child-like naïvete about her, a desire to try new things, to get out and be part of the gang. Her devotion to her children can be excessive, pushing them away. And she has a tendency not to listen, she is so determined to get her own point of view across. But her actions are well-meant and her heart is big.

Agnes is social and flamboyant and enjoys being the center of attention, and Adam didn't like that. He was very old-country, and over the years denied her the freedom to do many things she might have enjoyed, like taking part in a play, or just getting out together more. Adam was very dogmatic with his family: when he laid down the law, that was that and there was no discussing it. In fact, he is pretty stubborn in general, and it's difficult for him to open up. When I first met Adam he was gruff, but with time he softened and I realized he was shy. Gradually I discovered he could be charming, even talkative when he felt comfortable. His sparkling eyes and boyish expressions give him a gentleness hidden in his more sullen moods. And his accent and manner of speaking are endearing. I later learned that he is embarrassed by his accent and sometimes doesn't speak because of it; he has that sense of pride which is sometimes appealing, sometimes aggravating. But always, even in his old work clothes, there is a dignity about Adam which is undeniably natural.

The scene at my house was one of subdued activity. The aunts were busy in the kitchen, Jimmy was on the phone, and others sat around the room. There was quite a crowd. I think there were four sets of aunts and uncles, John's sister

Marian and her son Adam, Billy, Sandi, and John's parents.

When I arrived, a charge of energy shot through the room. The Albanian women all started crying, and there was a tremendous pull on me coming from Agnes. As I crossed the room I could see that her eyes were puffy and she looked weak. We embraced and someone gave me a chair. Tears were shed and my mother-in-law wailed in grief; it took some time before she calmed down, worn out by the process. As is customary with John's family, there was vocal concern about how thin I was, and I was quickly presented with a heaping plate of spaghetti. Much to everyone's surprise, I ate most of it. It was, in fact, the first time in three days that food had been at all appealing.

I don't remember talking with John's father. His face was sad and the circles under his eyes were very dark. We hugged and he cried briefly, seeming embarrassed by the emotion. He pulled a white handkerchief from his back pocket and dried his eyes.

I went to the bedrooms to look for Jimmy and Billy and found them having an argument with Marian. John's sister was so upset that Jimmy wanted her to take a Valium. She didn't want to. Billy sensed my distress at this situation and put his arm around me protectively and led me to another room. He said he loved me and held me for a while. When Billy spoke tears ran down his cheeks. "Everyone's going crazy," he said. "I just hope we can make it through this."

When Jimmy and I finally spent time alone, I don't think he cried right away. I do remember what it felt like when he finally did. Jimmy is about six inches taller, and much bigger than I, so I felt small in his embrace. But there was a power beyond size that surged from him as he sobbed. The energy pulsated from his chest, right through me. It was very painful, but I felt it would be okay; it wouldn't kill us. In fact, if he didn't let it out, it was clear it would be much more dangerous.

Just before we left I looked in John's drawer for my ring. I remembered a day in L.A. during the fall. I was with Tino and we'd stopped at a jewelry store to pick up something of his. Tino saw me admire a ring with a red stone heart and asked if I were going to get it. I didn't think it was the kind of ring you'd buy yourself, but he said if I liked it I should buy it. That evening, when John noticed the ring, he became quiet and seemed disturbed. "Is something wrong?" I asked.

"Where'd you get that ring?" he asked. I told him and he responded, "I wanted to get you something like that. I wish I'd given it to you."

A short time later, John and I were back on the Vineyard. As we lay in bed reading one night, I recalled the incident. I took off the ring, saying, "I have an idea, John. I want you to keep this, and some day in the future, when you think the time is right, you can give it to me." He liked this idea and gave me a kiss. He then reached over and put the ring into a drawer.

It was still there. I slipped it on my finger and headed out to the car. The night seemed especially black. It was dark and cold and I had nothing to look forward to.

MARCH 9

The morning of John's funeral no one needed to wake me. I lay in bed and tried to visualize the service. It was a technique John had explained to me to prepare for a show. He said to sit quietly and go through exactly what you would do; if you could do it in your mind, then you could do it onstage. Yes, I would approach this like a role. I'm The Widow. I should be strong, composed, carry myself with dignity. My husband had been a good and loving man, I would focus on the positives in our life. I imagined the service. I saw the open coffin in front, the body that was once John, now motionless, lifeless. I saw the pallbearers standing in a line, their solemn faces masking their hidden emotions. The image dissolved to Nena's funeral: we were filing past her coffin. The first, her son, kissed a picture of Jesus on the altar, then gave a final kiss to his mother. I felt a rush of panic, wondering if I was expected to do this, imagining the cold lips of my own grandmother. But I soon saw that this was a matter of choice, mainly observed by the older members of the church and Nena's own children. I brought myself back to the present. *I won't kiss John,* I thought. *I can't.*

In the chill of the winter morning I showered and cried. James had decided to sing "That Lonesome Road" after all, and the song had been going through my mind all morning.

> Walk down that lonesome road
> All by yourself
> Don't turn your head
> Back over your shoulder
> And only stop to rest yourself
> When the silver moon
> Is shining high
> Above the trees

I was nearly paralyzed by the idea of leaving the warmth and protection of the shower. I resented the fact that John wasn't there with a towel to rub me dry while I shivered in the bitter air and he laughed. He knew how I hated getting out of a shower on a cold day. How could he leave me like this?

Smokey knocked on the door and said that if I wanted to have time at the funeral home I should hurry. I drew a deep breath and turned the water to cold. John always tried to convince me I should let the cold water run on my head just before getting out. That's what a football coach once told him; gets your circulation going so the change in the air temperature doesn't seem so drastic. Numb, my heart pounding, I stepped out of the shower to face the day.

I was slow moving, so there wasn't time for Laila to put up my hair. Now, the hat and the veil didn't work, so I grabbed a floppy hat instead. It looked terrible, but I didn't care, I just wanted to get going.

Downstairs there was a lot of activity. Foremost was James's family rehearsing. His mother, his sister, Kate, and two brothers, Alex and Hugh, were singing harmony. Their voices blended together like that of a choir singing a hymn. When James sang out, his voice sent a chill up my spine.

If I had stopped to listen once or twice
If I had closed my mouth and opened my eyes
If I had cooled my head and warmed my heart
I'd not be on this road tonight

The song completed, James came over and gave me a
gentle, warm hug. I intentionally tried not to cry; he had a
difficult task ahead, and I guess I thought the more emotionally in control I was, the easier it might be for him. We
hugged a long time, then James pulled out a small pin and
handed it to me. "A fan of John's gave me this for you at my
concert last night," he explained. It was a small gold cross. I
was touched and surprised by the gift. The first piece of
jewelry John had ever given me was a cross. I pinned it to
my coat.

When I arrived at the funeral home, John's family was
already there, most of them sitting in the room with his
body, praying. My main concerns were to make sure that
John looked appropriate, and to place the heart ring in his
hand.

I spoke to Laila about John's hair not being right and she
felt she knew how to fix it. Jimmy was also aware of my
concern, and at one point I saw him make an attempt to fix
it. He stood next to the coffin with an expression that looked
like he was about to do something he shouldn't. After surveying the room, and determining that no one was looking,
he quickly, yet gently, stroked his brother's head, trying to
flatten his unruly hair.

John's hair had always been unmanageable. I had a vivid
image of him when he was about twenty. His hair was
shoulder length, but it seldom touched his shoulders. It seemed
to grow straight out from his head, as if he were a cartoon
character who'd just stuck his finger in an electrical outlet. I
frequently experienced this image going up the stairs to an
apartment I had in college. I would look up and, for a moment, see John standing there, smiling at me with his electric hair. It sometimes startled me it was so real. And I
always smiled back.

An undertaker informed us it was time to go to the church
and a numbing sensation shot through me. I felt like I was

on some horrible amusement park ride hurtling uncontrollably off its track. I was strapped in and there was nothing I could do but hope for the best. I shut my eyes and took another peek at that smiling boy. Okay John, this is it.

My parents traveled to the service with me, but I wasn't conscious of them. The limousine seemed motionless. I stared out the window aware of nothing but the scenes in my mind. I remembered how John looked as he leaned over to give me my first kiss; I watched the joy on his face as we galloped on horseback across a desert stream; I delighted in a day at the beach, observing the affinity he had with the ocean. "Come on, honey. You can do it," he taunted as he coaxed me into the freezing water. "I love you," he whispered in my ear.

Suddenly we were in front of the church. It seemed as if someone had simply changed sets when I wasn't looking. The West Tisbury Church was storybook Americana: white clapboard with a tall steeple and a clock in front, surrounded by a white picket fence. People lined both sides of the walk to the front door. The scene was slightly out of focus. The lyrics to James's song kept repeating:

> Carry on
> Never mind feeling sorry for yourself
> It doesn't save you from your troubled mind . . .

As the crowd came into focus, Bernie's snowy white hair and beard stood out. He was with Mitch and Klenfner. They wore only their suit jackets and I thought they must be cold. My legs felt weak when I stepped from the car. Bernie came over and as we embraced, the others encircled us. I felt we were being shielded, although I had no idea why. When Bernie let go of me I felt lost, unsure of where to go, what to do. I noticed that most of the people outside were press and police. "We should go in, they're waiting for us," someone said.

The room was smaller than the Albanian church in Chicago. Much smaller. The pulpit barely offered enough room for the two priests to stand, much less perform their rituals. There was activity in the back and I turned to see the casket being brought in. I was disturbed that it wasn't being carried by the pallbearers, but by two men who I at first thought were limo drivers. I asked Smokey what was going on and he said the funeral director thought the aisle was too small for everyone to carry the coffin. "I don't want these men to remove the casket," I said. "John's friend should carry him." Smokey nodded and quietly slipped out. Things were off to a bad start.

The casket wouldn't fit up front and was set in the aisle to the left of me. The priests entered, dressed in their ceremonial robes. I heard a faint gasp when the lid was raised, exposing John's body to the room. A cross and a picture of Christ were set on the coffin.

I looked over at John repeatedly throughout the service. He didn't appear to me to be sleeping, but was most definitely a body with no life. His head seemed larger than normal. Maybe it was because all his facial muscles were relaxed. Or maybe it was because he'd recently shaved off his sideburns. I still wasn't used to that.

For the first ten minutes or so I felt anxious. The priests seemed out of place in this stark interior. The incense was too strong for such a small room. There was no stained glass to provide warm colored light. This was not at all as I'd imagined. Maybe this mixture of Gothic America and Albanian Orthodox was too surreal.

As the priests performed their rituals, I soon found myself transformed by their magic. The ceremony freed me in some way and the tears flowed easily. There was no need, no desire, to hold them back. I had been afraid of becoming hysterical, but I needn't have worried. There was a protective energy in the air. While the priests recited the prayers in a hypnotic singsong manner, I chanted to myself, my eyes resting on John's expressionless face: At least the pain is over. At least the pain is over. . . .

Father Katre, the archbishop from Boston, gave a brief eulogy in his heavily accented English. He spoke about John as a son and brother, the boy growing up in Chicago, the young man becoming a husband. He commented on his importance to the Albanian community and the business community, then concluded, "We can hear the call of his solitary warning: 'Wise up!' " It was so unexpected to hear this distinguished gentleman suddenly say something funny (and he gave a good delivery!) that it caught the mourners off guard. How did he know that was one of John's catch-phrases? After a quiet moment of surprise, the room filled with laughter. I had wondered if I would feel John's spirit in the church, and although it wasn't the supernatural being I was thinking of, there was no doubt that the spirit of John Adam Belushi was very much with us.

It amused me to see the funny mingling of people witnessing an Albanian funeral in the middle of New England. Probably a third of the people there were Jews. The rest were fairly evenly divided between Catholics and WASPs. Maybe John was having the last laugh after all.

It was time to file past the coffin. Rob was on my left, so he was first. He kissed the icon, then took a long, last look at his brother-in-law. His face showed sadness, maybe some anger, but mostly disbelief. He took a deep breath, shook his head, and moved on. As I watched Rob, my fear of this moment left. I kissed the picture and looked at John. Unexpectedly, I realized I wanted to kiss him good-bye. I took his head in my hands and tenderly placed a kiss upon his forehead. My lips touched his hair, and to my relief I did not feel the cold of his body beneath it. For that moment I was totally unaware of anyone else in the room. I turned and went to my brother who held me as we stood waiting for the rest of our row to pass the coffin. I knew now, maybe for the first time, really, that John was dead. I could feel my heart pounding in every inch of my body. Suddenly I became aware of a commotion. John's mother was at the casket, sobbing uncontrollably. Jimmy and I helped her to her seat.

We sat again while the rest of the congregation filed past. It was painful to watch, so I stared at the floor. Every once in a while I looked up and noticed someone, often a friend I hadn't known was there: Anne Beatts, John Landis and his wife, Deborah, Treat Williams. Billy Murray's hair was tousled and the expression on his face told me that John's death was just sinking in for him, too. James Taylor stopped and took a long, very intense, sad look at John. There was something deep and gut-wrenching about his stare. At one point I saw an old friend with very new wave, very orange hair. If I weren't so unhappy, that hair would give me a chuckle, I thought. Maybe someday I'll remember this and laugh.

The five miles to the cemetery seemed endless. Danny headed up the motorcade on his Harley, followed by a police car from *The Blues Brothers* movie, the hearse, then us. We traveled at an impossibly slow pace.

The cemetery was bleak and cold. It was the gray season. The trees, ground, sky, water, and, here, even the people were all shades of gray. Along the fence that separated the cemetery from the road stood a group of forty or so people. My eye fixed on three Vineyard artists we knew. Allen, Doug, Zak! What are they doing over there? I gave a feeble wave for them to join us. They didn't see me, couldn't read my mind.

The pallbearers carried the coffin to the grave, Bernie leading the procession. There was a moment of confusion when Father Katre asked which direction was east. I had no idea. We wisely listened to the islanders among us, who pointed toward the ocean. Of course. John and I watched the sun rise over the ocean. It seemed not so long ago. My stomach tightened. I turned and searched the faces in the crowd. Could it really be true that John was no longer with us? The coffin was placed so that John's head faced east, in the Orthodox custom. Teta Dolly was concerned that everything be proper, and we assured her it was. With that decided, the fathers burned incense and began their blessings.

I was anxious for everything to be over. I had often driven past the cemetery, but never visited it. It always seemed like such a pretty, peaceful place. Now it was awful. None of the old trees graced the area where John was being buried. We stood in a large open field, with the wind ripping across the barren ground. I pulled my coat tight, but it was not the wind that made me shiver. This final act of putting John into the ground—this cold, hard ground—was one I hadn't envisioned, didn't want to accept.

I tried to lose my thoughts in the priest's chanting, that secret language with which they speak to God. I was comforted by their calm manner, which I thought must come from their belief in everlasting life. I imagined John's spirit leaving his body when he died. I saw him look down and, to his surprise, see himself lying there, dead. I imagined his reaction: "Holy shit!" Hmm, no. If there was a continuation of consciousness, I hoped it wasn't a difficult transition for John, that he accepted it with enthusiasm as a new experience. I hoped he was on a path with no memory of what went before, no knowledge of what was going on here. Or if he did know, that he had a new understanding which freed him from the kind of pain I was feeling.

I had asked Harold Ramis to say a few words at the grave. He and John had worked together at both Second City and *National Lampoon*. Harold's voice quivered slightly as he began, "I have known John and loved him ever since I saw him on the stage eleven years ago." I remembered that night. John had been excited, and a little nervous, because Harold was coming to the show. Harold, who left the cast before John was hired, had quite a reputation at the theater. Was it really eleven years ago? Now Harold was speaking at John's grave. It was all so weird. Harold said something about John being a good angel and I was startled, then realized he was talking about a scene where John had played the angel Gabriel. He was right. John had been a good angel. It was hard not to smile at the memory. John wore cardboard wings on his back and walked with a bounce so the wings would flap. Harold's words were sweet and brief, and then it was time for the song.

The Taylor family stood in a tight line and James began playing. Big Alex, the oldest brother, had tears rolling down his face. He shifted his weight, unable to sing. In fact, I think only Kate joined in. Huey, I remember, stood silent with the most endearing smile on his face. At the moment James raised his guitar, a helicopter that had been hovering nearby moved in and stopped directly overhead. Without missing a beat, James shot an admonishing glance at the intruders, and with great self-possession and respect, sang out loud and clear. His dignity made him by far the tallest man in the crowd. Almost as if it had been shamed, the helicopter retreated, and James's voice, sweet and warm, cut through the cold, crisp, March afternoon and fell upon the hearts of the silent mourners.

As the final chord vibrated, I shut my eyes and took in a long, deep breath. My chest tightened from the cold air and I felt weak. It's almost over. Hold on. The priests said another prayer and I wished they would finish. Then Father Katre nodded at me and I recalled that we had placed flowers on Nena's coffin at the end of her service. I stepped forward, selected a red rose from the flowers beside the grave, and laid it on John's coffin. I rested my hand on the lid a moment. It was cold. Lifeless. I turned and quickly walked away. Don't look back, I told myself. It's over, walk on, walk on . . . From dust to dust . . . Good-bye John. I retreated to the darkness of the limousine and waited for my parents.

I don't remember the drive back to the Flanders House, or the others arriving. My first memory is standing in a doorway with Larry, hugging and crying. Larry Bilzerian was John's best Vineyard buddy. In December he'd gone on a three-day trip to L.A. with John and had seen what it was like for him: a constant onslaught of people who wanted something. Mostly they wanted a piece of him—contact, an autograph, a lunch, a phone number. They had an idea for him, they wanted an idea from him, they just wanted to hang out. Some of that John enjoyed, he liked the action and the attention to a point. But it was constant in Los Angeles. And the pressure of his "star" image was strongest there. It sometimes seemed that everyone you met in Los Angeles wanted to be a star. And they wanted to see their stars *be* stars. Los Angeles, town of dreams, the ultimate fantasy spinner, encouraged John Belushi to be bigger than life. People looked at him and saw someone who created excitement, money, power, good times. He evoked feelings of friendship, awe, respect, even resentment. Everyone felt they knew him. He was a man of the people, he wasn't an unreachable star. And they expected him to be the image they had of him, were disappointed if he wasn't! I guess he just wasn't strong enough to deal with it all, especially if he was there alone. I think the combination of having so many people's attention, and yet feeling lonely, was confusing. He wanted to feel good, he must have told himself that he deserved to feel good! So he turned to drugs and those who offered them.

"Those bastards!" Larry kept repeating, tears streaking his face.

"I know, Lare, I know . . ." was all I could say. Why had I let him go back there alone? Why, why, why . . .

I'd held up fairly well, but was tired, empty. I recall Father Katre taking my hands, looking me in the eye, and saying, "You're young . . . Life goes on . . ." I tried to be receptive to his words, but all the while I was nodding in agreement I was thinking, he doesn't understand. Yes, I was young and might have a long life ahead, but it would never be the same without John. I would never feel happy again. The older, the wiser ones, kept telling me to give myself time. Time? It was ironic, almost insulting. The best anyone could offer was vague and immeasurable. It was something to say when you didn't know what to say. Give it time? I don't have time! I have right now. What am I supposed to do now to keep from dying? Yes, I thought I might die. It was hard to know, I was only just getting over the shock, but there was a big hole in me and it certainly felt deadly.

My plans were to fly home that night. I was leaning against a window when Smokey said, "If you want to go back on the plane, we'll have to leave soon because of the snow."

"The snow?" I questioned, turning to see a flurry of white flakes. I shivered. John wanted to be here this year for the snow; how many times had he said it? Well, here he was. I suddenly wanted to stay another night. "Tell them to go without us, Smokey. We'll drive back tomorrow."

As things were winding down, John's sister, Marian, told me that she and her son Adam were going home to Chicago. She said the experience had been very trying for Adam, and the memorial would be too much. Adam was only eleven, and I had worried about him, too. He looked so confused. "It's not just Adam," Marian admitted. "I really can't take any more myself. I hope you understand." Of course I understood. Marian and John, only two years apart, had been great buddies as kids. Although she was older, John had been kind of a big brother to her. What would she do without him? Everything was so sad.

That evening at sunset, Danny organized a twenty-one-gun salute off the cliff at our house. He, Smokey, Huey Taylor, and four others made up the squad. Only a handful of friends remained. As we waited for any stragglers, I began to worry that there was going to be a gun accident. I was sure one would go off in someone's hand. Finally everyone was ready and we all bundled up and went out for the ceremony.

The men stood in a line along the cliff, facing out to sea. There were seven honor guards, so each was to shoot three times, pausing three counts between each shot. Danny gave the signal, and one by one each of the men fired into the air. For over a minute the repetition exploded over the waves, resounding across the sea. Just before Danny let go of the twenty-first salute, he lowered his rifle and yelled into the night, "This one's for you, Johnny!" His voice rang out like a battle cry; the "Johnny" lingered, then united with the reverberation of the final blast. We listened to the echo as it faded into infinity, zig-zagging across the heavens in search of our friend. Good luck, John, I wished into the night. Good-bye.

Chapter 3

FOR A DANCER

TUESDAY, MARCH 10

We left for New York before noon. Knowing that the coroner's office might have the autopsy results later that day, Pam told them she'd phone every few hours. She reiterated that we would need a little time after receiving the information to reach family members before a general release was made. Most of the drive, I wondered if Pam already had the results.

As we drove down the West Side Highway into Greenwich Village, the sun was low in the sky. Morton Street was quiet. Inside, the apartment was dark and shadowy as the early winter darkness set in. Some family members were already there and Pam arrived just behind us. The phone rang. It was the coroner's office. Pan ran in to take the call; however, when she picked up, the line was dead. She rang back immediately, but was told that Noguchi, the coroner, was unavailable. He was at a press conference. Within moments, Jimmy called on the other line. He had the official results of the autopsy: death from an injection of heroin and cocaine. The coroner's office had phoned Bernie.

The television was on and simultaneously a news flash announced the autopsy report. It was a very confusing and painful moment, rather as if we'd just learned that John had died. Everyone cried again. I didn't understand why they'd first told us there was no sign of drug use, when clearly there must have been evidence. But heroin? I couldn't believe John would shoot heroin! And just as bad, he broke his promise.

It was during the binge in L.A., the one that sent me to

49

Dr. Cyborn, when he made the promise. The evening had begun with an argument and I nearly stormed off to catch a plane to New York. John insisted we talk it out and we finally did. I expressed my anger and fears about his cocaine use during the previous two weeks. John listened and apologized. He agreed with almost everything I had to say, but pointed out that he had been doing darn well the last year and a half, clean most of that time. He considered it a slip, and assured me he would stop using coke as soon as he returned home. In fact, he couldn't wait to get home, as soon as he and Don completed *Noble Rot.* "But if you'd leave town for a few days and rest up, come back straight, you'd work so much better," I said.

"If I don't do this now, it will be too late!" John was adamant. "The work will be over in a few days."

"John, I can't help you do it this way," I said. "I've told you before I won't be a part of this any more."

We agreed that I should go home the next day and he would return when he was finished with his project. Later, as I was reading in bed, John coyly entered the room with his best bad-boy-trying-to-make-good face. When I smiled in response he came over to the bed and hugged me.

"I love you, honey," he said.

"I love you, too."

"I know why you're worried about me, I know I get crazy when I do this stuff. But I'm okay, honest I am."

I was in a difficult position. We'd communicated on a good level earlier, and I wanted to let go of my anger so we could move on, but it would not be instantaneous. I knew John wanted to complete our making-up with making love. I didn't feel that way yet. John was still coming down from the cocaine, and I wanted to wait until he was straight. It was emotionally difficult for me to be close to him physically when he was high, since I had such bad feelings about his being that way. I had told John all this before, and didn't want to get into it again right then.

"John, I just feel . . . I can't even explain . . ."

John suddenly became very serious. "I know what it is, I know what's worrying you. You think I'm doing heroin."

I was taken by surprise and let out a short, nervous laugh. "Well, no, I wasn't . . . Should I be?"

I looked at him suspiciously. I hadn't been worried because of his attitude about heroin. John always reacted strongly when people talked about it, emphasizing that it was stupid to even fool around with heroin. Why had he brought it up now?

"I want to tell you something," John said standing up and beginning to pace. "When I got out of the hospital after my knee operation, and was having all that pain, and I finished my prescription but they wouldn't give me any more pain-killers . . . I did heroin for a little while."

I was stunned. So that explained his behavior then. It was early 1977 when he'd hurt himself during a college lecture. While performing his samurai character, he made an overenthusiastic lunge from the stage and tore the cartilage in his knee. Recovery had been slow and John's drug use increased. I'd thought at the time that John was mixing coke and quaaludes. It was a terrible couple of months.

"That's why I wanted to go up to Danny's alone that time, because that's when I cooled out."

Yes, it was spring when he'd visited Danny in Canada. I wasn't sure how I felt about John's confession. The fact that he had quit on his own—and I was certain he did quit since there was a drastic change and no other comparable time— was good. I think what bothered me most was learning of the deception. But at least, even after all these years, he had finally shared his secret.

"I never used all that much, mainly I just snorted. Once a dealer shot me up. I didn't like it. I threw up."

I just listened in silence. I really didn't know what to say. It was hard to imagine John letting someone shoot him up. Even when he was getting B-12 shots it was a big deal. Sometimes he'd change his mind after the doctor had the needle ready. He even passed out once when he had a blood test.

"I quit doing heroin in Canada, honey. I haven't been into it at all since. Believe me, I know I want to stay away from that stuff."

I don't remember what I said next, but I remember John's reaction. It was not said in the childish, flirting manner he'd so charmingly used earlier. This was a grown man, sitting up tall, holding my shoulders to give me a gentle shake, who said, "Honey, I don't want you to worry about it. I promise you I will *never* do heroin again. Okay?" He pulled my chin up with his hand. "Look me in the eye. Come on, I'm promising you." Interestingly, I began to cry. "Hey, now," he said, pulling me to him, "have I ever let you down on a promise? Have I?"

"No," I admitted. It was true. There wasn't a solemn promise John ever made me that he hadn't kept. There had been a lot of broken drug promises over the years, though, but I didn't consider most of them sincere. The serious ones had been "to try" and he always did try. And there was progress from those times. Was this a solemn promise or a drug promise? I didn't know and cried into John's embrace because I was scared. Scared enough to call Dr. Cyborn for help. Help that was too slow, too late . . .

This memory was outrageous! How stupid could I be? The man needed help. Oh, God, why did he put on such a good act? Why did he make the promise? Had he wanted to make his word good and just failed? Was it all just a lie? Did it mean he hadn't loved me any more? That he'd been angry with me?

I was tired and weary and didn't know what to think. At least now I was certain as to the "mystery woman's" role. I didn't understand what happened to John in the last week of his life, and I clearly hadn't understood his drug problem, but I *knew* my husband. I knew he did not have a secret habit of shooting drugs prior to that week. And I knew he could not put a needle into his own arm. This woman, whose name I didn't even know, must have given John the fatal injection.

About half an hour later John's brothers came by the house. There was more crying and hugging, then we collapsed on a couch in exhaustion. Jimmy dug into his pants pocket and pulled out a crumpled piece of paper. "I have my notes for tomorrow," he said, wearily unfolding his outline.

"Do you want to hear them?" Jimmy raised his eyebrows as if they held his eyes open and looked to me for encouragement. It was as if we had just completed a tremendous journey, only to be told we had to set out again immediately. I smiled and nodded for him to go ahead. Like a child denying he needs sleep by insisting on telling you one last story, Jimmy went over what he intended to say at the memorial. I told him it sounded wonderful, which it did. But I hoped he would have the strength to tell it with the grace with which he'd written it.

THURSDAY, MARCH 11

The morning of the memorial predicted another gray day. I had a light breakfast and went over arrangements again with Smokey, leaving enough time for Laila to put up my hair and fix the veil. Full widow garb this time.

Before we left, I asked my sisters to join me in the sound room to listen to the song Rhonda would sing at the service. I thought it might help release some of the emotions it would stir. We closed the doors and put on the record, then the three of us stood there, arm in arm, crying while we listened. Afterwards, the image of the three of us standing in front of the sound system, as if we were worshiping it, struck me as funny. John would like that idea, I thought. He loved a good sound system. In fact, had I thought of it, I would have taken the damn thing to St. John's, put on one of his favorite songs, and cranked it up!

The procession to the service began from 60 Morton. The street was lined with limousines, and Smokey had everyone in their cars, ready to go. When he came for me I noticed the house seemed oddly quiet. I wanted to have a word with John's mother before we began our drive, to share a moment together. Smokey explained that everyone else was already in their limos, and suggested we talk in her car.

Once on the street I was surprised by the crowd. I had looked out and seen them gathering, but until that moment I

didn't realize that they, too, were sad. I felt it as soon as I
stepped out. It was quiet and still. These were not people just
trying to get a glimpse of a tragedy, they were mourners.
Many of them were neighbors. I saw the three ladies who
often sat on the stoop next door. "How are you this evening,
ladies?" John would often ask them, and they would smile
and respond and the look in their eyes showed their approval
that the neighborhood "star" was a gentleman. I saw an
elderly lady who always walked her dog on our street. She
was standing there, her pet at her side, wiping her eyes with
a hankie. A familiar couple stood together, the husband's
gentle embrace comforting his wife.

I slid into the back seat with my mother-in-law and took
her hand. She looked very tired. "Mom, this is going to be
another hard day, are you going to be okay?"

"Well, I'll do my best."

"We're going to be okay. You know there are going to be a
lot of people there, and you and I are the women who represent John. I want us to be strong, to show what we're made
of. Okay? I'm not saying we shouldn't cry, just try not to lose
it. Jimmy, Dad, Billy, everyone needs us. Let's try to remember how lucky we were to have John in our lives for as long
as we did." We embraced for a while and then my mother-in-
law pulled herself up.

"Okay, honey, don't you worry about me."

"I'm not worried. I just wanted you to know I'm thinking
about you."

As I switched to my limo, someone grabbed my arm. It was
Sally, a local character, an older woman whom I often hired
for odd jobs. "Judy, can I come up to the church with you?"
she asked. I explained that the front cars were for the family,
but said I'd find someone to take her. I looked around and
grabbed Peter Aykroyd, Dan's brother, and asked him to
help.

The drive to the church was slow and indirect since I
wanted to drive past certain landmarks. First we headed
downtown to Tribeca and past the Blues Bar. Next we wound
our way up to Fifth Avenue and Twentieth Street where
Phantom Enterprises, the production company I shared with
John was located. We continued on up, past the NBC build-

ing ("SNL" headquarters), through Central Park and on up to the Cathedral of St. John the Divine. Smokey chuckled to himself as we arrived at a back door without a hitch. To avoid the press, he'd told everyone we would come up a different entrance out front. Sure enough, they were all set up where he'd said.

The service was set for noon and we started almost on schedule. The thousand or so people there were closely packed into the front section of the church. When I entered from the back, I could feel the room react to my arrival. People sensed we were beginning and the motion in the room settled down as people who were standing took their seats. The walk down the aisle to my seat in the first row was most unreal. I felt that people could only look at me briefly, as if the act were painful. I fixed my own gaze on the altar. The organ music seemed to float through me. My aunt, my father's sister, was playing, and even though I could see the organ pipes, I had no idea where it was that my aunt was creating the sounds. Rhonda, Paul Shaffer, and Tom Scott were seated in the front near the piano. They looked rather like children at an important recital: respectfully quiet, sitting erect, solemnly concentrating on their parts.

Bishop Moore walked across the pulpit as the music concluded. In his robes, Paul Moore was a striking figure, tall and regal in manner, with sterling silver hair. He welcomed the crowd and the service began with prayers and hymns. I was anxious to get through all that and on to the speakers and the song, not only because that was the heart of the service, but because I was nervous for my friends. They were all professionals who could certainly bear up to the pressures of performing, but none had ever been tested under the stress of grief. Finally, Bishop Moore introduced Jimmy.

He rose and went to the podium. Most of the people there didn't know John's brother, hadn't ever seen him. I think to many the similarity was startling.

Jimmy unconsciously pulled up his pants from the belt, a habit he shared with John, and surveyed the room. "What a beautiful hall," he commented before getting into his prepared address. "I can't help but think that John would have loved to play this room. I can see him doing somersaults down the aisle. I think he still believes he really did those flips in *The Blues Brothers!*"

Jimmy had broken the ice and was off to a good start. He still looked a little uncomfortable, however, as he stuffed his hands into his pants pockets and continued. "Older brothers are sort of like fathers, and John's approval was like sunshine."

I was most nervous for Jimmy. After all, he was trying to carry on in the face of his brother's death; his older brother, not an easy one to live up to. Jimmy had followed John's reputation from grade school to high school, then to Second City and into an acting career. John was hard on him in terms of making sure that Jimmy made it on his own in the business. Not because he didn't think Jimmy was good; he was very admiring of Jimmy's talents, but said he wanted Jimmy to know that whatever work he got was because of who he was, not because of who his brother was.

As Jimmy spoke, I anticipated what he would say next, hoping he could keep up his energy, while keeping his emotions at bay. About midway through I relaxed. Jimmy was nothing short of wonderful. As he spoke about John, his eyes lit up with admiration. He shared his memories with warmth and humor and charmed the room.

"I think one thing everyone remembers about John was his generosity. He was always giving. To the family, to the public, sometimes to people he didn't even know. Yet it seems he never needed anything, it never seemed there was anything you could do for John . . . except maybe get him an ashtray."

Jimmy made some comment about how many people benefited financially from John's work—not only the family, but agents and lawyers and theater owners and large corporations. "Why, even now, the press is still making money off John," he noted.

Jimmy closed with a story about his first visit to the Division Street Baths with John. "One time when John was in Chicago, he said he wanted to take me to this great steam bath 'to *schvitz*,' he said, to sweat." At this point there was some laughter from the audience. John had taken many friends to *schvitz*. "So I went with him and he dragged me into this hot, hot steam room. 'John,' I said, after we were there a little while, 'I think I'm gonna pass out.' So he grabbed me and put me in a cold tub. Then he made me lie down on a table where this guy rubs you with oak leaves that have been soaking in scalding hot water. I was beginning to think this was some kind of test, but when he made me go into the cold tub again, I doubted that he liked me at all. Now, after all this, we took a shower. And as we were standing there, side by side, he began washing my hair. Here I was twenty-five years old and my brother was washing my hair! John never said 'Hey, I love you, Jim,' but that day he did. Not in words, but when he washed my hair . . ." Jimmy paused a moment, smiling to himself. "When we finished we went upstairs and had a big meal. Then John turned to me and said, 'Got any money?' "

Laughter and tears followed Jimmy's stories. When he was finished, the trio members quickly took their places. Paul sat at the piano, Tom picked up his sax, and Rhonda stood at the microphone with the most angelic look as she waited for the music. I hadn't heard them rehearse, but I never doubted for a moment that the performance would be perfect. Paul, who normally looks somewhat impish when he plays, had a more serious demeanor than I'd ever seen. His piano playing was as beautiful as ever, though, solid and emotional. Tom's solo was wonderful, seemingly effortless. It wasn't a wailing sax sound, but crisp and soulful. And Rhonda was amazing. Her gaze was fixed on some distant point we could only imagine, and she had the most unusual smile. Her attitude combined with her clear, steady voice, brought a forceful, positive sense to the lyrics. The overall effect was powerful.

It felt odd when the music ended and we didn't applaud. It would have been natural to give a rousing ovation to such a lovely performance. Instead we were left to contemplate the seriousness of the occasion as the final notes of the music echoed in the great cathedral.

Now Danny walked up to the podium, carrying a cumbersome bag which he placed on the floor beside him. He began with an uncharacteristic softness: "I wrote many things for and with John. I know this is one assignment he'd rather I didn't have to take on." Then his voice became deep and brisk, as Danny tends to sound when he is serious. "Although I had a close, head to head, arm to arm, working relationship with John, that proximity never affected the fact that from the moment I met him, through all the work, I remained his number one fan. He was a brilliant performer, writer, tactician, business strategist and, most importantly" —Danny's voice softened again—"he was the only man I could dance with.

"He was a great—a world class—emissary of American humor. John was a patriot, a resident of the most wide open, liberal society on earth, and he took full advantage of it." Danny's speech was crisp and he spoke with authority. "In some cases, real greatness gives license for real indulgence; whether it's as a reward, as therapy, or as sanctuary. For as hard as John worked, there had to be an additional illicit thrill to make the effort all worthwhile.

"John was a nighthawk, true, but he was not an immoral individual. He was a good man, a kind man, a warm man, a *hot* man." The word "hot" sizzled. He paused a moment, surveying the room. "What we are talking about here is a good man, and"—Danny leaned up closer to the microphone and spoke very deliberately—"a bad boy."

Danny paused again, referring to his notes briefly. "John visited me in Canada one summer. He was, naturally, allowed to cross the Canadian border without having one piece of identification. He rarely carried I.D. He didn't have to. First of all, his word was good, his handshake honored, and he was the kind of guy you just wanted to give to. All the doors on the continent were open to John. He would walk into the homes of complete strangers—I watched it happen and I heard a number of stories about it—go into the kitchen, open the refrigerator, have a sandwich, turn on the TV and go to sleep on the couch while the lucky home-dwellers watched in amazement and delight. I once told him, and he liked it, that he was America's Guest. And he hadn't yet worn out his welcome."

Danny spoke briefly about John's dislike of playing a bee, a character he was forced to do several times on "Saturday Night Live." "The first blues number we ever performed was a song called King Bee. Although John hated being a bee, he didn't mind it under those circumstances because he was able to be the King Bee.

"Last summer on the Vineyard, John was the happiest I'd ever seen him. We were out one morning in his Jeep and I played an instrumental by the Ventures on the tape deck. He asked me what it was called. I told him. He laughed, I laughed, and we promised each other that we'd force it upon a churchful of people at the time of our respective deaths. Whomever went first." Danny leaned over and pulled a tape deck from his bag. He placed it next to the microphone, turned it on at full volume, and made good his promise. "So here it is, for the King Bee, a little closer by The Ventures called the '2,000 Pound Bee.'"

It was quite funny, Danny standing there, slapping his leg to the beat. People began to laugh, looking around to see how others were reacting. It seemed to get sillier the longer it lasted, and Danny wasn't about to stop before the last note filtered across the vast room into silence.

To many, it brought back the memory of John's enthusiasm for music. "Wow!! You've got to hear this one," he would say in his excitement as he pulled out yet another record, absorbed in his fury to share all new music he enjoyed. Many had spent evenings with John while he played records, and gave a history lesson about each song, composer, and group. Around the apartment, when he asked new "victims" into the sound room to hear some song or artist they didn't know, Mitch, Laila, and I would laugh and joke that we'd see them later—if they survived.

We listened to the music until it faded, then it was the laughter that lingered. Danny stuffed the machine back into his bag, then waited a moment for the room to quiet. "So there, Johnny," he said, picking up the bag. He looked out at the crowd again. "And you can be sure that I'll have my antennae out for the paranatural and the spiritual, and, believe me, if there's any contact with him, I'll let you know."

Danny sat down and Bishop Moore returned to the pulpit. To my surprise, he, too, had a story to tell. One afternoon the previous summer he had stopped by our house on Martha's Vineyard. "Well, I was only there a short while, when, before I knew it, John was handing me this pink electric bass and suggesting we jam! 'But, I don't play the bass, John,' I informed him. 'That's okay, I'll teach you.' Well, he showed me what to do and in a matter of minutes we were playing 'Louie, Louie!' " Of course, at this point, most of us were laughing pretty hard. It was funny to imagine the Bishop with a pink bass, playing "Louie, Louie." He closed commenting on the eagerness to teach and the willingness to share that were so typical of John.

The service ended with a prayer, and my anxieties returned. I had escaped for a while there in the church—become lost in the unity of the people, been uplifted by the music, comforted by the strength of the speakers and the memories they shared, the laughter they evoked. Now it was over and I would have to return to my own reality. The reality of life without John. Smokey stood and offered me his arm. I needed the support as I took that long walk up the aisle.

An image struck me, of walking up a church aisle on the arm of a man. It seemed an old familiar image. But wasn't it supposed to be a wedding? I felt shaky, but I kept moving. I tried to find whatever it was Rhonda had focused on. Maybe it would give me strength. Then suddenly, as I was almost up the aisle, I saw Sally, from our neighborhood. She nearly lunged in front of me to wave and let me know she'd gotten there, which startled me and brought me back to the moment. I realized what a remarkable event had just transpired, what an incredible mixing of people, what a warm display of love, what a wonderful remembrance! I felt pretty good as I walked out of the church.

All that was left now was the reception and I was going to be up! I was suddenly concerned that people might not know where to go. Smokey assured me they did and suggested we wait for the traffic to settle down before leaving. We sat a short while, but I was too impatient, couldn't sit still any longer, and I almost jumped out of the car to tell someone something that Smokey convinced me could wait. As we headed out, I saw Duck Dunn, the Blues Brothers' bassist, standing alone. I rolled down my window, leaned out and yelled to him. "Duck! Do you need a ride?" He looked at me and he was so sad, he just stood there and shook his head. "No, I'll see you there," he said softly. I came back to earth a little, realizing the day wasn't over, yet.

Downtown, in front of Danny's building, a small crowd had

gathered. The limousine seemed to excite them; they moved closer to the car, leaving a small path to the door. But when Smokey opened the door and helped us out, they were disappointed. "Oh, it's nobody," an observer remarked.

Danny's loft was huge and quickly filling with people. Shortly after we arrived I found myself feeling tired, already crashing from the brief high after the service. And I felt so unattractive. I'd had the hat and veil to hide under in church, but it was too much now. I kept my sunglasses on, however, even though the loft was so dark I could barely see.

For what seemed like hours I stood and spoke with a steady stream of people. I tried to visit with those I hadn't seen throughout the week. There were so many: Dan Payne, John's high-school acting teacher, the man who had helped him get into summer stock; Juanita Payne, Dan's wife, with whom John had become very close after he graduated from high school; so many people connected with Second City, including the producers and John's fellow actors, Brian Doyle-Murray, and Joe Flaherty's wife, Judith; Matty Simmons, the Chairman of the Board of National Lampoon; Laraine Newman, one of the members of John's "SNL" cast and Lorne Michaels, their producer. The parade went on: Penny Marshall, Paul Simon, Carrie Fisher, Christopher Reeves, and Carly Simon. The flow seemed endless. At one point I turned around and two friends from high school were standing there. I couldn't believe they'd come. So many friends had come.

I wanted to spend more time with guests; well, more to the point, I wanted to spend a different time. Everyone was awkward and unhappy. I was exhausted and hungry. I hadn't had a moment to eat, hadn't really had the desire, but I was in need of food now. I just wanted to get away and sit down in some quiet restaurant. I told Smokey it was time to go, and he said he wanted to check out what was going on outside first. The crowd on the street had grown considerably and people complained it was hard to get through.

Before I left I wanted to say thanks to Peter Aykroyd, on whose shoulders much of the party had fallen. Peter and his girlfriend had moved from Toronto to New York City about 1976, during the second season of "SNL," and the four of us quickly developed a strong friendship. John felt an instant warmth with Danny's brother, and it was nice to have friends who were a couple. We hadn't had any close "couple" friends for some time, and they were welcomed by us both.

Peter was in L.A. the week John died, and had returned for the services. I finally found him darting about the room, trying to keep up with the needs of the guests. "Peter, I'm leaving soon, but I wanted to thank you for handling all this, and for staying and helping with the services."

"Don't be silly," Peter said softly. "I had to be with you and Dan."

I said my good-byes as well as I could, while Smokey collected the friends who were going with me. Soon Laila, Kathryn, Judith Flaherty, and I were following Smokey down a back stairway and out onto a side street where we easily made our getaway.

Once again it struck me that I must have drunk quite a lot but wasn't the least bit high. Just kind of numb. Well, at least the pressure of the group activities was over. I didn't feel relieved exactly. I didn't really know what I was feeling, I just felt empty. And I felt tremendously heavy, yes, I think that could describe it. It was as if the air all around me was thick and heavy and pushing in on me.

Once in the car, Smokey asked where I'd like to go, a difficult question. Where could I go? Certainly none of our usual spots. In fact, every place I knew was wrong. We finally settled on a Greek restaurant in Tribeca. It held no memories. It was safe.

I don't particularly remember the meal or the conversation, although I do remember I wanted to drag it out. There was a certain unrealness to our time there. We had no more obligations, we were tired and silly. Smokey made several phone calls and we looked for things from the day we could laugh at. We teased Smokey for being so official all the time. In general, we just avoided the obvious. We had spent the day remembering John. For now, we were keeping thoughts of him to ourselves.

Later that night, Smokey, Laila, Hunter Thompson, and I sat in my living room and talked. Hunter, author of *Fear and Loathing in Las Vegas,* lived in Aspen and, although he had said he would come, no one really expected him to make it. (Hunter has been known to miss a plane now and then.) He surprised a lot of people by showing up, but then, he's always been unpredictable. I noticed he was more subdued than usual. As his books would suggest, Hunter enjoys creating confusion and doom whenever possible, but that night there was a gentleness. He was thoughtful with his words. He seemed genuinely moved by the events of the day, uncertain what to make of the whole situation.

The week had taken its toll and I went go bed quite early. Upstairs Hunter, Laila, and Smokey talked, while I was lost in another dark and dreamless sleep.

Chapter 4

LIMBO

MARCH 12–18

Smokey had an early afternoon flight, so I hurried out of bed to catch him before he left. Throwing on a robe, I thought how lucky I was to have had his help during the past week. Considering our unusual working relationship and friendship, I knew it must have been important for him, too.

Smokey was first hired by John, specifically to help him stay away from drugs. Although it had been John's idea, he did everything in his power to get away from Smokey for the first two weeks, once even physically struggling with him. I guess this was John's way of testing him. Smokey proved himself quickly, recognizing John's tricks and outsmarting him. That gained John's respect and their relationship changed: John trusted Smokey and followed his recommendations, such as when to leave a situation, or what people to stay away from. But I think Smokey helped John most by being there, at all times of the day or night, when John got an urge for cocaine. It was as if there were moments when the urge would be so strong that it was nearly impossible to combat. But if John could just hold out long enough, he would be okay again. Smokey was successful because he was so available to help John. Not to physically fight him, but to talk things through until the urge passed. With time, these urges happened less often, until it seemed that John had lost the desire. Then Smokey's job became more that of a basic security person: living with us to ease various stresses, being with John in public excursions or at work, managing our travel arrangements. Within six months or so, Smokey's role had changed completely. John was turning down drugs on his own and seemed to have control, and Smokey's days become fairly routine. In fact, by the time Smokey left our employ, he was helping me more than John. Yes, Smokey'd been a good friend over the years, and I wanted to let him know that I appreciated that.

Upstairs, I found him already gone. But he'd left me a note:

Judy,

I really won't go into details about this past week, however, only to say that I'll miss John so very much more than words can say. I know everyone said much about him, yet I never did, only because . . . I could see how hard it was for you to listen and thank everyone. I would like only to say that there will always be a void inside me without him here with you. Inside I loved and wanted only the best for John, in my eyes he could always be the ideal person to be with. . . . It is only now that I can and will feel the emptiness of him not here, to allow the tears to flow from my eyes—because I just don't want you to see that side of me. Lord knows you've had enough tears around you just this past week . . .

I want to thank you for all that you've ever done for me and for letting me be a part of your life and somewhat a part of your family.

Remember, I'll always be there for you . . .

Love, Smokey

As I read, tears filled my eyes until they overflowed. I knew how much Smokey loved and respected John, but in my dependence on his strength, I hadn't really considered his emotions during the week. Smokey was a good man and he'd come through, as both a professional and a friend.

Showering before a meeting with my business manager, I wondered what was so pressing that we had to meet on a Saturday. Again, I counted my blessings. Mark Lipsky was another good friend, I was lucky to have him manage my finances. It made me feel a little less alone.

What to wear? The question was debilitating and I stood looking at my clothes a long time. I had no feeling for who I was, no feeling of being the least bit attractive, no desire of any kind that had anything to do with why people wear clothes. All I knew was that I should wear black. I noticed an extra dress that Sandi and Laila had bought. Well, there was the answer. I heard the doorbell and knew it was Mark, right on time as usual.

Upstairs, I was surprised to find several people seated around the kitchen table. Beside Mark and his younger brother were Mark's father (a senior partner of the Lipsky firm), Bernie, Pam, and Rob. Mr. Lipsky had never before been involved in any of our meetings, in fact I'd only met him in passing. When I entered, the men rose and I was reintroduced to Mr. Lipsky, who offered his condolences. We all sat down, except Mr. Lipsky who pulled papers from his briefcase and began, "You are all here today to witness the reading of the last will and testament of the late John Adam Belushi . . ."

My heart began to pound, I was so startled. I felt panicked. I was familiar with the will, of course, we had written it together. I knew I was sole heir, and what our finances were. I just hadn't thought about it. I guess I never expected to hear the reading of John's will; not as a young woman, anyway.

Mr. Lipsky continued with some legalese and read from the will. It was odd. We'd spent a lot of time deciding what would happen if we both died—there were several pages to cover that possibility—but only one brief paragraph dictating what would happen if one of us died. Everything simply remained with the survivor. Suddenly I realized Mr. Lipsky was talking about life insurance, another thing I hadn't thought about since John died. Mr. Lipsky stated the amount I would receive and I felt the most unusual revulsion.

It is difficult to express, for I'm a middle-class kid, and not unaware that I inherited a lot of cash. Perhaps it was precisely because I did know, intellectually, how much money it was; perhaps because, subconsciously, money is supposed to be a good thing, something to make you happy; perhaps because there is no way to put a price tag on human life—for whatever reason, I felt a tremendous rush of sadness and anger. I wanted to slam my fist on the table and scream, "No! That isn't enough! I will not accept this as a trade for John!" My brother, sensing my distress, crossed the room and put his arm around me. I rested my head against his body and closed my eyes to hold back the tears. No, I don't want this money . . . I want John back!

Later that night I phoned my mother-in-law and assured her my financial situation was sound and that I would continue with the support to the family. I said things would be slightly altered since my income was, at least for the time being, "fixed." I also had a question for her: "Mom, I was wondering if there were any Albanian customs widows follow that might be appropriate for me?"

"Well," she exhaled, weighing the question. "In the old country, a widow wore black for the rest of her life . . . but here, widows wear black for forty days."

I felt like I'd been sentenced to life, then reprieved. The way she'd put it, forty days seemed like nothing. I decided immediately to wear black for that length of time.

I went to Florida for the week with Laila to meet James and Kathryn at some resort. It seemed to make others feel better to know I was getting away. I couldn't have cared less where I was. We headed out with minimum luggage, a portable tape deck, and a bottle of Jack Daniels. I always prefer to travel light, but one mustn't ignore essentials.

The time in Florida was most unusual. Kathryn insisted on buying three blue and white maillot swimsuits, and as a project had us dye three white T-shirts pink. While she and James were buying these, they also purchased him a blue three-piece J.C. Penney suit, which he modeled on the beach while we sported our new, identical outfits. A casual observer could easily see we were misfits, although I doubt they'd guess the root of our peculiar behavior.

If an activity wasn't forced on me, I sat in a beach chair staring out to sea, lost in memories, mainly reliving incidents leading to John's death. The vast expanse of ocean became a screen on which I'd rerun these images. Where had things gone wrong? The previous two years had been good. The 1980 Blues Brothers summer tour was a tough test on

John as far as staying straight, but he'd done it. With that completed, we'd traveled for a month in Europe, just the two of us again, driving at our leisure. Then John filmed *Continental Divide;* he was very proud that he'd gone through the entire movie without cocaine. We agreed that when he'd been straight a solid year, he'd get a new motorcycle. But shortly after the completion of filming he had a slip.

The film wrapped in January, but we kept our rented house in L.A. an extra week so John could attend some business meetings. I was out back playing tennis with Tino when Danny drove up. I knew John was looking forward to seeing him again, since we hadn't really seen Dan since the tour. Moments later John yelled that he and Danny were going out for a while. "Don't forget dinner at seven, then we'll all go to that play," I reminded them. John blew me a kiss, waved good-bye, and hopped into Danny's car. He looked great and was obviously happy to be with Danny again. I felt good, too, and went back to my game.

It was late afternoon when Danny returned. He seemed startled to find me alone. "Didn't John come back?" he asked.

"No," I replied. "I thought he was with you."

Danny said that they'd stopped by a friend's house, and while there, had a drink. Then he and John decided to go to a movie. In the car, something John said made Dan realize that John was drunk. "I think he only had one drink!" Danny said, forgetting that John had drunk very little in the past year. At any rate, at the theater John seemed to be enjoying the movie, but after he borrowed a dollar and went out for cigarettes, he never returned.

Smokey lived with us at the time, so I checked with him to see if he'd heard from John. He hadn't. The three of us ate dinner and passed on the play. Naturally, we were concerned about John. Getting around with no money or transportation was a talent of John's, but it didn't make sense that he hadn't called by now. We couldn't help but consider kidnapping, although it seemed silly to think someone could quietly abduct John from a public place. It was more likely that he'd felt sick and wandered outside, met someone and went off with that person. Still, why hadn't he called? Even if he had fallen in with someone who had drugs, which was, of course, the most likely explanation, it wasn't like him to just disappear. Only in our most combative times did he not keep in close communication. Something was wrong.

After Danny left I watched TV, waiting anxiously by the phone. Before going to bed, I knocked on Smokey's door. "Well, what are we supposed to do? How long are we supposed to wait?" Smokey said the police wouldn't do anything until a person was missing for twenty-four hours, so we should be patient. I promised to try.

The phone rang about five-thirty in the morning. Both Smokey and I picked up simultaneously. I spoke. "Hello." There was a silence, and then John exploded, "Honey, I don't know what happened, I don't even know where I got the coke."

When he got home I ran a hot bath to help him come down. I was trying very hard not to blow up. He had sounded so upset on the phone, I felt I should hear him out before I reacted. While he lay in the tub I sat on the side and we talked. He said he didn't remember the movie or much else until about three, when he found himself on a sidewalk in Westwood. In his pocket was some money and a little bit of coke. He said he knew I'd be worried and was afraid I'd be angry, so he phoned a friend, who came and picked him up. They went for coffee and something to eat. Once he felt more together, he phoned.

I couldn't forget the way John looked in the tub. He seemed achy, exhausted, and tense. And this blackout really had frightened him. He held my hand and shut his eyes, lying back in the oversized tub and saying he was so glad I wasn't mad. I told him how scared I'd been and he said it had scared him, too. Why hadn't he gone for professional help after that? The thought pounded in my head. The next day he had marveled at how bad he felt, wondered how he could have once spent so many evenings similarly indulging. I took his observations to be good signs. It was only a one-night binge, he continued working out, he seemed fine again. Damn it, I knew there was something wrong with him physically, maybe a chemical imbalance or a vitamin deficiency. That blackout wasn't a normal reaction. I should have made him go to a doctor. Damn it, damn it, damn it . . .

I couldn't stop the onslaught of bad drug memories: binges, drug arguments over the years, my own participation in bad situations. I couldn't stop going over how John's drug use had picked up again during the last half year, now seeing it so clearly as a progression.

One day, I remembered that the week before he died John had made a flippant remark about heroin. The memory was startling. It was after our argument about his being out of control. A little while later he apologized and admitted I was right: he was abusing himself again and needed to stop. Sitting on the couch he rubbed his face as if trying to wake up. "I don't know what got into me this morning. What did I take last night, heroin?" He'd said this in such a funny way that we both laughed, and that seemed to diffuse the tension between us. But what were we laughing at? I laughed because I thought it absurd; it was John making fun of himself. What had it meant to him? Was he already doing heroin? Maybe he was trying to tell me and I was just too stupid to put it together. The thought made me sick to my stomach.

Later I had an equally disturbing realization. John had had an idea for a movie about a middle-class man (John) who was unhappy with his successful but boring, predictable existence. His character starts checking out New York nightlife, becomes involved in the punk scene, and eventually gets talked into shooting up. I didn't much like the idea and, when he said it would be important to actually shoot up on screen, I objected strongly and we disagreed. The discussion was on the level of truth in art, not personal desire. Ultimately I decided that no studio would let him do it, so I didn't pursue my argument. Now I saw this idea as an attempt, probably unconscious, to disguise his obsession, or urge, so he could play it out in his work. I was angry with myself for seeing all this now. Too late. It was all so frustrating.

I was sad all the time. Although my companions would distract me for a while, I was never free of my grief. I began functioning on at least two levels. I could be talking or taking part in life, but at the same time I'd be intensely involved in a memory, as if I were watching two movies at the same time. Then there were moments when I would be on a third level as well, thinking, What am I saying to this person? I'm carrying on a conversation in which I feel like an observer, while I'm reliving this memory much more intensely than this moment that exists right now. I didn't seem to be in the same reality as anyone else.

My focus on the past was isolating. It was a comfort, though, to know that Kathryn understood, and a new bond was formed. I would automatically do anything she suggested —go in the water, get out of the sun, have a massage, eat something. I trusted her instincts implicitly.

Doug Kenney had first introduced us in 1975. I was very taken with her. Eight years my senior, pretty, with soft auburn hair, Kathryn sparkled as she and Doug went off on some humorous idea. I liked her right away, seeing her as a sophisticated actress and a woman of her own mind. I was close to Doug for some time before I really got to know Kathryn well, however.

I enjoyed many a late-night talk with Kathryn. She has a deep, resonant voice and a wonderful way of articulating things. When serious, her pronouncements are often very dramatic, and when amused, she radiates a sense of the whimsical while maintaining a caustic wit. After Doug died we grew even closer sharing the pain of his loss.

The time I spent with Kathryn after Doug died seemed so ironic now. I had loved Doug and missed him terribly, in a manner more intense than any loss I'd known. I thought I knew then how Kathryn felt—like me, only worse. Now I realized how different it is to lose your mate, how emotionally and physically consuming, as if a large chunk of you has been yanked from your body, and there you are, dazed, confused, frightened, struggling to maintain yourself. And then there is the constant threat of a crying attack. "Attack" is a good word for it, a sudden intense bodily assault.

The week in Florida seemed interminable, as if I'd been exiled, or was serving time. I could think about nothing simple or happy. One thought that kept entering my mind was, Where did John go?

I examined my past, searching for the development of my concepts of life and death. My parents didn't believe in any religious doctrine, in fact, my father was emphatically antireligion. As a kid I learned about Catholicism from my neighbors and cousins and it was especially troublesome to hear all the restrictions to getting into heaven. It frightened me that maybe my parents were wrong. I worried for a time about not being a christened Catholic and briefly attended church in seventh grade. Later, I tended to agree with my parents' basic disbelief in God as a power who sat in judgment, sending you special struggles or rewards for your actions. I began to understand that my father was an agnostic; to him, a person who believed in God and the concept of heaven was someone who was afraid to face the fact that life as we know it is all there is. My father liked nothing better than a good "discussion" about religion (as opposed to an "argument," although in truth there was little difference). His reasoning was usually logical and supported by historical and scientific examples, but ultimately deteriorated into dogmatic pronouncements which always brought an abrupt end to debate. Still, my father instilled in me a sense of mistrust in religious doctrines and institutions.

My mother, although not a supporter of organized religion, did believe in a creative power. I remember asking her once if she believed in God and she said something like, "Well, when I look at the heavens, the ocean, the mountains, I believe there is a God, some power that created them." My mother seemed to innately trust this power, accepting her lack of understanding without anxiety, just as she rejected formal religion without anxiety. She was always respectful and interested in nature, and it was that which she passed along to us kids.

By the time I went to college in 1969, the synthesis of my parents' beliefs formed a foundation on which my own ideas and ideals grew. I didn't believe in a wrathful God, and I wasn't really sure I believed in God at all. He either existed or He didn't, and if He did, I figured He must be magnificent and certainly wasn't going to hold it against me for not being sure. I no longer concerned myself with what I considered the fear tactics of organized religion, and simply tried to lead a good life as my heart defined it. In my more cynical days, I joked that I was better off never to have been christened, since if I had I would be assured a place in hell. Just in case the Catholics turned out to be right, I had my ticket to limbo.

In Florida I discovered I had no firm thoughts about what death meant, other than the obvious. But seeing John's body had made clear that whatever breathes life into us is not of the body. I knew that the energy which had been John did not just end—hadn't Einstein proven that energy could not be destroyed? It was clear John's energy moved on. I could feel it. It might have transformed into electricity or an animal or the wind; I couldn't say *how* it moved on, I just knew it had. I tried to find solace in my strong sense of this, but it was little comfort. My problems were with the here and now.

Laila was a good companion. When we'd first met in New York in 1974, I wasn't sure about her. She'd struck me as cocky and self-centered, and the fact that she was pretty with large, sultry, brown eyes only made her more annoying. When I discovered she was only nineteen, I began to perceive her differently. She was still a teenager! (At twenty-three, I had been the youngest of our group at the time.) Because Laila had traveled a great deal and was well-read and smart, it was natural to think she was older. After we were more comfortable with each other, and spent time alone, I found her open and candid, very funny and sweet. Laila's father is an Arab and her mother is from Kansas, an unusual heritage to say the least. She's been known to have what one might call a "bad attitude," and is a very trying adversary. On the other hand, she is a fiercely loyal friend.

With her ethnic roots, wit, and rebelliousness, it was natural that Laila and John would also become close. Soon after she and I became friends, Laila moved to Perry Street, just around the corner from where we lived on Bleecker Street, and quickly became part of our "family." I think John was also a bit of a father figure to her. Obviously she, too, was very affected by his death. Still, she didn't show me her sad side that week, but maintained a steady and good-natured attitude. In fact, on our trip home, we even managed a good laugh recalling some of the events of the previous week and making fun of our situation and ourselves.

After we returned from Florida, Laila lived with me for six

weeks while working in the city on a film called *Nothing Lasts Forever*. The irony of the title did not escape us.

Before I'd gone away, I decided to move from the bedroom I'd shared with John to one in the back. When we returned, I found that my sister Pat had not only moved me, but had painted the room and hung things on the wall as well.

I was very pleased with my new bedroom. It was two rooms, actually. One was scarcely bigger than the queen-sized mattress on the floor, and held nothing else but a built-in bookshelf and a TV that looked much too big in the tiny space. Two large windows opened onto the courtyard. The adjoining room, which had been John's workout area, housed my clothes. Blouses and dresses hung on his chinning bar, and the cabinet that once held boxing gloves and extra weights now stored sweaters and pants. This space became, in essence, my new apartment, as I largely ignored the rest of the house. I was comfortable in my back bedroom. It fit me well—small and isolated.

Chapter 5

STARTING OVER

MARCH 19—EARLY APRIL

In 1978, John and I realized the necessity to divert business from our home: the phone was constantly busy, messengers and business associates were in and out all day, and when I was designing, my art work took over the apartment. With the success of *Animal House* we felt we could finally afford to open an office, so we formed Phantom Enterprises, Ltd. While I was hunting for office space, Danny expressed an interest in sharing it with us, so I looked with all our needs in mind. I found a suite at 150 Fifth Avenue that fit us well, with a front room for our secretary, three offices for us, a storage room, and lounge. Finally I had a good space for design work and writing. John and I were excited about forming a company and wrote a declaration of principles. Phantom was a commitment to our work, the marriage of our business and artistic sensibilities, and we vowed not to extend into businesses outside our instinctual realm. The office would serve as a base through which we could work, although it was not the physical reality, but the spirit of the company that was important. Thus "Phantom." The name was also appropriate because we wanted to play down the fact that it was John's company—our phantom—thereby avoiding people dropping in for autographs, to leave scripts, or whatever. To further this goal, I designed the reception area to look like a travel agency. The rest of the office, however, was homey and very us. We were all pleased with the situation; the atmosphere was comfortable and our secretary, Karen Krenitsky, was quickly becoming indis-

pensable. It was a change that made our personal lives much
more manageable.

Shortly before John's death, Anne Beatts, Deanne Stillman, and I had begun work on *Titters 101: An Introduction
to Woman's Literature,* a sequel to our first book. It was a
parody of a college textbook, for which we invented authors
throughout history. Now we had to write introductions to the
writers and their work, as well as a sample piece. Once that
was completed, we would commission art and I would design
the book. The due date was early 1983 and we had just
begun outlining our individual tasks. After the funeral Anne
and Deanne suggested we wait a few weeks before getting
back to work. They'd talk to the publisher about a short
extension.

The first day after my return from Florida, I hurried to
Phantom. There had been a few condolence letters at the
apartment, but since most of our mail was directed to the
office I expected more letters there, and was pleased to find
several large piles of envelopes neatly stacked on the couch. I
tore into my missives eagerly, but Karen soon interrupted
with a call from the Brillstein office. That evening "20/20"
intended to air a taped interview with Cathy Smith, the
woman arrested at John's bungalow. Bernie felt she was
taking advantage of John's death for publicity, and that
much of what she was quoted as saying in the L.A. papers
was untrue. His lawyer had already sent a telegram to ABC,
requesting that the airing be delayed until they were certain
of the veracity and accurateness of Ms. Smith's remarks.
ABC responded that they would proceed as scheduled.

I hung up and immediately phoned my sister at her law
firm in Portland, Oregon. I was emotional, confused, and
frustrated. My concern about the interview was strictly fear
of the unknown; I had no idea what Cathy Smith would say.
But I couldn't understand "20/20"'s callousness. Pam said
she'd talk to Bernie's lawyer and call right back.

Within minutes we were talking again. Pam's voice was
soft and steady as she explained she felt everything had been
done that could be at this time. First Amendment rights,
concerning freedom of speech and of the press, were very
complicated, but were written to protect one of the funda-

mental privileges democracy champions and may therefore, at times, seem unfair to the individual in defense of the ideal. Since we did not know what Cathy Smith said, we had no claim for an injunction; we were only speculating. After the interview aired, we could review it and discuss what to do. Pam hesitated, then asked, "Do you want to watch it? I could have someone make a transcript."

My stomach tightened and a chill ran through my body. "No, Pammy, I don't think I want to see this woman, yet."

That night I spoke to my mother-in-law, who had watched "20/20." She wavered between sounding very low and very angry. She told me they also interviewed Dr. Noguchi. "Did you see that? Did you hear what they said?" She was crying. "That doctor made it sound like John was a junkie. He said he had needle marks all up and down his body! . . . They showed a chart, too, and said there were fifty or sixty injections!"

The report couldn't possibly be that erroneous, I thought, and assumed that Mrs. Belushi was so upset she'd misunderstood. I assured her that John was not a heroin addict. "I saw him the Sunday before he died, Mom, and believe me, he didn't have needle marks all over his body."

"How can they do this? Why do they say these things?" Mrs. Belushi was inconsolable.

The next day, Pam relayed an assistant's account of the show. Apparently, Dr. Noguchi said nothing specific about John, but was interviewed about his temporary suspension as head coroner while his conduct concerning other recent celebrity deaths was under consideration. Following this interview, "20/20" showed a drawing of a body, which they stated was from the coroner's office, showing that John had multiple track marks on his arms. The visual had the numeral "24" next to one arm, and "12" next to another. On the legs and stomach were markings which seemed to imply more needle holes. The overall effect of the report was that John had shot up for years.

Cathy Smith's interview was described in detail. Her attorney was present and she appeared to be stoned. She said she'd been with John for most of the last five days of his life. The night before his death they were at On the Rox until approximately one-forty-five in the morning. John was drinking wine, but she didn't think he was excessively drunk. There was no mention of drugs.

Smith said that when they'd arrived at the bungalow John hadn't felt well and went to his room, saying it might have been something he ate. When he returned, he looked better. John went to bed and Smith stayed up writing a letter in the living room. She later fell asleep on the couch, until awakened by John's abnormal snoring. Concerned, she went into the bedroom, woke him, and asked if he was all right. He said he was fine, asked for a drink of water, and went back to sleep. The next day before she left, Smith checked on him again. He seemed okay.

Cathy Smith contended she had known John for about five years, but had never met me. She stressed that her relationship with John had been platonic, that I was the most important woman in his life. "He was just that kind of guy. You could tell."

So went the first scenario of the last night of John's life according to Cathy Smith. It certainly wasn't a full explanation, however. My gut feeling was that Smith had only recently met John, no doubt as a drug connection, and that her function on that night (and perhaps for a few previous days) had been to handle the mechanics of injecting drugs (most likely for both of them). I was grateful that she'd said something about John's love for me. For one, it was a familiar reaction from someone who'd spent time with John, and so it helped dispel my fear that possibly John had stopped loving me. For another, many women in Smith's situation might have tried to protect themselves (from more serious drug implications) by saying they were having an affair. I interpreted this as a sign of respect. Maybe their relationship was more than just two sick people using each other. After all, I loved John and preferred to think there was some decency in this person with whom he'd spent his last week. Still, I had problems with Smith's story.

We found it interesting that Smith hadn't mentioned Robert DeNiro and Robin Williams. Was she protecting them? If what Nelson had told me were true, they didn't need protecting. But then, since they themselves had not communicated with the family, nor made a public comment, maybe it was logical to assume they did have something to hide. And there was no mention of John and her leaving the Chateau. But most noticeably missing from Smith's story was any explanation of how, where, or when John had injected the drugs that killed him. There was no doubt in my mind *who* had injected them. It was painful that this woman was appearing on television stoned, giving interviews about John. Perhaps it served him right for being so stupid as to get involved in the whole mess. But then he was dead, he wasn't affected. I was. Our family was. John's friends were and I suppose even some of John's fans felt the same disgust from this perverse display. I turned my anger on "20/20": "What was this business with the drawing?"

Pam made some calls and was back with more information. It seemed that the drawing was from the coroner. The numbers represented how many hours old the needle marks were: one arm had four to five marks which were no more than twenty-four hours old, and the other had approximately four to five marks which were forty-eight hours old. The other indications on his stomach and legs were to show where John had a rash. Unfortunately, "20/20" hadn't explained this clearly.

I was furious and wanted to sue for defamation of character. But I was still a new celebrity widow and had much to learn. A dead man cannot be defamed, at least he rarely is in the eyes of the law. My only recourse was to ask "20/20" to make a correction. Besides Pam, I also spoke with Bernie, and we all agreed a correction would not bring much satisfaction. Going over it again meant more people would see it, and the average viewer would probably focus on the issue of shooting up, not the mistake. We decided to let it go and hope it would be the last of such problems. I also naïvely hoped this would be the last we'd hear from Cathy Smith. It seemed to me she was extremely lucky not to be in jail. Maybe she would be smart enough to keep quiet and not rock her precarious boat.

Another nagging and persistent thought was what to do with John's grave. I knew I wanted to do some planting. I'd quickly decided on lilacs, since that was his favorite bush, and a couple of beetlebung trees, because he loved the grove behind our Chilmark house. I couldn't even begin to contemplate a gravestone, however. I was unable to form a visual image of one in my mind; I had no idea what it should be, how it should look. I finally decided to ask Rob to design one. My brother was then assistant county manager of Aspen, but he had been a jeweler for years. His work was beautiful—little sculptures, really—and I knew John had liked and respected Rob as an artist. In fact, Rob made my wedding ring. It was odd that he should make two such momentous symbols for us.

Since it would be some time before the stone was installed, I needed a temporary marker. On my next visit to the Vineyard, friends and I lugged some large stones from our yard to the cemetery where we arranged them in a mound at the head of John's grave. I felt surprisingly good about the marking; it was solid and well-balanced. Like John. Yes, this would do for now.

I continued going to the office daily, where I spent my time reading or writing letters and making phone calls. Karen was always pleasant, helpful, protective. Concerned that I was losing weight, she took it upon herself to make sure I ate lunch, repeatedly asking me what I'd like until I'd commit to something, then ordering it for me. I took over John's office because mine, set up for art work, was the largest and his was small and cozy. And blue. I felt good in John's office.

My condolence letters fascinated me. I would read and reread them, leaving my favorites out to read yet again. There were letters from relatives and friends, many from fans. Often what they said made me cry. My mother's cousin wrote, "We only met John once and I remember how helpful he was. . . . But I'd surely heard his praises sung by one of the greatest of the Keller aunts, your grandmother. She was always telling us how you two would come to her little apartment and clean it up and do the laundry and help her get lunch and play cards with her. I thought that was wonderful for young people to do."

A young girl wrote, "Dear Judith, I know you don't know me, but I feel I almost know you. I am 13 years old and I thought John was a very funny person. I just couldn't believe the news when I heard of his death. I'm so sorry he didn't value his life any more as he did make thousands of people laugh and he would still be here today if he hadn't taken those terrible drugs and drank so much." So simple and to the point. Was it true John "didn't value" his life?

Another fan wrote that John "gave my family and me so much laughter and good feeling when we desperately needed it . . ." She went on to explain that John's humor had helped her get through the difficulty of nursing her dying mother for four years. "I swear to you, the man actually helped me keep my sanity."

Some people reminisced. A woman crew member from *Neighbors*, whose husband had also worked on the movie, wrote, "Gary would come home giggling and say, 'John runs up to me all the time and hugs me!' His unique shyness and sweetness will always be remembered . . ." Our dental hygienist wrote: "I will always remember John's visits fondly, he turned our office upside down and made my day. And he always made me feel that he was interested in my family. When he found out I was pregnant, he hugged me and kissed me and spent his whole visit thinking of names, some of which were really outrageous and gave us a good laugh."

Hearing from people in John's profession made me feel good, proud. Richard Pryor's words are an example of this support: "I loved and respected your husband very much. He was one of the funniest men ever. I share in your grief of his leaving us. A friend and a fan . . ."

Writer William Styron wrote the most beautiful letter: "Dear Judy, I was deeply saddened about John, and torn with a sense of loss that I've only rarely felt about anyone. During those past summers on Martha's Vineyard he shed a glow of absolute brightness—my heart leaped up with joy whenever I saw him strolling down across my lawn. He brought such great pleasure—such pure unleashed hilarity—to me and to so many others. . . . John was a clown, indeed, in the Shakespearean sense, which is to say he was utterly imbued with a feeling of both the joy and the sadness of being human. I will miss both his genius and the golden light of his friendship . . ."

At times I would have to stop; energy would surge through me and I aimlessly paced the office. All around me was proof of the worlds John had created, that I helped to create. Displayed in the lounge were framed posters and magazine covers featuring "Saturday Night Live," his movies, the Blues Brothers and the band. On one wall hung a neon Blues Brothers logo, a gift from Stephen Spielberg, surrounded by the Blues Brothers gold and platinum records. Also hanging were several awards: Emmy nominations for writing and performing, Grammy nominations, the "Jack Benny Award" from UCLA, my own design and graphics awards for my book *Blues Brothers: Private*. There were mementos from projects, photos, autographs, and notes from John's fellow actors. In a corner hung a large card that Gilda Radner (a co-star of "SNL"), had given John when he was in the hospital. It was handwritten in large block letters: "In loving memory of John Belushi, who can hit me without hurting me, and who can hurt me without hitting me." I found myself standing in front of that for a long while, staring, seeing beyond it into a haze. The words ran through my mind like a chant, while I evaluated their prophesy. Something John had said in an interview returned to me: "It's easy to make people cry," he stated. "I want to make people laugh." Yes, it was easy to make people cry.

Many letters came from schoolmates, grade school through college, full of the love they'd had for John, as well as for me. One wrote, "Thank you for sharing [John] with so many—too many—people." Another closed, "When you get ready to come home, we'll be here for you. You'll always be little 'Jutes' to us—some things never change."

Occasionally, stories were upsetting. Nelson Lyon's wife, Vivian, told me, "That Thursday night after you telephoned me from New York, John called, maybe an hour later. He was very concerned about you being sick when I related to him our earlier conversation. . . . I told him you were going to sleep. . . . John said he wanted to go back home as soon as possible and that he loved you and missed you very much. John was very proud of you and you were the love of his life. He was always talking about you . . ."

The mother of a friend, Mrs. Stitt, who had known us both since we were teenagers, wrote: "I had a very nice, and rather lengthy, conversation with John not too long ago . . ." [He'd called to ask her husband a question to do with insurance, some research for *Noble Rot*.] "He also told me how much he missed you, Judy, and mother to the end that I am, I just said, 'Well, hop on a plane and get to New York!' But I guess there were deadlines to meet with the movie. . . ."

That fucking movie, stupid deadlines—how did we get to a point where those were more important than us? It didn't seem real, it just seemed impossible that things were so screwed up. And there was no going back, no chance to try again. I wished and wished to go back, like a skipping record, I'd beg to be given another chance, to wake up and find John's death a bad dream. But every morning I'd wake up and find that my life was the nightmare.

Days were easier than evenings; it was hard to stay home alone at night. TV was impossible. I'd turn the set on and within minutes I'd be hysterical over a commercial about phoning home, or because a game show contestant won his dream vacation. Then there were the constant news flashes and reports. Anything from a fire sweeping a building to a boy losing his dog left me shattered. Also, John was in the news and on reruns of "SNL." I was unable to watch him at all. Often, between eleven and midnight, when "SNL" aired, I felt bothered knowing John was on TV. It was a temptation to watch, but I knew I wasn't ready to see him looking so alive when I was still trying to get it into my head that he was dead.

How I spent my evenings those first months is somewhat foggy. I saw a lot of Kathryn, usually at her apartment until I was tired enough to go home. Often Laila would join us and sometimes James. Kathryn was very important to me; through her I could confirm that my suffering was not unusual, but a part of the mourning process. She constantly recommended things to make me feel physically good, like taking hot baths or exercising.

I also saw a lot of Rhonda. She was in the process of a divorce, and we found we shared many common problems: adjustments to living alone, fright, anger, depression, sadness, guilt. The obvious difference was that Rhonda had chosen to separate from her husband.

Rhonda and I met in 1973 when she was in *National Lampoon's Lemmings*, an Off-Broadway rock'n roll comedy review. John was directing, as well as performing in the road version, and was looking for one woman to play roles which previously were performed by two. This was not an easy task and he was getting discouraged. Then he came home one day brimming with excitement about a former Miss Arkansas who had been in the original L.A. production of *Hair* and did a perfect Joni Mitchell imitation. Rhonda Coullet was a pretty, sexy, long-haired blonde, with a golden voice to boot. She was hired and that, technically, was the beginning of our friendship. But it wasn't until about a year later, when Rhonda and her husband moved to our neighborhood in the West Village, that she and I became close.

A love of music was the common thread that brought us closer. Rhonda had been a closet songwriter, but she eventually played one of her songs for me, a sweet, emotional song that I loved. In time, Laila and I became her fan club, encouraging her to pursue her natural calling. My fondest image of Rhonda is of her at her piano, singing, her eyes closed, her head turned toward heaven, one foot tapping the floor.

We also shared a similiar sensibility about life. After John died she expressed this unusual perspective to me in a letter: "At the risk of making you sad, I just wanted to remind you of the Bigger Picture. You are a patriot. John is a patriot and I thought this [an enclosed article about John] might remind you of what his life means to America and why we'll miss him, putting human frailty aside as we all must in order to acomplish something grand for everyone. You both made great sacrifices on the personal level to cheer up America. She needed it and she still does. To me, it's like losing a brother in the war. . . . Nothing will ever shake my Faith in the Grand Scheme of it all . . ."

Now, our conversations often turned to spiritual matters. Rhonda understood and believed in the strong feelings I had that John had moved on. We talked about the importance of nature and the interrelations of all entities composing the universe. We'd drink and talk late into the night. Discussions often ended with Rhonda playing me a song of hers I'd never heard that expressed whatever we'd been talking about. Then I'd beg her to indulge me with sad songs. Rhonda would play and I'd sing along and afterwards I always felt better. Maybe it was the sharing, maybe it was the wine. Maybe it's just good for the soul to sing.

There were other friends who kept tabs on me. Michael Klenfner phoned nearly every day. John had been his daughter Kate's godfather and now Michael became mine. Mitch Glazer and his wife Wendie lived around the corner and we often had breakfast. But they were newlyweds, just starting a new life together, and I was struggling just to keep it together. Tim Kazurinsky, a Chicago friend who was then an "SNL" cast member, called and visited often, as did Steve Jordan, who had been in the Blues Brothers band. My sister Pat and her husband John Brewster invited me out to their house in New Jersey almost weekly. Pat always made fabulous meals; I think she was in cahoots with Karen to fatten me up. I enjoyed getting out of the city and driving. The trip took only an hour, but it was usually an emotional hour; being alone in the car was conducive to crying. Music usually started it. Every song had a John memory. Dr. Cyborn said it was natural for most associations to include John, since we'd been together so long. "With time," he said, "you'll have new experiences on your own and find that will change." There it was again, my new enemy, Time. What an interesting enigma Time is. We can waste it, spend it, not have enough of it; we can measure it, look forward to having more of it, lose track of it; but I couldn't for the life of me define it in terms of when or how it was going to help me.

Pam continued to deal with the police, the coroners, and my unanswered questions: Did Cathy Smith have a record? Could you tell from the needle marks if a person injected himself? What happens when you die from cocaine? From heroin? I wanted to know everything. The police weren't very receptive, and the coroner's office, which was helpful to a point, seemed to be getting annoyed. It appeared the only way to get answers was to request all official reports.

Although I hadn't read any of the press coverage of John's death, bits and pieces filtered down to me. For instance, a fan might write something like "I don't care what the *Daily News* says, I'll never believe that John Belushi was a heroin addict." Or a friend: "I hope you have not been hurt too much by the nasty attitude the press has taken." So I was pleased when Mitch phoned with news that Jann Wenner, the publisher of *Rolling Stone*, wanted him and journalist Tim White to put together a memorial issue on John. Mitch wanted to know how I felt and if I would help—he and Tim wouldn't do it unless I supported it. Mitch explained that Tim would conduct interviews with family, friends, and business associates, and he would expand an old article he had written. They would both edit with Jann, and Mitch promised something we would all be proud of.

I was pleased with the *Rolling Stone* idea and felt it was appropriate. John had been a cover story three times, and each was a big seller. He liked *Rolling Stone* and had been friends with Jann during the "SNL" years. I was glad he would be personally involved. I liked the approach—letting friends reminisce—and knew Mitch and Tim would present them properly. I was happy with the plan and agreed to let them use personal photos.

So began my first trip through my photo collection. I kept everything in a small, three-drawer dresser, one of the first pieces of furniture we bought when we moved to New York. Our first purchase was a mattress. Necessity. The next week we bought a television, John's choice. The following week's purchase was my choice and I dragged John to some Fourteenth Street stores where we bought a cheap but decent set of dressers. Now here it was, my oldest New York acquisition, housing the images of my past. I took my time approaching the search, respectful of the power hidden in that dresser. Finally one night when Laila was out, I pulled a drawer and entered the sanctum of the sound room to sort through my treasures.

I removed a handful of loose eight by tens from the top and quickly shuffled through them. These were professional photos, Blues Brothers, John meeting President Ford, movie shots. These were not what I was looking for, they wanted something more personal. I picked up an envelope that said "Vacation '74" and looked through it. Fascinated by the images of John, I looked at them long and hard. Especially his face: he had such nice, strong features. A classical nose, smooth skin, dark, thick eyebrows, beautiful big brown eyes. In these photos he had a good, thick head of hair and a beard. It was summer and he was tan and healthy—so full of life! In one photo he was pointing the way for our journey through New England, in another throwing a fish to a seal. The seal, I recalled, thought John was throwing something *at* him and took off. I took out some more: John sitting at the water's edge, playing in the sand, pretending to be tying a fishing boat to a dock, posing with his arms extended, American Indian fashion, worshiping the sunset. Each image flooded my mind with memories, but there was something wrong . . . something wrong . . . My eyes filled with tears and I wiped them away. There he was lying on the beach, hugging me, making a model airplane. But damn it, what was wrong was that John was dead. He would no longer raise an eyebrow to the camera, no more smiles for anyone. He would exist only on these flimsy pieces of paper, lifeless! I studied a large portrait, running my eyes over his face, searching out each scar, noting how the hairs of his eyebrows fell, staring into his gaze until the gleam in his eye seemed to twinkle. Unconsciously I raised my hand to stroke his cheek. The photo was cold and mean. Yes, it was mean because it was taunting me. I exploded with pain, rolling on the floor doubled up, crying from the pit of my stomach. How could John be dead? I wondered in amazement as every emotion in me raced to be released. I must have cried for five minutes, until I was exhausted. I lay still on the floor for a while, breathing in the stagnant air of the insulated room. Finally I got up and went into the bathroom. I just don't understand, I repeated, rinsing my face with shaky hands. I returned and set aside photos I thought would be good for the article: John as a little boy, John with various friends and family, John and me, John on the beach. I felt very low as I returned the drawer. A portrait on top stared up at me. "How could you do it, John? How could you go and die?" I asked it out loud. "How could you?"

I decided to take the train to Washington, D.C., to see Jimmy in *Pirates of Penzance*. It was my first trip alone, and I carefully packed a suitcase of black clothing. I was looking forward to seeing Jimmy, Sandi, and my nephew, Robert. Robert Belushi. Oddly, this was the name I used to say to myself with a big question mark, since there were five generations of Roberts in the Jacklin family. John and I once joked about what a child of ours would look like. A big belly and long skinny legs we decided, and laughed at ourselves. John fantasized a little girl and I a little boy. Robert Jacklin Belushi, I would think, and reject the name as incongruous. I never told John my thoughts, afraid that they would make it seem too real an idea, and at the time we were still far from that reality. Then Sandi and Jimmy had a boy and, of all things, named him Robert!

When I thought about Robert, I would wish briefly that I'd had a baby. No, I determined, it's better this way. It would be too difficult to be the child of John Belushi. How could a youngster handle the legacy? Seeing people idolize the man you never knew, singing his praises or expressing the joy he brought to their lives, while at the same time hearing cruel statements about his character or lifestyle. Feeling the emptiness of never knowing your father, perhaps confusing his drug-taking with not loving you. It was hard enough for me as an adult to deal with these issues. Yes, it was all for the best that we'd never had a child. Then I would remember the abortion I'd had at nineteen. That child would have known his father. No, we'd both made that decision long ago and there was no going back on that one either. If I'd had that baby, everything would be different now. Maybe better, maybe not. It was too much, too senseless to think about. I just had to accept things the way they were.

By the time I got to the hotel, Jimmy had already left for the theater, but Sandi was waiting. I changed quickly and we arrived at the National Theater shortly before curtain. I was uneasy and couldn't shake the fact that John should have been there with me. Jimmy must have felt John's respect when he told him he would be the Pirate King in the National Touring Company of Joe Papp's production. The Pirate King! What a great role! John had been impressed. This should have been Jimmy's night to show off for his brother. Instead, my being there alone shouted the injustice of it all. I knew this was going to be a hard night for Jimmy, and Sandi, and me.

My eyes filled with tears when Jimmy made his entrance. He looked great. He took command as he strutted the stage, tall and handsome, his eyes sparkling. His energy filled the room. I was impressed with his agility as he danced and performed the various acrobatic stunts from pratfalls to a graceful back flip. By intermission my emotions were welling up in my chest as I tried not to hear myself think, John would have been so proud!

When the lights came up Sandi started backstage. "Maybe we should wait till after the show," I suggested.

"Well, Jimmy said to bring you back at intermission," she said. Hesitantly, I followed.

When we entered Jimmy's dressing room, a pressure from within rushed to be released and I fought to hold it back, but Jimmy hugged me and we both began crying. We sat on the couch and cried for what seemed like several minutes. "I didn't want to upset you," I said, wiping my eyes, and we laughed. Crying and laughing, both felt good. I was glad I'd come to Washington.

It never occurred to me that I would note the first month anniversary of John's death, but I did. It seemed to arrive moments after Danny told me John was dead, and yet it was painfully slow in arriving. Time seemed so inconsistent. Minutes were filled with images of years and years. Days crawled by. But I never seemed to get any farther from the day John died. I still could not think through the actual exchange when Danny told me the news, was still unable to allow my memory access to that moment.

It was pouring rain on the fifth of April. I was to see a new doctor, an obstetrician. It didn't make much sense now, but I'd had the appointment for six months and it was time for my yearly check-up anyway.

I sat in the small reception room filling out a form for new patients, feeling totally out of place. This office was about birth and I reeked of death. Everything was white and happy. I was black and very low.

Dr. Nash was a pleasant, older man, soft-spoken with a cheery disposition and a German accent. He sat behind a large desk. A sheet of glass protected the many photos of babies displayed on top. Dr. Nash asked how I was doing, and I told him the truth—not very well. "Are you talking to someone about it, a doctor?" Yes, I told him, I was seeing a psychiatrist. He leaned forward and smiled kindly. "You are young," he said. "You are healthy, pretty. You will see, things will get better." He tapped his desk with his finger. "I will save this spot for you, someday, yes?" I forced a smile, but couldn't say anything. What could I say, that he was crazy, that he didn't understand? It was easy for others to be optimistic. To me, having a baby no longer seemed an option.

My perspective on life had changed drastically in one month. I was in pain and had this odd feeling that death was the only way to stop it. Odder still, the idea of dying didn't scare me. It was as if I were perched on the edge of a dark abyss, knowing I should hang on but not caring to. I was just standing there, looking down, unafraid, thinking how easy it would be to just fall forward and end it all.

If it were only that simple. But to act on such a course . . . I couldn't. I couldn't bring that pain to my loved ones. And so, although I didn't have much hope for the idea that "time heals," I resolved to trust in it. I would give time a year, maybe two. For the others, I would try to be patient. But if things didn't improve in two years, if this were all my life could offer, I knew there was no way I was sticking around.

A letter came, forwarded from Martha's Vineyard, addressed to the wrong town. Still, it found its way. It was a handwritten note, only one sentence: "You Can't Imagine The Pleasure And Delight I Have In Knowing That Slimy Cockroach (John) Won't Spread His Filth Anymore!"

Paralyzed, I stared at the envelope: no return address or name. My letters, the outpouring of love, had been violated. I threw the hate letter in the trash, but couldn't stop thinking about it. Later I decided to keep it, although I wasn't sure why.

Toward the middle of April, galleys for the *Rolling Stone* issue were ready. I sat reading in a small office at the magazine, Mitch and Tim next door.

Mr. and Mrs. Belushi had provided a pretty good history, and from all the Belushi reports an interesting family portrait grew: a proud Albanian family struggling in Middle America; a grandmother, John's "second mother," who was the "soul" of the family; a young boy telling his parents his dreams; a sister's adoration; the younger brothers' admiration of the older.

Hunter Thompson made me laugh when he said, "Even though he was a bit of a monster, he was our monster," and expounded, "as well as a damned good person you could count on for help in the dark times. . . . For me, John's epitaph is: THIS MAN WAS THE REAL THING. HE NEVER NEEDED PROPS."

It was difficult to read the tribute at the *Rolling Stone* office. As I became emotional over stories, I'd have to stop reading, my eyes tearing. I wore my sunglasses to hide my eyes and they kept fogging up.

Kathryn commented on John's friendship: "During my initial period of mourning [after Doug Kenney's death], [John] became very protective of me. He encouraged me to come to Martha's Vineyard last summer, and . . . to play the role of his wife in *Neighbors*, which got me back on my feet, emotionally and financially. There was a great, warm place in his heart for anyone who needed it."

I wished I had John to help me through *my* mourning. How ironic that Kathryn would turn out to be so helpful and important to me now.

I was also glad to see many nice comments from John's professional peers, people he admired. A director from Second City said, "My attention always gravitated to him onstage. He always worked at the top of his intelligence." Several people commented that the Blues Brothers resurrected many blues performers' careers. Singer James Browne said, "Through the film and their own records, they opened the door again for me and for so many other performers. . . . [John] knew I was having problems and he said, 'How can I help?' He was *there* for me, understand?"

John's "SNL" co-star, Laraine Newman, observed, "John was typecast as an uncouth, boorish slob with no discipline, so you were constantly impressed to discover he was just the opposite. . . . Granted, it was not the only side. He could be so damned dogmatic when he wanted you to share something with him . . ." Bernie noted, "He was much more of a traditionalist and a romantic than he'd ever care to admit . . ." And Klenfner made a throwaway remark about John that I thought was sweet. Talking about being at a health spa with John, he commented: "During the day we'd play water volleyball, which John could have gone on doing forever with no further ambitions in life."

Mitch's piece captured John beautifully, and he told many great stories. One was especially bittersweet: "Late summer of 1978. The backyard . . . was carpeted in yellow fuzz; thick curtains of it had blown down from the tree in the Belushi courtyard. The wicker couch and the man asleep on it were covered in gold pollen. After a while, John, a white cap covering his eyes, began to shift positions on the small couch. He kicked his legs: nightmare running. He bolted up abruptly, eyes open, yellow fluff sticking to his eyelashes, to his hair. 'I gotta get off the island . . . I don't wanna be here!' he shouted. Then calmer, now awake: 'Shit, I just had the weirdest nightmare. Did you ever see *Pinocchio*? Remember,' he said, brushing the flowers from his face, 'remember that island for bad boys that Pinocchio went to? All those kids cursing and drinking. . . . Pretty soon they all began turning into donkeys. God, it was horrible. I mean, in my dream it was happening to *me*.' John jumped up from the couch. 'I kept telling 'em I didn't wanna be a bad boy anymore, but they wouldn't listen. My tail and ears kept growing.' He tugged his cap down over his eyes, grabbed his Vantage Blues, and disappeared into the house."

I was surprised that Danny chose to address John's overdosing, but I was not surprised by his honesty or clear sense of the situation. He began: "The thing that killed John was not a habitual element in his list of pleasures. I believe that he was being led into an experiment, and that he was being assisted in a flirtation with this new and dangerous substance. Three packs a day, a bottle of Courvoisier, la Cocaina, maybe, but Jones was not his Jones. The *Los Angeles Times* reported that two 'movie producers' claimed John was shooting this stuff for two years. People, the man who grasped me, danced with me, met my eye and planned the future was not a junkie. As a prop the hypo made us laugh. It was not a tool in his life."

Danny concluded: "The full rewards of knowing and being with John will never be totally understood by even those who loved his work, don't care how he died, and are just sorry he's gone. To these people I say, his sweetness and generosity were as big as his appetite for life.... This is the John I'll remember—a powerhouse with a big, warm, sensitive, vulnerable guy inside."

Danny's words seemed to jump from his heart to the page. John was a lucky man to have such a friend, so many good friends.

I had been in this tiny room much too long and was cold, shivering. I needed to get out, to be alone. I returned the galleys and spoke briefly with Tim and Mitch. I told them I liked the tribute very much, but couldn't say much. I left abruptly.

Once on the street I had to keep moving. I had held back my emotions so long that my body ached. The cold air stung my nose and drew tears to my eyes. I walked briskly down Fifth Avenue, my eyes continuing to tear, blurring, so the activity on the street looked like bouncing blobs of color. I walked faster. I was crying now, tears streaking down my cheeks. I ran into someone who swore at me. I wanted to yell back, "My husband is dead!"

I returned to Phantom and asked Karen to find an issue of the *L.A. Times* that quoted some producers as saying that John was a junkie. I went into John's office, closed the door, and cried.

One night around midnight there was a rap on my apartment door. It was Billy Murray. I was a little surprised to see him at that hour, since his wife had recently had a baby. I was pretty tired, but happy to see him. I asked him in and offered some tea.

I first met Billy when John worked at Second City with Billy's brother, Brian. Brian took us to his mother's house for dinner one night with several Murray siblings. The dinner table was clearly a place for the brothers to spar with their humor, and Billy led the pack. It was some time before

I got to know him well, when he was in the *National Lampoon Show* with John. Over the years I witnessed a lot of growth in Billy, and became very fond of him and his girlfriend, Mickey Kelly. I remembered how happy John and I were when they married.

Waiting for the water to boil, I asked about Mickey and the baby. Billy paced restlessly. When we sat in the living room he was distracted, as if trying to figure something out. After a long silence, he stood and wandered the room. I assumed he wanted to talk about John, and figured he would when he was ready. Finally he turned and looked at me, his head cocked to one side, a perplexed expression on his face. "Have you felt John around here?" he finally asked.

"No," I replied quietly. "I haven't felt him at all." Thoughtfully he shook his head in agreement. "Yeah, I don't feel him at all."

I found it endearing that Billy was in search of John's spirit, and maybe a little sad that he, too, could not find it.

Chapter 6

DARK DREAMS

APRIL

Dream: John and I are sitting peacefully in a cabin in the woods. He is reading in a big old comfy chair and I am drawing at a table. There is a glow in the room, a warmth, and the day is crisp and clear. Autumn colors surround us.

A sudden rap at the door startles me. I look up and much to my distress see a drug dealer at the door. He holds up a large baggie filled with white powder. "Hey, man, want some coke?" I run to the entrance and try to shut the door, but he sticks a foot inside and forces his way in. People are coming out of the woods toward the cabin. They walk stiffly, ghoul-like, and all carry similar bags. I try to keep them out, but they overpower me, tearing the screen and knocking me down. "Leave us alone!" I yell, then see that John is gone. The dealer sits at the table, a mound of cocaine piled in front of him, a straw up his nose.

I sit up in bed, eyes wide open, heart pounding.

It's a terrible thing, waking up depressed, alone, early in the morning. The first month I just stayed in bed, going over and over the events leading to John's death. The bedroom was cold and I'd curl up under the covers, holding extra pillows close to my body. Finally I'd drag myself to the kitchen and force down some breakfast.

I often wondered how the average widow, one with a family or a nine-to-five job, carried on; I couldn't imagine how anyone in mourning could handle serious responsibility. Sometimes I cried for that "other widow." How did she do it? Then again, maybe I'd be better off with responsibility to something or someone. I fantasized about joining the army. Now there was a way to put some order in my life.

At times I caught myself forgetting that John was dead. A man's shirt in a store window might catch my eye and I'd stop, thinking, This is perfect for . . .

Everything made me think of John. An old Volvo: that was *his* car. A man with a beard: *he* was so huggable with a beard. The Chicago Bears won? *He* loved the Bears. Seeing a couple walking hand-in-hand made me jealous. Something as inconsequential as a pocket flap accidentally pushed inside the pocket of a man's suit jacket nearly sent me into hysterics. I would flash on an image of John, all dressed up and smiling, standing with his hands in his suit jacket pockets, unknowingly stuffing the flaps inside. It was one of those unimportant things I would fix. I'd reach for his pockets and he'd grab me and give me a kiss and a hug. Damn it, how could he be dead and be so alive in my mind? It was as if he *did* live in my mind! Like a genie in a bottle, he was trapped there until I could find the secret to letting him out.

My forty days of wearing black came to an end April fifteenth. It was a nice change and an even bigger relief to my friends. I had been slowly losing weight, and was pale and drawn. The noticeable addition of color to my wardrobe gave the impression of improvement.

I wondered if forty days was an amount of time by which one *should* feel some improvement. "Give it time!" people said. Well, forty days marked little change. I was still unable to mingle with people, still unsteady with my emotions, still miserable. I was always aware of March fifth, and yet it was still too painful to think through the moment Danny came and told me. I'd imagine myself in the living room, lying on the couch—so unaware—wondering what time John would get home. Then I'd hear the click of the downstairs lock, someone pushing the combination to open the door. That "click" triggered a rush of emotions: fear, pain, sadness . . . I would explode in tears. Clearly, forty days wasn't *enough* time. Nothing was any better, really. Well, except my apparel. So maybe that was the point of the ritual. At least *something* about my life as a widow was better.

In November 1981, John and I bought a house in New York City, very different from the one on the Vineyard. That was a beach house, a summer house. This was going to be *home*.

Fifty-six West Tenth Street, an 1832 landmark building, was a lovely old one-family building. It needed a lot of work, but I had wanted an old house to restore and redesign to fit our needs. It was perfect for us.

The basement was typical of its era, a stone wall, dirt floor, and low ceiling. This would be the music room. If it couldn't absorb the sounds we'd produce, nothing would. The ground level was being opened into one large living/kitchen space. The kitchen work area would be completely redone, including restoring the walk-in fireplace and enlarging the window to the courtyard. Old paneling gave it the feel of a country farmhouse.

Most of the courtyard was given up to a one-room studio. It was a cozy, light room with French doors, a fireplace at one end, and a tall ceiling with a large skylight. John wanted this to be an all-purpose space, a recreation room, a place to hang out with friends.

On the parlor floor, the formal living and dining rooms were divided by a wet bar and dumbwaiter. We loved the old wooden dumbwaiter, and designed the new kitchen around it. Off the dining room was a very small library, just big enough for a couch and small desk or comfortable chair. John had his eye on this room as a personal sanctuary.

The third floor had two rooms which would be combined to make our bedroom, walk-in closet, and bath. On the top floor were two little guest bedrooms with dormers and another slightly larger room overlooking the courtyard. This would be my studio, for art work and writing.

Construction was halted the week after John's death. I needed to make a decision as to what I wanted to do with the house, but I found it difficult to think about. This was our dream house and represented our future, a future that died with John. Now I wondered if the house had upset John; maybe it was too much, he always had difficulty with an "upwardly mobile" move. Each time we made a decision about a new place to live, he was up and down about it. "Just ignore me," he would say. "I'll be fine once we're settled." And he always was.

In 1974, during *National Lampoon Lemmings*, we got our first decent apartment in the city. When we looked at 376 Bleecker Street, John was adamant that it cost too much. At three hundred twenty-five dollars a month, it was high. But after more apartment hunting, and going over our budget on paper, we decided to give it a try. Everything worked out and we loved living there for a time. By 1979, however, we'd outgrown it. And John's salary from "Saturday Night Live" and movies would allow a much higher rent. When I took him to see the Morton Street apartment, he walked through it too fast to have absorbed a thing, mumbling that it looked like the Reich palace. The rent, eighteen hundred a month, was the top of what we could afford, so I didn't want to push it. I'd find something else. A few days later John phoned from work and said, "Let's go with the Morton Street one." We never regretted it, but two years later we wanted to buy. Then when I found the Tenth Street house, after looking for nearly a year, John was very hesitant. It would take a lot of work, and time, before we could move in, and to afford another house John would have to commit to several movies in a relatively short time. Once again, I let him think about it. Then one day, out of the blue, he turned to me with a big grin and said, "Let's buy that house, honey!" "Are you sure?" I asked. "Are you sure you don't want to take off and travel . . . wait on a house?" "No, I wanta work," he said enthusiastically. "I want to do three films next year, and I want to get that house!"

There was an incident around Thanksgiving which bothered me now. John was angry that I was seeing a psychiatrist. "He's going to tell her to leave me," he told Laila. She assured him that wasn't why I was going to therapy. Unaware of the conversation, I came home and found John sitting on the hall stairs, just inside the street-level entrance, his chin on his fist. He looked sad. He raised his eyebrows in greeting. "What is it?" I asked, hugging him.

"I don't know . . . I was just thinking about the Tenth Street house." I sat down and we leaned against one another in silence. I knew he would love the house. I could see him proudly showing friends around, pointing out what work we'd done. I could see him sleeping peacefully on his couch in the little library. I could hear his laughter filtering across the courtyard from the studio. I said something to try and boost his spirits. "Don't worry about me," he said placing a kiss on my forehead. "You know how I get."

What had the house represented to John? Couldn't he trust the security he hoped it might bring? Did he feel he didn't deserve it, or that he didn't want the financial burden? Maybe he thought I was just staying with him because of the house? God, he couldn't have thought that, could he?

Mark phoned one day, suggesting I decide what to do with the Tenth Street house soon. I surprised myself by responding immediately, saying it was not right for me, it was too large and too expensive. What I didn't say was that it held too many fantasies which could never become reality. All the hours I'd spent in the big, empty house—designing rooms, running up and down the stairs, meeting with the various workmen—had been just a waste of time. I didn't want to think about it any more. I hated the house. It was suddenly an easy decision. Sell it.

In March, Pam had requested the various police reports and coroner records on John. We expected them within a week, but they didn't arrive. Pam phoned a few times to check out the delay, and on one such follow-up call an officer angrily told her, "Look, we've conducted a thorough investigation and we're confident that he shot himself up." This kind of response, combined with a quote from a officer who stated, "He was just another fat junkie landed belly up . . ." and Chief Darryl Gates's reported statement that John was "a horrible person," not only left me cold, but made me angry.

Meanwhile, Cathy Smith not only waltzed away from the police station, but left the country for Canada. In an attempt to find a missing guitar of John's, we contacted her lawyers and were told, "Cathy doesn't have it, she only has a few items of clothing, but don't worry, she won't auction them." They also informed us she would be out of the country "indefinitely." It was just as well. A courtroom drama would be hard to take, and John would probably end up on trial. But my questions persisted: I still wanted to know what had happened in Los Angeles.

By Mid-April, we received the official coroner's report. Pam reviewed it and said that much of it was meaningless to her. She suggested asking an independent agent to interpret, which sounded best. What she could tell me from the report was minimal. There was a reference to "multiple fresh needle puncture marks present on each arm," but there was no indication of how many. "It says a 'partially erased tattoo is present on the left upper arm.' " Pam quoted.

"A partially erased tattoo?" I repeated.

"Yeah, I wondered about that."

"He didn't have one when I last saw him," I said and thought a moment. John had been threatening to get a tattoo for the past few years. I put it in the same category with his talk about getting an ear pierced or a Mohawk hair cut: not likely. It struck me as odd that in five days he could have gotten a tattoo *and* had it partially erased. "Maybe that wasn't John," I half-joked, half-wished.

Another section listed "evidence found at the scene," including: "White powder on dresser drawer," a "green leafy substance" and "a syringe reported to be at the scene." I felt angry, remembering the police originally said they found no drugs.

The case report, information from the detectives at John's bungalow, as well as additional information taken at the police station, told us the most. There were three pages of description, beginning with a brief identification of John. Things of interest were: "Since 3-2-82, during the evening, the decedent had been in the company of an unidentified female with the exception of 3-3-82. . . . The female friend stated to the above detectives that on Monday night she and the decedent had stayed up all night drinking wine and inhaling cocaine through the nasal passages and injecting the drug into the antecubital fossa.

"On 3-4-82 during the evening . . . it is reported that the decedent was drinking heavily . . . the decedent asked somebody else to drive because he was unable to. Upon arriving back at the bungalow, the decedent immediately went to the bathroom and vomited. The female friend stated that he appeared pale and sweaty. Soon after the episode in the bathroom, the decedent began to partake of the wine and cocaine again. Other friends arrived at the scene at about 0300 hours, leaving at 0330. . . . At 0630 hours the decedent took a shower, emerging from the bathroom in a towel. The decedent stated that he was cold, turning up the heat. At approximately 0800 hours the decedent went to bed. He laid on his right side and was seen to be shaking and wheezing. . . . The female friend . . . at 0930 hours . . . heard a loud wheezing coming from the bedroom. She awakened the decedent asking if he was all right to which he replied he was. She then gave him a glass of ice water and he went back to sleep. . . . At 1050 hours she looked in on the decedent, saw he was covered with a blanket and appeared sleeping. She then left the location to get something to eat. . . ."

The coroner's report left us with more questions: Why were the police referring to Smith as an unidentified woman? Did they really question her without identifying her? And why had they lied to us about the drugs in the room? It would have been one thing to say they couldn't comment, but why mislead us? We hoped that the official police version would clear up some of these questions.

One thing was clear now. The drawing from the coroner, used on "20/20," indicated there were two episodes of shooting up, and now Smith confirmed that. So, somehow, John first got involved on Monday night, then again on Thursday.

On the other hand, the description of John shaking and getting hot and cold disturbed me. I didn't know much about heroin, but I would think those were signs of an overdose. And it's fairly common knowledge that someone who has taken too many drugs shouldn't go to sleep. Why didn't it occur to Smith he was in trouble? The word on the street was that she was a notorious user, she should have known. And I'd heard that a heroin overdose can be prevented by an injection of some other drug, which a paramedic or an emergency room can administer. It left me cold to realize that Smith not only injected him with the fatal drug, but was probably been too drugged-up herself to understand what was happening. It was such a stupid, stupid, senseless death.

I called Nelson with more questions. He reiterated he didn't think John drank any liquor, and said that he definitely was not drunk nor drinking at the bungalow. He had no knowledge of John throwing up. Cathy Smith had driven, but not because John couldn't.

Nelson asked me a lot of questions, too, about what was going on with the police. A detective had come by his house looking for him, but Nelson didn't speak with him. He seemed very nervous about his possible involvement if an investigation continued. I asked what he was afraid would happen and he became agitated, his voice rising as he speculated. He was afraid to admit he'd been doing coke with John, he feared it could hurt his career. "Nelson," I said, "your involvement can't be changed, that's happened. And I think it's really important for you not to hide anything and get it over with. DeNiro and Williams, too. I think it looks worse than it is when you won't even speak to the police." Nelson adamantly disagreed. "Can't you see what that would mean to me? I'd become the 'mystery man.' There would be press people following me, coming to my door. I have my baby to think of. I don't want those scum scrounging around here when Vivian and Natalie are alone!"

I thought Nelson was overreacting, his fear of the press seemed particularly paranoid. It was difficult, with my complicated feelings on the issue, to see his perspective.

I thought back to when we'd first met Nelson. He was drunk and abrasive, and neither John nor I much liked him. But he was a friend of writer Michael O'Donoghue, who was a friend of ours, so we chanced to meet again. We were on a month's vacation in Europe, and Michael, who was staying with Nelson in a chateau in France, asked us to call when we were nearby. We thought we'd have dinner and move on, but everyone in the house was in such great spirits and so welcoming that we ended up staying almost a week.

The most pleasant surprise about the trip was that Nelson had quit drinking and was quite a different fellow. He was remarkably happy and charming and living with a really great, radiantly beautiful French woman named Vivian, who had just given birth to the equally beautiful Natalie. Our visit was lovely and Nelson and John became fast friends. I think John appreciated Nelson's intellectual fervor and sense of humor, but they also shared an inner struggle and spoke about the difficulties and benefits of quitting their respective vices. They supported and encouraged each other, and it seemed that an important bond was formed between them.

A description in the coroner's report troubled me, kept coming back to me. Bill Wallace was quoted as stating that when he entered the bedroom, John was lying on his right side in a "tight fetal position." The image was haunting. Many times I found myself lying in the dark, visualizing John on the bed, tossing and turning, not feeling well, breathing heavily. As the end drew nearer, he'd slowly curl up, finally finding relief in a peaceful sleep, until . . . I wasn't sure. There were a couple of versions. If it was a heroin death, I had learned, the brain shuts down and you stop breathing. If cocaine caused the death, it could have been a heart attack or respiratory problem. I wondered if John had been frightened, if he realized he was dying? What if Smith knew and left him there alone? Maybe he'd given her a message for me! These thoughts were too painful.

The phone rang. It was Laila; she sounded agitated. "I'm sorry to be the one to have to tell you this, but I just saw an advance copy of *Rolling Stone* . . . They have an interview with Cathy Smith. I just thought you should know."

Laila was furious: how dare they use everyone to do a tribute, then turn around and follow up with this! Mitch and Tim were also angry. Jann (Wenner) had wanted to run an interview with Smith in the tribute issue, but they'd opposed him, refusing to work on it if he did. Jann said he'd forget the whole idea. I wasn't very happy to hear about another Cathy Smith interview, especially in *Rolling Stone*. I did, however, understand Jann's desire to cover different angles. But not the way it had been done. I didn't like the deception. I could have taken it as an insult, but it wasn't really; it wasn't that personal. It was just the rotten way things were done.

People told me not to read the interview; it was just more

of the same attitude, the same story Smith had been telling.
I wondered if there were a photo of her. She was still faceless
to me. I considered looking at the issue, but decided to ignore
it. It would go away, that's what everyone said. It would go
away.

At the end of April we finally received a copy of the police
report. Pam read the five-page document over the phone. It
was written in the same style of questions and answers. Most
of it overlapped the coroner's records, but there was some
new information. In this report, Cathy Smith stated that on
the morning of the fifth she took John's car and went to a bar
to meet a friend (whom she only knew by his first name) for
lunch. Smith also admitted that she'd given the drug paraphernalia to John. She said he asked her to, so he could shoot
cocaine. She stated she'd last shot cocaine on Tuesday, March
2, but took the works with her when she left because she
didn't want the maid to find it.

I was angered by the lack of police curiosity evidenced in
these reports. I had assumed the police version would be
more thorough, in terms of Smith, than the coroner's. Instead it was worse. They didn't even slap her hand when
they took the syringe away. If it was worth an officer's time
to ask her questions, why not ask pertinent ones? Like, who
was supplying the drugs? Or how about a little verification
of where she'd been that morning? How did she get to this
bar, perhaps she could give directions on how to get there?
And what about her friend? Wouldn't you think the police
would want to talk to him? If she met him for lunch she must
know some way to communicate with him. Even a bad episode of "Kojak" wouldn't allow so many holes. Clearly the
police had no real interest in knowing anything about Cathy
Smith's whereabouts or her possible involvement in John's
death.

And why had they arrested her in the first place? That was
the only logical step taken. Something must have happened
after she got to the station. All I could figure was that she
was a police informant; they probably only questioned her for
formality's sake. But that seemed too stupid. Certainly the
Los Angeles Police Department knew to anticipate the interest a celebrity death would bring. It just didn't make sense.

It took a few weeks before Pam was able to obtain the aid of an Oregon medical examiner, Dr. Larry Lewman, to interpret the autopsy report. He concluded from microscopic study of the tissue that John had only been involved with injecting drugs over a two to three day period before his death. Any serious involvement with shooting up over the years could be eliminated, since that would have left scar tissue and thickened veins. The report stated there were some recent needle marks on each arm and the evidence suggested that John was mixing cocaine with heroin—speedballing, something coke users sometimes do to cut the edginess. Dr. Lewman placed the time of death around ten in the morning, an estimate which could be off by an hour either way.

We asked Dr. Lewman to consider Smith's story and give us his opinion as to its veracity. He was quite certain John's death did not happen exactly as Smith described. Assuming John had no drugs after 3:30 A.M., as Smith contended, she could not have awakened John and given him water when she said she did. If the drugs had been sufficient to cause a fatal overdose, John would have been in a coma or semi-coma, by that time. He also doubted that at six-thirty John had taken a shower, based on the fact that his bladder was full.

We asked Dr. Lewman if the autopsy showed John to be in terrible physical state, as several journalists had contended. He said there appeared to be a history of sinus problems and that the lungs showed typical wear from smoking. The heart was slightly enlarged, which suggested high blood pressure. But he pointed out that John's vessels were wide open, which would imply he was not subject to having a heart attack any time soon. John was not in tip-top shape, but he appeared basically healthy.

We asked if the needle marks gave any indication as to whether John could have injected himself. Dr. Lewman said it was technically possible, but he doubted the injections were the work of a novice, especially on the right arm. (John was right handed.)

Dr. Lewman's final conjecture was that John was not a heavy chronic user of intravenous narcotics up until the days immediately before his death. However, there were

signs of abusive cocaine use over the years. He said the
amount of morphine (a by-product of heroin) in the blood was
technically enough to kill someone, but it was not a massive
amount. When combined with the cocaine however, death
easily could result.

Dr. Lewman suggested a plausible scenario. He explained
that cocaine users sometimes erroneously believe that heroin
will bring them down. It was possible that John was uncomfortable from taking too much coke, and he or Smith mistak-
enly decided a shot of heroin would help. Unfortunately, this
is a fatal mistake. Death from heroin, however, is usually
within the hour. This meant that if John died from a shot of
heroin, he would have had to recieve his last injection about
nine, the same time Smith said she left the bungalow.

It was creepy to go over this kind of information. But there
was a certain relief in having a professional explain the
medical evidence. Now my belief was supported, not just
blind faith; John did not have a secret habit of shooting up.

In early May, Alan Sonnenschein, a writer from *Penthouse*, contacted Pam. He said they felt something was wrong
with the circumstances surrounding John's death, and they
intended to investigate. He wanted to know if we would
cooperate. Although I was pleased that somebody else was
suspicious, we declined. I didn't want to see my first involvement with the press on this issue positioned between the legs
of naked women.

I had been hesitant to get back to work on *Titters 101*.
Anne, Deanne, and I had begun working on it when John
was in L.A. writing *Noble Rot*. In fact, that was one of the
reasons I chose not to go to California, a decision I felt guilty
about now.

John's intellectual self and functioning self seemed to be
at odds with the issue of my working. On one hand, he
believed I was talented and should work, and at times was
very influential and helpful in my meeting that goal. But it
seemed that whenever I was involved in a big undertaking,
he resented the energy it took, time and attention he wanted.
Titters projects had a history of being time-consuming, so he
wasn't happy with the idea of a new book. That meant

he wasn't very happy with Anne, who he saw as the deal-maker, the one who solidified the projects.

When we'd first met, Anne was working at *Lampoon* and living with Michael O'Donoghue. They became our first close "couple" friends after we moved to the city. They were very New York to us: intellectual, witty, and fashionable. Anne was intimidating at first because she is exceedingly sharp and quick to express her opinion in a manner which is often abrupt. But she's also very funny, giving, and actually very sweet. At their apartment we saw Anne's softer side; she wore flowing satin robes and catered to Michael's whims.

Michael and Anne were two of the first writers hired for "SNL" and they both fought fiercely for John to be cast as a player. They split up just after we finished our first *Titters*, which had been a trying time for all three of our spouses. For nine months, during which Anne was also writing for "SNL," the project had taken most of our time. One evening while we worked, the three men went out together and dubbed themselves the "Titter's Widowers." This coincided with the beginning of John's problems with Anne. He once said, in the middle of a mad rage about why he had difficulty working with her, "And she's trying to take you away from me!" I think he also felt threatened by her moving out on Michael, as if I would follow her lead. John was concerned that two professionals could not make a marriage last in our world.

I tried to be clear with John as to my own interests and let him know our relationship came first. But it was important to me to continue working, since I enjoyed it and so much of his time was filled by his work. I had shaped my career so I was able to work around his schedule fairly well. Overall—since the first *Titters*, anyway—our plans were rarely inter-rupted by my work. I think an unconscious part of John was that ethnic man who likes the idea of his wife at home in the kitchen. On a conscious level, however, he wanted an equal, someone who took an interest in life and lived it to the fullest.

John didn't know Deanne very well, and maybe he didn't try to know her better in keeping with his dislike of our working partnership. He used to call her "the drill sergeant." Deanne is a deadpan humorist with a cutting wit, an attitude which is often misread as cold in women. Underneath her armor, she is sensitive and caring. During the last year of his life, John was much friendlier to Deanne; he was clearly beginning to like her because he started joking with her. One day when she phoned for me, he answered and said in mock desperation, "I'll give you fifty thousand dollars to stay away from my wife!" Then in a sweet voice to me, "Honey, it's Deanne."

It was with all this excess baggage that I reentered the *Titters* project. We had divided the work so we each had two chapters to write alone and several to write together. Anne, who had been spending a lot of time in L.A., was now in New York, so it was a good idea to take advantage of being able to work together. We chose to begin with a piece which was a parody of the style of Notzake Shange's *For Colored Girls Who Have Considered Suicide When the Rainbow Is Enuf*, while satirizing the story *Washington Post* writer Janet Cook invented (and presented as fact) about a little boy who was a heroin junkie. This exposé won Cook the Pulitzer Prize, which was retracted upon discovery of her fraud. Our piece was called, *For Pulitzer Prize Winners Who Have Considered Fiction When the Facts Weren't Enuf*.

The three of us began working daily at Phantom. It felt good to work with my friends again, to have a purpose outside myself. It was also very tiring. My concentration was off, but Anne and Deanne were patient, sometimes gently bringing me back from my own world to the task at hand, other times leaving me in my fantasy. Our work was going well when Anne unexpectedly had to return to L.A. to produce "Square Pegs," a television pilot she had written. Deanne and I agreed to complete our piece.

The story Janet Cook wrote included graphic descriptions of drug injections, which we incorporated in our parody. The images it conjured were bizarrely interwoven in my mind. I'd find myself in memory, such as my first date with John, while at the same time feeling disturbed by visions of John experimenting with needles. Still, somehow I continued to help Deanne write, perhaps more to my amazement than hers. When we finally completed the story, and its descriptions of "Little Jimmy" shooting up, I sat at the table in the Phantom office and felt sick to my stomach.

I had been dreaming about John when a gentle rain against my bedroom window made me aware that I was suspended between dreaming and waking. I felt heavy, sad, aware that I was tortuously searching for John, not finding him anywhere. I knew I could end this nightmare, shake myself awake, but maybe I *would* find him. Awake, I knew I wouldn't . . . The phone jolted me up; a woman speaking in broken English, looking for Hernández. I don't even know where John is. . . . "Hernández no aqui." She accepted my response. Oh well, time to give up this dream.

I discovered the best thing I could do when I woke up early was to read. I was reading *The Human Season* by Edward Lewis Wallant, about a widower's anguish after the loss of his wife of forty years. It was odd, I'd just pulled it from the bookshelf one morning, started reading, and that's what it was about. I found I related very closely to his pain, fears, and confusion. As he delves into his grief, his daughter repeatedly tries to share his mourning, until he finally cuts her off: "You talk about sad, about mourning . . . What you got is like a sad movie. You think about the old times, about the things that are over and done with anyhow, and you're sad . . . It's not that way with me, . . . I'm not crying for the good old days. I'm crying because I'm dead . . . worse than dead . . . in Hell. I feel only hate. Oh, how can I tell you? . . . I can't help you *mourn*, I can't be *sad* with you. I'm a million miles under sad."

Yes, that was how I felt. And I felt guilty about it, because I knew things could be worse; people suffered worse tragedies. But this was my tragedy and it was killing me. I didn't want to have fun anymore, I *couldn't* have fun anymore. I wasn't interested in music, unless the lyrics were about life and death. I had no sexual desires. I didn't want to meet people or even be with most. I just wanted to be in my own hell.

The Human Season stirred some rumblings of life in me. I saw for the first time that the ugliness and hatred, the depression and exhaustion I felt, were part of a process that must be universal. I began to feel an enthusiasm for this idea and suddenly knew what I must do. Since this experience consumed me, why not write about it? I could keep diaries, chart my own progress. Maybe it would be a book. Then I could share the healing—if it ever came.

Chapter 7

WALKING IN CIRCLES

MAY

Odd information about John's death and its reverbera-
tions continued to filter down. A persistent rumor was
that a member of the narcotics division was somehow involved with Cathy Smith. One story went that Cathy
Smith phoned a friend who was with the police officer the
morning John died, and told him John was dead and what
had happened. The officer supposedly told her to return to
the Chateau Marmont, he'd take care of everything. I didn't
altogether believe any specific rumor, but thought there must
be some such explanation for the police's nasty attitude toward John and unexplainable attitude toward Smith. Pam
told me that California was one of the few states to have
prosecuted people suspected of injecting another with drugs
where death resulted. Why were the police so uninterested in
questioning Smith more thoroughly? Why so intent on cast-
ing John as the bad guy?

About this time, Don Novello sent me an interesting arti-
cle. It was from the May 1, 1982 edition of the *Revolutionary
Worker*, and titled "The Killing Things About the Death of
John Belushi." I sat in my office and read with interest.

The article was severely at odds with the "official" version
of the events surrounding John's death, stating, "The only
thing consistent about it is its pattern of deceit." It noted
that the L.A.P.D. initially reported John died of natural causes
and no drugs or paraphernalia were found in his bungalow.
Then, ". . . a temporary freeze was declared on any further

statements as the coroner's office stepped in. A routine autopsy and toxicological analysis, normally taking little more than twenty-four hours, this time required six full days to complete." The article pointed out that not until John's "body was deep in the ground" was the official ruling released, along with an admission that the police had found drugs and a syringe on the premises, after all. The article surmised: "Conveniently this ruling automatically implies self-destruction, relieving the state of any legal obligation to investigate further . . ."

The article also noted that "this alleged involvement with heroin stands in marked contrast to everything Belushi's close associates know about him."

I had to stop at this point and take a breath. Here, finally, was someone who saw the obvious and trusted in the basics, like believing that what John's family and friends were saying might be the truth: that although John may have had a drug problem, he wasn't a junkie; it was not his habit to use needles or heroin. The author observed that only "two unnamed sources, 'Hollywood producers'" were on record (in the *L.A. Times*) stating that John was a heroin junkie. And for the first time, as far as I knew, it was reported that this was contradicted by the coroner's report. I was exhilarated that someone had bothered to check this out.

And other matters bothered the author, like Chief Darryl Gates's response at a March 11 press conference to a question about whether John injected the drugs voluntarily or was injected by someone else. "Gates replied: 'Our investigators are pretty well convinced that it (the drug-*RW*) was something he wanted administered.' *Wanted administered*? What about Cathy E. Smith's testimony to police that Belushi retired alone to a back room of his bungalow to take care of 'his private concerns?' Do 'self-administered' and 'wanted administered' suddenly have identical meanings? Or is this simply a poor choice of words by Chief Gates, a mere slip of the lip as it were?"

The author then focused on the holes in Cathy Smith's story, including that her scenario requires us to "believe that

Belushi . . . actually woke up in the middle of over dosing to drink a glass of water. . . . Cathy Smith's credibility comes not from the coherence or accuracy of her story—how could it? On the contrary, it is *the story* she tells—combined with her checkered past, her alleged drug connections, her near-nodding performance on "20/20" and her seemingly half-memorized lines noted by the *Rolling Stone* interviewer—that make her so exceedingly *convenient* and *necessary*. . . . For [the authorities] are relying on and evoking all the mainstream images of the Hollywood party scene, hoping to create confusion with their conflicting reports and to elicit disgust . . . enabling them to pass over Belushi's death with a cynical 'That's life in the fast lane, that's Hollywood.' . . . Smith provides a very useful conveyor to reinforce such imagery."

The article contended that Smith had been arrested twice recently for "possession of drugs/syringes," citing that the previous January 4 she had been "held in jail for a month—even though court records indicate that a friend had paid her $300 bail—until she pleaded guilty and was released on twelve months probation." This was information I had asked of the police, who had never responded.

Lastly, the article questioned the "official story of a depressed Belushi who really had nothing to live for." For contrast the article quoted Bernie Brillstein's excerpt from *Rolling Stone* describing John during his last month, a portrait of a very active man, involved in the planning of future projects, excited about his prospects. The author concluded: "This is hardly the image of a man depressed and demoralized about life, hardly the image of a man seeking death. But it must be asked: Was his death being sought and by whom? As for those who celebrated the occasion, there is plenty of evidence.

"Belushi's loyalties and enthusiasm were precisely with the oppressed and with people who went against the grain, in the arts, and in general. Coming out of the '60s and through the '70s, his in-your-face irreverence prompted millions to embrace him as 'one of us.' . . . The night of Belushi's death, Ted Koppel of ABC "Nightline" was prompted to say of Belushi: 'He attacked the establishment with a zeal bordering on vengeance.' And in the weeks following, they certainly took their revenge, combining some highly political character assassination with a broadly aimed threat at those who don't want to turn down the music—that such 'excesses' will, one way or another, lead to a bad end."

The article ended: " 'It was just the Hollywood scene, really, nothing out of the ordinary.' So says Miss Smith. But for those who find the all too 'ordinary' and 'business-as-usual' nature of such things as the mysterious deaths of progressive artists and the oh-so-casual acceptance of these crimes to be intolerable, this case will not be so easily closed."

I got up and paced my office. Energy surged through me, I had to be in motion. Even though I recognized the antiestablishment bias of the writer, it was a shock to see my own concerns and fears neatly spelled out. So what was the article saying, that John was intentionally murdered? I had heard stories like that about Hendrix and Joplin. Rumors that they had been killed by a government agency because their counterculture ideas and lifestyle were affecting too many people and were viewed as a threat. A part of me believed such a theory could be true. Could it be that Cathy Smith was instructed to become involved with John and see that he overdosed? The thought was chilling. No. Now these kind of thoughts must mean I'm over the edge. I said that to myself, but deep down I wondered. Although I had no evidence, I was certain Smith was an informant. She was probable assigned to collect information on the drug habits of celebrities, perhaps John specifically. I conjectured that during this assignment, John accidentally overdosed. Perhaps when her police contact realized Smith was actively involved in the death, steps were taken to avoid an investigation. Or maybe it was even worse than that. Maybe the drugs that caused John's death were given to Smith by her police contact. Now this would be worth covering up.

That night I lay in the dark, a singsong ditty annoying me the way a catchy commercial won't leave you alone:

> John is dead,
> John is dead,
> Thought keeps running through my head,
> Was he killed by a Fed,
> And left to die in his bed?
> That's not what the papers said,
> But I don't trust them a fuck anyway . . .

The following morning I woke with an idea that excited me. I decided to approach a reporter, a writer with an honest, straight-ahead style, to investigate John's death. I would provide our information and records, and he could take it from there. I decided it was best not to ask a friend; I didn't want the results to be "an article a friend wrote." It had to be a nationally respected writer, someone people trusted.

Who would John select, I wondered? Who did he like to read? Royko! Mike Royko was John's favorite newsman. His style of talking to you, his heart, his gut-level smartness, were perfect for this. On an impulse I decided to phone him right away. I'd met him a few times in Chicago and knew he was fond of John. Royko used to frequent John's father's restaurant, back when John was a busboy. He once wrote an article featuring Adam Belushi and his brother: first-generation immigrants who found a piece of the American dream through hard work and enterprise. Then he later wrote a column about the immigrant's son making good.

In a matter of minutes I had phoned the *Chicago Sun-Times* and had Mike Royko on the line. As I began to explain my idea, I suddenly felt very sad, very strange, almost in another dimension. Mr. Royko spoke highly of John and said he hadn't read much about what happened. I started to say something and began crying as I spoke. As if it weren't me talking, I heard myself say, "I just want people to know the real John." Mike Royko was silent while I pulled myself

together. He apologetically declined, explaining it wasn't
really the sort of thing he did, he was not an investigative reporter. I thanked him, my voice sounding a hundred miles away. When I got off the phone, I cried for some
time.

"What about Bob Woodward?" I asked Pam. There was no
immediate response; she often didn't say anything while she
thought through questions I asked. I waited impatiently,
twenty-five hundred miles away, the receiver not quite to my
ear until I heard her speak.

"Well, sounds like a great idea. As far as an investigative
reporter, we couldn't do better. But do you think he'd be
interested?"

"I don't know. It just seems we should decide who we'd like
first, and then see. No harm in asking, right?"

After my experience with Mike Royko, I knew I wasn't
emotionally able to approach anyone. So Pam made the call,
explaining to Woodward that we felt there was a story in all
the unanswered questions surrounding John's death, and
asking if he would be interested in going over what information we had. Woodward was interested. They arranged to
meet May 17 in Washington, D.C.

After meeting with Woodward, Pam came to New York.
She arrived just in time to accompany me to a financial
meeting with Mark to go over my budget. He informed me
that my current spending was dipping into my capital, which
eventually would eat up my ability to live off the interest. He
determined I could proceed this way without much damage
for a while, but that within three to five years I should
reevaluate. A new budget could then be determined, based on
what kind of earnings I was able to generate, what monies
came in for John's work and the selling of the Tenth Street
house. And there were some business deals in the works
which Mark felt were very promising. I felt comfortable with
the plan.

I was much more interested in what Pam had to say about
the meeting with Woodward. Once home, she gave a detailed
account. Bob Woodward was reserved and businesslike, yet
friendly. They chatted briefly about Wheaton (our common

hometown) and she told him our bother had been in some classes with him. He responded politely that he thought the name was familiar. They then got down to the business at hand, Bob listening intently while Pam went over the reports and information we had collected. When she finished, he was pensive, soft-spoken in his response, saying he found the situation very unusual and agreed that something was wrong. He said he felt there was a good story in this, and that if he took it on he would go to L.A. to investigate. But he would want to write about more than just John's end; he would want to write about John, the man, really look into his life and who he was. He was interested in understanding how someone like John ends up where he did.

I was disappointed with Pam's news. To have to talk to someone about John, to try to make sense out of what had happened, to ask friends and family to talk to a reporter . . . No, it was too much. If the Los Angeles story wasn't enough for Woodward, then it wasn't. We would think of someone else.

An article on John was underway at the *Chicago Tribune*. Staff reporter Cheryl Lavin approached several of my family members for interviews. She even tried to persuade my brother to convince me to talk with her, saying her focus was on John as a young man in Wheaton and Chicago; something to counter the bad image being portrayed in the press. I was turning down all interviews and never considered talking to Lavin, but Rob and other family members were tempted as she made the positive angle very appealing. In the end, everyone declined for the simple reason that the loss was still too painful.

I don't remember who phoned first. I remember my mother-in-law crying, telling me about the article on John in the Sunday paper. She said she phoned the *Tribune* after reading the article, giving an earful to the fellow who took her call. "Why do you do this?" she said. "My Johnny never did anything wrong."

"Well, he's dead, isn't he?" the man replied coldly.

Someone sent the article and I read it in my bedroom. I found it so upsetting I couldn't read it straight through.

I spoke out loud to the author, appalled at what I saw unfolding, calling her on this and that, wandering the hallway, the sound room, returning to continue reading. I shivered uncontrollably.

The portrait Lavin painted was of a man on a self-destructive path since he'd graduated high school, when he stopped being "the best little boy in Wheaton" and became a hippie. From there on his life became a constant search for a better high—until March fifth, when "he banged his head against the floor until he died."

I grabbed a pen and started making notes in the margin and underlining offensive items. The second paragraph stated: "He was only 33, but he had an old man's body—an obese old man's body—with hardened arteries and swollen, bloated organs." I underlined this and wrote on the side, "Did you bother to check out the coroner's report?" Another paragraph quoted a high-school classmate as saying, "He didn't even last a semester in college." Next to this I wrote, "Why don't you check records? John was at Whitewater State, Wisconsin, a full year, and received an Associate Degree from the College of DuPage."

Lavin says of John's hiring at Second City, "He was 22 then, weighed 170 pounds, and he wrote in his biography for Second City that the only time his life had ever been in danger was 'when I thought of suicide.'" Now, this was true, but totally out of context. He had also written silly answers to almost every question the form asked. For instance, John's response to "Have you musical interest?" was "Someday I'd like to buy a big stereo outfit and learn to play records at full volume," and his answer to "What would be your second choice of career?" was, "Commander of a star ship." As reported, however, the suicide remark fit her angle.

Lavin wrote that John became difficult as his fame grew, citing: "And then you demand things. The marble floor in his penthouse suite at the Ambassador East Hotel in Chicago seemed a little cold, so the management carpeted it. He wanted a phone in his favorite booth at the Pump Room—where he would shovel in double orders of caviar followed by a hamburger—so they put in a jack." Hmm. Well, the marble floor was actually in a bathroom, and I phoned and, quite politely, requested a throw rug because, indeed, I found the floor to be cold. We would be in the room for over a month, so it didn't strike me as an unreasonable request. I myself was very impressed when the following day the bathroom floor was carpeted. As for the Pump Room story, yes, we had a favorite booth, one in the back where we had more privacy. One day the maitre d' asked John how he liked the service, and John graciously replied that it was wonderful. He added that it would be perfect, except there was no phone. We all laughed and the following morning the maitre d' one-upped John by presenting him with a phone at the table, which we thought was very funny. I was under the impression that the plug was already there and it was just an extension, but, regardless, it was never requested, much less demanded. As for the food mentioned, I *was* pretty big on caviar with egg and onion on toast, and I think I did once get a double order when I took several high-school friends to lunch. At any rate, John was being criticized for things he didn't do—in this case probably because Lavin had him confused with Bluto, his character from *Animal House.*

Many of her comments were inane. "He didn't object when Aykroyd yelled at a photographer, 'Just take the picture, pal. Guys like you are a dime a f—— dozen.' " As if John were responsible for any rude thing Danny might do or say. But, again, this is out of context. Perhaps the photographer deserved such a comment. I suspect if Danny said something like this, the photographer probably had been rude himself.

The article added up to a contrived portrait, but I was especially disturbed by Lavin's conclusions and prejudiced account of an incident I hadn't thought about for some time:

It was mid-August 1977 when John went to Durango, Mexico, to film his first movie, *Goin' South.* He accepted the role of a Mexican deputy as a last-minute arrangement, mostly because he wanted to work with Jack Nicholson, but also because he expected to be filming *Animal House* in the fall and thought it would be good to have a movie under his belt. The job cut short our summer vacation on Long Island, but the opportunity for John professionally, along with that of getting a chance to spend time in Mexico, made it worthwhile. The biggest concern was that John be finished filming before the "SNL" season began again in late September, and the producers, Harry Gittes and Harold Schneider promised that he would.

Time past pleasantly and quickly in Mexico and soon mid-September was upon us. One night, going over the script with John, it struck us that he still had a lot to shoot. The next day John brought it up with one of the producers and was told there would be no problem getting him home in time for the show.

However, when the week ended, John still hadn't completed his scenes. He flew home to begin the second season of "SNL," but had to return to Mexico the next weekend, which meant a very difficult schedule for him. He had to catch an early plane on Sunday after doing the show Saturday until one in the morning, spend the night in Mexico City, and get up for an early plane to Durango on Monday. He would be on location Monday and Tuesday, then back to work at "SNL" Wednesday evening. He returned only to complain that he had still not completed, he'd have to go back.

The next week when John came home he was very angry. He had hardly worked while in Mexico and again had to return. He hated making the trip, he hated being in Mexico alone, he hated the food, the hotel. And he was not feeling well. Needless to say, John returned to Mexico with a bad attitude. He began drinking and got into an argument with the producers which ended in a shoving match with Schneider.

The next day the rest of his scenes for *Goin' South* were completed, but the conflict wasn't over. Several months later, when he was in L.A. on business, he was asked to do some dubbing for *Goin' South*. He was scheduled to return to "SNL" the day *Goin' South* wanted him. John balked at the idea, since he wouldn't get back to New York until the Thursday before the show. This was not only difficult for him, but not much appreciated by his co-workers. Bernie thought it was a good idea for John to cooperate with the

Goin' South producers, to get beyond their dispute. He explained that John owed the movie a reasonable amount of overdubbing, and recommended getting it over with. He could request a per diem and transportation for the day. Bernie worked this out with the producers and John stayed in L.A. to dub. The next evening he phoned on his way to the airport. He was very upset as he explained that he'd been humiliated by the producers: angry with his request for a car and per diem, they sent a small, extremely dirty car and a hundred dollars in change. Did Nicholson know they were doing this? I wondered. John didn't think so, was quite sure it was the producers. "Even the poor girl who was sent with the money was embarrassed," John said.

Lavin made a brief reference to this incident. "Drugs were the place where Belushi went when he needed to get away. His appetite and his demand grew together. . . . A story buzzed through Hollywood about the time Belushi had to do an hour's worth of dubbing on a completed film, and he demanded $100 for it—the price of a gram of cocaine—and a limousine to chauffeur him. He was making $350,000 a film by this time, and the producers were so disgusted they sent a Subaru and a sack of nickels and dimes."

Needless to say, Lavin's viewpoint on this struck a very sore spot. I found it odd that this story had surfaced. Could Gittes and Schneider be so vindictive that they would bring this up now, when John was unable to respond? I even wondered if they were the "two Hollywood producers" who labeled John a heroin addict. Oh, probably not, but I didn't know what to think.

A few nights after reading the *Tribune* article, I lay in my bed, unable to sleep, going over some of the things said about John. Finally, I got up and wrote:

YOU KNOW WHO YOU ARE

Leave me shivering in my bed
Make me wish that I was dead
Go on, write your slime, your trash
Go on, fit the crime, the dash

To make sure what you write is read
Even if it's on my head
You leave your sting, your words, your lies
You don't have to hear my cries

This is not fiction
This is not comedy
This is my life
So fuck off!

Chapter 8

LIFE GOES ON

JUNE

Life dragged on, really dragged, as if I were carrying John on my back. In a way I was; at least, he was always on my mind. And my thoughts didn't get me anywhere, they just went round and round. My attitude was blasé at best. I didn't care if I lived and I didn't care if I died. There was a certain freedom in that, a kind of ability to do anything without fear. I never thought twice about living alone in New York. I'd come home to the dark apartment unafraid; a creak or unfamiliar sound at night piqued my interest instead of frightening me. Maybe it was John? I moved on with no sense of direction. Occasionally there were moments when I felt good, but feeling good made me uncomfortable. I'd find myself laughing at something, sense my mood lifting, then *crash*! I'd have recognized the change in my feelings and remembered why it was I suddenly felt odd. *How can I feel okay when John is dead?* My body ached.

I was also experiencing various unexpected losses. My focus was on John, but I was becoming aware that the basic structure of my existence died with him as well. Not just the scheduling of life, which was obvious, but my deeper sense of self. I'd put a lot of thought and energy into defining myself as wife and artist. Quite clearly, I was no longer a wife, although I didn't feel any different; I still loved John, was still devoted to him. Everything that changed was physical; emotionally nothing had changed. But how to stop thinking of yourself as someone's wife? My ring was still in place on my left hand. I considered taking it off, but the idea repulsed

123

me. I just couldn't. As far as being an artist, I certainly wasn't feeling creative. And I had no love for life, so what could I offer?

My pace was also totally altered. The whirlwind of activity that had surrounded *our* life was gone. We'd often had friends living with us, or spending so much time that it was as if they lived with us. Now, not only were the people gone, but so were all the various household tasks and personal concerns that come with even a somewhat atypical "family" unit.

The most obvious missing family member was Danny. He'd been such a constant, coming and going like a kid in college. During a project we often shared living accommodations; I'd wake him for work, include him in our meal plans, take care of his laundry. We all got along well, worked together well. If we fought, we always made up. And how we laughed! Sometimes we laughed so hard we would roll on the floor until we were too exhausted to move. I would suddenly have an image of us laughing and wonder what we ever found so funny . . .

Mainly we laughed at ourselves—our antics, the way we looked, worked, lived. Our lives were absurd and we knew it. We fancied ourselves gypsies, bandits; traveling to towns, dazzling people, taking their money. At times we would "hide out," just take off and get away. If we needed supplies, I was the one to get them because my face wasn't on any "wanted poster." If we stayed at a motel, we often registered as Johnny Friendly, the name of the union boss in *On the Waterfront*. We kept our curtains drawn, preferring to go out at night. You can become a prisoner of fame, or you can use it to your advantage. We got plenty from it and appreciated that. We tried to keep a sense of humor about the rest.

Over the years, our lives became comfortably intertwined. Following our lead, Danny hired Mark as his business manager and Bernie as his personal manager. We shared Phantom. We rented the Blues Bars in New York and Chicago together. And after John and I bought the Vineyard house, Danny wanted a house there, too. They were filming *The Blues Brothers* at the time, so I went to look for him. Rhonda accompanied me and we took Polaroids of the choices. On

returning to Chicago, I met Dan at the Blues Bar to go over
what I'd seen. He liked one very much, it was solid and on a
hilltop. As I described it in detail, he stared at a photo,
listening intently. When I finished, he took a long, thoughtful swig of beer, held out the Polaroid, and said, "Okay, I'll
take it." He didn't even want to see it first. "It's beautiful
there and you'll be five minutes away," he stated matter-of-
factly. "What more do I need to know?"

John loved Danny from their first meeting at Second City
in Toronto. When I'd arrived a few days later, John imitated
Danny's scenes from the show; he already admired Danny's
talent and knew they would work together someday. "He's a
great guy, honey, you've got to meet him!" When "SNL"
began, and John and Danny were finally working together,
they quickly grew close. New to the city, Danny took up
residence on a foam mattress on our living room floor.

Who's to say what makes people friends? It seemed that John
and Danny were attracted by some similar energy, almost
like magnets. They were on the same wavelength, and understood each other, although they didn't always think alike.
They felt good together and their comedic senses clicked.
Both were disciplined about their work and both worked
hard. Yet, in many ways, they were very different. Like yin
and yang, they were opposites that together made one. Danny
was controlled and studied, John chaotic and spontaneous.
Danny held things in. John wore his feelings on his face.
Actually, there was a similiar attraction to that between
John and me, except that John and I were partners in life,
whereas John and Danny were partners in business. Still,
each overlapped. And each had a future

Now I seldom saw Danny. He was mostly on the West
Coast, popping into the city occasionally, always very busy
when he did. He no longer came by the house. I didn't blame
him. It was a sad house, it barely resembled the home he had
known. Every once in a while we'd run into each other at the
office. I felt it made Danny sad to see me.

One day when I was at Phantom, he came in to meet with
a writer who was interviewing him for a book called *The
Best of Friends*, in which a chapter was devoted to John and
Dan. When the author arrived, Danny introduced us and

asked me to sit with them. They got right to work, so after a short while I excused myself, thinking they'd rather talk alone. A few minutes later Danny came back to my room and asked me to join them again. I was pleased that he seemed to really want me there, and feeling more comfortable now, I enjoyed listening as Danny passionately talked about John. He was animated, pacing the room as if his own motion might help to convey the energy he was trying to describe. Suddenly he said in his deep, booming voice, "You know one of the things I loved about John? I loved the way he loved my brother." As he said this, his voice cracked and he began to cry. "As soon as he met Peter, he loved him because he was my brother, and I feel the same way about his brothers." Then Danny sat down across the table from me and sobbed. Tears streaking my face, I gently put my hand on his and we finally shared our grief. I sensed the author's emotions as he sat, motionless, in silent respect.

At night, when I entered the darkened Morton Street apartment, I often didn't bother to flip on any lights until I needed them. It used to be the first thing I'd do, but now it seemed unnecessary. The light was almost an intrusion, an offense. Sometimes I would sit in the living room, my cat Whisper on my lap, and let my mind wander. I saw John and Danny in the kitchen, devouring a leftover chicken while standing in front of the open fridge door, laughing, as they continued to work on a scene. I saw John and myself lying on a rug in front of the fireplace, remembering exactly how the light played on his face, how the warmth of the fire complemented the warmth of his caress. I remembered the apartment when we first moved in, the big rooms awaiting more furniture, the sound room not yet built, but set up for music. We had a party to kick off the first official Blues Brothers tour, just the band members, their wives, and a few others. Some of us were still getting to know each other, so it was good to have a low-key time together. After dinner, most of the party was in the courtyard, but a few of us were dancing inside when someone put on Otis Redding. Steve Cropper and Duck Dunn had played with Otis, and for a moment I sensed a sadness in them. Mitch must have noticed, too, because he asked if they minded listening. They said no, and we all danced to the slow tune. Afterward, Duck said it was the first time he'd listened to Otis since he'd died. I remembered not being able to imagine what it was like to have such a personal loss. Another record was played, an up number, and the sadness was left behind and the mood was joyous. Paul Shaffer played piano, Steve Jordan improvised some drums, and people sang along. The house was rockin'; it was finally initiated.

Now the house was deathly quiet. Yes, I thought, it *is* exactly that. *Deathly* quiet. The origin of the expression was suddenly clear. I began to think I should look for a new place to live, something to buy. A change would be good.

Walking along Morton Street I was surprised to see that spring was in full bloom. The air was fresh and I almost felt good. Taking in the beauty of the block, I saw a large sign attached to the front of a brownstone: "Co-Ops Available." The prospect of buying on the block was too good to be true!

Excited, I rushed on to Shopsin's. The deli was in its usual state of family activity. Charlie, the oldest son, buzzed in and out. The twins, toddlers now, played in a corner. Eve sat behind the counter nursing the baby, while Kenny prepared an order.

Shopsin's was one of the reasons I loved my neighborhood. It was a constant; you knew they'd be there, you knew they'd have plenty of great food, and if they weren't busy, they liked to talk. I enjoyed Kenny and Eve; they were hard working, I admired them. And the store was a hotbed of neighborhood information. I sat in the rocker and asked if they knew anything about the co-op.

With the sale of the 10th Street house, I could certainly afford a co-op, I realized. This was one situation I was truly grateful for. In that instant, I knew I really did want to leave 60 Morton—the sooner the better. The feeling of emptiness in the large upstairs rooms was encouraging and exaggerating my own feelings of emptiness. I was so keen on moving, I was ready to rush over and put money down. Talking with Kenny and Eve cooled my heels. They knew of another co-op for sale on the block, and suggested I look around.

I spoke to Dr. Cyborn about moving and he thought I should take it slowly. He suggested I wait a year before buying, to give myself time to see how I felt. There was that old obstacle again—time. Well, I concluded, I was planning to move before John died, so I already knew how I felt about it. The real problem would be finding a place. After having looked for a year before finding the Tenth Street house, it was depressing to think about looking again, especially when I was selling the best place I'd ever seen in the city. Well, that was the way it was. I would look again. At least I was lucky to be able to afford the luxury of buying in the city.

I contacted the broker who sold me the Tenth Street house and said I was interested in buying a brownstone duplex in the West Village. The first two weeks of June, I looked at everything available that fit my requirements, mostly co-ops. It was a tiring undertaking and quickly began to get me down. Nothing had that special feeling. I began to think that perhaps I wasn't emotionally ready to move. I realized I was comparing everything to the Tenth Street house; I wanted something that was as perfect for me, alone, as the Tenth Street house had been for the two of us.

I was losing my enthusiasm for moving when the broker threw an idea at me. It wasn't a co-op situation, but an 1880s brownstone with a coach house. It was nearly three times my budget, but it would be a rental investment with income potential. I had never wanted to be a landlord, but the more I heard about co-ops, the less I wanted to be involved with them. Some friends had been trying to sell their co-op top floor loft, and now Rolling Stone Keith Richards wanted to buy it. He'd agreed to add a rooftop sound room, in reaction to fears that he would play music and disturb the building. The anti-Keith movement was being led by a transvestite song-writer (who lived with a woman, which always made me wonder if that made her a lesbian) who felt Keith was "unde-sirable." (I love New York!) Anyway, descriptions of the board meetings and the manner in which things were de-layed made me apprehensive. Why not look at the brownstone?

The realtor sent a description. The main building had four apartments, which all sounded nice. But the coach house was the kicker! Situated in the courtyard, with entrance through the brownstone, it consisted of three rooms downstairs and a bedroom and bath above.

I dreamt about the building the night before I looked at it. In my dream, the brownstone was long and winding; I couldn't find my way through it. I was alone and lost and wanted so much to get to the coach house, which sounded so perfect for me—if only I could find it.

Not surprisingly, 52 West Ninth was situated on its block in nearly the same position as 56 West Tenth was on its block. As I walked across Sixth Avenue at Ninth Street, I remembered what made me like this area of the city so much. On the corner was Balducci's, one of the world's finest groceries, with beautiful fruit, pastries, and home-baked goods. Wonderful smells floated onto the street from their kitchen. The buildings along Ninth Street were quaint and well kept, mainly brownstones or row houses from the 1880s. I recalled walking around the area with Doug Kenney, admiring houses and talking about the future. We would all live in this neighborhood one day, all our friends; we'd be a community, we'd have *homes*. Of course our careers would be fabulous. New York was *the* place to be and someday it would be ours: we would own the city! Well, for a brief moment we had. But Doug was gone, John was gone. . . . I realized I didn't hate the Tenth Street house, I really loved it. That it didn't work out was sad, but maybe this would work. Maybe I would still complete the dream and live in this area that had attracted me so many years before.

The broker met me at the door and filled me in on the building, which was owned by Marie Morgan, who, as a young woman with two children, had lost her husband in World War II. On the advice of her cousin, Eleanor Roosevelt, she'd purchased the building with her inheritance. Mrs. Morgan didn't like to show the house unless the prospective buyer was serious and understood that her price was firm. Standing in the hallway, I felt that this building would soon pass from one widow to another.

Mrs. Morgan was a small, graceful woman with creamy white skin. Following her around the building, I was taken by the way she moved, as if she were walking on air. The coach house was smaller than I'd imagined, but it did have a light, homey quality, most unusual for New York City. And it was quiet. Set in the courtyard, the noises of the city were silenced. I loved it immediately; it was perfect.

We entered through a makeshift room, sort of a summer room that would need work, but had potential. A step up and we were in the kitchen, which by city standards was great, then another step down into the living room. One end had a very high ceiling, probably twenty-five feet, with two large skylights. The other end was about nine feet high, with a brick fireplace surrounded by bookshelves. The original tin ceiling was nicely set off by a white carpet. I followed Mrs. Morgan as she seemingly glided up the stairs, wondering if that would be me one day: an old woman living alone in the coach house. Would I wait to sell until I found another widow?

The bedroom was cottagelike and warm, the bath was small with big, old-fashioned fixtures. There was an opening, once a window through which hay was tossed, on the wall overlooking the high end of the living room. I noticed a photo of a young attractive Marie Morgan with her cousin, Eleanor. I was an admirer of Mrs. Roosevelt. I liked the idea that I might someday own the home she had suggested for her cousin, which she herself must have visited.

The next day I went over figures, trying to assess the financing of the Ninth Street property. The mortgage would be high, but rents would help with that. I phoned Mark. It was the first time since John's death that I'd been excited, happily excited, about something. I told him the price and described the building in detail, speculating on what a great investment it could be. I knew Mark was making notes; he was quiet, considering. "I think it could work," he slowly, deliberately stated. Of course, he wanted to see it, have a survey done. But my heart soared, I knew this was going to be good. I knew it would work out!

James was going on tour again and asked me to design a T-shirt for him. I was flattered, but admired his work too much to even be involved peripherally and not do a good job. Not feeling up to the task I hedged, looking for an excuse. I could hardly say I was too busy. Finally I just admitted I wasn't up to it. Both he and Kathryn refused to accept that, insisting I come over and discuss it.

James wanted three shirts. One would be a photo portrait; another, art work of a touring bus and map; the third was undecided. I had an artist in mind for the bus, and suggested I could create a montage of the states he was touring, so they would look like a country. James liked that. The portrait was black and white, which I suggested coloring. I saw that the job wasn't really difficult and agreed to do it. A few days later, James phoned to say he wanted me to come up with an idea for the third shirt.

As I worked at Phantom, pulling together the elements for the T-shirts, I tried but couldn't concentrate on an idea for the third design. When a week passed and still nothing had come to me, I felt low, unsure of myself. I couldn't think of some silly idea for a T-shirt with John on my mind all the time! I'd sit at my drawing board to work, then realize I'd been drifting in my memories for almost an hour. Sometimes I'd wander aimlessly. Once I found myself standing in front of Karen's desk, wondering what I was doing there. My gaze rested on a spot on the desk where John had drawn a heart with a wide magic marker. Inside, using a different pen, he'd written "JB and JJ." For the first time, I noticed that the initials had worn away; all that remained was the heart. It was just like my life.

Penny Marshall was in town and asked me to a screening of *E.T.* I knew nothing about the movie, but it seemed like a good idea to get out and do something different. Toward the end of the movie, when our hero appears to die on us, I found it very difficult not to burst out crying. That passed quickly, however, and, as several hundred million people know, E.T. lived. It was a nice movie and I was glad I went. And it gave me an idea. Someone there was wearing a T-shirt with "E.T." in bold letters, under which was written, THE EXTRA-TER-RESTRIAL. On the back it simply said, "Welcome him." The next day I worked up a rough design for James's T-shirt: "J.T., justa terrestrial," on the front, and on the back, "Welcome him."

When it came to showing James and Kathryn my work, I had no confidence in the new design idea. Maybe it was stupid. I'd need permission from Steven Spielberg, and maybe he wouldn't give it. Oh, well, it was all I had.

I first showed them the map, which really had a wonderful look. And the portrait was fine. Handing over the new design, I suggested that maybe it wasn't right, but they found it amusing and appealing and were quick to give it a definite yes. I was so relieved. I could still function under a deadline. I could still work!

Over the months a few people had contacted Pam to express an interest in writing an authorized biography of John—or threatening to do an unauthorized one—and now there was a rumor that Lavin was attempting to use her *Tribune* article as a proposal for a book. It was suggested that I write the John biography, but that didn't appeal to me. I had begun to write about my process, my experiences since John's death, and nothing seemed more important. Also, my agent said that if I sold my story as a book, my contract would prohibit collaborating on another "John" book, so an authorized biography was out for the time being. Still, I was feeling pressured to attempt to see that certain aspects of John's story be told. I began to wonder if maybe Woodward would be the answer. This was appealing on many levels. At least my suspicions about a police connection to the drugs that caused John's death would be substantiated or put to rest. But I was also thinking about the broader picture Bob wanted to explore.

Of late, I'd been trying to put John's life in perspective. What made people so enamored of him? Obviously, his humor drew people to him. And they seemed to appreciate that he was a real, gut level, American individual. But there was more to it; he seemed to represent something people wished they could be, the part of them that wants to revel in freedom of self-expression and an uninhibited lust for life. There was an aspect of danger to him, a disregard for playing it safe, but at the same time a sense of joy. Maybe it was the dream of the sixties, the innocence and explosiveness of youth that people saw in John. In the dry, uninspired seventies, I think he represented this "Woodstock generation" ideal. In him, the spirit lived on.

John was an artist, in that he performed his work as if it were an art; he employed a system of principles and methods, based on instinct and learning, with a high quality of conception and execution. He had a brightness and a vividness which, like Van Gogh's sunflowers, remained clear in your mind: a vibrant symbol of life bursting with energy. I have always felt I learned more about a society from its artists than from historians. If you want facts, go to the historians. If you want the essence, the spirit, of a people, look at their art.

In his work John reflected the energy of the time, the confusion as well as the caring. A close look at his life's work indicated as much concern for the world as it did a "fuck it, let's have a good time" attitude. He was very political, very socially influential. He was, indeed, a phenomenon.

And so it was not only sad, but scary that John destroyed himself—and in essence he did destroy himself. Not intentionally, not because he wanted to die, but because of bad judgment. And if he did reflect a generation—what did that say? What John represented was worthwhile. And the bad judgment needed examining.

I was especially concerned about John's young fans. Rather than beating the idea into kids' heads that people who do drugs are bad, or attempting to frighten them by impressing the fact that drugs are dangerous (which I believe becomes part of the appeal), a more constructive approach might be to focus on the *struggle* people have with drugs. Let them know how John thought he could control drugs, but how the drugs controlled him. Talk of his decision to stop, and his inability to follow through. Share the pain drugs create, the heartache of the battle.

Maybe Woodward's idea of a fuller portrait was good, maybe that was the way to deal with these issues. If I were going to talk to a reporter, it would have to be someone of his stature. In order to carry the weight the issues warranted, there should be no "underground" tones. I decided to meet with Woodward and feel him out.

Passing a newsstand on Sixth Avenue, I caught sight of a *National Enquirer* headline: "I KILLED JOHN BELUSHI." A photo of John was on the front page. I realized it was the interview with Cathy Smith I'd heard about. Still, I was shocked, and felt as if I were simultaneously speeding up and slowing down. I rushed away, my heartbeat inordinately slow and the pounding in my body especially loud. I realized I was heading nowhere, went back home, and burst out crying. How could they print a headline like that? How could freedom of the press mean that Cathy Smith could say anything, yet be responsible for nothing? I felt sick to my stomach. I wanted to know what was said, yet was afraid at the same time.

Not having the nerve to buy the article, I asked a friend to get one for me. It was the first time I'd seen a photo of Smith. She wasn't at all what I'd imagined. I don't know *what* I thought she'd look like, but this wasn't it. They had superimposed a photo of her over a particularly unflattering, distorted photo of John, so it seemed as if she were standing in front of a big poster of him. I found her frightening; she looked heavy, dark-haired, puffy-faced, and mean.

After reading the article I was sure I could sue the *Enquirer*. Once again, I was advised not to. I could demand corrections for inaccuracies, but why bother. Fortunately I don't recall much of the article. But I do remember the manner in which Cathy Smith was quoted, the unpleasant way she talked, and the ugly things that were said about John.

Before the *Enquirer* article, Cathy Smith's involvement in John's death was almost a side issue to me. I had been emotionally incapable of thinking about her in terms of responsibility; she was obviously a junkie and didn't know what she was doing. Now here she was, saying she provided the "coup de grace," the final injection that killed John. I was finally mad at her! Well, if she wanted to make money by admitting her role in John's death, then she could take the consequences. As far as I was concerned, I hoped she'd hung herself with this one.

The following Sunday, the *Los Angeles Herald Examiner* ran another story about John. It provided no new information, but the viewpoint was different. The author finally asked the obvious: Why did the police let Cathy Smith go? There was a subtle suggestion that it might be a perfect crime to murder someone who has a drug history. After all, who would think twice? Although the *Examiner* referred to the *Enquirer* as a sleazy publication, the article was based on Smith's *Enquirer* "confession" and quoted heavily from it.

The next morning Pam's secretary called to say the Los Angeles District Attorney would make a statement pertain-

ing to John's case that day. Later in the afternoon Pam
called. District Attorney Michael Montagna was reopening
John's case, and had said he would question DeNiro, Williams, and Cathy Smith. Pam's phones were jumping with
calls from reporters wanting a statement.

When I spoke with Pam again, she told me about an odd
call she'd received. A man with a mature voice phoned and
introduced himself as Marvin Markovitz, an L.A. businessman with interests in real estate. He said he owned a Hollywood restaurant where he had come across some information
he thought would be of interest to us. He said he never knew
John, but that he was a fan and had been "obsessed" with his
death because he could see something wasn't right. Then he
heard about a taped interview Smith gave to some underground reporter a few days after John died. Somehow he'd
tracked it down and heard a brief section. He said, "I'm no
lawyer, but . . ." he believed Smith had admitted to manslaughter. She'd apparently said that John hadn't known how
to shoot up, and admitted doing it for him. Markovitz said
he thought the tape could be bought, maybe he would buy it
for us, or maybe the interviewer would even give us a copy.
He'd find out and get back to us.

The whole conversation was odd. He would buy it for us, or
maybe he could get a free copy? I was interested—I had
heard rumors about such a tape—but I didn't want to be
sucked into a scam. Pam tried to check out Markovitz through
a business bureau and other sources, but found no information on anyone named Marvin Markovitz. Then she phoned
the number he had given her which was answered "Mr.
Markovitz" by an answering service that had no information.
There was nothing more to be done, except to wait and see
what Mr. Markovitz came up with next. I expected a suggestion that I buy the tapes.

Pam had another odd call, this one with the L.A. coroner's
office. She asked for some additional information and was
told John's records had been taken to the archives. Was this
routine procedure? she inquired, and was told that normally
records are kept available for two or three years. There was
no explanation for John's records being handled differently.
Yes, something was rotten in L.A., that was for sure.

I was planning to spend July on the Vineyard and wanted to make a trip to Nyack to see Mickey and Billy Murray and their baby before I left. The drive was soothing and it was good to see the Murrays in peaceful surroundings. Homer Banks Murray was beautiful, just old enough to respond with a smile or a chuckle. Billy already had a routine using him much as if he were a prop, holding the baby above his head in one hand and saying things like, "Look out, everybody, it's Homer, the biggest man in the world. Oh, no! He's taking up the entire roooom!" Homer laughed at the funny way his dad spoke, as did Mickey and I. The new parents were very happy.

Mickey told me of a dream she'd had about John. She said he looked good and was in great spirits. When she woke she felt as if John had really visited her. It sounded a lot like a dream I'd had of Doug after he died. I thought it was interesting that several people told me about nice dreams of John, dreams which were described as very real. Everybody said that John looked good, some even said radiant. And I had the feeling that people felt a need, almost a responsibility, to tell me these dreams, as if John had given them a message for me.

The three of us shared memories of John and laughed. It was good to reminisce with old friends, to forget the hell of John's death. Later, Mickey said that when Homer was born, they received many letters from people saying congratulations, and that many people included condolences for John. "They seemed to want to say it's good to see that life goes on," she said. For that moment, while I sat with Mickey as she held her baby, I believed they were right.

Chapter 9

ANOTHER POKE IN THE EYE
(WITH A SHARP STICK)

JULY

*A*ll that spring, I was often restless to go to the Vineyard —I had a nagging feeling of having left John out there alone. My calendar shows I made several trips each month, usually only staying a few days at a time. Now, I looked forward to spending the month. I was planning to set aside time to write a piece for *Titters 101*, but mainly I hoped to relax and have fun. To spend a summer month in the Chilmark house would be good for me. Laila was coming to visit for a couple of weeks. It would be great to see her again under less stressful circumstances. Also, Kathryn and James planned to be at their house in Chilmark, Mitch and Wendie took a monthly rental nearby, and Danny lent the Klenfners his house for the first week of July. Things were shaping up for a terrific Independence Day celebration.

The Chilmark house was a perfect place to be on the Fourth of July. The summer before, it had been a gorgeous day; the light sparkled, the air was fresh and warm, the water turbulent and cold. Tino and his wife Dana, and Sean Daniel, a friend and Universal Studios executive, were visiting from L.A. Larry Bilzerian and a few other Vineyard friends had joined us and we spent the day between the beach and the house, body surfing, sunning, playing croquet, and preparing the cookout. The night was clear and filled with stars, so we dragged out the telescope and searched the sky. Exhausted by the sun and salt air, we went to bed early.

Larry had been with us on two or three Vineyard Fourths. About an hour before sunset he and John would barbecue, the only form of cooking John really enjoyed. The two of them milked the process for all they could, talking up their "formula" sauce, cooking a couple of quick "dogs" to test the coals, and debating which had been their most successful barbecue to date. Later, the two of them would set off fireworks, shooting small rockets over the cliffs, while the rest of us watched from the deck.

Recalling these times was like floating down a cool, gentle stream, bathed in the warmth of sunlight. Now the legacy of the Fourth seemed important. It was important to have the barbecue, "to go on." It would be okay, I wasn't going to let it be sad.

Laila and I arrived on the Vineyard the evening of the second. It had been hot and muggy in New York, and the embrace of the fresh, cool air when we exited the airplane was a wondrous relief. We were tired and went to bed early.

The next morning I organized a writing area in an extra bedroom. After lunch, Laila napped and I settled down to write in my new "office." I had just begun to organize my thoughts when the phone ran.

It was my father. At first he made small talk, but it was strained and I realized something was wrong. Then his tone changed and his voice quivered. "Honey, I don't know how to tell you this, what with all you've been through . . ." Mom's dead! I thought, my heart racing.

"I don't know if you knew, but Rob and Liz went on a rafting trip this weekend . . ." He hesitated, unable to go on.

"What is it, Dad, what happened?"

"Well . . . Liz is dead," he blurted out and began to cry. He put down the phone. I was stunned. My mother picked up and with a perplexed, sad voice took over.

"Boy, can you believe this? I just don't know what's happening to us."

"How's Rob, Mom?" I asked. I was shaking.

"Apparently he's broken his foot. Another girl on the trip was killed, too."

My parents didn't know any more, but they had a number where Rob might be reached. I sat on the bed and took some deep breaths. What *was* happening? Jesus, it was unreal. I sat paralyzed for a few minutes. Finally, I went to the living room where Laila was sleeping on the couch. "Laila," I said a little too loud, pacing in front of her. "Come on, get up, Liz is dead." I couldn't stand still and the more I thought about it, the angrier I got. Laila opened her eyes, not sure she was awake.

"What?"

"Liz is dead," I repeated and told her what little I knew. She sat upright, digesting my words. Liz and Rob had stayed at her house in Colorado the previous winter when she was away. "I have to try to reach Rob," I said unclenching the little piece of paper with his number on it. I stood motionless at the phone for a moment. What would I say? Oh, shit, it didn't matter, I just had to reach Rob.

A woman answered. I asked for my brother and she was uncertain he was there. I waited anxiously while she checked. Suddenly Rob was on the phone, crying, talking. We only spoke briefly. "Please come soon," he sobbed. "I'm really gonna need help." When we hung up I felt as if I couldn't move, as if I'd be in danger. Then an explosion of grief overcame me like a wave capsizing a boat. Laila came over and hugged me and we cried into each other's arms. I wasn't sure if I was crying for Liz or Rob or John or me.

My parents, Pam, and I went to Aspen to be with Rob. He'd smashed several bones in his foot and was hospitalized for a few days. Liz's family wanted to bury her in California, where she grew up, so we had a memorial in Aspen before we left. Rob was released in a wheelchair to attend the service—in a pretty little chapel, the same one where Rob and Liz had planned to be married.

We flew to San Diego, a very sad cortege, and were joined by my sister Pat. Liz and Rob were to have brought the family together again, but not this way. My dad often said that life wasn't fair. I always hated the notion of seeing life that way. Now it seemed the only way to view it.

We stayed with my father-in-law, Adam, at the ranch in Julian. The day before the funeral, Pam had a message from her office that a man, who refused to leave a name, had phoned for her per Markovitz's suggestion. He had important information and would call again.

It took some doing before Pam was actually on the phone

with "Mr. X" (as we called him). He identified himself as Chris Van Ness, and claimed he'd taped an interview with Cathy Smith—sober—six days after John's death. He said that what Smith said definitely "took John off the hook" in terms of his involvement with heroin. He'd been trying to sell the tape, and it looked as if an anchorman from NBC was going to use a section. He read the transcript of the section, which went something like: "Van Ness: 'Did you shoot him up?' Cathy Smith: 'Yeah, I shot him up.' Van Ness: 'Was he a junkie?' Smith: 'No, no way was he a junkie.' " NBC wanted to know if I would be interested in making a comment?

A few calls later it was confirmed that NBC would air the tape the following day. It finally seemed like the time to make a public statement. Pam spoke to the anchorman, who was anxious to have my statement on the same broadcast. Obviously, I couldn't go to L.A. the next day, but NBC wanted the statement enough to helicopter a crew to a hotel near the funeral home. I would record my statement before the funeral.

During the hour's drive to Escondito, we finished writing the statement Pam and I had started the night before. Once in town, we had trouble locating the hotel, but a helicopter in the parking lot helped identify our destination. My mother and father, my brother, who was now on crutches, my two sisters, Billy Belushi, Adam, and I all hurried into the hotel. As we entered the room set up for the interview, I noticed we outnumbered the TV crew. I suddenly felt uncomfortable, realizing we were all dressed in black.

My statement was brief:

My family and I are confused and frustrated by the police inaction since John's death. Our attempts to ensure a thorough investigation have been fruitless. Instead of investigating competently and pressing charges for obvious criminal wrongdoings, the Los Angeles Police Department has responded with an unbelievably vile, vicious, and slanderous attack on the character of my late husband. I am as baffled as anyone as to why this should be happening. But from the information available to us, we can only conclude that the Los Angeles Police Department is either incompetent or is involved in some sort of a cover-up.

We taped my statement twice and were off at a run for the funeral home.

The week Liz died, Pam had a meeting planned in Los Angeles with the District Attorney, which was rescheduled for the week after the funeral. Now Van Ness wanted to meet as well. After the funeral, as we all discussed our travel plans, I decided I would like to meet this Van Ness. I was a little nervous about going to L.A., however, after having just accused the police department of incompetence or worse. Or maybe I was just uncomfortable about L.A. After all, it was the place where John had died. I decided not to let anyone except Tino and Dana know I was going to be there. We chose not to tell Van Ness, either.

We had a small suite at the Beverly Wilshire, where Pam and I spent most of the day on the phone. In the early afternoon we had a call from Alan Sonnenschein, the *Penthouse* writer doing the article on John. He told Pam he'd spoken with a Chateau maid, Isabelle Chavez, who reportedly said that at approximately eleven o'clock on March fifth, she saw a black and white police car in front of John's bungalow. An officer told her to forget ever seeing it.

We wanted to talk to Isabelle Chavez ourselves and Pam tracked her to a new job at a hotel in Westwood. When I phoned the hotel and asked to speak with an employee named Isabelle Chavez, however, the woman hung up on me. This happened twice.

That evening Pam and I met with Van Ness at our hotel room. He arrived promptly and seemed taken aback, perhaps uncomfortable, when he saw me sitting on the couch. He was a tall, heavy man with a black beard, dressed casually. I was uncomfortable, too, and didn't say much.

Van Ness gave us some background. He had worked for an underground newspaper, the *Los Angeles Free Press*, some years before. There wasn't much money in it, so he finally got another job. When John died, he saw news clips of Cathy Smith and realized she was someone he knew from around town. Thinking there was a story in Smith's side of what had happened, he approached her with the idea of doing an interview, perhaps for an eventual book.

Finally Van Ness talked about the tape. He reiterated that Smith made it clear that John was not an habitual user of heroin, and said she reproached herself for what had happened, saying it was all her fault. Pam asked if he knew anything of Charles Pearson or someone named April, names that kept surfacing in connection with John that last week. Van Ness told us that Charles was a part-time musician/part-time dealer, and that April Milstead was his girlfriend. Leslie Marks was another person from that circle. Van Ness also said there was "at least one other person" shooting up with John and Cathy. He quoted Smith as describing this person's reaction, saying something like, "I want it all over me." My stomach turned when he said this, the unusual phrasing sounding very Nelson-like. A part of me was sure it was Nelson, while another part thought Van Ness was just trying to bait me, to make his tape more intriguing.

As I listened to Van Ness I felt cold. I realized I was fixing him with an icy stare and tried to warm up, but it was hard. I felt he was playing games, telling me things without telling me specifics. This wasn't a game to me.

After about an hour it was clear I was not going to hear what I wanted. I had always known Cathy Smith had injected John. That he had a tape of her admitting it was good on one level, but I was hoping for more: an explanation of how John got involved with heroin or what Cathy Smith's connection to the police was. Or better yet, some insight into John's thoughts and feelings on the last night of his life. From the answers Van Ness gave to Pam's questions, I doubted that there was anything I wanted to pay for on this tape.

Pam asked what was going on with NBC; they had aired my statement but said nothing about, nor played anything from the tape. Van Ness said there had been a snag in the legal department. The NBC lawyer who listened to the tape felt that the sound quality was not good enough to be sure of what was said, or that it actually was Cathy Smith. He still thought he could sell the tape to a magazine or another paper, he said. It was clear he also hoped we might buy it.

I didn't really trust Van Ness. I wasn't sure I hadn't been set up to make a statement; maybe there never was any intention to air Smith's segment. I figured Van Ness would find a buyer for his tape, but it wouldn't be me.

The following day I flew from Los Angeles to Aspen. Rob wanted to take me to one of the country's finest marble deposits in Marble, Colorado, to help select the piece for John's gravestone. He'd made a drawing of his design when we were in California. It was a rectangular shape, which would be cut in half, lengthwise, in a twisting motion. It would stand upright, the two halves separated only by inches, the inside of the cut area remaining rough, the outside smooth. The design had nice proportions and a solid, yet graceful feel. Rob felt it represented the separation of life and death, or on a more personal level, the separation of John and me.

I felt worn out by the past week, as if the weight of my emotions were too much for my body. But I felt I should return to Aspen now because Rob was anxious to get to work on the stone, and I knew how important it was for him to have something he wanted to do at this time.

He looked no better than when I'd last seen him a few days before, which I guess was no surprise. He was glad I'd returned. The ride to Marble took a few hours, and we talked a great deal. At one point he said, "You know, when I came to New York for John's funeral I had a lot of mixed feelings. I was angry with John and I was sad that he was gone . . . and I was very sad for you. But I thought I had some idea of how you felt. Now I realize I had no idea. No idea at all."

Chapter 10

SEARCHING FOR CLUES

MID-JULY–AUGUST 4

I didn't return directly to the Vineyard, but stopped for a weekend in New York. Mostly I wanted to talk to my psychiatrist, but I also had an appointment to meet Bob Woodward.

A loud, crisp knock on the upstairs door at 60 Morton sent a chill down my spine. Woodward. I put on sunglasses. The better to see you . . . As we introduced ourselves, and I introduced Billy Belushi, who'd also just arrived in town, I was aware of a staleness in the apartment. It was dark and quiet, as if no one lived there. I suggested we go to a restaurant to talk.

Woodward was wearing a suit jacket and tie, not overly pressed, but neat. Smartly casual. He struck me as a type of guy I'd known in high school, not surprisingly, since we did go to the same school. He was someone who would have been on student council, the honor roll, and probably played varsity sports, although not necessarily well. His leadership standing in the class and dedication would have kept him on the team. He probably hadn't changed much.

I guessed Bob to be about forty-two. His dirty blond hair, cool blue eyes, and square jaw gave him an All-American look. His mid-western accent was somewhat homogenized, but recognizable. He had a habit of speaking in a soft voice, something I've noticed many lawyers do, so you have to listen carefully to hear what they're saying, and he was deliberate with his phrasing, signaling important thoughts with a subtle hesitation and then a slight emphasis on key words. I felt he was being delicate with me, respectful. He said he could see, from what Pam showed him, why I was interested in having someone investigate in Los Angeles; but he was also interested in using John to study fame and its effects on individuals and society. "I know what it is to have an early success," he said thoughtfully, looking out the window, tapping the palm of one hand with a fork. "I know how hard it is to follow up with anything after that, how people treat you. It's kinda like . . ." Bob paused, as if he questioned whether or not it would be appropriate to say what was on his mind. "I hate to say it, but it's kind of like . . . you're dead." He made a slight grimace as he completed his sentence, a look that seemed to say, "I hope my choice of words is not upsetting." It wasn't and he'd made his point—something I hadn't considered. Yes, he and John did have that in common. *All The President's Men* was Woodward's *Animal House*; silly as that might sound, what each success meant to each man would be similar. It's the thing everyone wants you to repeat, the thing you can never top, the thing you'll never be allowed to put behind you.

"I see this story as a series of articles," Woodward continued, "my part being not unlike that of the reporter in *Citizen Kane* . . . I would collect information from friends, business associates, acquaintances, and from those people's recollections, a portrait would evolve. And of course, foremost would be my obligation to offer to you an explanation of what went on in Los Angeles."

I liked the analogy to *Citizen Kane*, it gave me a feeling of what Bob would be doing. "I think that John was an important American artist," I began, and explained my theory about how he reflected our generation. I talked about drugs and how necessary I felt it was for us as a nation to begin to talk honestly about the situation.

Woodward made it clear that, as a reporter, he worked for no one. It would be *his* story. I would have no control, I would receive no money. I told him I was not interested in control or money. "What I want is to see this story told fairly and accurately," I said. "That's what I'd ask from you." Bob looked me straight in the eye—or rather, in the sunglasses—

and told me that this was something on which he prided himself.

Before we left I told Bob, "I feel quite strongly that there is some greater good that can come from John's story." I wasn't sure what that was, and wondered if Woodward could find it.

I liked Bob Woodward. I thought he was straight ahead, insightful, and intelligent. He seemed sincere in his fondness for John as a performer (mainly he knew him from "SNL"). I leaned toward trusting him with John's story, but wanted to think about it on the Vineyard. Things were always clearer there.

The night before we left New York, Billy and I had dinner with Rhonda. Afterward we went to her apartment and she played some of her songs. About a month before, Rhonda mentioned that she'd written a song for John, but she'd been hesitant to play it for me. I knew she would when she was ready—or thought I was ready. Now, suddenly, she offered to.

Billy and I sat back, the open door to the garden allowing a gentle breeze to enter. Rhonda sat erect at her piano and concentrated on her song a moment. "This is called 'West Heaven,'" she informed us, then tapped her foot a measure and began a long musical introduction. Her eyes were closed and the upper part of her body swayed rhythmically. Rhonda's voice was sweet, the music sad. The song began:

> Gone, gone, gone
> Gone like the wind
> But some good-byes never end
> I'll look for you when leaves are falling
> It's me, long distance calling.

The tempo increased slightly.

> Gone, gone, gone
> Gone like the day
> But the moon still shines, it lights the way
> I'll watch for you where stars are falling
> It's me, long distance calling

The verse took on a more "up" melody. My emotions were swept along with it.

> Calling West Heaven
> Where the outlaws never die
> They ride into the sunset
> No time to say good-bye
> But I know your spirit is somewhere running free
> And that's good enough for me

Tears rolled down my cheeks. Billy put his arm around me and I leaned into his embrace.

> Hearts can break
> Or turn to stone
> But hearts like yours head home
> To that home in West Heaven
> Where the outlaws never die
> They ride into the sunset
> See them turn and wave good-bye
> And I know their spirits are somewhere running free
> And one day my soul will see

Billy and I were both crying, gently rocking.

> Gone, gone, gone
> Gone like the tide,
> Rushing in on the other side.
> I'll write your name where waves are falling
> It's me, long distance calling

> Long distance call
> Long distance call
> Long distance call . . .

Rhonda repeated the refrain for some time, Billy and I letting our tears flow. When she finally stopped she remained motionless, her head bowed, her eyes still closed. Finally she turned her head and sheepishly looked at us. "That's beautiful, Rhonda," I said in a tiny, squeaky voice and we all burst out laughing, the laughter as intense as the crying. It's the sharing that makes you feel better, I thought. How would I work through this pain alone?

I returned to the Vineyard a weary traveler and took to my bed for a few days, sleeping and reading. Sometimes I'd just lie there, staring at the ceiling, thinking about John, Liz, my life. If Billy hadn't been with me, I probably would have spent several more days that way. He encouraged me to get out at least some of the day and walk along the shore. The walks were refreshing, although I was still exhausted and depressed in general.

At times, when I was alone, I'd roam the house, *feeling* the different rooms. It was *our* house! That made it different than anyplace else in the world. Not because we built it—which we didn't—or even changed it much. But we'd loved it. There was a sense of comfort, of peace I'd never felt anywhere else. Below, on the beach, the ocean churned and crashed on the shore, but from the house the distant roar was subdued, a lulling melody. The house was lined with windows, through which the outdoors became a part of the living space. Birds fluttered in the crabapple tree. Rabbits grazed on the lawn, unafraid. An occasional deer wandered out of the brush and into the yard. The house was beautifully designed to take best advantage of the property, which was, indeed, in an extraordinary location. The vista was filled with shades of green and blue, while the magnificent cliffs were streaked red and gray and brown. The gentle terrain of the yard was in marked contrast to the beach, where the fine, beige sand and occasional large boulder withstood the constant assault of the Atlantic. And the beach, the ocean, were magical. I realized that—ever so slowly—I was being rejuvenated at the Chilmark house. To move back to New York in a few days would be premature. Liz's death had changed everything, the events of the last few weeks had eaten up my summer. Now, more than ever, I needed the healing powers of the island.

Fortunately, I was able to rearrange my schedule to better fit my needs; I would remain on the Vineyard through mid-August. It would mark another first, as well. Billy was leav-

ing and I hadn't invited anyone to join me. It would be the
first time I'd stay alone at the Chilmark house.

Walks on the beach became an important part of my day.
The cliffs, from the top to the sand, form a dramatically
sloping fifty-foot obstacle. We'd developed our means of de-
scending the first summer we owned the house. Larry provided us with a good, thick piece of rope which he and John
tied to a sturdy little shrub and threw down over the edge.
Holding onto this, we worked our way slowly down the cliff,
rather like mountain climbers. It was fun; we enjoyed scur-
rying up and down several times a day. Now it was an effort
for me to make the climb at all, but I forced myself. Once I
was on the beach, the effort was rewarded.

A sizable width of sand separates the foot of the cliffs from
the ocean. The waves are biggest on this, the south side of
the island, perfect for body surfing. The water is clean and
cold. Those days, I'd hit the sand and begin walking to the
west. The air was always cooler and the sound of the waves
exhilarating. Still, my mind raced with troubled thoughts. I
wanted to leave them behind, but there they'd be, taking me
over. I'd walk faster and faster, as if I could get away from
them if I just walked fast enough. Then I'd feel that familiar
darkness closing in on me. Down I'd go, hugging my knees,
crying into the wind. Once cried out, I'd wipe my eyes and sit
back on the sand. The rhythm of the ocean would soothe me,
enthrall me, and for a while I'd feel nothing but its presence.
Soon I'd be up, wading into the ocean, then back to walking
along its edge. I'd become interested in a shell or some
treasure washed ashore. Inevitably, I would even forget the
pain that had just overtaken me.

The ocean was invigorating, once I released my anguish.
Just as the waves ebbed and flowed, so did my thoughts.
Only now they were inspired and curious. I thought about
nature a good deal and wondered if John had become part of
it. I often heard Rhonda's song in my head. I had been
thinking about making a video to express my feelings, and
after hearing "West Heaven" I knew it was the right song for
it. Before returning to the Vineyard, I'd talked to Rhonda
about my plan, and she'd agreed to produce her song for the
video. I felt as if she'd read my mind and provided me with a

music track on purpose. I wondered if gifts could come to us from . . . I don't know, from God, heaven, nature? On the beach I felt, more than I understood, that I was just a little part of a bigger energy. It was so obvious there, it made such sense.

I thought about more concrete matters as well. When I saw Penny Marshall in New York, she had posed a delicate question. "When ya gonna take off your wedding ring?" she asked. I hesitated. I'd thought about it, blocked it, didn't want to deal with the issue. No one had ever said anything; I had begun to think no one noticed. I answered honestly.

"I guess, when I don't feel like I'm married anymore."

"But you *know* you're not?" she stated more than asked.

"Yes, I know. But I still feel like I am."

Penny let it go at that, but she started me thinking about it. Visiting the cemetery one day, I understood that I couldn't be married to John's grave. I phoned my mother and asked her what a widow was supposed to do with her wedding ring. It was a hard question for her. "I don't really know, honey," she admitted. "Your grandmother always wore her ring, but she was older and had children, and hers was a different generation. I don't think she ever expected to marry again." I raised the idea of moving it to my right hand, which I'd been hesitant to do because I'd associated this with divorce. My mother didn't think it was appropriate for divorced women to continue wearing their wedding rings, but thought it was a good solution for me. I hung up, unsure that was the answer. Oh, well, I wouldn't do anything. Who cares? Then—just like a scared kid on a high dive who realizes he's also afraid to back down the ladder, and so without thinking any more suddenly jumps—I removed my wedding ring from my left hand and put it on my right.

The examination of "issues" was underway and I was easily consumed by endless dilemmas. At times the process was frustrating and my mind rebelled, the way your eyes do when they can no longer deal with an intricate puzzle. Thankfully I found solace at the beach, and gradually resolutions to some of the quandaries began to take shape.

Many of my mental efforts focused on trying to figure out how something "positive" could come from John's death. I knew that cocaine was a popular drug and believed that most users were as misinformed as John and I had been, especially in their belief that coke was not addictive. I had read numerous reports that stated, and John himself had often pointed out, that coke was not physically addicting. Now something he had said one day struck me. He'd refused some coke, saying he didn't do it any more, and the person who offered it responded, "Don't you miss it, man?" John replied, "There isn't a day I don't think about it." At the time, I was annoyed by the remark, as if he were embarrassed, afraid he wasn't cool if he said "no" to cocaine. It didn't occur to me that he was telling the truth. If, technically, cocaine wasn't physically addicting, then it must be psychologically addicting. And when it gets down to it, what's the difference? John's story could help get that message out, could help change the attitude that cocaine is not addictive.

I thought about the way John had been portrayed in the press, and about how the average coke user might react to that. Would they see the danger and be moved to stop? I imagined many would read about John as he was being portrayed and say, "I'm not *that* bad" when possibly, if the up and down pattern were presented, the user might see himself in John and realize, "I *do* have the same problem." I was becoming more and more convinced that the best way to reach users was to focus on the struggle; they would sense the honesty in that. But there was so much more to John than the fact that he did drugs. Maybe a fuller picture would make John easier to relate to and ultimately be more valuable.

Another subject I weighed was that of fame and its repercussions. We hear a lot about an individual's inability to deal with fame, but little about society's inability to deal with fame. I became aware of some of the difficulties while John was alive. People's own lack of self-worth was sometimes obvious in their dealings with famous people, in their desperateness, their need to somehow, in any way, be close to fame. I saw everything from people simply putting themselves down, "I'm just a nobody, but . . ." to women becoming hysterical, grabbing on to John, kissing him while he tried to push them away, to the hostility that such an inferior feeling could foster. Once, at a music club in Los Angeles, we were sitting at our table waiting for the show when I heard someone behind me say, "Excuse me, John." Suddenly John was wrestling with some man and as they rolled across the floor I thought I saw John's face bleeding. I jumped up and ran to where they continued to fight on the floor. John was holding the man down and, afraid he would hurt the guy, I yelled to let him up. He did and the man scampered off.

"What happened?" I asked. "Who was that?"

"I don't know." John was breathing heavily. "The guy tapped me on the shoulder, and when I turned, smashed a hamburger in my face."

What is it that makes someone so angry, so hurt, that he will physically attack someone he doesn't know just because that person is famous? This was not, of course, as extreme an offense as in the case of John Lennon, but it had an element of the same disease that warped Lennon's killer.

All these thoughts were ultimately part of the same basic question: what could be learned from examining John's life and death? Could Woodward write a study of fame and shed new light on this American obsession? Could he present, through the story of John's involvement with drugs, a lesson of value? Most importantly, could he reflect both the dark side *and* that sense of John which was inspiring, warm, and caring? Could he portray the talent, the hard work and dedication? And what of the issues that led me to Woodward in the first place? What was going on in L.A.? If it were true that there was some, however insignificant, tie between John's death and the L.A. police, then that was important to uncover. And if my worst fears were true, it was essential.

The idea of trusting this story to a reporter was a gamble. If I went with Woodward, I would succeed—or fail—big time. It was a tall order to expect anyone to fulfill all my hopes, especially in a series of articles. I was hoping for too much, the odds couldn't be good. But I felt it was my responsibility to try; I'd have to trust someone. So I looked for the bottom line. If the result of talking to Woodward—whatever that might be—could help save the life of just one person, then it would be worth it. I was leaning heavily toward taking the risk.

Jimmy Belushi was joining the Broadway cast of *Pirates,* so I went to New York for his opening night.

His entrance into the Broadway production was well attended by friends from Chicago, New York, and Los Angeles. He stole the show that night, singing better than he had in the Washington show, surrounded by a better cast. It was a terrific performance in general.

Afterward, we invited a small group to a party at Central Falls, a Soho restaurant. Jimmy looked happy as he accepted people's compliments, and he was touched that several of my friends had come to the show. It was good to see him have a great evening. Still, I couldn't help but feel sad at times. Broadway was a goal John had never reached. Maybe if he'd stopped doing movies, gone back and done some theater, maybe everything would be different. Jesus, how long would I go on finding things that would have made everything different? I had a funny thought: John being dead takes the fun out of everything. It didn't strike me as funny at the time. It was painfully true.

The next night I went with Kathryn to one of James's concerts on Long Island. Before the show, James told me the "JT" T-shirt had sold out at every show so far. It was even mentioned in his Boston review.

When James performed, Kathryn preferred to be backstage, but I wanted to sit in the audience. Long before I ever met James I was a fan of his music. I considered him a Renaissance man: a true artist, poet, musician, philosopher. He had a great time onstage and it showed; his face beamed and his energy was up. But I couldn't concentrate on the show. I remembered instead how much John loved to perform, how happy he was onstage. Especially with the Blues Brothers, he just glowed. During filming of *The Blues Brothers* John *was* Jake Blues—the down and out blues hipster—he wasn't John Belushi in a suit. But when he was Jake onstage, singing with the band, he felt so good he couldn't hold the image. Especially when he spoke to the audience. Then he was a hundred percent John, introducing people in the audience or suggesting to the fans to "buy as many blues records as you can find." Sometimes he giggled, he was so happy.

I thought I might get lost in James's music at the concert,

but instead every lyric sent me into another corner of my mind. "I need four walls around me, to hold me in, and keep me from slipping away," James crooned, and my thoughts turned to John, alone in Los Angeles, slipping away . . .

The next morning, I saw in the mirror a sadder, older face than I remembered. My brow was tense and I had to concentrate to relax it. Shit! I bet I get gray hair this year, I thought. *She used to look so young . . . before . . . the tragedy . . .*

A friend, photographer Lynn Goldsmith, accompanied me back to the Vineyard for a few days. I used her as a sounding board, verbalizing many of the things I'd been thinking about in terms of going with Woodward or not, especially about fame and drugs. "I never really thought of John so much as a drug taker, but as a risk taker," Lynn commented. Yes, he was that, I thought, a risk taker. I have to remember to tell that to Woodward. Like a flash I heard myself think, "remember to tell Woodward." I realized my decision was made. I would take the risk. I would talk to Woodward.

Chapter 11

TAKING A RISK

AUGUST 4–10

Footsteps on the deck of the Chilmark house signaled Woodward's arrival. Other than the fact that he was carrying a pad of paper, he looked more like a vacationer than a reporter. I, too, was more relaxed than when we'd first met. After a brief tour of the house, we sat at the dining room table and got down to business. He suggested I simply begin reminiscing, which I did, basically chronologically. Bob occasionally interrupted with questions and took notes continuously.

As I described our courtship in high school, I found it easy to talk about that period, since Bob had grown up in Wheaton, too, and knew the setting. I could say, "John and I first met at the Little League field," or "our first important encounter was at Herrick Lake." It was nice to think back to this time, late summer 1966. I saw a young, healthy John, shy and quiet that first night. A few days later, I went to Herrick Lake with my girlfriends to meet some guys. I was happy to see John with them; I kind of liked him and didn't think he had a girlfriend. We rented two boats. John and I were in the same one, and a water fight broke out. In his enthusiasm, John accidently hit my arm on a backswing with his oar. He immediately dropped the oar and began gently rubbing my arm, his face showing concern, almost anguish, that he might have hurt me. He apologized repeatedly. That night he phoned and asked how my arm was. I said it was fine and we talked briefly. The next night he called again with the same question, and I laughed. We talked for

some time. Calling and asking about my arm became a
running joke for about a week. Finally, John changed his
question and asked if I'd like to go to the Homecoming
Dance. I said I would.

John was co-captain of the football team and a Homecoming King candidate, which added an element of excitement to
the weekend. The king was announced at the dance and
John seemed embarrassed when he won. The crown was too
small and he felt silly posing for photos with the queen. His
main interest was football; he was a serious athlete with
ambitions to play professionally or coach.

Bob often responded with a smile or a laugh. It felt good to
share memories, and he seemed interested in my observations. He was curious about what it was like for John to grow
up in such a WASP community. I thought it was sometimes
difficult for him, kids being kids and making cruel jokes
about his family; he seldom had friends to his house. But I
couldn't recall John ever saying anything specific. His parents were proud of his awards and write-ups in the newspaper,
although they didn't really understand his interest in sports
or music. Still, they bought him a set of drums when he
wanted them, taking out a loan to do so.

I told Bob that John had entered my life at a time when I
was heading for trouble. Shortly before our meeting, I had
begun drinking secretly with friends. We would stockpile
liquor stolen from our parents, then drink on weekends.
Occasionally there would be a party at someone's house,
which meant their parents were out. Often it was some boy's
house, so sexual tensions and pressures were on, and, of
course, impaired judgments were made. Or else we'd drink in
the car, then drive around looking for friends, which resulted
in more than one fender bender. Not surprisingly, two of my
friends from this time later died in separate car crashes—
under the influence—before they were eighteen.

We didn't drink as often as I would have liked, mainly
because getting alcohol was difficult, but we also discovered
a cough syrup which made you high if you drank an entire
bottle. (This thrill wore off quickly as it was disgusting to
drink.) John disapproved of both habits and my participation
became a point of contention between us. A few times I didn't

go out with him, in order to go drinking instead. One such night John came looking for me and I hid under a bed so he wouldn't find me.

After we'd been dating about six months, we had an argument and broke up. I was glad at first. I wanted to go to a party I knew he wouldn't go to. But within a few hours I felt really sad; I would miss John, I would miss the closeness we shared, the special way we got on. He was so sweet and he really cared for me. And there was something else, something I couldn't quite put my finger on. A feeling in the pit of my stomach. To my surprise, I decided it must be love. I loved John!

As I reminisced, certain events seemed very clear, as if they'd just happened. When I talked about the breakup, for instance, although the telling was brief, I was totally in touch with how empty and unhappy I'd been at that time. I remembered sitting in a chair at the party that night, depressed, a mutual friend comforting me. "Don't worry, you guys are made for each other," he said. "You're always gonna be together." I thought, No, I've blown it. The next day I wrote John a note and said I loved him. I was thrilled when he responded; he felt the same way. We began spending all our free time together and soon after he asked me to go steady.

That year John took his first drama class. His teacher, Dan Payne, gave him a fuller sense of what it was to be an actor and encouraged him. It was Mr. Payne who arranged John's first professional audition, for Shawnee Summer Theater in Indiana, which led to a job as the youngest paid performer the theater had ever hired.

The separation that summer was difficult, but it strengthened our relationship. And John learned a lot at Shawnee; the hard work and rough schedule had been worth the effort. He also now knew he was committed to a future as an actor. "You should leave me now," he said shortly after returning, "because it's not going to be easy. I'll probably never make any money, so you'd have to support us." I told him I didn't care. "If I can't make a living as an actor by the time I'm thirty, I'll quit and get a job," he promised.

John was not only introduced to the rigors and techniques

of professional acting in summer stock, but to an entire way of life. He was comfortable with the family atmosphere, the camaraderie of the actors. He liked the late-night schedule and the impassioned discussions that seemed to bloom in the night, the emphasis on the importance of details. In the debating of current issues he heard different viewpoints and reached new conclusions. He was introduced to authors and playwrights, and recited Shakespeare with a friend. It was during one such get-together that John first tried marijuana. His dislike for alcohol continued, and his transformation into a hippie was underway.

In the fall, he went to Whitewater State in Wisconsin. At college he grew his hair long and became involved in the antiwar movement. He had no interest in joining a fraternity, which I thought he should, and we often argued over issues. I basically repeated things I'd heard from my parents, and couldn't understand what I viewed as unpatriotic criticism on John's part. I was especially angry when he stood up for student rioting, or, even worse, talked about the possibility of being a conscientious objector.

Bob asked when I'd discovered that John was smoking marijuana. Although John told me he had tried "pot" at summer stock, I didn't find out he'd continued using it until the following Christmas. He had taken to burning incense in his car before picking me up, which I thought was odd, but knowing nothing about drugs, I never guessed it was to cover the smell of grass. I found out by accident, basically. I heard John talking secretively to a friend, and only understood him say, "Did you get it?" The only "illicit" item I could think of was a condom, and I was embarrassed that he would ask a friend. Why, it was admitting we *did it!* (Which, frankly, we had only *done* a few times at this point.) I was angry on the drive home, quiet, looking out the window. Finally John asked what was wrong and I said I'd overheard he and his friend. I was shocked when he responded, "I just got a little pot." I was so surprised that I just continued to stare out the window while he said he didn't smoke much and promised he wasn't doing any other drugs. He said a lot of kids on campus smoked pot and compared it to alcohol, insisting it was less harmful. He was adamant that there was nothing to worry about, but I wasn't very happy about it.

When did I first try grass? At the end of my junior year, after many arguments with John, I agreed to try it sometime to see what it was like. One night at a drive-in, he pulled out a joint and lit it, reminding me of a pusher in a movie I'd seen at school. An old image flashed before me of my father, during a dinner conversation, pounding his fist on the table and saying, "I don't know how anyone can be so stupid as to try marijuana, when everyone knows it leads right to heroin." The pot was harsh and I coughed as I tried to hold it in. We shared a joint, but it didn't seem to have an effect, not like drinking did. In fact, I didn't feel anything. Suddenly I found the movie totally incomprehensible. We decided to get a soda and were astounded at how bright the snack bar was. Waiting at our table for someone to take our order, we wondered why the waitresses ignored us. They just stood behind the counter, talking. Then we realized you had to go to the counter to place an order, and we burst out laughing. A school friend came in and I was certain she knew we were stoned. Back in the safety of the car, we laughed, feeling we'd escaped some danger. When we kissed, I felt very warm and light headed.

The next day there were no ill effects, no overwhelming desire to run out and get more pot, nor an urge to try heroin. We had fun, actually. I felt as if I'd been let in on a wonderful secret; pot was okay. But I told John I didn't want to do it again, at least not until after graduation; if anyone knew I had smoked marijuana, my reputation would be ruined! Drinking was one thing—it was frowned upon, but ultimately acceptable. Drugs were taboo. I didn't know of anyone, other than John, who didn't think so and I was still very much influenced by that. But it no longer worried me that John smoked pot.

About this point I diverted from my history to describe a scene from a movie I'd seen in grade school: a small group of teenage boys smoke a joint; their eyes get glassy and their expressions turn wild. They go out and spontaneously steal a case of Coca-Cola and run into an alleyway, laughing. One of them grabs a bottle and breaks off the top by smashing it against a brick wall. Still laughing, he drinks from the bottle, cutting his mouth; blood gushes down his chin. The black and white image of his face, the blood, the maniacal laughter, was very frightening.

I told Bob this story because I felt it was this kind of *Reefer Madness* misteaching that backfired on our generation. We were frightened instead of given real information about drugs. So, when we first came in contact with marijuana, it was clear that what we'd been told wasn't true. With a little more experimentation, we assumed that none of our drug information was right. "Not long ago, I thought my father's statement about grass leading to heroin was ridiculous," I said. "But that is the progression my husband made; only it didn't happen overnight, it took years." I clarified that I wasn't saying that everyone who smoked grass would eventually go on to heroin. But the possibility of one experiment leading to another was real. I strongly believed the drug situation warranted—demanded—open, honest communication. That, I emphasized, was one of the goals I hoped we might reach through Bob's articles.

Bob encouraged me to ramble, saying it was all helpful, it put things in perspective. I tried to be direct when answering questions and to keep my opinions to a minimum, not wanting him to think I was trying to shape his story.

In the fall of 1968, my senior year at high school, John transferred to the College of DuPage, a junior college in the Wheaton area. The move was largely due to a lack of money, but our desire to be together was reason for choosing C.O.D. Now that he was living at home again, his father began to pressure him to become a partner in his restaurant, even offering to sign it over to him, but John refused. He wanted to be an actor, would be no good at anything else until he at least gave it a try. Always moving toward his goal, he started the West Compass Players. His commitment to his dream was very strong.

The following fall, I went to the downstate campus of the University of Illinois. The night before I left, John and I hugged in my parents' driveway, holding on to each other, not wanting to say good-bye. I started to cry and John held my face and wiped my tears. With a gentle laugh, like a man who laughs at the innocence of a child afraid of the dark, he comforted me with words of love. "I'll come see you almost every weekend," he assured me, "and I'll phone whenever I can. We both have things we have to do right now, so work hard and do well. That's what I'm going to do." He pulled my chin up and looked into my eyes. "Come on, now, say you love me and it will be all right. Come on, you can do it," he teased. We hugged for a long time. "We have to think it will be okay for it to be okay," he said with determination. "We'll be okay, honey. I promise."

I couldn't describe that moment to Bob or I would have cried. Instead, I described how John worked at keeping us together: writing, phoning, coming to visit on weekends. My roommate was a friend from high school, and John would usually stay with her boyfriend.

At college I began to explore life. We began an active sexual relationship, as my concern about "what people will think" became secondary to my own thoughts and feelings. There were lots of new ideas in the air and our split in political viewpoints was mended with my own radicalization. A campus film series offered a wide selection of movies, many by avant-garde filmmakers, which we often attended. Movies like *The Battle of Algiers* and *Z* were very powerful and provided insights and a different perspective on politics. The Vietnam War and our own government's role in it was under heated debate and we often went to rallies or to lectures on the subject. We didn't drink liquor, so we never went to bars or drinking parties. We occasionally went to a concert, although our budget seldom allowed it. It didn't much matter what we did, we were happy to be together.

Bob was interested in our level of drug use. First semester I was very disciplined, smoking mostly on weekends. Sometimes, smoking grass and listening to records *was* our activity. Grass was still pretty underground; we didn't think anyone else on our dorm floor smoked, so we stuffed towels under the door, covered the cracks with tape and opened the windows. Then we'd turn off the lights—except for a red one that flashed on and off—and turn up the stereo. One weekend we played only the Rolling Stones. Next weekend, the Beatles.

I was trying to touch on any experience with drugs I

remembered, so Bob wouldn't think I was hiding anything. John was experimenting with hallucinogens, but I was afraid of them, passing up many opportunities to try some. I first tripped on LSD on New Year's Eve in Wheaton, my sopho- more year. I was nervous, afraid I'd taken too much, but John kept me close and assured me I was fine. When it began to wear off I relaxed and decided I liked it, wishing I'd taken more. It expanded my perception, not only making things look different, but making me feel different about what was important in life. I understood the Beatles song, "All You Need Is Love," in a new light. Still, I retained a healthy fear of hallucinogens, never taking any again until after I moved to Chicago.

Speed (amphetamine) was popular at that time, and John used it for a period, but I didn't really know much about it. The only other drug I ever tried in college was cocaine. A friend gave me some, but it wasn't any good, I didn't feel any effects. I never even saw cocaine again until we moved to New York, which was when John first tried it. By the time I left college, I smoked grass almost daily.

Ironically, the first person I ever knew to actually try heroin was a relative of Bob Woodward's. I didn't bring it up, but I knew his family member's problems with hallucinogens (he only briefly dabbled in heroin) had led to years of frustra- tion and concern to his relations. I suspected that was the crux of Bob's interest in this whole subject.

There was another memory I didn't discuss: my pregnancy and subsequent abortion during my freshman year.

I'd been meaning to go to the University Medical Clinic for birth control pills, but had hesitated out of fear. I was afraid they might call my parents. Now my period was late and I was waiting the results of a pregnancy test.

The doctor entered her office, reviewing my file. She sat at her desk, faced me, and said simply, "Your test results are positive." I sat quietly, trying to read her face before I asked, "Well, what does that mean?"

I phoned John with the news and he came down the follow- ing weekend. He was wonderfully supportive, concerned that we make the right decision. "Whatever you think is best, whatever you decide, honey, I'll be there," he promised. He thought we were still too young to have a baby, since he wasn't capable of providing much of an income; maybe it would be smarter to give it up or have an abortion. "But I'll marry you tomorrow if you want to have the baby." I agreed we were not ready to be parents, and the idea of having a baby and then giving it away didn't even seem real. An abortion also seemed unreal—and it was certainly illegal—so I wasn't sure what to do. A few weekends later we talked about it some more. John said he knew I was having trouble making up my mind, and admitted he thought an abortion was our best solution. It was what I thought, too, but I hadn't been able to say it.

Finding a doctor was harder than we expected. We knew a friend who'd had an abortion, but her doctor had disappeared. We found out that abortions were legal in Puerto Rico, which would cost something like four hundred dollars in air fare (for one) and two hundred for the surgery. We saved all the money we could and borrowed as much, and it was clear we couldn't afford a ticket for us both. I was terrified by the idea of going alone, and probably wouldn't have, when at the last minute John stumbled upon someone who gave him the name and number of a woman who arranged abortions. Arrangements were made for the week of my nineteenth birthday.

We both went to an address in Hyde Park and met Sharon, our contact, who was very nice and offered to put us up for the night. I was nervous as we waited for another contact to phone Sharon's apartment. Finally a man called and gave me instructions on where and when to meet him. John and I grabbed a cab to a restaurant near the airport. It wasn't exactly comforting that the restaurant was named The Bum Steer.

John was outwardly more nervous than I, both of us searching the faces of all who entered to see if they were "the one." We had arrived a little late and began to worry that we might have missed the contact. Finally, after about an hour, a woman rushed in, came directly to me, and asked if I were Judy.

"Yeah."

"Good, come with me. He'll have to wait here," she said,

indicating "him" with a glance. John's eyes widened; I never saw him look more frightened. He started to protest.

"I'll be okay," I said. I was too naïve to be frightened. I just wanted to get this over with.

"You'll bring her back here?" he told the woman more than asked. She nodded and he handed over a wad of bills about three inches high. It was five hundred dollars, much of it in the five and ten-dollar bills loaned by friends. John kissed me, promising he'd stay right there.

The abortion took place in a nearby hotel. When I came back to The Bum Steer, John was jubilant. He kept kissing my hand, my cheek, and holding me, not wanting to let go. That night, at Sharon's, he nearly floated across the room as he ran to get things for me. Later, in bed, he gently put his arm around me. "I love you, honey," he whispered in my ear.

I wondered if I should tell Bob about the abortion, about John's support. But neither my parents nor John's knew anything about it, and I felt it would be especially upsetting at this time.

The following day Bob and I spent several hours together. I spoke fondly of Second City and what an important learning experience it had been for us both. In January 1972, after John had been there about a year, I moved in with him and transferred to the Chicago campus of the University of Illinois. While I took art classes at school, I also learned a lot from my contact with Second City: how to put a show together, scene structure, timing, and many things which would later help me as a writer. I also learned what it was like to live with an actor.

John's days were somewhat routine. He slept late, going to a local restaurant about noon to meet up with co-workers— Joe Flaherty, Harold Ramis, and Tino, usually grabbing Brian Doyle-Murray along the way. They often sat there for hours, drinking coffee, reading the paper, and talking. It was here that their work day began. Keeping up with the news was a must, since after the show they did an improvisational set in which the audience suggested topics for scenes, and a broad knowledge of events was essential. Then they were off to rehearsal, to work on scenes for the next show or possibly to put together a benefit. I was home from school in time for dinner, and if John were home, he was glued to the TV news. It took me a while to get used to the fact that his job didn't end at a specific time. He was good about phoning to keep me informed as to what time he *thought* he'd be home, but at first it was difficult not to feel secondary to the work.

John didn't finish work until about midnight, so I'd try to have my homework finished in time to go to the improvs at eleven; then, after the show, we'd get something to eat and go with Brian or Harold or Tino to one of our apartments, where we'd watch movies and hang out. Everything we did had the potential of becoming a scene. A bad "B" movie was a favorite for John's cast to parody. At commercials, John would jump up and phone Joe Flaherty to make sure he was watching the same thing, laughing about what they might do. Once I was surprised to hear something worked into a scene that I'd said to John in an argument the night before. And I was pleased when John would try my suggestion for a line or a new way to say something.

The drug scene at Second City didn't strike me as unusual, mainly we smoked grass; at night after the show, it was that, not drinking, that we enjoyed. I made it clear to Bob that not everyone in the cast partook, and didn't get into who else did. John and I took psychedelics for a while, on Mondays, his day off. At the time, because the work schedule was so full and there was only one day off—not enough time to get away—tripping was an appealing break. We didn't do it every Monday, but several. John once tripped on a work day, but his timing was off during the show and he was terrible on stage. Also, Joe embarrassed him during a scene, which helped him realize he wasn't any good, and he never did it again. In fact, soon after that we stopped altogether.

In the fall of 1972, John negotiated with National Lampoon for a role in *Lemmings,* a job that would call for a move to New York City. Listening to John talk about it, I was unsure what it meant in terms of *us.* Would I go? He never asked if I'd like to go. Finally I broached the subject. John was emphatic that of course he wanted me to go with him; he thought I knew his life would call for career moves and that he wouldn't go without me. Now the idea of the move was frightening. We didn't know anyone, what would I do? It was too late to enroll in school. John had an answer; he'd just read an article about corporate businesses providing jobs for wives when an employee relocated. John insisted that *National Lampoon* magazine hire me for their art department! I wasn't sure about the job or living in New York, but I knew I loved John and wanted to be with him. Plans were made to move.

John left a few days ahead of me. The first night he phoned to say things were going well; he was learning his bass guitar parts and playing drums on a couple of songs. "And guess what? I tried cocaine, it was great!" Someone had given him cocaine at the first rehearsal. We had been interested in trying coke, it sounded like a cool drug: euphoric, nonaddictive. I never saw it around *Lemmings* much, nor remember having any there, although I might have. Cocaine was too expensive for us, although John may have used more than I knew. He went through a relatively short, but bad period of abusing quaaludes. Thinking back, it was probably a combination of downers and coke. But basically, our new drug in New York was liquor.

New York was less friendly than Chicago. The cast didn't get on the same. People never invited you home; going to a bar for a few drinks after the show was more popular. So we began drinking. We met a lot of people that way, including some who became friends, like Doug Kenney (who was peripherally involved with the show) and Penny Marshall. But it took over a year to feel comfortable in New York.

The show itself was good. It was hip, irreverent, funny, sometimes even poignant. John got rave reviews, and the show was the toast of Off-Broadway. Chevy Chase and Chris Guest were also strong, and they all made a good team, especially Chevy and John. They looked funny together and were both good at physical comedy. Off stage Chevy put John down a lot, probably due to his own insecurities, but I don't think he realized how sensitive John was or how often he hurt his feelings. Still, they admired each other's work and had a lot of fun onstage.

About the time John finished *Lemmings*, at the end of 1973, I switched from working at the magazine to the "National Lampoon Radio Hour." John convinced Brian Doyle-Murray to move to New York from California, so Brian took up residence on the floor of our Bleecker Street apartment. John was happy to have a buddy again. They would both sleep late, then spend hours at breakfast, poring over the paper, drinking coffee, and smoking cigarettes; it was suspiciously similar to life in Chicago. They both hated to audition. I don't recall either of them ever actually going to one; no, they preferred to spend their afternoons at the living room table, writing and planning new projects for themselves. It was fun to come home from work and have them perform their material for me.

Meanwhile, I pushed Michael O'Donoghue, who was creative director of the "Radio Hour," to hire John and Brian as actors. Michael refused to use John as a matter of principle. He had a serious feud going with Tony Hendra, the director of *Lemmings,* and was certain he wouldn't like anyone Tony had "discovered." In fact, it had taken him a long time to warm up to me because of my connection to the show. Anyway, the fear of never working again had taken over John and Brian, and they decided to enroll in an audition class. It was a sweet time, helping them rehearse for class, sending them off to school in the morning, and hearing about it later.

Finally my not-too-aggressive-but-consistent approach to getting John and Brian work at the "Radio Hour" worked. We were scheduled to record a scene which called for a Peter O'Toole voice, and our actor cancelled at the last minute. "John does Peter O'Toole," I said matter-of-factly. Shooting me a doubtful look, Michael said to give him a call. The funny thing was, John didn't really do a very good impression of Peter O'Toole. He did a terrific version of one line from *Lawrence of Arabia*—"I want two large glasses of lemonade"—so I assumed he could do O'Toole. He wowed them with his one line, but had difficulty with the scene. With work, however, we got what we wanted. And there was a bonus: John impressed both Michael and the producer, Bob Tischler, and soon Brian and John were working at the "Radio Hour" as both writers and actors.

Within a few months, after O'Donoghue and *Lampoon* parted ways, John was hired as the new creative director. I worked

closely with Bob Tischler, organizing and helping at recording sessions, and enjoyed learning and growing in my job,
eventually becoming associate producer. It was a full schedule for the core group to produce a weekly half-hour radio
show—getting it written, cast, recorded, edited, embellished,
and out. The end result was brought vividly to life by the
wizardry of Tischler's sound work. In fact, poor Bob was
seldom seen out of the studio for a solid year.

We worked with a variety of interesting and talented people. Chris Guest, Rhonda, Chevy Chase, and Anne Beatts all
worked fairly regularly. Doug Kenney loved the show and
often wrote for us, including a two-parter entitled, "High
School: Confidential," which highlighted Doug's particular
brilliance for finding humor in the American school system
and teen insecurities. Many aspiring actors like Billy Crystal and Steve Collins and, occasionally, established ones like
Peter Cook and Dudley Moore passed through our doors.

I thought John's work on the "Radio Hour" was as impressive as any he had done, so I played Bob Woodward a show
entitled, "Welcome Back: The Death Penalty." I chose it
because it was entirely written by John and Brian, and
because of its decidedly anti-death-penalty position. The show
had several scenes, some just little snippets:

(SFX: Gavel pounding. Background crowd quiets.)
    BAILIFF: Will the defendant please rise.
    JUDGE: Mr. Capone, I have decided to show leniency in
your case; therefore, I shall not sentence you to death.
However, I hereby sentence you to a dose of syphilis.

And:

(Crowd applauding.)
    MAN: Miss North Carolina, what are some of your
favorite things?
    SWEET, SOFT, AND SOUTHERN MISS N.C.: I like cookin',
makin' ma own clothes, and the death penalty. (Cheering.)

I had forgotten that there'd been a Nixon scene on the
show. It seemed an odd twist of fate that I was playing it for

Bob Woodward. The Nixon imitation was excellent. John was the Aide.

(SFX: Crowd of reporters. "Mr. President . . ." etc. Clicking of cameras.)

NIXON: Oh, no pictures, boys, not today. Ziegler!

ZIEGLER: Yes, Mr. President?

NIXON: Ziegler, when I tell you to get those reporters out of here, I mean get them out! Now move, you idiot!

(THUD! Silence)

AIDE: He's dead, you killed Zeigler when you pushed him, Mr. President.

NIXON: I didn't push him, Mitchell pushed him. Of course, that's it, Mitchell pushed Ron and he hit his head on the corner of that marble table. Don't blame me for everything that goes on around here.

AIDE: But, Mr. President, Mitchell isn't here. You were the only one close to Mr. Ziegler. We all saw you push him.

NIXON: Push Ron? Me? Why, it was just a friendly shove. I push all my advisors, just like Hank Aaron pushed that ball right over the fence to break Ruth's record. How about that hit? Wasn't it terrific?

AIDE: But, Mr. President, you just signed a bill reinstating the death penalty. You said, "If anyone takes a human life, he should be willing to pay for it with his own life."

NIXON: Sit on this and take a spin, Mister. I didn't say that. Don't tell me what I said. I know what I said, I know what I meant, and I know what I did. Besides, I'm not sure the death penalty works. If it did, Ron would be alive today. Just like that Larry Csonka making deals for 1.4 million dollars to play football in Canada. He made out all right, didn't he? I'm the President of the United States and I don't make that much. Why should he make all that money? I want money, too!

AIDE: Mr. President . . .

NIXON: A million dollars isn't too much to ask for, is it? If Magnavox can give Hank Aaron a million dollars for a

lousy baseball bat, then Howard Hughes should give me
a million!

AIDE: All right, take him away.

(SFX: Clinking of locking handcuffs.)

NIXON: He only gave me a hundred thousand stinking
dollars and everyone's upset about it.

(SFX: Clicking of cameras. Reporters: "Mr. President . . ."
etc. continues under . . .)

NIXON: He won't miss it. If he wants to give it to me,
who cares? It's his money, all I want is a million dollars,
that's all! . . . Perch on this, pal, and take a ride.

Bob seemed to enjoy the show and I was glad I'd played it,
because it brought back the feeling of the time. And it was a
wonderful time in our lives—1974—the year before "SNL."
We had an outlet for our work, the creative freedom to do
pretty much what we wanted, friends we liked working with,
and decent money. It was especially nice that John and I
worked together. Within a few months, Lampoon asked him
to direct a new live show, and so John lured Joe Flaherty,
Harold Ramis, and Gilda Radner to New York with job
promises. (Danny was asked, but was otherwise committed.)
The three of them, along with Brian and John, became the
"Radio Hour" stable of actors for several months before they
opened *The National Lampoon Show.*

It was great to have a group of friends nearby. Joe and
Judith sublet an apartment down the street, and Gilda moved
into the neighborhood. Brian got his own place a few blocks
away and his brother Billy (Murray) soon came to stay.
When we had free time, we often went out as a group—we
even briefly got into bowling.

I hadn't known Gilda before this, except through her work
at the Toronto Second City, but she and I became instant
friends, sharing a similar sense of humor and fashion. John
and Gilda hit it off, too, especially onstage, where they mas-
terfully combined their talents. They could make anything
work. In one particular scene from *The National Lampoon
Show,* Gilda played the blind "Rhoda Tyler Moore." Her
theme song set up the mood: "Who's always the last one in
the room/The one who poked her eyes out with a broom/Who's

the girl who likes everyone she meets/'Specially if they help her cross the street." Gilda would skip onto the stage, cane in hand, banging into everything, never losing her smile or exuberance. John was her unmerciful boyfriend, who constantly played jokes on her, like pretending to be her dog and humping her leg. The balance between Gilda's peppy, youthful innocence and John's ability to be adorable one minute and sadistically funny the next, was extraordinary.

Although it had been a long day, I felt energized when Bob and I concluded. I'd been invited to a party on the beach, and decided to go down early to watch the sunset.

The beach was deserted except for a couple taking a walk along the shore. I found a comfortable spot and for a while just stared out to sea, remembering how much John had loved it here. How he loved the ocean, could spend hours at a time in the water. I was the opposite. One of his missions in life was to make sure I never got away from any bathing situation without going in the water. Sooner or later he would force me in, and with time he actually changed my attitude: the Atlantic no longer seemed too cold, and I enjoyed floating around, holding on to John, who stood solidly in the turbulent waves. Usually when we first arrived at the Chilmark house, I took my time going down to the beach, afraid John would drag me in. The previous summer, after a few days, he'd come up to me in the kitchen, kissing my neck from behind and resting his head on my shoulder. "It's okay for you to come down to the beach with us," he promised ever so sweetly. "I'll give you a week to get used to the water before I throw you in."

Now the ocean seemed unfriendly again. Without my anchor, I was hopelessly tossed about, not a very strong swimmer. In Bali, John had actually rescued me from the waves.

It was funny to think of him as a swimmer, but he'd been quite good. As a kid he'd joined the Wheaton public pool's swim team, because it was an opportunity to meet girls and, better yet, see them in swimsuits. He had an infectious, boyish excitement when he was around water, and was especially good with children, watching their achievements, encouraging them, teaching them new things. In a pool, he could be a terror, regressing to high-school antics, such as performing one cannonball too many. Or he could amuse you with stunts, like his famous "butt" dive: standing motionless at the end of the board, with the complete concentration of a professional diver, Belushi gracefully bounces into the air, stretching, defying gravity as he rises. The legs are thrown out in front, he forms a perfect right angle, and drops to his butt—landing seated—on the edge of the board. The board responds, now he's in flight again, into a head-first dive. Truly unbelievable!

I focused again on the beach. The sun was setting on the far side of the island, the sky streaked brilliant red, orange, and gold. I walked till I came to a spot where the cliffs leveled out and the sunset was in full view, then sat again to face the colors of the fading day.

How to express who John was to Woodward? How could anyone describe the rare powers he seemed to have? The instant connection he was able to make with people, the devotion he gave and received? He seemed to have it all, and yet . . . What was it that sometimes made him unhappy? I don't think he knew. I stood up. I wouldn't think about this now. I don't want to feel sad, I thought. I want to enjoy this, it's so beautiful. This was a moment to appreciate life, not dissect it. I turned to see a magnificent, orange, full moon rising from the edge of the water. It was huge and sent a wide stream of sparkling light toward me across the ocean. The sky was simply spectacular. I sat down again in that privileged spot, and tried to take in the expanse of quickly changing sky. When the sun finally dropped below the horizon and the moon was well established, I recognized a familiar feeling: somehow John's energy was there. It was not a strong sense, perhaps only a wish, but he was with me, one way or another.

The next day Bob had some questions, and we worked on an overall chronology. He was impressed with my memory for dates, and I myself was somewhat surprised at my recall, but attributed it to the fact that I'd been thinking about the past so much. We picked up where we'd left off the day before.

"SNL" was difficult to explain; it was the best of times, the worst . . . It was fun, fast, exciting! A show every week for (usually) three weeks of the month, a new host every week, a new guest band. Some of the biggest stars of the day appeared on the show and the list of those watching in the studio was equally impressive. The live element of the show meant unbelievably long hours, and there was always the fear that it wouldn't come together.

I thought back to the early days. At first, The Not Ready For Prime Time Players were one of several elements of the show; the host was considered the draw, then the guest band; there was a weekly film by Albert Brooks; the Muppets were making an attempt to find an adult audience on this, their foray into nighttime television; there were commercial parodies (which sometimes used cast members, but as often employed extra actors); and there was a slot for a comedian (early participants were Billy Crystal and Andy Kaufman) to do several minutes of stand-up. With all these competing elements, the air time alloted to scenes was probably only about half an hour. And some of the writers often wrote themselves into scenes. In fact, Chevy Chase was originally hired as a writer, not a cast member.

From the beginning, scenes often developed around issues the cast or writers were struggling with, and the second show made fun of the fact that there wasn't enough time for scenes. The cast, all dressed in bee costumes, began a sketch, then were "interrupted" and told they were short of time, but promised they could do the scene the following week. After the first few shows, John, in fact, had still had very little air time, and much of it was as a bee. He felt the show was suffering from a lack of good scenes and made his feeling known. He didn't like the Muppets, he didn't think the short films were working, he didn't see a need for stand-up—that was like a variety show, they were supposed to be different. In a relatively few shows they had already repeated the bees instead of developing new characters. He argued for The Not Ready For Prime Time Players to be a larger focus of the show. The result was that some of his complaints were written into a scene, which John addressed to hosts Rob Reiner and Penny Marshall, dressed as a bee. The truth was, he looked so funny in the bee suit—he had a way of making the antennae move around his head in circles while he talked, and his stout legs looked cute coming out of the round bee body—that he only made the bees more popular. In the scene John complained that all the Not Ready For Prime Time Players needed was a break, and in fact Penny and Rob did give John one that show. Having seen him in *Lemmings,* they insisted that John do his imitation of Joe Cocker singing. He finally had a performance he felt proud of.

Meanwhile, Chevy had almost instantly gained fame from the show, largely because he was featured as himself, as the anchorman for a weekly segment, the "SNL" news. His introductory line was clever and catchy: "Good evening. I'm Chevy Chase and you're not." Chevy was also being featured in roles for which John felt he would be better. John attributed this to the fact that Chevy had worked before with producer Lorne Michaels, and was able to pitch his ideas over dinner or while hanging out with Lorne after the show.

I mentioned to Bob that I had read comments about John being jealous of Chevy's early fame; they implied that John was being childish or somehow lessening himself. I didn't think it was an unhealthy rivalry; after all, in the entertainment business, fame is a measure of success. John thought that Chevy was good, but he believed *he* was a better performer and wanted a chance to prove himself. As a result, he began writing his own scenes and by the second year wrote a fair amount. This created another point of contention since John felt he should be credited as a writer. Although he would occasionally sit down and write out a solo piece, most of his writing was improvisational, that is, he would suggest something to a writer, improvise it, then, remembering the good beats, work on it with the writer. He didn't like to actually write out the result; perhaps this was laziness, but I think he was frustrated by that side of the process. Regardless, his point was that if he, or another actor, said lines that he invented in a scene that was his idea, he should be credited as a writer. John was finally given writing status, but only under pressure to be involved with the final piece, and after a year, he dropped this position although he still contributed to his scenes as much as ever.

I wasn't interested in getting into all the different friendships and rivalries at "SNL," but I did want to touch on one issue I thought drew unfair conclusions: John's infamous problems with the women on the show.

From the reading I'd done, I knew that John was being portrayed as not working well with women, an idea that I found upsetting because it simply was untrue. "SNL" was only one story, there he did have trouble with Anne Beatts and Rosie Schuster, and for a while refused to do their scenes. And he never got along with Jane Curtin. But at Second City, John was often the "guy" to do the "women's scenes," and during all the various Lampoon projects, John had few problems with women co-workers. *Continental Divide* was as much Blair Brown's movie as John's, and they got along wonderfully. In fact, John got along well with women in general. Interestingly, during the summer of 1981 he'd watched a few reruns of "SNL" and commented that he'd been wrong about Jane, that she was really very good on the show.

How was our life together affected by all these changes? I left Lampoon shortly after "SNL" began, since free-lance work allowed me to better arrange my time around John's irregular schedule. I told Bob about *Titters* and the problems it had caused. During the second season of the show, when John began doing movies on the West Coast, our lives became even more hectic. The work week at "SNL" was mostly late afternoon to early morning, in keeping with the late hour of the show. The week was fast paced and gained in momentum, culminating at showtime. While filming a movie, John was expected to put in eight to twelve hours, usually beginning early in the morning. There was a lot of waiting, and it was often boring. It struck me that one of the difficulties for a film actor is having to wait, wait, wait, and then, suddenly, pull up your energy and put yourself in character at that unpredictable moment when the director is finally ready for you. Flying back and forth between two jobs was exhausting, but having to deal with two agendas was equally disconcerting. For a time, it seemed that cocaine helped make that schedule work. Ultimately, of course, it made it impossible.

As John's fame grew, the city became wide open to him. For a time that was fun, but by the beginning of the third season—after *Animal House*—it became difficult for him to go anywhere without drawing attention and being approached. So we started the Blues Bar. Soon we were having a party every Saturday night after the show, which quickly became the hippest place to be. On occasion, it was the greatest party on earth! But it got too crazy—too many people and too many drugs. Cocaine was available and plentiful, which ultimately led to disharmony in our personal life; misunderstandings, arguments, and one brief separation. Somehow we were able to pull ourselves back together during the show's off-season, when I would once again see the John I liked best.

Without trying to make excuses for the drug abuse, I did think that John's problem was compounded by his fame. Sometimes it seemed as if everyone we met had cocaine. During periods when he was trying not to use it, he had to be especially careful where he went and with whom. On the other hand, if he wanted to use it, there was always someone who had some or could get more. The time he was hospitalized with his knee injury was a good example. On morphine and Demerol, he was pretty out of it, still he very much wanted to do the show and was angry that the doctors were taking so long to decide whether they should operate or not. He was also in pain a lot of the time and complained that he needed more painkillers. Then one night I realized that a visitor, a movie producer, was bringing cocaine. I took the man into the hall and told him not to bring any more. "Can't you see that it works against his medication? It might even be dangerous," I said angrily.

I tried to trace, for Bob, the up and down progression of John's drug use over the next few years. It seemed there were three phases to our drugging. For a while, when we were trying a new drug or using only occasionally, it was fun. Then it would become routine, sometimes fun but sometimes unpleasant. There'd be misunderstandings, arguments over money spent on drugs or concern about taking too much. Finally, I would back off, as John eventually would, but often not until after he'd crossed the line and was out of control into outrageous, sometimes dangerous, behavior. Bob asked for some examples and I told him of the four or so times I felt John had become most desperate.

In the spring of 1979, John quit "SNL." After much deliberation, we decided he had to choose between movies and the show; the pressure of both was too much. At that time we also had some very important discussions about drugs, the result of which was that I quit using cocaine in May and John was using very seldom. In June, we spent a wonderful month on the Vineyard, and it was then we decided to buy a summer house. The following month, we flew to Chicago to begin work on *The Blues Brothers*. The six months of filming were difficult. I saw some good steps on John's part, but mostly he was moving backward. He was repeating the drug cycle every other month; he would not use for a brief time, then fast spin to stages two and three. Things improved when the production moved to L.A., and within a few months of the film's wrap, I finally believed he was on his way to being drug free. Our marriage grew stronger; we were healthy, happy, and life was good. A binge after six months did not disturb me, since it was only one night. Another, several months later, seemed no worse. Hearing myself describe John's binges, it was difficult to believe I didn't know how serious the problem was at the time. But the idea of "backing off" drugs seemed possible; it took years of repeated patterns for me to see the truth of John's addiction. In fact, although I recognized the problem, I never thought of it as an addiction until after his death.

Bob and I concluded our "history" with the last year and a half of John's life, that period when I thought our problems with drugs were behind us. The Blues Brothers last tour had been exciting and fun, and the shooting of *Continental Divide* went very well. I spoke fondly of our trips to Europe and Asia, each bringing us a great sense of being on our own, unhindered by the pressures of our lives at home. I described some of the problems John had with director John Avilson on his last film *Neighbors* and his binge during that film. I expressed John's love of the Vineyard and talked about the peace he seemed to feel when there. And I tried to make some sense out of his progression back to drugs and the binging that went on during his last months.

Bob and I talked about the press and the manner in which John's death had been handled. I pulled out the *Chicago*

Tribune piece as an example, pointing out errors, especially the *Goin' South* incident. He skimmed the article and agreed with my conclusions about it, but made light of its importance. His reaction made it seem less important to me, too.

Before Woodward left, he said he planned to go to Los Angeles soon, and that he figured it would take anywhere from six weeks to four months to complete the story. He thought he was getting a good feeling of John and hoped he would soon have some answers for me about L.A. "Oh, by the way," he said, "I've done enough of this sort of thing to know what will happen now. You've heard of the game 'telephone?' Well, that's undoubtedly what you're going to experience. I'll talk to someone who'll tell someone else about it, and by the time it gets to you it may not resemble our conversation at all. So any time you have questions, please phone me. *Any time.*" The wind blew his hair over his forehead, giving him a boyish look when he smiled, a marked contrast to the serious man I'd been talking with the last few days. I felt Bob Woodward was an honorable man and I trusted him.

Playwright Tim Mayer, an old friend of Kathryn, and a Harvard buddy of Doug Kenney, whom I'd known since Lampoon days, came by one night. He was roaring drunk and wanted to talk about Woodward. "You can't trust him, Jacklin. You can't trust reporters."

"But I'm not trying to hide anything," I said, "I'm being totally honest with him. You know who John was. Do you feel that, if he captures that, if he gives a fair balance of the positives along with the negatives, do you think that would be anything we wouldn't want to see?"

"No, but he'll never do that! That's not what's interesting to people."

"I believe it is. I think there's been enough bullshit, and what people want to see is something that resembles the man they think they knew."

"Woodward will never understand who John was."

"Well, that may be, but I've made my choice. I have to trust someone."

Glassy-eyed, Tim attempted to focus on my face. "John loved you so much," he said. "He really did. I know, I spent a lot of nights out with him after you'd gone home. He wasn't like the rest of us, trying to pick up some woman. Don't you see, the reason it's so difficult for people to understand what you're talking about is because *most* people don't have good relationships! *Most* people can't relate to what you had." Tim was emphatic, gesturing wildly and pounding the table. He had a rich, deep voice and, when in good form, was perhaps the most wonderful orator I've ever heard. But he was drunk now, and getting emotional. I cherished what he was saying, but felt the anger he was expressing was probably misdirected. I certainly didn't think there was any validity to his fears.

The following week I began contacting the people Woodward wanted to interview, explaining his approach and asking if they would cooperate. I told each person that I looked to these articles to provide a full portrait of John, and stressed that I'd been totally open when we talked about drugs, believing it was important to do so in order to understand John. I added that I believed Woodward would be able to solve some of the unanswered questions surrounding John's death.

Danny sounded good and was positive about the idea. "I'm sorry that you've had to spend so much time talking publicly about John since he died," I offered.

"Oh, that's okay," Danny said softly. "I like talking about him."

Sean Daniel and John Landis, director of *Animal House* and *The Blues Brothers,* were less enthusiastic. Because of the terrible helicopter accident on Landis's last film, in which actor Vic Morrow and two children had died, he was then under a vicious attack by the press, who blamed him. "Ya know!" Landis's voice was energetic, as it usually is. I had an image of him as a cartoon character with an "!" at the end of every sentence. "I'm not sure this is a good idea!" His voice became softer, deeper. "You know how I feel about the press."

Although both Sean and John were anxious to help, they were uncertain that Woodward could be successful. Finally Landis said to me, "I don't care, I'll do what you want."

"I can't guarantee that this is going to work out the way I hope," I said. "It's a gamble."

"Do you want me to do it?" Landis asked.

My instincts told me not to encourage anyone who was hesitant, and I hadn't with anyone else. But I knew Landis had a unique understanding of John as an actor, and felt there would be a big gap in Woodward's insights if they didn't talk. "Yes, I wish you would."

"All right, then," John replied. "I'll talk to him."

I spoke to Tino, Mitch, and Bernie, all of whom were positive, although Mitch did whine a little, much preferring to be on the asking end of an interview. I explained the situation to my secretary Karen, and told her to do anything that would help Woodward. I talked to about twenty-five people in two days.

Michael Klenfner said he'd take Woodward to the *schvitz* that John had frequented in New York. I had to laugh at the idea. One thing about Woodward, he's definitely purebred WASP. The *schvitz*—which I myself only went to twice but heard countless tales about—is about as ethnic and funky as you can get. It's located on the Lower East Side, on a block where you'd expect to see the "Bowery Boys" hanging out— the "Bowery Boys" at the *end* of their careers. From the hallway it seems to be a deserted building, with only the warning BEWARE OF DOG. If you have the nerve to try the next door, a gruff old Jewish guy shuffles out, takes your money, and gives you a robe, a towel, and some slippers. The slippers are designed so that everyone who wears them has to shuffle. Near the entrance is a counter where exceptionally good Kosher food is served. Off to the side are two rows of lockers and cots.

Downstairs is where you "*schvitz*." There is a steamroom, a sauna, a cold dip, and a table where the ritual "rub" with oak-leaves-soaked-in-hot-hot-hot-water takes place. After my first trip, I dragged myself upstairs and fell asleep, only to awaken feeling that I had somehow gotten myself into a state mental institution. Until I had something to eat. Then I thought I was in heaven, or wherever it is that good Jews go. Yes, Bob would get close to the heart of John at the *schvitz*.

I thought a lot about my conversations with Bob; was there anything I'd left out that I should tell him? What more might he ask of me? I knew that eventually we would go over the events of the night John died, and I'd have to tell him about Nelson Lyon. I knew Nelson would prefer to be left out of it, so I was in a quandary. Rhonda didn't think it was fair of Nelson to put me in this position, and said, "I don't think he should expect you to lie for him." I thought about what John would do; he wouldn't want to see anyone involved in this mess if it could be avoided. I felt like Joey, the Marlon Brando character in *On the Waterfront,* after he's realized that what his friends have done is wrong. If he rats on them, it will put an end to their power and justice will be served—but his life will fall apart. Joey spends a lot of time debating what to do. At one point, Brando does one of his classic, pained, "I'm thinking" looks and says, "I don't know about this conscience stuff." That line kept popping into my head. But like Joey I knew I had to sacrifice my feelings, and maybe some friendships, to follow my conscience.

Chapter 12

SQUARE PEG

AUGUST 15–AUGUST 21

I was on my way to Kennedy Airport for a plane to L.A. Anne Beatts had commissioned Tino and me to write an episode of her TV show "Square Pegs," and, although I didn't really want to write for TV, I figured it was wise to take on more work. Anne was going out of her way to make everything easy, letting me stay at her house, offering the use of her car. It would be good to see her and Deanne, and we'd work on *Titters 101*. I was also looking forward to spending time with Tino and Dana. With them, I would find a familiar feeling I longed for.

As I stared out the limousine window at the streets of New York, the beautiful day gave way to images in my mind. How many times had John and I made this trip, how routine had it become to us? I remembered returning from the filming of *Continental Divide*. We had so many pieces of luggage that I took Polaroids of everything to help Smokey collect it. A funny contrast to my first arrival in New York, when John had met me at the train to help lug the two suitcases and several bags full of our possessions. My mind continued to wander, until an abrupt stop brought the expressway slowly into focus again. It was disturbing to realize I was nearly at the airport with no sense of time passing. I decided to write in my diary. No sooner had I begun an entry than I found myself overcome and crying: I had flashed on being in Jimmy's dressing room a few days before, when he showed me an interview in *Newsday* entitled, "Another Belushi Carries On." It made me sad and I tried not to show it, but Jimmy knew and hugged me and I cried briefly. "Does it make you sad?" he asked, patting my head. "It makes me sad, too."

The sun through the window warmed my arm and it felt good. I made a note in my diary, "Sitting in an air-conditioned limousine, sun on my arms, listening to good music, on my way to California, *shouldn't* be so depressing. I *hate my life.*"

On the plane my mood continued. I was nervous about how I would react in L.A., seeing people I hadn't seen since the funeral, visiting places John and I had frequented. Another limo met me at the airport in L.A. I was staying with Penny Marshall my first evening, before settling down to work at Anne's. I gave instructions to the driver, then sat back, lost in thought most of the ride. When we were off the freeway and in a familiar area, I rolled down the window. The heat rippled off the sidewalk, creating an illusion of distorted feet on the people walking by. The air was thick and smelled of gas. I looked up at a street sign. Sepulveda. My heart ached as I remembered John teasing me about my inability to say it correctly. "What's the name of this street?" he baited me. "Sep . . . Seplavada . . ." I attempted and he laughed. It was a playful joke. "C'mon honey, you can say it," he said squeezing my cheeks in mock pretense of helping to form the word properly. I played along, making monosyllabic utterances, and we both laughed at the silliness.

A shudder ran through me. This was where John's spirit had left his body! It hadn't been a conscious thought before, but now the idea pulsated through me. A fantasy flashed of John's spirit coming to me. Maybe his spirit was still here, maybe that was the real reason I had come.

At Penny's that night we talked until early morning; mostly I listened to Penny complain about her sitcom. I found it difficult to be sympathetic. She encountered the same problems with the show every year, the same you go through in any production. I wanted to say, "Don't you see you're wasting precious time? If you hate this so much, stop doing it. Why do you let these things make you crazy year after year?"

Later, in my bedroom, I felt very isolated. A little voice in my head was going over what I should have said to Penny and I suddenly realized the advice was for me. I was the one in a rut—going over and over my situation without resolving anything. But my insight fell short: I recognized the problem but didn't know what to do about it.

The next day I moved to Anne's. She was renting a large, Spanish-style house just up the hill from Sunset Boulevard. Anne was out and I wanted to go by Tino's, but the only route I knew was to drive down Sunset, a path that led me past the Chateau Marmont Hotel. I had mixed feelings about this. Just thinking about seeing the Chateau made me tense. But I couldn't avoid it forever and didn't really wish to; a part of me wanted very much to confront the place where John had died.

Driving toward the Chateau from the west, I knew I would first see a familiar restaurant, the Imperial Gardens, and then, just past that, the hotel. As I approached I moved on "automatic pilot," apprehension grasping me as if I were about to see some horrific sight. Passing the Imperial Gardens my stomach dropped, then the Chateau loomed above me. Unconsciously I took my foot off the gas and forgot to breathe as I slowly glided past. It looked larger than I'd remembered, and spookier; it towered over the boulevard like a haunted castle and seemed to lean toward me, slowly following my movement with its window eyes, daring to be more alive than I was at that moment. I was going terribly slow and somebody honked. My heart pounding, my body stiff, I drove on.

Tino and I worked together at Anne's every day while she went to her office. I liked being with Tino. I guess it was his energy. I just felt good with him, or in this case, better. He was sensitive to my lack of consistent productivity and kept plugging along. Writing tired me out and I'd need to have a midday break, sometimes a nap. One afternoon I dreamt about John, a nice dream, just the two of us hanging out together, and as I began to awake I thought for a moment that John's death was a part of my dream. I wrote in my diary: "I still can't believe it. John seemed so alive in my thoughts. His manner of pulling up his pants from the belt loops, the way he tucked in his shirt, walked, smiled, fixed his hair while looking in the mirror; it was all so clear, he must have been here."

One morning when Tino arrived to work he told me he'd canceled his upcoming appointment with Woodward. He just didn't want to talk about John with a reporter. I was disappointed, but didn't say anything. I could understand Tino's position. Still, I hoped he'd change his mind.

I didn't get out much while I was in L.A., but basically stuck with Tino and Dana or Anne and Deanne. Getting out in L.A. meant running into people John had worked with or knew, people who asked how I was doing, and cared, but didn't really want to hear that I was miserable. People looked at me in an uncomfortable way. I was a reminder of the inevitable, that we all must die someday, a fact the very nature of Hollywood works to obscure.

One day I went to see Danny at Universal where he was shooting *Dr. Detroit*. He tried to be welcoming, but was distracted, not because of me, but because of work. Still it was disappointing that he was so busy. I felt strangely at home and out of place at the same time. Before I left, we agreed to have dinner one night.

We finally got together at the Imperial Garden because it was close to the Chateau, where Danny was staying. When we spoke on the phone, he said, somewhat as a warning, "I'm at the Chateau, you know. I know it sounds weird, but it's a good location for me. I can't run from these things, Judy. I have a bungalow right across from Johnny's." His voice warmed a little. "I'm quite comfortable here, really."

Dressing for dinner, I was nervous about the night. I was joining Danny at a business dinner with Sean Daniel. I would have preferred a more casual meeting, but it was Danny's only "free" time. He was likely to invite us to his bungalow after dinner, and if he did it meant coming awfully close to the very spot where John died. Maybe I'd even have a chance to check out bungalow 3. Maybe I'd walk right up to it, ring the bell, tell them who I was, and ask them to let me in. Or maybe the Chateau wasn't renting it out yet, maybe no one wanted to rent a room where someone died. No, they probably got more money for it now . . .

I recalled Kathryn's experience when she went to the cliff where Doug died. As she and two friends stood overlooking the edge, a beautiful rainbow had appeared. She was certain it was a greeting from Doug, they all felt that, I guess. Well, I didn't expect to find a rainbow in John's bungalow, but then, one never knows.

Dinner was another experience of isolation. Sean and Danny talked about Danny's next projects, movies he'd been writing to do with John—*Spies Like Us* and *Ghostbusters*. It was upsetting to hear these projects mentioned so casually, continuing so easily, without John.

Afterward, Danny did suggest that we go to his bungalow. I was somewhat numb as we walked up the hill to the Chateau. He took us past the main entrance to a locked gate that led to a group of bungalows I'd never noticed before. Unlocking the gate, Danny told me that the number on John's had been changed from 3 to 63. So much for the idea that the hotel was taking advantage of John's death. As we walked up to Danny's bungalow, I glanced over at the old Number 3. The door was open and a man was sprawled on the floor in front of the couch. My stomach dropped and I looked away. I looked back and saw that my mind was not playing tricks, that there was, indeed, a man lying on the floor, sleeping.

Danny told us to make ourselves comfortable while he made a few phone calls. I wandered the bungalow, checking it out. It appeared to be identical to the one across the way, but was not at all what I'd expected. For one thing, it didn't strike me as worth three thousand dollars a week. I'd imagined the rooms to be larger, the bungalows farther apart. The set-up didn't afford much privacy. And I thought I'd been told there was a garage, and this certainly didn't have one. Funny how you can create such a strong image of something in your mind that when you see the real thing it just doesn't seem right.

I wandered back into the living room and saw that the man from bungalow 3 had joined us. Danny introduced him, and his name, coincidentally, was Johnny. I wanted to ask if I could look at his bungalow, but couldn't muster up the nerve. He left and I focused totally on my desire to go there; my heart raced and I debated different ways to go about it. Finally, when Danny got another call, I simply walked up to the open door, knocked, and asked if I could come in. Danny had introduced me as Judy, so I didn't assume he knew who I was or why I was there. "I'm sorry to bother you," I began, not sure what I would say, "I just wanted to see this bungalow . . . my husband died here."

Johnny stood erect, more serious now, and politely invited me in. "Let me show you the place," he offered, and we made a quick tour. When we got to the bedroom, I stood a moment looking at the bed where Bill had found John. "Let's smoke a joint," Johnny suggested, and lit one up. My entire body pounded, I was "stoned" already, but accepted the joint. We sat and smoked in silence. My mind ran in circles and yet I had no thoughts of substance. "This place has a real good vibe," he said. I nodded. I didn't feel John there, but I agreed, there was a nice feeling and I was glad of that.

I returned directly to Anne's, and finding her on the phone, grabbed my diary and began to write. As soon as she hung up, I took a deep breath and told her, "I went to bungalow 3 tonight."

She seemed somewhat surprised. "Well, how do you feel?"

"Okay, I guess. Kinda speedy."

Anne looked concerned. "How was it?"

"It was odd, because the bungalow wasn't at all as I'd imagined." I described the location of the bungalows.

"Wait a minute," Anne interjected. "I know those, that's not where John was." She had been staying at the Chateau when John died.

As I told her more of the evening, we began to laugh. I returned so intense about this bold move—*I'd gone to the place where John died!*—and now I discovered I wasn't at the right place. It was a little as if some kind of supernatural practical joke had been played on me. And it must have taken some setting up—clearly Danny and the others believed bungalow 63 had once been the infamous 3. All the emotion and tension of the experience came out in laughter. It was pretty funny really, not a bad joke at all.

Chapter 13

RIDING DESTINY

LATE AUGUST–EARLY SEPTEMBER

I was on a plane to Montana, heading to a remote cabin on a lake. It wasn't exactly a vacation; my parents, Pam, and I had arranged to be with my brother on what would have been his wedding day. Rob was driving up in his van so he and I could take a trip through some areas of the Northwest he wanted to show me. I worried about his making such a long drive alone, concerned that his concentration must be off.

I grabbed a magazine to divert my thoughts. Mindlessly flipping the pages, I came upon a photo of Robin Williams. My stomach turned and my shoulders tensed. I tried to read the accompanying article, but couldn't focus on the words; they were blurred, unreadable. I turned my gaze to the photo. Why did his life go on? Why not him instead of John? I was jealous of him for being alive and envious of his wife for having him. I knew my thoughts were irrational, why was I reacting this way? Feeling I might cry, I closed the magazine, shut my eyes, and tried to think of something else. Nelson popped into my mind, then Woodward. Not that, I thought. Then I saw John on the bed at the Chateau, dying . . . being carried from the hotel . . . in his coffin . . . I felt panicked for a moment by my inability to stop these awful images. I took a deep breath and slowly exhaled. What would I like to remember? I saw John lying on his back on the beach, his head propped on a towel. He wore sunglasses and a cap pulled down to shade his eyes. He was very brown and, although he had a scruffy beard, looked good. I entered the memory and John looked at me and smiled. Yes, this was much better. I could sense the day; the ocean was calm and the air was cooled by a gentle breeze. I knew the smoothness of John's skin, the solidity of his body, and longed to touch him, to feel that sweet softness, that closeness you only feel with someone you love. I lay down next to him and rested my head on his shoulder, put my arm around his belly. I enjoyed the contact, even if it was just an illusion, even though it was ever so brief.

Our two cabins were nestled on the shore of Lake Placid. It was a quiet setting among tall trees, cool on a hot day. The cabins, originally built for loggers, were rustic and cozy. Rob arrived late the day after I did. That evening, as we barbecued together, we had our first moment to talk alone. He said he was having a difficult time, he'd been bothered by the feeling that Liz was trapped somewhere. I could appreciate how disturbing that would be. I think Rob was grateful I didn't try to negate the idea or say it was silly, that I took his concern to heart. He gave me a big hug. "It's good to see ya, kid."

It didn't take long for the outside world to invade my retreat. I talked to Jimmy who had just read an early copy of the *Penthouse* article. He said it wasn't bad, at least it wasn't a slam, but it was sad. They didn't really capture John, but portrayed him as a victim. Pam spoke with the author, Alan Sonnenschein, and he asked if either Danny or I would do an interview. My first reaction was to say no, but I said I'd think about it.

Later I had a message from Bernie that Woodward was doing a book for Simon and Schuster, not a series of articles. My stomach dropped, but I decided not to assume anything until I spoke to Bob. When I finally reached him, he calmly assured me he had no plans to do a book at this time. Shortly after we hung up, the words "at this time" jumped out at me. What if he later turned the articles into a book? Would it get in the way of an authorized biography? No, Bob's approach was different, it wasn't really a biography. And if, when all was said and done, he thought it was book material, I felt confident it would be an important book.

We also learned that the Los Angeles Police Department was planning to release a statement about their investigation into John's death. Most sources believed they would drop the case. I felt that I should have a statement ready, in case they did, but I had no idea what to say.

August 26, 6:45 P.M.

Feeling depressed today, can't shake it. It's hard being with my family when I feel this way—yet I want to be here. Can't think of anywhere I'd rather be right now.

August 27, Noon

I woke this morning feeling rested. . . . Before my imagination could go to work, I grabbed my book and continued reading [*Hotel New Hampshire*]. Funny what things work their way with my emotions. In an innocent enough passage, the father says, "I love you" and his wife says, "I know, I love you, too," and this exchange brings on the old pain in the chest, tears begin to flow. How many times did we say that? Hundreds at least. Not often enough. . . . As I try to think about what I'm saying—how do I feel?—I realize I'm not breathing. And there goes my brow again.

Talked to Woodward yesterday. . . . Said there were many strange things in connection with John's death, but [before going over everything] he wanted to get his notes typed up. Said he has found out, by talking with friends, as well as people who worked with or knew J. briefly, that J. was a wonderful man, and that this was a story that must be told. I said that was how I felt.

He brought up the whole "book" problem and said that he hoped I believed that he was just working toward a series of articles for the *Washington Post*. He said it was important that we trust each other. I do trust him, but I guess mainly I trust *who* John was. After all, he was a wonderful person. Even though, I'd like to kick him in the ass if he walked up right now, I still love him and respect him and am thankful for the time we had together.

Pam also talked to L.A. District Attorney to see when they

would announce decision of J.'s case. Said press was jumping the gun, they wouldn't be ready for another week.

August 28, 10:15 A.M.

This was to be Rob's wedding day. There is a dark cloud over my mother who wants to make Rob feel better, but knows she can't. He's been off by himself mostly. I'm on the verge of tears most of the time myself. Reading last night about New Year's Eve [*Hotel New Hampshire*]: someone announces midnight and "Mother runs for father" put that damn pain in my chest. I've wondered about New Year's Eve—I'm aware it will be hard on many levels. Mostly because it is our anniversary, partly because it's a new year with *what?* to look forward to. But I hadn't imagined that moment until then. . . . I can't think of anything that will make New Year's Eve not be hard. That's how today must be for Rob.

11:45 P.M.

About three, Rob wanted to go out in the canoe, alone, for a while. I took a nap. When I returned to the main cabin I discovered that Mom had made "memory boats" for both Liz and John. She used a piece of bark as the base, then added moss, flowers, a good luck stone (Liz's had a ring around it), and stuck four little candles into each one. She made John's "like a Viking boat" and wanted more daisies for Liz's. I went and got some. When Rob came back, he added a white heart with "Elizabeth Forrester Jacklin 1957–1982" written on it. Mom put a Blues Brothers button on J.'s.

After dinner we went down to the dock. The night was bright, a three-quarter moon hung over the lake. Rob and I took the memory boats out in the canoe and the others sat on the dock with the tape deck. We lit the candles and gently set the memory boats in the water while "For a Dancer" played from the dock. We all drifted for a while—the little boats and the big. Liz's candles burned bright and beautiful; John's began strong, then flickered on and off in a teasing fashion. The music Rob selected for Liz was put on. The music and the flames seemed in unison: as the music swelled, the moss caught fire and burned, and as the music grew softer and slower, the flame became smaller until finally it was out. Through the pale darkness I could see its smoke rise toward the moon. We watched quietly till all was a memory. Then Rob toasted "My brother-in-law and my beautiful wife" and we returned to shore. Without words we put up the canoe and filed up the path, all but Mom. "I want to sit here a while," she said in a soft voice.

*   *   *

The next day we all headed out. Pam had to get back to work and Mom and Dad were winding their way home via Canada. Rob plotted our route from Yellowstone through Wyoming, Utah, and on to Colorado. I wasn't too excited about the trip, but Rob had been so enthusiastic that I couldn't say no. Anyway, it didn't seem to matter much what I did; I was just passing time.

We were all up early, packing and cleaning the cabins. Watching Mom and Dad slowly pull away, I worried that the drive might be too much for them. I imagined it must have been how they felt when we kids first started driving. And just as they had to smile and let us go, I stood there and waved, trying not to look concerned.

The day was stormy with occasional streams of warm sunshine breaking through the clouds. At one point we saw one of the most colorful rainbows I've ever seen. As we drove, we talked mostly about Liz and John.

"I don't know if I ever told you how I found out about John's death," Rob said. He hadn't and I was very interested.

"I'd gone to a conference for the day and had neglected to tell either Liz or my secretary where it was, not thinking it much mattered since I'd be home that evening. Toward the end of the conference a man walked in and said, 'Is there a Mr. Jacklin here?' I knew from his voice that something was wrong. He said I had a call and I honestly went to the phone with trepidation, sure I was going to be told that Liz had died." Rob paused a moment, a pained look on his face. "When I head Liz's voice, I was greatly relieved. Then she said, 'I'm sorry I have to tell you this,' and I thought she was going to say Dad died. But she said, 'Rob, John is dead.' I was totally caught off guard and I thought of John Brewster. I was shocked, I couldn't believe it and said, 'John . . . We just saw John. He was in great shape, how could he be dead?' There was a long pause, then Liz said, 'John Belushi, Rob.' " Anger and hurt were in his voice as Rob relayed his first reaction. " 'That stupid son-of-a-bitch!' I said and burst out crying."

I immediately wanted to tell Rob my reaction when I first learned that Liz was dead. As I told about Dad phoning— how I knew something was wrong and thought Mom was dead, how I had to pull the information out of Dad—I began to relive it. I heard myself recounting, "Dad, what is it?" with the same frightened urgency I felt that day, and I couldn't go on. Suddenly tears began streaming down my face. Rob began crying, too. He reached out his hand and I took it. It was rather surreal, barreling down this endless stretch of empty highway, us holding hands, the beautiful panorama blurred by tears. Jesus, I thought, this is real. This is life.

*　　*　　*

September 4, 9:00 A.M.

Arrived in Aspen last night. Will stay at Rob's house next few days. Our trip turned out to be good for both of us. . . . Rob has brought me up-to-date regarding John's gravestone. He talked to a man from the cemetery commission before buying the marble, and discovered that there was a height restriction of two feet. This nixed Rob's design.

September 5, 3:30 P.M.

Talked with Pam, then had an intense anxiety attack . . . It's taken me about two hours to calm down. Thought I'd jot down conversation while I'm waiting for R.

She had some questions Sonnenschein wanted me to address. . . . [She also] spoke with the coroner who did the report for *Penthouse* and he gave us some new info. He feels that very possibly John died of a heart attack. It appeared to him that the coroners in L.A., probably due to their knowledge of drugs being found on C.S., only did tests that involved looking for drugs. For instance, a test on tissue from the heart could have at least ruled out a heart attack. The test is not expensive, so it is odd that they didn't do it. He said that when Pam asked the coroner's office for test results, it was unusual that they didn't send everything. [Pam suggested that perhaps it was because she hadn't checked the proper box on the request form and] he said that the exchange of information is very common, and that, "this isn't a guessing game. They should have sent you everything they did, including the test on the heart."

September 6, 1:15 A.M.

Spent the evening at Laila's. SCTV came on and we watched, not knowing it was the show with the tribute to John at the end. It was kind of nice to see. I was startled at first and thought it would make me cry, but it didn't. Laila cried. It made me feel a little sad, but mostly I enjoyed seeing the photos. I wonder, is it only a coincidence that they aired that show on the 6-mo. anniv.?

September 7, 10:15 A.M.

Have felt tired since I've been in Aspen. Am ready to go home, which I will tomorrow. Last night, when I went to sleep, an interesting thing happened. I was too tired to write, but my mind was racing. At some point, I began to *feel* how much I love John still. I thought to myself, "I am unabashedly in love with John, and I guess I always will be." I felt light-headed and there was a feeling in my chest I find hard to describe. It was similar to anxiety, but it felt good—it didn't make me uncomfortable. I felt lucky to still *feel* love— not to be left empty.

September 8, 1:00 A.M.

Laila jokingly asked me to marry her tonight. I told her,
"No, because I love you too much to have people saying that
you married me for my money."

Pam phoned. . . . Danny is going to do an interview with
Penthouse and they want to do a separate one with me. At
first I was thinking of doing it—answering Sonnenschein's
questions from the other day. Actually, I'd love to answer
those questions. But I'd have to depend on *Pent.*'s promise of
total editorial control. Woodward said that he'd had a few
problems with Guccione. That G. sometimes edits after the
authors/editors have made promises. I feel I should put my
trust in Woodward. It may pay later.

Chapter 14

FLOUNDERING

SEPTEMBER

I was glad to find Sandi back at 60 Morton Street. (She, Jimmy, and Robert had been living at my house since Jimmy had begun *Pirates* on Broadway.) Robert was already in bed and Jimmy was out picking up a pizza. Soon Jimmy came bustling in, smiling and full of energy. The aroma of hot pizza filled the room. It was nice to return to this family situation.

Jimmy and I sat up late, filling each other in on the past few weeks. He was especially happy to hear that the D.A. was moving ahead with a grand jury probe; they were not going for manslaughter, but for furnishing drugs. At least the case hadn't been dropped. We wondered if Woodward's involvement had influenced their decision, and talked about the disquieted reaction to Bob's arrival in L.A. It made us laugh to imagine how much John would enjoy the commotion.

That night I wrote in my diary: "When I think of how I've structured the next few years (video tribute, documentary, book, etc.) around these things connected with John, I feel that it's something I do as a sort of unspoken promise . . . almost a tying-up of loose ends. At any rate, it's a way to go on. And when that's done, if I find there are enough other reasons to go on, I will. If not, I'll probably die of a broken heart. Not to sound dramatic, but I believe one can."

The next day I had a meeting uptown, then returned to my house and met Woodward. He was self-assured and easygoing; I was growing fond of him. He suggested we talk over dinner, so I took him to one of my current hangouts in Soho,

196

Wise Maria's. It had an intimate atmosphere and, because it was relatively new, was not very busy. We talked about John, and again Bob appeared to be impressed with how people spoke of him. He felt it was the pressure of John's last week that drove him to heroin, and he was certain it wasn't a usual part of his drug habit. Bob commented on the *Penthouse* article, saying it really hadn't gotten to the bottom of anything. And he wasn't so sure the police were actually at John's bungalow before they said they were, as *Penthouse* implied. Still, Bob found an inordinate amount of bungling—and/or lack of interest—by the police and the D.A. For instance, he made reference to some jewelry which was confiscated from John's room, but never checked out. (Except in a phone call to me, three months after the fact.) These items may or may not be of importance, he pointed out, but it was curious that things weren't followed up.

I was very interested in Bob's reactions to the people he was meeting; he was delving into our world and, I was pleased to see, coming up with positive reactions. He seemed to appreciate how much John did in his short life; in fact, I felt he even respected him. I was totally at ease.

The following day Woodward conducted more interviews, including one with Jimmy. The two of them sat in the courtyard and talked for some time. Afterward Jimmy felt good; he'd talked about the family a lot. Woodward asked if he might interview his parents and Jimmy said we would talk about it. We both agreed it was a bad idea. They were still very emotional, sad, angry. Since we had no control over what Bob was doing, we didn't feel they should take the risk. If he insisted, we would reconsider.

Jimmy said he felt a certain relief having talked to Bob. "He asked me"—imitating Bob as he repeated the query—" 'What is it about Wheaton that fucked us all up?' " Jimmy laughed. "Boy, he really hates Wheaton."

I had noted it, too, and found it curious. Of all of us, Bob had had the most going for him as a kid growing up there. A big house, prominent family, the proper WASP looks, manners. Money didn't seem to be a problem. But all that was just outward appearances. His parents were divorced when he was in his teens. Maybe that was why he "hated Wheaton."

Later that evening, Jimmy and I sat in a little park near the house and played checkers on a cement table where the old men play by day. He brought up his interview again. "I was telling Bob about Nena," Jimmy said, his expression showing he'd slipped back to the past. "I was describing the day you and John came to see Nena in the hospital, and all of a sudden, I realized that the two people who influenced me most in my life . . . were dead. And I cried."

Walking back home I told Jimmy about the problems Rob had encountered with the design for the gravestone. His initial reaction was similar to mine. Now I took Rob's attitude that a fieldstone might be nice. As we turned onto Morton Street, a thought occurred to me. "Say, Jimmy, what do you think if, instead of a gravestone, we put a checker table like the one at the park on John's grave? Of course, it could only be two feet high, so people would have to sit on the ground."

"Yeah, I like that idea. That way people could go visit John and play a few games of checkers. Spend a little time."

"I know Larry would like it," I added. Larry Bilzerian and John had become avid checker adversaries the summer before.

"Oh yeah, Larry and I could have some good games out there," Jimmy agreed. We laughed at the image. Jimmy unlocked the door and held it open for me.

"So, it's decided?" I asked, entering the house.

"I think," Jimmy said, holding his finger up for emphasis, "we should sleep on it."

In my diary, I drew a sketch of a checker table, writing "1949" on one side of the base and "1982" on another side. On the thick edges of the tabletop I wrote "John Adam Belushi" and "He always left a mess." The joke was silly and it made me laugh.

Jimmy completed his run in *Pirates* on the thirteenth, and went to the Vineyard with his family. After they left I lay down to nap and cried; separations always seemed to make me cry now. A few hours later, a woman who worked on John's *Noble Rot* project in L.A. phoned. Woodward had contacted her and she wanted to check with me before talking to him. She began to talk about John, how much she enjoyed working for him and how badly she felt the studio had treated him. Then she mentioned the day John died. "I went over to the office with another secretary after we heard. We didn't know what to do. When we got there, it was as if they didn't know he'd died, which of course they did. Finally, we suggested we should send a card or flowers, and someone said, 'No! We've already wasted enough money on Belushi!' "

I was quite startled. John was in L.A. working for Paramount the day he died, but they didn't have enough respect for him even to send a card to his family. It was an insult to John. Thinking about it later, I became very angry; I vowed never to forgive them. I had never made a vow before. In fact, it struck me as, well, rather Albanian. Yes, it was an old world vow. It felt right.

On September eighteenth I went to the closing for 52 West Ninth Street. When I returned home, there was a message from Steve Jordan. He had four tickets for a Sinatra concert at Carnegie Hall that evening. Wendie, Mitch, Steve, and I had talked about going to Carnegie Hall, and none of them had ever seen Sinatra. So, before I knew it, I was seated in the balcony, watching Ole' Blue Eyes strut his stuff.

Steve, Mitch, and I had been to Carnegie Hall when the Blues Brothers appeared in 1980. What a crazy night that had been! I remembered going backstage and being struck by the plainness of the dressing rooms. I had imagined grand dressing rooms to match the splendor of the theater. John was excited just to be there, I'm sure he never thought twice about the dressing rooms. "Did you see the stage?" he asked, a big smile on his face and an energy vibrating from him. "It's a great room. This is going to be fun!"

Sinatra's show began fairly close to schedule. As the lights went down and the room quieted, my thoughts returned to the Blues Brothers concert. Scattered applause had signaled the start, as the Blues Brothers band members took their places on the darkened stage. The lights came up and the nine-person band, all wearing similar dark sunglasses, broke into a hot version of "Soul Finger." From offstage, Danny's voice had boomed out, fast paced to match the driving music: "Good evening everyone and welcome to the United States of America. And indeed, we have congregated here at this time to celebrate a most treasured wellspring of contemporary music. It is the sound which historians in the far future might catalogue under Twentieth-Century pre-light-emitting-dioeuphoria. But today the sound lives, and tonight, assembled exclusively for your entertainment pleasure, from the music capitals of this continent, this is the heart of the all-star show band of Joliet Jake and Elwood Blues. Ladies and gentlemen, these are the Blue Brothers!" The crowd cheered as Jake and Elwood strutted on stage wearing baggy black suits, white shirts with small collars, thin black ties, black porkpie hats, and dark glasses. Danny carried a black leather briefcase handcuffed to his wrist, and John followed nonchalantly swinging a key on a long chain. John unlocked the handcuffs, Danny set the briefcase down, reached in, and pulled out a harmonica. In perfect time with the music, John gracefully—seemingly effortlessly—turned a roundoff (a movement that begins like a cartwheel and ends like a flip), landing at Danny's side, motionless, on the final beat of the song. It was a brilliant move for a man in a suit and hat to suddenly turn himself upside down. It was cartoonlike; it happened so fast and John looked so nonperplexed that it didn't seem real. It was a great opening and I had been proud of them.

Now I watched Sinatra working the audience. He was cool. He had their total attention, their love, their respect. Oddly, I saw a similarity between his stage personality and John's. They both had their little inside jokes with the band members and both respectfully noted the composers of the songs they sang. And they both chatted with the audience, sharing a bit of themselves, although John was more naïve in his manner. But I was overwhelmed by one big difference, overall: when the Blues Brothers played there'd been a crackle in the air; there was excitement, energy was high. Sinatra's audience was enthusiastic, but it was not electric—at least not that night.

As we headed from the theater down to Mitch and Wendie's, Steve started talking about the Blues Brothers concert. Back at the apartment, he and Mitch had a new energy as they reminisced; the memory of the show pumped them up. I enjoyed listening. Steve, as a band member, recalled how it had felt to be on the stage, his hands pantomiming playing drums while he talked. His face lit up and his wiry body doubled over in laughter at something Mitch reminded him about. Wendie put on the Blues Brothers tour album. At first, it was a little difficult for me to have John singing in the background, but before I knew it I was so interested in what Mitch and Steve were saying that I forgot about it. When "Guilty" came on, I thought for a moment I was hearing Joe Cocker, then was startled by the realization that it was John. "Life is really strange," I wrote in my diary that night. "I still wish John would come back."

I drove up to Martha's Vineyard with Kathryn and James to take care of some cemetery arrangements. On the drive we listened to John Prine, and once again I was a lump of memories being dragged along for the ride. I pretended to watch the scenery, but saw John as a young man in Chicago, working at Second City. During intermissions he enjoyed going across the street to the Earl of Olde Town, an established club for folksingers. It was there, after he made friends with various performers like John Prine and Steve Goodman, that he first began singing. Usually he'd do a Cocker or a Stones song. If he felt he wasn't winning over the audience, he would fall back on his improvisation talents and make them laugh instead. He was also a good audience, for the other performers, clapping, whistling, and talking up the act. There was a nice camaraderie at the Earl. I hadn't heard a John Prine song for a long time and was surprised at how many of his lyrics I remembered.

Jimmy picked me up at James's and we decided to stop at the cemetery. Some items had been left at John's grave. One was a nicely hand-chiseled rock that spelled out BELUSHI. The other was a note engraved into a small block of wood: "He could have brought us more laughs—but nooo!" For a moment it sort of stopped me in my tracks. We stood silently, looking at it. "What d'ya think?" Jimmy asked.

"It's okay, I think, don't you?"

"Yeah, I think it's okay. It's from a fan. This one is really nice," he said, picking up the name rock and giving it better placement at the mound of stones marking John's head.

The next day I went sailing with James and Kathryn. It

was a beautiful, clear day; the water was calm and a deep, rich blue. James played his guitar. The light that day had a captivating brilliance, and I lost myself in a dreamlike trance, imagining the notes from the guitar and the light sparkling on the water were one. Then the memories began . . .

John and I never sailed a lot. I guess our "sailing life" was pretty well established at an early date. We went to a lake with my sister Pat and her boyfriend who owned a little sailfish. The boyfriend asked John if we knew how to sail. "Sure!" John said with enthusiasm. I hopped on behind and sailed off with my captain. It was easy going until we got to the other side of the lake and tried to turn. Boom! Down we went. After three failed attempts at getting upright, John asked if I knew how to sail.

"No," I replied, "I thought you did."

"Well, no," he admitted. "Actually, I didn't think it was so difficult."

Further attempts at sailing on bigger boats led us to the discovery that John often became seasick. Needless to say, we didn't sail much. I wish we'd tried a small sail just off the island, I thought, like today; John could have handled this. When Kathryn brought me back from my own world with conversation, I felt sad; I missed John. It was such a beautiful afternoon, I felt guilty for not being able to shake my down mood. I wanted to feel good. But I didn't.

After the sail I stopped to get flowers for John's grave and found that the florist was closed for the season. My first thought was, Oh, no, now what am I going to do? Then my stomach dropped, and for the first time I thought, I really don't want to go to the grave. It was an uncomfortable feeling, but I couldn't deny it. I drove home a longer route to avoid passing the cemetery. I'm not going to let myself feel guilty for this, I thought. But I did.

That evening, I wrote in my diary: "I wish I believed in heaven. It's such a lovely idea. Tonight Tim Mayer joined us at dinner. He said he'd been going to church some since his mother died. He said, 'I told my father, "I don't believe it, but I like it!"' I guess we all think these things when we've lost someone we love. Hoping the best for them—peace, happiness, energy—and wanting desperately to believe you will find them again." On my feelings about the grave I wrote: "It worries me. Am I going to get resentful of giving too much now that he's dead?"

It was much colder when James, Kathryn, and I drove to Boston the following day. Kathryn and I had lunch before I took the shuttle to New York. I had a couple of drinks at lunch, and another while waiting at the airport. In line for the plane, I chatted briefly with the man behind me. On board, he asked to sit next to me. He was about my age, a businessman type. I didn't really want to have a conversation with a stranger, but I didn't really want to read a magazine, either. As it turned out, the hour passed quickly and enjoyably; we didn't talk about much of a personal nature. He was stopping over in New York and staying at an airport hotel. He wondered if I'd like to join him for dinner. I felt lonely and vulnerable and wanted to talk to someone, but not someone I had just met. I figured I could catch Rhonda at home, and said I was meeting a friend in the city.

Once we'd landed I phoned for a cab. Because it was raining there were none available, and the line for street cabs was outrageously long. My new friend was trying to convince me to join him for a drink and wait out rush hour. I was feeling pretty high, almost sociable, and didn't really want to return to an empty house. I phoned Rhonda, but there was no answer. Oh well, maybe I'd get something to eat . . . What the heck.

We crossed the parking lot to the hotel restaurant and ordered drinks. I thought he was a nice guy, and wondered if he were interested in me. Sex was definitely not on my mind, but it was nice to think that someone found me attractive. I hadn't felt attractive for some time. I kept the conversation on him and pretty well avoided talking about myself until the question "Have you ever been married?" I said I was a widow, hesitated, then told him John had been my husband. After that, I opened up. Several times I was ready to leave, but was pulled back into conversation. Finally I collected my things. In the lobby he took my hand and said, "Is there anything I can do for you?" I was embarrassed, shook my head, and said nothing. We stood there and he rubbed my hands gently between his. Unexpectedly, I realized I wanted to be held and to make love. I told myself I was drunk, I should leave right away, but I just stood there. He took my hand and led me to the elevator.

Alone inside the elevator, we hugged for a while. Then we kissed. "I didn't expect this to happen, although I admit, it did cross my mind," I acknowledged.

"I didn't expect it, either," he said and smiled.

Suddenly I felt very sad; it swept through me like a drug rush. I burst out crying. He held on to me, stroking my head. After I'd cried myself out I felt a little better, and said I wanted to call a cab. "Are you sure?" he asked. "Please stay. I'm a good listener." I had to leave, it didn't feel right. I knew if I stayed I'd wake up and wish I weren't there.

On the way home in the cab I cried again. I knew how much I still loved John, and felt that I would belong to him in my heart, if not in the flesh, forever.

The next day I was nervous waiting for Dr. Cyborn, debating whether or not to tell him about last night, but I was embarrassed, maybe even ashamed. I heard his footsteps and knew my deliberation time was up. I don't have to tell him everything I do, I told myself. It's not that important anyway.

Walking into the office, I decided to ignore the events of the preceding night and tell a dream, instead. Dreams were always interesting. I'd had one a few nights before that I still remembered clearly. After probing into my associations to various images in it, Dr. Cyborn rested his elbows on the arms of his chair and brought his fingertips together, usually a sign that he had something to tell me. "You know, Judy, I see this as a dream about masturbation. It's not the first one you've told me. Now this week you have a dog biting at your hands. In dream analysis, this kind of image implies a guilt about masturbation. You know, sex is a drive, and it's there to help keep you alive. So the reawakening of this drive is a positive sign. That you are feeling guilty about it at this time is not unusual, and that is what we have to work on."

I was taken aback by what Dr. Cyborn said; wasn't this what I didn't want to talk about? I told him about my encounter and my hesitation to tell him. Dr. Cyborn told me that these actions supported what he'd just said, that when we have subconscious problems we often do things, like drink alcohol, to suppress them, then act on impulse and feel bad about it as our guilt surfaces. "You're reacting as if you'd cheated on John, as if he were still alive," Dr. Cyborn pointed out. "Or you may even be feeling guilty that you are still alive." He thought a moment. "Let me tell you something, Judy. You are an attractive, sexual young woman and you need a sex life. It's still too soon, perhaps, but with time I would like to see you in a new marriage and maybe with a family. That is up to you, of course, but you at least need to be loved and to love someone. Do you have a goal for yourself in mind?"

"Well . . ." I hesitated. All this seemed to have come up so unexpectedly, I couldn't really imagine myself in love and remarried, much less with a family. "I liked being married and I guess I'd like to be married again. But at this time, I don't feel that it's very likely."

"Well, that's a natural reaction. At this time you need to feel the sadness and the loss. And we need to work on keeping you in touch with your feelings."

I left Dr. Cyborn feeling better about myself. I had felt my impulses to be reprehensible; now I realized I'd just been human. And I'd been able to turn it around and learn something. In fact, I realized I was drawn to someone and had been denying it; I was very attracted to Steve, but for several reasons could not, until this time, admit it to myself. There were the reasons Dr. Cyborn brought up. And maybe becoming involved with a friend was confusing. But I knew a big reason for my denial was because Steve is black. An old, deep-rooted thought ran through my mind. *It would kill my father!* It was out of the question.

Chapter 15

SHELTERING ARMS

LATE SEPTEMBER–EARLY OCTOBER

I was at Phantom when Pam called with interesting news from the L.A. District Attorney. Nelson Lyon was going to plead the Fifth at the grand jury. Van Ness's claim that another person had been shooting up with John came to mind. It was Nelson, I was certain now. It was disturbing to realize that my only direct contact to someone with John that night was not telling me the whole story.

Karen buzzed me to say that Robin Williams's lawyer was on the phone, returning a call I had placed to Robin. He introduced himself and said it was his counsel to Robin not to talk with anyone about John's death until after he'd testified at the grand jury. I couldn't help saying, rather snottily, "Yes, I'm sure there are things Robin shouldn't talk about." Very lawyerlike in his choice of words, he denied that Robin's silence implied illegalities. I knew he was right and felt silly for having said anything. It was just that I was still angry that Robin had never contacted us after John's death. He continued, "Of course, if you want to talk to Robin about any other personal matter, I don't want to get in the way of friendships." I bit my tongue on that one and explained that Woodward was interested in talking to Robin about the eve of John's death. That led to a circular conversation since, obviously, Robin couldn't talk to Bob. "However," the attorney said to me, "I wouldn't mind talking to Bob myself, because as a lawyer I'm interested in the truth and I like to conduct my own investigation regardless of what a client might tell me." What a strange thing for Robin's lawyer to say to me, I thought. Everything around this whole affair seemed screwy. I was glad that Woodward was out there looking into things.

Karen buzzed again; MTV was on the line. I had placed a call to an executive I knew to see if they would be interested in airing my *West Heaven* video. He seemed to be caught off guard at hearing from me, and choked up as he expressed his sorrow about John's death: "Even though I didn't really know him that well, I had an affection for him. . . . I really miss him." I explained that I was planning to make a video with a song a friend had written for John, something that would reflect the kind of sentiments he had just shared—only it would be my personal statement, with snapshots and symbolic images. He was immediately enthusiastic; MTV wanted to do something special for John, and this sounded perfect. We agreed to talk when I had something to show him.

I made a call to check up on my parents. My dad answered; he'd been about to call me. They'd been looking for something to do in memory of Liz and John, and thought it would be nice to plant a tree for each of them in the yard. They wanted to have a dedication and invite friends. I thought it was a very good idea, and said I'd arrange my schedule to be there. "That would be great!" Dad said. "You know, Judy, so many people here have been so thoughtful and helpful to us, what with all that's gone wrong this year. We just wanted to do this thing with the trees, well, to share something with them. Mom will get a ham and we'll make some of your grandmother's German potato salad, you know, have some beer and wine and all. I think it'll be nice."

I was moved by my parents' sweetness. My eyes stung from the bittersweet touch that accompanied it. An image of those trees, full grown, came to mind. I wondered how I would feel then.

September 23 4:00 P.M.

Today I really feel low . . . depleted, like I just have enough in me to finish these projects. I feel there are more death visits coming, maybe soon. I imagined my parents dying, and thought, "Maybe I'll kill myself then. I can't take much more sadness." I imagined taking pills, I even thought, "I shouldn't tell Dr. C. this, because if I do, he'll watch out for it and try to stop me." And I realized I wouldn't tell him. This is the first time I think I've ever remotely considered suicide. I can't tell how I feel about that yet. I don't think it scares me.

At my next session with Dr. Cyborn, I admitted my attraction to Steve. "Do you think you could have a comfortable relationship with a black man?" he asked.

"I don't know," I said. "One difficulty is that it would hurt my father."

"Your father's a racist?" Dr. Cyborn asked.

"Well, the truth is that he puts down every race and religious group, but when he deals with individuals, he's always very fair to people."

"So you think he might like Steve?"

"Sure, if he met him out of the blue, but I don't think he could think straight about Steve if we were involved."

Dr. Cyborn said that dealing with John's death had taken over my therapy, and that we needed to start focusing on me and my family involvement more because "there's a lot of unfinished business there." He said every family has dramas they play out, and we needed to find what patterns I was repeating. For instance, I didn't marry the nice WASP man of my father's dreams, but fell in love with an Albanian. In a sense, I "got back" at Dad by doing this. An interest in Steve could be a healthy attraction to someone who might offer many good qualities, or it might be a subconscious, repeating pattern. "I'm not saying your marriage was not a good marriage," Dr. Cyborn was quick to add, "because I think it was. I'm just saying that it is important to understand these patterns so you can consider them when you're making choices."

On Rhonda's birthday there was a little party and a lot of champagne. I came home about two in the morning with a strong urge to hear "For a Dancer," headed straight for the sound room, and pulled out my Jackson Browne album. As the record spun and music filled the room, images filled my mind. The song has a waltz rhythm, and I began to dance.

The champagne had made my head light, and the twirling felt good. The song ended and I put it on again, continuing my slow, flowing dance. Whisper the cat ambled into the room, sat on the couch, and watched with mild interest. When the song was over I made my final spin and landed on my knees in front of her. "There, I must be getting better if I can listen to this and not cry," I said aloud. Looking at the large fluffy cat I remembered the little kitten John and I had taken home on our first day in L.A. for *Continental Divide*. John had chosen her because she was the most alert of the litter, the most adventurous. "You remember John, don't you, Whisp? Don't you?" I burst into tears and buried my face in her fur until she could no longer stand being held and ran away. I rolled onto the floor and lay there crying in agony until I was cried out. I looked around the sound room, the vault, the nearly airtight tomb; after I left the apartment, this room would be torn down. Then it too would be just a memory.

I dragged myself to my feet. Jeeze, I felt heavy. And sluggish. There was a noise as if something had fallen upstairs. I didn't care, so what if someone had broken in. I went into the bathroom and washed my face. I guess I used to be afraid of dying, I thought. It's kind of nice not to be afraid. Suddenly I looked at myself in the mirror. Here I was, exhausted, yet taking the time to wash my face with cleansing milk, following that with toner, then gently applying night cream. Shit! If I'm doing this, I must be afraid of something, I thought. Maybe I'm afraid I might live.

Steve phoned and asked if I would like to see Peter Tosh and Jimmy Cliff in concert at Madison Square Garden. As usual, I hadn't made any plans for the weekend, so the invitation was welcomed. I was also excited about the opportunity to see Steve alone.

We took a cab uptown, got out, and walked a block to the entrance. As we crossed the street Steve took my hand, almost in a protective manner. I wondered if it was an affectionate or just a friendly gesture. I felt like a seventh grader.

The concert was fun, the music really felt good. My mind wandered, however, and I found myself often thinking of

John, although more philosophically than usual. Afterward, we went downtown to Steve's loft, a corner space with twenty-foot ceilings and full-length windows overlooking Fifth Avenue and Eighteenth Street. It was light and open and always in a state of transition. This month, drums were set up on a large round platform in the middle of the room, surrounded by about ten guitars on stands, various amplifiers, microphones, and other equipment. A stand-up bass looked a little lonely in a far corner. Instruments definitely took priority over furniture. The most accessible places to sit were the drum stool or an old bathtub (decorative only) filled with pillows. A sleeping area at the back of the loft was separated from the entrance by a tall stack of crates filled with clothes. Two impressive speakers hung securely from the ceiling. When Steve wasn't actually making music, he usually blared recorded music through these monsters.

Steve put on some music and I sat at his drums and played. It felt good to drum again. I should have been embarrassed, since I had hardly played the past few years, but Steve was encouraging and made me feel at ease. He picked up a guitar and we improvised. I had a natural sense for drumming; I had been able to play a basic rock 'n roll beat from the first time I sat at a drum set as a little girl. But drums weren't an instrument a girl was encouraged to take up, and there was little access to them. A friend's brother once caught me playing his drums and told me never to touch them again. It wasn't until we were filming *The Blues Brothers* that I finally began to really play. I bought a drum kit for the Blues Bar, thinking it would be fun for John, and hoping he would teach me as well. He taught me some basic patterns and I began playing daily to the accompaniment of the juke box. I improved quite a bit and got good enough to jam with other musicians. I became interested in playing bass guitar and that Christmas John gave me my pink bass. I didn't think about all this as Steve and I played, however, but concentrated on the music. We played for a while and then I called a cab, thinking it was good to end the night on an up note.

Steve came down to the street with me and, before I got in the cab, gave me the same friendly kiss he always had. I felt confused; I liked him very much, was very attracted to him, but didn't feel he had any interest in me beyond our friend-ship. It's too soon for me to even think about getting involved with Steve, I told myself. Look at how much of the night I spent thinking of John. But then, when we were at his place, look how long a time I forgot about John. Anyway, one thing was for sure, I felt good with Steve. Almost as if it were worth being alive. Maybe I should be satisfied with things the way they were.

Jimmy and Sandi had returned from the Vineyard for a few nonworking days in New York before going home to Chicago. After a nice breakfast with Sandi and little Robert, I went to my office, where I took care of a lot of business calls, including talking to an artist about a storyboard for *West Heaven*. About four, Steve phoned and asked what I was doing. I said I felt a little harried and he suggested I come over to his place and smoke a joint, which sounded good to me. I told Karen where I was going and was out the door and down the two blocks to Steve's in a flash.

Not long after I arrived, Rhonda's boyfriend Zo-Reller called and asked us to join them at a nearby restaurant. Rhonda had just been offered a role in a Broadway show called *Pump Boys and Dinettes* and they were celebrating.

Outside the restaurant, we walked around a TV crew that was using it as a backdrop for filming. Inside, Rhonda and Zo-Reller were already enjoying a bottle of champagne.

We were a funny foursome. The differences among Rhonda—the outgoing, southern blonde from Arkansas, and Steve—a hip, New York black, and myself—a pasty white, fragile-looking midwesterner, were silly enough. But Zo-Reller put us into the absurd. A new-wave musician who was also a disciple of the guru Sri Chinmoy, he currently sported shoulder-length dreadlocks. He was also a strict tropical-fruitarian (he only ate fruits found in the tropics).

As we opened our second bottle of champagne, the camera crew began to move their equipment into the restaurant. The management explained to the scattered tables of diners that they were a Japanese TV crew shooting a documentary on American restaurants. They hoped no one minded. We cer-tainly didn't, although I thought they might prefer that *we* weren't there. We were a celebratory group, after all, not your typical early evening diners, and I worried that perhaps we were a little too noisy. Of all the people I know, Rhonda and Steve have the loudest laughs; they have great laughs, but loud. And Zo-Reller is right up there with them. I'd have rated us at somewhere between amusing and obnoxious. Regardless, after the hostess of the show filmed her intros, the producer came over and asked if our table would like to join in tasting the food. Obviously, they recognized our charm. We said we'd be happy to, although, of course Zo could only eat tropical fruits.

We left the restaurant giggling, and not wanting to break up our foursome caught a cab and headed to Steve's. There, Zo-Reller picked up a guitar, I sat at the drums, and Steve grabbed a bass. We played some of Zo-Reller's songs, all of which were insanely fast, impossible for me to play without cutting the beat in half. Then Steve and I switched instruments and he showed me what to play on bass. After about an hour's workout, Rhonda and Zo headed home.

I stayed another two hours, debating what kind of a relationship I wanted with Steve. I knew the situation was sensitive and Steve would never put me on the spot. All the same, if he was waiting for me to make a move, I was still uncertain. I phoned a cab and went home.

The next day I had a late breakfast with Rhonda to talk about the video. I was working out images and described my ideas to her. The heart of the video would be a photo montage, personal shots of John being himself, doing the things he loved other than work. To lead into this, there would be a shot of me sitting in my living room—which would be empty—looking at a scrapbook. This shot would be moody, dreamlike, the camera swooping down over my shoulder to a close-up of a photo in the book which would begin the montage. But before all this we would see Rhonda, the storyteller, sing the first verse in the sound room. I was still working on a way to include various images, like leaves blowing and waves crashing.

Our conversation shifted to talk about her new show, and then to Steve. I expressed my feelings and fears, and Rhonda said not to analyze it so much. "I think he's good for you,"

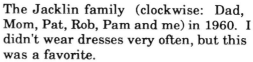

The Jacklin family (clockwise: Dad, Mom, Pat, Rob, Pam and me) in 1960. I didn't wear dresses very often, but this was a favorite.

Robert Leslie Jacklin and Jean Buchanan on their wedding day, November 7, 1940.

A 1983 family portrait. (*L.G.I.*)

Wheaton Central High School,
Wheaton Illinois, 1969 year book:

JUDY JACKLIN
Honor Roll 1,2,3,4; Class Council 1,
2,3,4, President 3; Student Conference
3,4, Vice-president; Girls' League 1;
Play and Crew 2,3; Monitor 3; Homecoming Court 4; Tiger Turnout Chairman 4; School Spirit Award 4; High
Honor Roll 4.

Above: My guy,
captain of the football
team, from John's
senior year book. The
caption read, *"Then I
grabbed him..."*

Right: My Senior Prom.
My sister Pat made my
dress.

As a member of the Homecoming Queen's Court. That's me on the left.

After John graduated high school in 1967, he became a resident actor at Shawnee Summer Theatre in Bloomfield, Indiana. But not before he shaved his new beard.

John points to his first professional credit. It was an exciting time, but our first big seperation: a long, lonely summer.

While at Shawnee, John played a variety of characters, from Cardinal Wolsey in "Anne of A Thousand Days" to this role as a jazz musician in "The Tender Trap."
(Courtesy Shawnee Summer Theatre.)

A rare photo from a West Compass Players performance, about 1970.

Left: A year later, John at Chicago's Second City, as the Angel Gabriel, explaining the Immaculate Conception to Mary.

(Courtesy 2nd City)

Top: Harold Ramis, Joe Flaherty, John, Bob Tischler and Christopher Guest after a "Radio Hour" recording session.

In 1973, we moved to New York City and worked for *National Lampoon;* John as an actor/writer and I as an art assistant for the magazine. Later, I became Associate Producer of the Radio Hour. Sometimes, as above, we modeled for the mag.
(Courtesy National Lampoon)

John Belushi as Joe Cocker

In *National Lampoon's* "Lemmings," John found an audience for his Joe Cocker imitation. *(Courtesy National Lampoon)*

My first job as an art director was for *Titters: The First Collection of Humor by Women* in 1976. Our features were often painstakingly created, as shown in these shots for a parody of a rock group. I modeled as a guitar player, first with short hair (mine), then long hair (a wig), and finally with no hair at all (make-up!). Our piano player was Rhonda Coullet. *(Lynn Goldsmith)*

The late Doug Kenney lived in
our West Village
neighborhood during the
mid-seventies. He introduced
us to Kathryn Walker.
(John)

Left: Laila at a
"Girl's Tea" thrown
by Gilda Radner (in
the background).
We all dressed up
and were requested
to wear hats.

John as sun-worshipper,
during our first visit to
Martha's Vineyard, June,
1974. *(J.J.B.)*

John and Dan Aykroyd horsing around during "Saturday Night Live" days, 1977.

Girl talk backstage at "SNL": Jane Curtin, Laraine Newman, Gilda Radner. *(J.J.B.)*

John took this picture of Billy Murray, who shows characteristic unfaltering concentration and exceptional style at the plate.

The Samurai !

Opposite: A promotional photo as
co-author/designer, proudly
holding my book, *Blues Brothers:
Private.* (Lynn Goldsmith)

In *Animal House,* I was Bluto's dancing partner at the toga party. In *The Blues Brothers,* I was a waitress along with *SNL* writer Rosie Shuster. *(Courtesy Universal Studios.)*

On our way to the premier for *Animal House,* 1978. John received so many congratulatory slaps on the back that night, his shoulders ached the next day. *(Mitch Glazer)*

At a ceremony in Chicago with Mayor Byrne. John Landis is standing behind Danny, and Bernie Brillstein and Sean Daniel are behind me. That's producer Robert K. Wise on the right. *(Steve Kagan)*

Top: During a party after a
Blues Brothers concert,
everyone wanted John's ear,
including Penny Marshall
and Walter Matthau.
*(Courtesy Universal
Studios.)*

Center: John pauses for a
photo with brother Jimmy.
(Courtesy Universal Studios.)

John as fighter-pilot Kelso in
the film, *1941*. Nice jacket.

Visiting John's parents, Adam and
Agnes, and brother Billy, at the ranch
in California, 1980.
(Billy Belushi/J.J.B.)

We bought the
Chilmark house
in late 1979.

Mitch Glazer
and John
researching
possible
material for a
new script.
(J.J.B.)

"Hey, isn't that
your jeep out
there?" John
with J.T.
somewhere off
Martha's
Vineyard.
(John Landis)

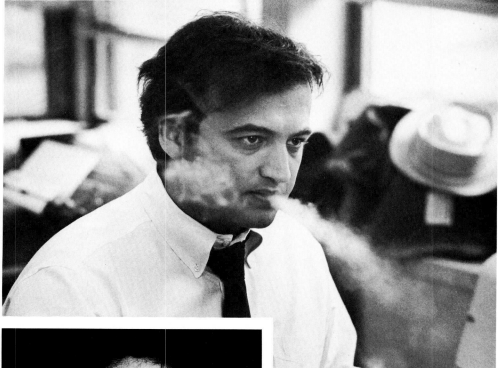

Above: As reporter Ernie Soucheck in *Continental Divide*, 1980. He went after this role because my mom, my sister Pam and I all liked the script very much. *(Courtesy Universal Studios.)*

Center: While filming at the studio in L.A., Whisper joined our family. John made her feel at home by holding her in his mouth like a mother cat.

Christmas tree trimming with friends, Christmas 1980. Rangy Tino Insana caps the tree.

We were fortunate to go to Japan in February, 1981, to promote *The Blues Brothers.* John and I then traveled alone for another three weeks in the Orient.

Late summer, we attended a family picnic in upstate New York. Here with John's mom, Agnes, nephew Adam, and sister, Marian.
(Bill Samaras)

Late January, 1982, on a leisurely drive via Highway 101 from San Francisco to L.A., we stopped to watch the sunset. This is my last photo of John before he died.

Working on *West Heaven,* at
the Morton Street apartment,
1983: sorting through photos
for the montage and
rehearsing with Rhonda in
the sound room.
(Lynn Goldsmith)

Right: The living room
cleared out for filming.

The week *West Heaven* aired on "Saturday Night Live," I moved into 52 W. 9th Street. Here with Agnes, who visited me in the spring.
(Passerby)

The coach house (behind 52 W. 9th) where I resided was cozy and protective.
(J.J.B.)

My dining room, a favorite writing area for Anne Beatts, Deanne Stillman and myself. *(Lynn Goldsmith)*

Judy and Rhonda, out on the town...
my last night as a New Yorker.
January 1987.

Although my move to the Vineyard
was during the biggest snowstorm
in years, the house was happy and
warm. Danny said this house
always feels like Christmas to him.

Then, the most unexpected turn of
events...I fell in love.
(Agnes Belushi)

A Vineyard Thanksgiving: Victor, me, Mom and Dad, Victor's girls (two
recently released from chains), and one perfectly cooked 24 pound turkey.

My office is upstairs in the
back of the house, Victor's
is downstairs in the front.
We walk to work.
(Bob Gothard)

My guy, writer/producer!
(J.J.B.)

One gray day, for fun, we had a photo session
with the girls: Jessica, Rebecca and Vanessa.
Vanessa's fanciful pose served a purpose...it
helped to keep her hat on. *(Victor)*

After an offshore fishing trip, Victor caught Jimmy posing with the biggest bluefish of the day. It turned out to be Victor's...or so he claims. The dispute may rage forever!

Agnes and Victor's girls shared a common love of the Oak Bluffs Carousel...the oldest in the country. Aggie said this was her favorite photo. *(Victor)*

Danny, Donna, Victor and I at a local bistro. "A night out on the Island!" Even the waiters giggled. *(Bilzerian)*

(Bob Gothard)

Second chance...

she told me. "Last night was the first time I've seen you look like you were having fun since John died."

"Yeah, well, I'm not sure that Steve wants anything more than a close friendship," I said.

"Don't you think he's been a little more aggressive than a man who just wants a friendship?"

"What do you mean aggressive?" I asked.

"Well, he's been around an awful lot," she pointed out.

"I don't know. He just doesn't seem interested in me sexually."

Rhonda laughed. "Well, honey," she said in her best southern accent, "I saw how he watched you get into that cab last night, and I can tell you, he's interested!"

I spent that evening with Sandi and Jimmy, taking them by 52 West Ninth Street after dinner for their first official tour of my new digs. Their faces lit up as I showed them around. "It's so perfect for you," they both said, and I knew they were really happy for me. Later, I wrote in my diary "Everything is double-edged for me now. I feel pretty happy about the place, and then it makes me sad because it's *my* house and not *ours*."

Steve phoned in the late afternoon and asked what I was doing. I said there was a friend's birthday party I was hesitant to attend because I didn't know her friends. He promptly offered to go with me. The party turned out to be quite nice, and at about eleven we headed downtown to meet Jimmy, Sandi, and some Chicago friends including Tim Kazurinsky at C'ent Anni, an Italian restaurant on Carmine Street.

Everyone was jovial and it was good to see Tim, who spent most of his time working at "SNL." Jimmy had emceed an event at St. John the Divine earlier in the evening and we joked that his career was over and all he would do now was emcee. It was getting late—the restaurant wanted to close— but it was Jimmy and Sandi's last night in New York. We moved our party to One Fifth Avenue, where Steve and I had something to eat, then dragged everyone to One University Place for a last drink. Jimmy and I discussed being an actor versus being a celebrity. "The less the public knows of you as a person, the easier they can accept you as a character," I advised. "John always said, you don't owe the public anything but a good performance." I felt very much like a big sister.

One University closed at four and Steve invited everyone to his loft. I was the only one who wanted to go, so we said goodnight to the others. "I'll see you in the morning," I promised Jimmy and Sandi as we waved and headed up Fifth Avenue.

I had pretty much decided that I was happy with Steve and would leave the boundaries of our relationship to him. That night we extended the boundaries. It was comfortable and sweet and I was happy being with him.

It was nearly noon the next day when I hurried down Morton Street. I wasn't sure what time Jimmy and Sandi had to leave, but I knew I was pushing it. Jimmy and I nearly collided as he came out the door with suitcases for the waiting cab.

"Ah, there you are," he said, looking at me in a way which seemed to take in the fact that I was still wearing the same clothes I had on last night. "We weren't sure if you were still sleeping . . ." His words trailed off as if something had been left unsaid. I helped finish loading the cab, feeling remiss for not getting back early enough to spend time with Robert. And I was concerned over what they would think about Steve and me. I felt Sandi would be okay, but what would Jimmy think? Would he feel it was too soon, that it was disrespectful of John?

The car loaded, Jimmy and Sandi had to get going. Our good-byes were rushed and it seemed as if we had much to talk about that had to wait. They pulled off and although I smiled as I waved, I felt confused. They'd been with me a while now and I'd miss them. I'd felt so good just moments before; I'd felt great! Why did I feel so weird? As I shut the door to the apartment, it seemed to close me into emptiness; as if the door had closed on my heart, I burst out crying.

That night Steve and I went to the Palladium to see James Brown. Steve was a member of the Letterman Band, and James had sung with them the day before. Backstage we met up with Paul Shaffer and watched the show together. Wilson Pickett, who was great, was the opening act, and then James Brown gave an amazing show. His energy, as always, was outrageous and his voice was strong. Afterward, I had a message from him; he'd heard I was there and had invited me to come to his dressing room. I felt funny about going up. I'd met him when he filmed *The Blues Brothers* movie, but I didn't really know him. "You should say hello," Shaffer encouraged me. "Will you guys come with me?" I asked.

James Brown was sitting under an old-style cone hair dryer, alone in the room except for a blond woman lounging on a couch. On seeing us he immediately stood, pushing the dryer up to reveal a full head of curlers. He crossed the room and gave me a hug. After a cordial hello to Paul and Steve, he pulled up chairs for the two of us and started talking about John, his face very close to mine. I was riveted to his eyes. "Your husband was a good man, of course I don't have to tell you that. He sure helped me an' I ain't never gonna forget that." His speech was rapid and his intonation like a Baptist minister's. "I talk about him wherever I go. Why just the other night at my concert, I talked up the Blues Brothers, I always do that, well you probably know . . ." I wish I could remember every word he said, but he kind of has his own language and it all came out so fast. "It's this business," he concluded, shaking his head. We were all totally focused on him. "It's the fans, they take you up, they just take you up!" James Brown hesitated, as if this were a painful thought. He stood. "Look at me, I do this every night." He went back to his hair dryer. "They just take you up. An' if you don't have it," he sat down again, "it's a slow death. An' if you do," he shrugged and put a hand on the cone of the dryer, "it's just a slower death." He pulled the dryer back over his head, and began a conversation with Steve and Paul.

Before we left, I thanked James for taking part in a benefit Peter Aykroyd had orchestrated at the Lone Star for the John Belushi Foundation. "Anytime," he promised. "John gave me a new life and I ain't never gonna forget it. As long as I'm alive, I'll be talkin' 'bout him."

Steve was coming down with a cold, so we went by the Pink Teacup and picked up some soup and food and returned to my house. It was nice to take care of someone for a change.

The October weather was crisp as I walked over to the Klenfners for a barbecue. At dinner, I was seated next to their daughter, Kate; it seemed as if every time I saw her, she was at least a half-inch taller. Her red hair was getting long, and she was a very composed little girl. "How old are you now, Kate?" I asked.

"Three and a half," she said unhesitatingly.

"Do you remember coming to visit John and me on Martha's Vineyard when you were little?" I tested.

She gave a firm nod of her head, and her big eyes got even wider, and she said, "Yes, we went to the beach and Daddy put mud on my face."

"That's right!" I laughed at the memory. "And remember how John put mud all over him?"

She shook her head again and a little hand came up to her mouth to cover a giggle. "He looked *so* funny." Kate's expression turned serious. "I know why John died," she matter-of-factly informed me, her brow furrowed. "Because he ate junk food and he didn't brush his teeth." Of course, I was surprised and mildly amused by this reasoning, but I was also uncertain how to respond.

"Well, Kate, junk food isn't good for you and it's important to brush your teeth, but I don't want you to think that if you don't brush your teeth you'll die. You might lose your teeth, but you won't die."

She considered this. "You know, I'm sad that John died," she said. At this point Kathryn, who was sitting on my other side, picked up on the conversation. Kate continued, "But it's lucky I had two!"

I could see Kathryn was confused. "Two godfathers," I explained. "John and Danny both were her godfathers." Kathryn absorbed this, looked at me with mock seriousness, and said, "And you only had one. How foolish."

A few days later, Woodward came to New York to go over more information. He suggested we go somewhere for a drink. I took him to the Buffalo Roadhouse, which was nearby and not very crowded at that hour. He had John's phone message book from Paramount, and phone bills from our house. He went over these, asking me various people's connections to John, and what numbers I recognized. Through cab bills at the Lipsky office, he'd traced John's movements the Sunday morning before he left for L.A., but there didn't seem to be anything to note, other than another confirmation that he was not doing heroin at that time.

Bob said he was already convinced that Cathy Smith was an informant, and he was trying to figure out if the police had tried to get another informant involved with John besides her. "What about Charles Pearson or April Milstead?" I asked. I had no idea who these people were, but their names were seared into my brain. "I don't know," Woodward admitted. "I still don't know enough about them. But I can tell you one thing," he said, sitting back and pausing as if considering his words, "if I'm on the right track with the L.A. police, I could end up dead."

When I saw Dr. Cyborn next, he said I was looking better. We talked about Steve and he asked how I felt about being involved with a black man. I said I didn't think about it most of the time, but there'd been a few times when we were out that I'd noticed someone looking at us oddly, and then I'd remember, ah, yes, some people don't like to see this. Dr. Cyborn asked what made me decide to try a relationship with Steve. I said that I'd recognized my feelings for him and decided to be open to them. I'd realized that I responded to the guy on the plane because I was avoiding my feelings for Steve. "Now you're getting smart, Belushi," Dr. Cyborn kidded, "and if we could get these feelings out of you before you start reacting to them, maybe we could really get somewhere."

That evening my brother phoned. He said he'd been feeling down the last couple of days, which was annoying to him because he knew that people expected him to be a man and be able to bounce right back. We talked about that and then I told him I had been feeling pretty good myself. "Well, I guess my biggest problem right now is Dad," I baited him.

"Dad?"

"Yeah. I'm worried about how he'll react to the fact that I'm going out with a black guy." I knew Rob liked Steve and could tell he was pleased. Before we got off the phone, he said he felt better.

I awoke with a terribly swollen throat, canceled my appointments, and made one with Dr. Gould. It was tonsillitis again. I was concerned about the fact that I was to leave in a few days for my parents' tree-planting ceremony and Dr. Gould had said it wasn't a good idea for me to fly.

I slept most of the afternoon, and when Steve phoned, told him what the doctor said. "I'm going to leave a day early so I can take the train to Chicago. I got a sleeper," I explained.

"That sounds cool," Steve said, then asked, "Are you in your bedroom? Because it's really cold back there and that's probably what's making you sick."

"Oh, I'm fine, I've got lots of blankets," I replied. There was no way I was going back to the bedroom I'd shared with John, I thought. I left it a long time ago.

Later that night, as I lay in front of the TV, flipping channels, I came upon "Entertainment Tonight" and paused. A photo of John popped onto the screen. "Cathy Smith's lawyers said today that she will not be appearing at the grand jury as requested."

"Yeah, yeah, yeah, big surprise," I said to the TV as I switched channels. She was still in Canada and wasn't about to give up her country's protection.

The next day Steve phoned to say good-bye and wish me a safe trip. I wanted to tell him I'd miss him, but the words would not come.

Chapter 16

ONLY THE YOUNG DIE YOUNG

OCTOBER

Traffic was slow, but I arrived at Grand Central in time to buy a few magazines before boarding the 6:45 to Chicago. I liked the sleeper. It was cozy and had the feel of a boat in its compact use of space.

After dinner I listened to a demo tape of a friend's music. I was a minor investor in the tape, and had just received my copy. I enjoyed the silhouetted landscape and illuminated towns as I rocked my way through the night to the music.

The tape was short, and on my second listen, a tune called "Hot Knives" caught my attention. Listening to the lyrics ("hot knives" is a way to take opium or hashish), I thought, I wouldn't mind doing some hash. As if I'd overheard myself, I was shocked. Would I really? I hadn't thought of "doing drugs" for some time, that is, other than my seemingly controlled use of alcohol and marijuana. The contention wasn't so much that the song was about "hot knives" as it was one of responsibility. I wondered how serious an influence a song might be on a listener, and if this was the kind of message I wanted to support.

How did I really feel about drugs? I thought cocaine, heroin, and opium were destructive, too addictive and dangerous. I liked grass, personally, but had seen others have bad reactions, from intense anxiety to extreme lethargy. Alcohol seemed to have an equally dissimilar effect on individuals. My gut feeling was that a drug, per se, wasn't the issue, but that problems within the user—emotional or physical—created the different reactions. Someone who took drugs to feel more

219

powerful, to rebel or express anger, to withdraw or as an excuse to be out of control, was probably heading for trouble. And everyone reacted differently.

But what could be done to deal with the drug problem? I felt communication was key and believed that by talking to Woodward I was at least making an attempt at progress. Maybe in the future I would find a more direct way. But now it was too complicated a problem for me to tackle. I opted to read a nice, escapist book instead.

My father met me at the station and as is my habit when I go home, I immediately observed him to see if he'd been drinking. He hadn't; I relaxed. Dad was always a drinker, but since retiring earlier than he would have liked, some eight years before, he'd found little to interest him and often went through phases of heavy drinking. I began to have problems with his drinking when I was about twelve, and by high school I was watering his vodka. As the youngest, I saw the progression more than the others, and was probably most affected. Although I really liked being with my dad, I had little patience with him when he wasn't sober. Anywhere in between left me in a state of anxiety, wondering when it would turn.

We put my luggage in the car and Dad asked if I wanted to drive. This was a holdover from the days when I was a new driver and begged to take the wheel at every opportunity. My father navigated the route to the freeway. A salesman working out of Chicago for thirty-odd years, he reminisced as we drove past companies he'd called on, or areas that had "changed." Once on the Eisenhower Expressway, I had some memories of my own. The freeway doesn't pass the neighborhood where I was born and spent my early childhood, but I always looked for something familiar when I drove through Oak Park—a feeling, really, not a landmark. When I lived there everything was just beyond my grasp. Driving by, I tried to catch a glimpse of life through a window, searching for some little girl who would remind me of myself.

We picked up the tollway and continued through what was, when we'd first moved to Wheaton, largely open land. Now suburban growth had devoured it, eaten it acre by acre. On Butterfield Road, the final stretch to my parents' house, what had been nothing but fields when I was a kid, with perhaps three farm houses along this particular two-mile section, was now wall-to-wall homes. They still startled me, as if someone had slipped in during the night and set them all up.

Dad had been talking about some work they'd done around the house, "thanks to you and John," he would always say. After my mother retired, we offered to help finance a move and my parents checked out various parts of the country. After an exhaustive search, they concluded there was no place like home, so we gave them a loan instead to make repairs and improvements. Pulling into the drive, Dad quoted statistics about the heating capabilities of the house due to the new furnace and insulation. And the aluminum siding would last longer than they would! So it's come to this, I thought. I'd always hated aluminum siding, and now I was responsible for its yellow envelopment of my parents' home. And it would last longer than they would! Oh well, actually it looked good. If only I didn't know it was aluminum . . .

My mother welcomed us at the door. Glancing around I could tell my parents had already spent a good deal of time and thought getting things ready for Sunday. The dining room table was loaded with dishes, candles, and accessories for the brunch. From the kitchen I looked out back. Off to the side was a pile of dirt and two trees waiting to be planted. "They're cypress trees, their sprigs are used as symbols for mourning. They're supposed to be good sturdy trees. We thought cypress was a good choice for John," my mother said, giving me a hug. "I don't know that it's so appropriate for Liz," she admitted, then added, "Well, they're pretty trees and that's like Liz."

"Liz was strong, too," I said.

My father entered the kitchen. "I had the trees put in their holes, but we'll finish the planting on Sunday. I thought it was too much to dig the holes when everyone was here. I hope you don't mind." He showed me two gold-plated markers he'd had made up with Liz and John's names on them.

"They're nice, Dad, I think that'll be fine." I returned my gaze to the trees. "Have you selected which tree is which?"

"Well, I think the one on the left is John's," my mother offered.

"Me, too." I smiled. It was the tree with the bigger trunk, and it was a little shorter than the other. That was the way it should be.

As I unpacked, I remembered our move to Wheaton on a rainy day in early spring. The yard was extremely muddy, a rusty colored, claylike mud. The property had been part of a cornfield, there were no trees or bushes whatsoever. The house was much smaller than the one we'd left and the more the movers carried in the tinier it looked. I was cold and in the way. I was six years old.

The farmland our property was on had been originally owned by the Wiesbrocks. John Wiesbrock and his family were the ones we'd run to for some butter, a cup of milk, or help—like removing a mouse from a trap—when my father was out of town. They were a good old-fashioned Catholic family with five healthy and attractive kids. David, a year older than I, was one of my best friends throughout grade school. He once kissed me on a dare: he chased me around the yard, wrestled me to the ground, and sat on my belly while holding my arms in order to plant the triumphant kiss. But generally our relationship was innocent, one of endless hours of play. We made rafts for the pond at the farm, built forts in the hay, and had a tree house in his backyard. On summer nights we'd run behind the truck that sprayed for bugs; our parents told us not to, but it was hard to resist playing in the clouds of smoke the truck left behind. I imagined it was a peek at what heaven must be like.

We often played with David's cousin, Shelly. The Al Wiesbrock family lived about a quarter-mile down the road, right next to the grade school. Wiesbrook School was a two-room schoolhouse, three grades in each room. Shelly and I were in the same class, and for several years shared a fascination with horses, she more than I, but then she actually had a horse. I can remember all three of us, David, Shelly, and I, trying to ride her horse, Jeannie, at once. We tied a blanket to her back with a rope around her middle (Indian-style!), stood her next to the stall so we could climb on, and away we went. Well, Jeannie started to trot, and we slid off in unison, each holding on to the one in front—just the way Mo, Larry, and Curly would fall off a horse!

My thoughts returned to the house and my family. The guest room was originally Pat and Pam's bedroom. Since they were only a year apart they always shared a room, each wishing she could have a private bedroom while I wished I could share one. I always thought of my room as small, until I moved to New York and discovered how small a bedroom could be. Rob was relegated to the semi-basement of the tri-level house. It was humid and dark, and for a number of years, flooded after a big rain. Still, it felt like an apartment because it had a door to the outside, which made it attractive to me during my teenage years. As a high-school senior I was finally allowed to move downstairs. I imagined I would sneak out and meet John at night, but never did.

Now the extra bedrooms had been taken over by my mother's rare books and first editions. Since her retirement, she had begun a small book business, which didn't seem so small anymore. Makeshift bookshelves lined the walls and desks and files had replaced the beds and dressers. Mom had become my greatest source for research material, and I enjoyed browsing through her collection.

I felt good, excited actually, about being home. My parents seemed to be doing well, and my sisters and brother were all coming for Sunday; the whole family would be home, although briefly, for the first time in at least twenty years.

That night I watched TV in my bedroom. I'd had a strong desire to see John all day and decided to watch "SNL." Steve Martin was host, and I settled back to enjoy the show. After about fifteen minutes, however, I was upset that John wasn't on yet. (The reruns were an hour, edited from the hour-and-a-half live version.) When the show ended, and John hadn't been on, I was furious, insulted; they'd edited him out! I was all worked up. *Oh, no! The network is cutting John out of all the shows!* Then just as suddenly I realized that Danny hadn't been on either; the rerun was from the fifth year of "SNL," after John and Danny had left. I realized I was reacting the way John would have if one of his scenes had been cut from a live show. Well, I reasoned, I was frustrated because I wanted to see John and hadn't. I thought a glass of warm milk might help me relax.

Cup in hand, I wandered the downstairs. The house was a good size for my parents. How in the world had six of us ever lived here? The kitchen had been redone recently and now the sink was under a window overlooking the backyard. I remembered when the Vincens had moved in. I was thrilled to learn they had a teenage girl, nearly ecstatic to discover she was my age. I'd been feeling very isolated by the distance we lived from the junior high, many of my new friends lived within walking distance of school, and were able to take part in afterschool activities or go home together and hang out. The summer after seventh grade was especially miserable because I'd often been stuck at home alone. I ran down the road to meet the new girl, worrying, what if she's a creep?

Debbie was wonderful. We became fast friends, sharing our intimate secrets and dreams and making each other laugh. I was deeply entrenched in the social scene in school, but Debbie seemed beyond it. Still, she was quickly accepted by my peers and became one of us. We were the socialites, the ones who were supposed to have it all. Most of my other girl friends were cheerleaders. Debbie and I seemed to be the only ones who felt foolish trying to smile on cue and be peppy. We were both elected to student council, and I was constantly inventing projects and dragging her into them. When I started to fool around with alcohol, Debbie didn't understand the allure. Her rejection of my involvement (along with John's) helped pull me away from it.

The end of our sophomore year I ran for class president and convinced Debbie to run for vice president. We both won. When we returned our junior year I imagined we would run our class. And in many ways, we did.

Debbie was dating Alan, who was twenty, which caused problems at home; she often wasn't allowed to see him. John was away at school, and I didn't date other boys, so that left us more time to spend together. Talk of college threatened to separate us. Debbie wanted to go to Berkeley or an Eastern school, she was definitely getting out of the Midwest. I didn't feel strongly about where I went, I just wanted to be close to John. But that seemed a long way off. Then life was school, parties, and fun. We were the Class of 1969 and I felt there was something new and special about the times and about us.

At the semester, I ran for vice president of the school. I won, thereby vacating my class president position, which Debbie took over. But she was sick a lot that semester and her family moved to a new house, about two miles away. One day I stopped there on my way home from work and got bad news: Debbie wouldn't be going to Wheaton Central next year. I was stunned, I couldn't believe my ears as she explained, "because Alan and I are getting married." I don't remember how I responded. How should a child respond when her friend drops such news? I'm sure I smiled and acted as if this were great. I knew it meant she was pregnant; there had been rumors, but I never listened, they just made me angry. I do remember driving home, at breakneck speed, crying, reacting as if I'd just been jilted by a lover. It was, I guess, the first time my heart was broken.

Debbie married in June 1968. The most memorable thing about the wedding was a row of crying teenage girls. I wanted to continue as her best friend, and told myself I could. But our lives were separated first by miles and then by degrees. I saw her from time to time, but she and Alan moved around a lot. Once when we were in San Francisco for a Blues Brothers show, I took her in a limousine on a shopping tour for a porkpie hat for "Jake." We had fun that day, just the two of us again. The last time I saw her she was back in the Wheaton area. She'd just had another baby, her fourth or fifth, and talked about going back to school when the baby was older. I hadn't heard from her since.

My father came into the kitchen, surprised to find me up. He'd fallen asleep in his recliner in front of the TV. "I woke up and wondered why the lights were on." One of my father's missions in life is to make sure lights are never left on if no one's in the room.

"I'll just be a little longer," I said.

"Do whatever you want. Just rinse out your cup and leave it in the sink when you're finished." My father must have said this to me a million times in my life, so whenever I finished using a dish, I heard him say, "Rinse it now, it makes it so much easier to wash later."

"Okay, goodnight, Dad."

"Goodnight, honey. Don't forget to turn out the lights."

Agnes Belushi's condo is about forty minutes from my parents, and since I was just in town for the weekend, I said I could only come by briefly. I was seeing her Sunday and only agreed to the visit because it seemed important to her. Agnes hadn't been doing well since John's death, calling me every week or so and crying. I talked things through as best I could—listened mostly. The previous month she'd gone to Albania, and since her return sounded much better. Her dinner was for friends from the Albanian trip.

When I arrived, Agnes had just run out to the store. Her cousin Gloria, who was always called "Aunt Gloria," introduced me to everyone. I was surprised at how young the other women were, probably in their late thirties. They were all very friendly: "We're so happy to meet you," "Aggie has told us so much about you," "She likes you so much," "She's always saying, 'Judy this' and 'Judy that.'" Marie, a small older Greek woman with a very sweet disposition, just beamed at me. I was a bit embarrassed by the whole situation, and was relieved when Agnes came bustling in to break up the focus on me.

She looked good, her energy was up and she seemed younger than her years. The women kidded about how much food she had prepared and I found an unexpected girlish attitude, a camaraderie among them. It was nice to see Agnes entertaining in her own element; when we were together as the family, she was always the mom. Now she was the life of the party, and her friends clearly appreciated that side of her.

Before I left, she took me aside to look at photos her brother had taken at a family reunion in 1981. I was thrilled at how great they were and happy to see John looking good.

On the way home I thought about my reaction to the photos and my desire to see John on television the night before. I figured it meant I was entering some new phase, maybe beginning to accept that he was dead.

Rob and Pam arrived Saturday evening and Pat, with her young son Robbie, came on Sunday. We all pitched in to get things ready for the brunch, except for Pam who had business to tend. My memory of Pam in that house is of her studying, so it was in keeping. Typically, Pat was a whirlwind in the kitchen, finishing ten chores to my one. She was the one who took over much of the housekeeping when I was in grade school and Mom began working.

As I clumsily helped with the potato peeling, it felt good for our family to be pulling together. My dad saw I was behind with my peeling and said, "Let me help you with that, Sunshine." The affectionate term sparked many memories. I thought of going to Kiddieland, probably my favorite childhood memory, just me and my parents, staying out so late that Dad had to carry me to my bed. Then I would struggle to wake up so he would tell me a story, about a little girl named Judy and her trip to Kiddieland. When he got to "and she saved the pony ride for last because it was her very favorite" I'd fallen asleep on cue.

Dad decided to have a beer and my heart sank. He didn't consider his drinking a problem and never saw it as having any ill effect on his life. I felt his viewpoint was due to the insidiousness of alcohol. At any rate, it had been a problem for me. It was a subtle problem; there was no horrendous bout or abuse to point to. There is an early memory of waiting for him to come back from a nearby bar to take me somewhere. This happened repeatedly; he'd be late and I'd phone and he'd say he'd be right home. I'd watch out the window, looking to spot his car coming down the long stretch of road. That's him ... no ... Another car, another hope, another disappointment. Finally another phone call and another promise. By high school I'd learned not to ask Dad for rides. And not to ask kids over to the house, because I never knew when he might come home drunk.

I was pretty angry with my father when I was in high school. I didn't know it at the time; I didn't know it for a long time. One of my first days in therapy, when Dr. Cyborn said I'd begun to drink because I wanted my parents' attention, I thought he was wrong. If I'd wanted their attention, then why did I do such a good job of covering it up? With time, I realized Dr. Cyborn was right. I loved my dad and was confused by my anger, probably even guilty about it. That shaped a lot of things in my life.

I also remembered a day shortly before high-school graduation when my father came home and handed me a box from a local boutique. It was a pretty pink dress. "I hope you like it, Sunshine. Driving downtown I saw it in the window and thought it looked like you." He hadn't brought me a non-holiday present since I was a little girl and I was emotional. Here I was excitedly making plans to leave home—I thought I couldn't wait to get away from my parents—yet while a part of me wanted to be independent and adult, I also wanted to be Daddy's little girl forever. I wore the dress to Honor's Day and when it was complimented I said proudly, "My dad bought it for me." Yes, the father/daughter relationship was sufficiently complicated.

I couldn't help but consider the connection in my life between John's drug use and my father's alcohol use. I remembered thinking I would never marry a man with a drinking problem. And John didn't drink, not as a young man anyway; he was straight as an arrow when we fell in love. And when drugs came on the scene, they seemed an alternative—a good one, I thought. Well, I was wrong; a drug is a drug and alcohol is just a socially acceptable one. And from my experience, I knew the man under the influence was not the real man, the true man, the one I loved. And in both cases, there was nothing I could do to help that man want to be himself.

Our guests began to arrive on schedule. There were relatives and neighbors and high-school friends, most of whom I hadn't seen for some time. Of course this meant condolences, but they weren't emphasized; there was much to catch up on and so little time. Once everyone was there, we gathered in the backyard and my father said a few words, heartfelt and to the point. I was proud of Dad for this uncharacteristic public expression of feeling. We then all put a handful of dirt into the holes and he attached the nameplates. It was a lovely autumn day, and my little nephews ran giggling around the yard. They were both dressed up and looking rather like little angels. Once inside again, Robbie Brewster showed Robert Belushi how neat it is to spit into glasses of champagne.

After an hour or two, the gathering began to break up. A high-school friend, Sue Stitt Keller, asked if we could go upstairs and talk. I was ready for a little break from the group, anyway.

We sat in my parents' room and Sue pulled out a cigarette. She was one of those people who made smoking look attrac-

tive. She lit her cigarette and with it still in her mouth as
she shook out the match, said, "Well, Jutes, what can I say?"
She took a long, thoughtful drag. "Ya know, John phoned my
parents the week before he died. Can you beat that? He
wanted to ask my dad about insurance, something to do with
what he was writing. Anyway, my mom talked to him for a
long time. She said he really sounded good, except that he
missed you." Sue laughed. "Ya know, he never really changed.
I mean, things changed a lot and all, but he always seemed
basically the same to me." I could tell that John's death was
still painful to Sue, and that it was important for her to talk
with me about him. They'd been friends since junior high
and had even gone to the College of DuPage together. She
reminisced a while, then talked about how important I was
to him. Tears welled up in my eyes. "You were his best
friend, too, and I know that it's really hard for you, and I
think you're doing great . . . Am I upsetting you?" she reached
for the ashtray.

"No, that's all right," I said, grabbing a Kleenex.

She laughed again. "You know what my mother said after
she heard? Well, she started crying, ya know, and when she
stopped she said . . ." Sue imitated her mother, nearly hysterical: " 'I feel so bad for yelling at Judy!' " We both laughed
at this reference to an incident which had taken place over
twelve years before. Sue settled back in her chair and took
another long draw on her cigarette. "What can I say, Jutes?"
she said, reflecting. "Only the good die young."

Deep in sleep, I realized the phone was ringing and woke
abruptly. For a moment, I wasn't sure where I was. My
parents' house? No, ah! My apartment in New York. I'd
returned late last night. I found the phone under a pillow.

"Hi, Judy. It's Woodward." I sat up and made an effort to
sound alert. "I'm off to L.A. Monday," he announced. He had
several appointments set up, and as he went over them with
me I began to have a feeling that he was talking to so broad
a group of people that he was getting off the track. But his
calm, reassuring manner cooled my concerns.

I asked Bob if he had read an article the *Soho News* had
run the week after John's death. I'd just read it, and was

upset by the derogatory tone. Bob was quick to dismiss the article as "bull." He also referred to some important information he'd dug up concerning drugs. "I'm going to be doing a lot of underground work while I'm out there," he confided. "So if I'm found floating somewhere . . ." He let the sentence dangle, the implications being clear.

I hung up the phone, wondering if this trail were really that dangerous. Sue's words popped into my mind: *Only the good die young.* Only the good die young? What the hell was that supposed to mean, anyway? I'd always thought that a dumb sentiment. Only the dumb die young. No, that wasn't fair, either. It had nothing to do with being good or bad or smart or dumb. Only the . . . young . . . die young. That was it. Only the young.

Chapter 17

LOVE FOREVER

OCTOBER 20

*I*t had been on my mind for a while. I thought many times about going through my old letters, but knew I wasn't strong enough. Now I needed some contact with John, and his letters were a link, his voice. I felt ready.

After double-locking the front doors, I carried the brief-case of letters into the sound room. The service would answer the phone. There would be no interruptions.

I wanted to begin at the beginning and my letters were somewhat organized, bound by ribbons into groups. The ones from Indiana, where John did summer stock after graduating from high school, were the first "official" letters he ever sent me. I slid them out from the embrace of the faded pink sash and began to read.

June 25 (1967)
Dear Jutes,

Well, here it is 20 minutes to 10 and we're going through the reading for our first play. I don't have a real big part in this one, I play a general. The play is pretty lousy anyway, but I hope I get better parts so you can come to see me. We've been working like slaves. I'm building things, racks, stairs, the whole bit. I'm a real carpenter. I don't have much time to do things besides work. I can't believe it here, there is no supervision at all. At night every time I do something I always expect some adult to say "Hey kid you can't do that!" but no one cares. It's really great, I guess.

I haven't decided whether I like this place or not. It's okay, I guess. The directors are great and the members of the cast are okay.

I'm sending $20 with this letter (for you to save for me) because I'm spending money like crazy. The pipes broke on my cycle so I'll need money to fix it. The play is so lousy all the people who are reading are laughing at the stupid lines. There are 13 people in the room and I'm the only one writing a letter. I guess I'm lonely.

This is really Hicksville USA. I can't believe it. When I ride my bike in town the local yocals think I'm a Hell's Angel. They look at us like we're animals in a zoo someone let out. (dumb sentence)

I'm going to call you after I write this letter. It's kind of bad timing but I won't have time later. We have to be ready to work by 9:00 A.M. I have to go into town to get some change to call you. We have a pay phone.

I must be crazy to miss you so much, it's only Sunday. Judy, will you send me Mr. Payne's address if I didn't tell you on the phone. It's about time for my lousy part to come, so I'll have to end this letter. We have a director here who tells really stupid jokes so I'll conclude with this: What causes forest fires? Answer: Trees

Love, XOXOXOXOXOXOXOXOXO John

June 28, 1967
Dear Judith,

We are now rehearsing for "John Loves Mary" in the theater. I've got a good part in a bad show. In "Anne of 1000 Days" I play Cardinal Wolsey . . . a real good part. Maybe you can come to see that. I got your first letter . . . I got a big kick out of it. I was in a very depressed mood when I got it. It cheered me up. Sometimes I hate it here. . . .

I think about you day and night, I think about the fun we had. I miss you, Judy, as a person. I'll tell you something I never said before. I've never felt this way about another girl. I even like the way you get mad at me. Well, I guess it sounds a little stupid, you know how emotional I am sometimes. I ride my cycle alone at night and just think. Well, you know what they say, "absence makes the heart grow fonder." Well, absence makes my heart hurt for you (What?) I'll just go babbling on.

I have to shave off my beard for "John Loves Mary," but I'll take a picture and send it to you. We've really been working hard. One of my queer (fem) roommates is a good guy. This other cat, Tom Long, is a real good guy. . . . I like it here sometimes.

I love you more each day. I love you with all my being. I'll leave you with the words of Shakespeare, "Function is smothered in sunrise."

Love, John

A lonely July 8 Saturday Night 1967 AD
Dear Jutes,

I'm listening to the Beatles album, Sergeant Pepper. Another kid and I bought it. Whenever I hear it, I think of you, especially, "A Little Help From My Friends." Now I'm in my dressing room. I just finished putting my makeup on and am waiting for the show to begin. It's the last night of "John Loves Mary" and I'm kind of glad to see it over. We got some reviews from the papers. I got some good ones. Two papers said I was "superb." I'll send some to you when I get them. It's too bad you can't come to see "Ten Little Indians." It's a great mystery by Agatha Christie.

Well, I guess I better tell you, now, Judy, but I hope you won't try it because John did and I hope you don't think I'm a hypocrite because I want you to stop [smoking cigarettes]. I do, and I don't want you to drink, either, but I really must be in love to tell you this because most cats wouldn't say anything to anyone, especially his girlfriend, but maybe you won't care, I don't know. But I smoked pot the other night. It's really something. It is better than being drunk and doesn't do any physical harm to you. I might take it again, but I don't know. Believe it or not, I took it mostly because I missed you so much and I'm going crazy here. I was high when I called you Thursday. I didn't want to tell you then, but my conscience bothered me so much I decided to tell you, love. Please, I know you won't tell anyone, because it can lead to bad talk about goodie John Belu. There I told you. Are you satisfied? You must be in my head somewhere telling me what to do. You drive me nuts. Please tell me what you think, because, well, never mind . . .

Write when you can my sweet,

All my love, John

P.S. I'm growing my beard again.

July 12, 1967
Dear Judy,

I got two letters today from you and that brought me out of a long period of depression. I didn't hear from you for four miserable days. If I didn't get one from you today, I was going to "Strawberry Fields Forever" but I won't now.

Yesterday was the opening of "Anne of a Thousand Days." The play went real well and afterwards everyone wanted to go out and get drunk, but since I'm on a diet and don't like to drink, I didn't go. I didn't get to sleep until about 5 A.M. This place is the most depressing place in the world at night. Two other guys and I shot the bull all night. We talked about our philosophies of life. We decided life scares the shit out of all of us. If I didn't love you I don't know what I'd do.

I work out everyday and everyone else wants to work out with me. We're rehearsing now, so I must sign off.

Love, John

July 29
Dear Jewdy, Judie, Judi, Jute, Jutes, cupcake,

. . . You won't believe what just happened. I'm sitting on the porch writing and this guys drives up and introduces himself. He started talking to me and this other kid about going to church and God. Then he pulled out the *Layman's Bible* and asked me how much I thought it was worth. I said about seven or eight dollars. He said "Well, a lot of people guess more, it costs $12.50." He was a nice guy, but I just couldn't buy it. That was about the most exciting thing that's happened to me since I've been here.

. . . I'll call Mr. Payne soon and ask him to call you. Why don't you stop over there some night and talk to him . . . he'll tell you the arrangements on coming here with them. You can use as much money as you need of mine to come here.

I've got to get back to my lines so I must say good-bye for now, baby blue.

Your Hippie Dippie Boyfriend, John

Tears streaked my face, but I was most definitely enchanted. I was reminded with every page how our love grew through such communications, what things strengthened and bonded us. I wanted more. In a red ribbon were the letters John had sent when he went to Wisconsin State University at Whitewater. I read on.

September 11, 1967
Dear Judy,

I am now waiting for my first college class to begin. P.E. The teacher isn't here yet, so I'll write until he comes. I received your 3 beautiful letters. After I read them I sort of "floated" out of the room. I'm sorry I didn't write more often, but I thought you wanted it that way. I really felt depressed the first week, not that I don't like school, I do, just being away from you again. I didn't want to feel like I did this summer. I was miserable without you.

I didn't think you wanted my ring since when I came back I only saw you wear it about two or three times. I love you, Judy, I really do, so much. I'll love you until the cows come home (?). Well, anyway, I'll always love you.

College life so far is not bad. All the freshmen had to read a book the first week. I think I'm the only one on my floor that read it and understood it. (Class just started.)

I'm going to join the Karate Club this semester. It only costs $2.00 fee. Someday you'll be a beautiful mature woman. And every time I come home I get fatter and fatter, and someday I'll grow up to be a mature fat man. . . .

Well, it's been about 3 hours since I wrote anything. I love you and always will. See you October 13.

Love John

January 24, 1968
Dear Judy,

This morning I woke up to the crashing of snowflakes against my window. What lousy stupid Wisconsin Weather. I'm in my dorm now, I have to finish a 300 page book by tomorrow and I've got about 150 pages to go. I've got a headache, I think it's from not eating. I'm starting to lose weight again, but I'd have to lose about 30 pounds before you'd notice. . . .

I can't wait until the summer so I can spend more time with you. Today is only Wednesday and it seems so long since I've seen your beautiful face. I just wrote a poem. I haven't written one for a long time. It has no title, but it was inspired by you.

I wander through the dark forest of my mind
In search of something I must find
There is no purpose to this futile strife
To find the answer of what should be life
The bountiful monotony of this petty place
Is broken by an understanding face
For there the answer lies
The answer to my cries
      I am forever yours and yours alone
          John Keats Belushi

February 1, 1968
Dear Judy,

I'm in my theater class now and a lot of fruits are arguing about "what is art" which no one can explain. We have rehearsal every night. I'll write the rest of the letter when I get back to the dorm because I have to listen.

The play is going well. My director said I should keep the beard for the play. I guess a lot of people tried out for the play, but only three boys made it and I'm the only freshman. It should be a good play because there are few people in the cast and we've got an excellent director.

I've been dreaming a lot lately. Last night I dreamed I was going to join the navy with Craig Baker and Lorzel because you didn't love me anymore but I backed out at the last second because I wanted to go to school. It was real spooky.

I got this new Bob Dylan album, it's really good. It's called "John Wesley Harding." I'm listening to it now. I'm not sure if I'll be able to come home to see you because I'm in every act in the play and rehearsal starts at 1:00 P.M. Saturday afternoon. . . . I love you.

Love, John

(No Date)

Dear Judy,

It's 9:00 A.M. Thursday, I haven't been asleep all night. I can't sleep, Judy. I'm tired, but I can't sleep. I can't get you out of my mind. Ok—now I'm sorry I hung up the phone on you, it was very rude. I almost broke it off I was so uptight. I just couldn't take it. I asked you, I pleaded with you not to be upset with me, and all you could say was "Well, I guess it's all right," in a very complacent tone. BOOOOOM!!! I just exploded. I don't know what came over me, I don't usually do things like that and hope I'll never do it again.

I'll try to explain something to you. I'm not sure of anything right now in this whole damn fucked-up world. The only thing I was sure of is your love for me. This is something I know is real. You know, one of my faults is that I get too emotional, I guess. Another flaw in my character is that I love you so much. These are two of many. So when I hear you talk like that to me something goes click and I go nuts.

I'm kind of a nutty guy I think. Sometimes I like to grow my hair real long and my beard real long and smoke pot and cigarettes and eat a lot and other stupid things. Now don't you think I'm completely dependent on what you say at all times, but you kind of keep me down to earth. I quit smoking because it's bad for me and it made you happy. I cut my hair for you and I'll stop smoking pot and go on a diet for you *and* me. I will, it just takes time. I told you on the phone that all I wanted to do was make you happy and I do. Our relationship during this past year and a half has been one of helping each other. I know I'm emotional enough for the both of us and I know you're concerned about me, but please, as Bob Dylan says, "Why don't you show it?" I mean when I talk to you on the phone—well forget it, I don't know what I'm saying.

Don't think this is a letter of complete apology because I don't think that I should be the one to apologize all the time. I hope this letter clears a few things up. I don't know, maybe you'll hate me by the time you get this letter, but I just couldn't call again. SO—I'll apologize halfway—OK? I really hope you don't misunderstand this letter. Please, when you finish reading this messed up letter write me and tell me how you really feel. I need it. WRITE!!

Love, Your Thing

Report card for this letter:

Neatness	F
Spelling	D
Apology	C
Attitude	B
Love for Judy	A+ + + + + + + +

(John has been a good boy! from, all the girls at WSUW)

Today
(No Date)
All the way with R.F.K.
All the way with J.V.J.
Dear Judy,

I'm sitting in the student union now with my sunglasses on, looking cool. Last night I finished off that bottle of vodka with Grady to celebrate Johnson not running for president. Our next president should be Bobby Kennedy. I like Bobby Kennedy. I think he should be our next president no matter what your mother says. I might not get drafted now.

I've got a test today. Not much is happening. I'll see you Friday night. I must get to class. I LOVE YOU.

Love, John

(No Date)
Dear Judy,

Well how is my sweet little girl today? We started the play tonight. It went fairly well. You know something? I love you. Back to the play. I forgot a line in the play and we left out a whole page. The audience liked the play I think. . . .

I went to Madison to see a "happening," a type of theater where the audience participates. Out of 300 people I was nominated for President of the United States and had to make a speech. It was really strange, but interesting. It was a type of improvisational existential-istic "thing." I'm reading a book and some plays about existentialism. It's really fascinating. I'm starting to understand it, I think. As soon as I find out what it is, I'll tell you.

I'm getting an A in English and that's no bull. The teacher really likes me and I do a lot of extra credit work.

I miss you so much I can't stand it. I wish you could have come to see me but we'll spend the rest of our lives together. . . . Well, lover, I must go to bed now and have sweet dreams about you.

Love John

May 14, 1968
Dear Judy,

I've done a lot of thinking these last few days and came to some conclusions. Do you remember Mike? He broke up with his girl and dropped acid and speed and didn't go to class and really messed himself up. I'll *never* drop acid. I was thinking maybe I would, but I know what it's done to some friends of mine and it's bad news.

I don't know if I can explain how I feel now because I'm not sure myself. One thing I am sure of is that if it wasn't for you I'd be a mental and physical wreck and you're the most wonderful thing that's ever happened to me. I guess I'm going through what they call an "identity crisis." You know, who am I? What do I want to be? etc. Well, I've been searching and trying things, accepting and rejecting, the whole bit to find out who John Belushi is. I don't mean to alarm you in any way about me. It's just that I want to talk to someone and no one is here to listen. I'd rather talk to you, because I think you're one person who really understands me. Grass isn't really that great. It's ok and I'll smoke it once in a while, but some people on this campus make it a way of life. All this plastic hippy shit gets me down. You're right about a lot of things, but I've got to find things out for myself. I could go through life like [names deleted] and accept things the way they are, without finding out the truth about them. This type of person doesn't care and doesn't question, but they also have simple ideas. Do you see what I'm trying to say?

We gave our "happening" yesterday. I worked Sunday until 7:00, then got to school (my mother gave me $20) and worked on the project until . . . 2:30 . . . [only] had 3 hours sleep, [then] went to set things up for the "Happening." . . . The teacher loved it, some of the more hip kids liked it and the stupid ones didn't know what was happening.

If we're going to double to the prom with Dan and Steph, I've got to make arrangements. I'll call you this Thursday. I love you, miss you, and you're the most beautiful girl in the world.

        Love, your ex-hippy boyfriend, Master John
P.S. I'm sending you some pictures we used in our "happening." We flashed them on a screen to music and poetry.

(No Date)
Dear Judy,
    I think I made [my future with pot] quite clear.

[Although] you sent me the article it seems you did not read it carefully. I'm sending you a part to read again. You've implied I'm an unpatriotic, pot smoking anarchist. This summer I want you to read Mary McCarthy's *Vietnam*. Your mother will know who she is, she is a fine writer.

I often hear you complain about how your student government can't do anything. In college we are supposed to be adults and are treated like high school freshmen. Democracy is no good unless it is dangerous. We live in a country where we can speak out about what's wrong about the country *to make it a better place.* I try to get involved with issues and *facts.* Your own sister was a member of the so-called most radical student group, the SDS. Maybe you and a lot of people would like it if I didn't care about anything and was a frat rat who only thought about the next beer party and [felt that] all that "brotherhood" crap and being childish were more important than their own country. I don't agree with *many* of the riots on campus. Judy, you can't believe all you read about it. The ones with a purpose which help the school, students, and country are the ones I'm in favor of.

This country was founded by a *minority* of the people who wanted independence. I want you to *read* more about *both* sides of the issues. You will be involved in a couple of years with this problem, not your parents. If you want to sit back and do nothing and not to even try to find out what is right or wrong, then I'm much more of a patriotic American than you. I want this country to be a better place for *our* children to live in. Enough said?

I'll call you tonight, I'd love you if you were a communist or a John Bircher. There are no politics in love. No more letters about issues, just love letters.

Love, John

It was late and I was tired and knew I should stop reading. Each letter was another memory, and I wanted to be able to correct every wrong thought or move I ever made. Everything seemed so innocent then, and look where it had led us.

No, I couldn't stop now, there was no stopping until I'd read them all. The bundle in the blue ribbon were written during my college days at the University of Illinois. John was in his second year at the College of DuPage and living in Wheaton.

September 11, 1969
Dearest Judy,

You've only been gone 4 days and I'm almost out of my mind with misery. Writing helps some, but being near you or talking with you would be better. . . .

It's strange, much stranger than when we've been apart before. I've dreaded the thought of you going away to college for three years and now you are really gone. When you left you took a part of me with you, so will you please send my right foot back?

I helped the Paynes put down their new rug and fixed the bike. I now have a Sears 3-speed racer and sore legs. It should be good exercise.

I miss you so very much.

John

September
Dear Jutes,

I'm writing you from my parents' house. We worked overtime today so I came here to wash my clothes and see my mother. Last night I spent the night at Payne's. . . . Dan asked me if I ever wanted to be a coach. I said at one time, a long time ago I did, but I grew out of it. I also wanted to be a professional drummer in a marching band, I told him, but I grew out of that, too. He feels responsible for getting me involved with theater and thought I might want to have a secure job, like coaching. I could never be a coach for long. The administration would never like my attitude.

I have to go to bed now. Please write. . . . You're the best friend I've ever had.

Love, John XXX

October
Dear Judy,

I'm writing this letter at a party. . . . I'm coming this

weekend to see you. Sounds like a lot is going on. . . . If you can, BUY the new Beatles album, *Abby Road*—it's really fantastic. I'll finish this letter when I get back home.

I'm home. . . . Now, about your not studying and flunking your French test. It's about time I gave you some advice from experience. I think getting involved in the activities is a fantastic thing, and I'll try to be there the 10th. But if it interferes with your studying and [means you have to] cut classes (other than the 15th) then limit your activities. That was one of the reasons I messed up at Whitewater. DON'T CUT CLASSES. I did and fucked up. The other reason I had a hard time was YOU. I don't blame you, because I couldn't stop thinking about you, seeing you, writing you, missing you, and loving you. I couldn't do anything and that's called LOVE. BUT the only way either of us will be able to have peace of mind is if we both have *trust* in each other. I was messed up the first week you were gone, but after seeing you I knew how much you loved me and it helped get my head together.

I know I'm telling you a lot of things you are aware of. I have to tell you these things because they happened to me and I don't want them to happen to you. If we get married some day, we'll be together all the time for a *very* long time. I'll never forgive myself if I cause you to flunk out of school. I may be making too much out of this and maybe not, but I have to be as honest as I can be. That's the only way we can make it. Don't do too much dope. I smoked every day (almost) at Whitewater. It makes you sleepy and it will be hard to study. Try to keep up with your work, if you fall behind, see your prof. I guess that's all I can think of right now.

Whenever you feel super lonely or need some help, *please* don't hesitate to call me at any time collect. If I'm not here I'll get the message and call you.

Judy, I think about you because I know how you feel. College is not all studying (unless you fall behind), it's involvement and fun. Stay active.

I miss you and hope you understand why I wrote what I did. Stay as beautiful as you are. Don't worry about writing, just write when you can. I love every part of you.

Love forever, John

(No Date)

MY LIFE STORY

I was born in Chicago in 1949. I was a brilliant child. I loved to watch Creative Cookery with Franswa Pope on television. He also had his son, David, on his show. David didn't have an accent like his father. They were French, I think.

Chicago was a nice place to live, so I'm told. When you are a kid, any place is nice. Anyone could swim in the public pool for free. The pool and the park were a half a block away. Now the park cut down all the bushes because people would get mugged.

I used to wear a baseball uniform, I didn't know why, someone gave it to me and I wore it. I wore a Sox uniform and a Cubs hat. People laughed at me because of it. I would laugh with them not knowing why.

We had a phone you could pick up and the operator would say "number please." I called my mother one time when she was in the hospital having my brother. All I told the operator was that I wanted to talk to my mother. Everyone thought it was very cute. I still don't know how I managed it.

We moved out of Chicago when I was six years old to Wheaton. I didn't like it at first because it had a lot of mosquitoes. I went to first grade on the back of a patrol girl's bike. She lived across the street. I had the most fun in school when we would finger paint. Then I got older and died.

THE END

February 17, 1970
Dear Judy,

This is the second letter I've [written] to you this week, but I lost the first one. . . .

Saturday there's going to be a big demonstration in Chicago for the trial [the Chicago Seven], maybe you could come to Chicago Saturday and Sunday and we could stay with your brother? Good idea? If you don't come, I'll be there [U. of I.] Saturday night if I've got the money. I might not have a ride or the money, if not, I'll swim to your dorm room, unless the rain freezes the water. I'll have to have my blood pressure checked Thursday, Friday, and Saturday [for the draft]. Your brother invited me to stay with him, he's really a good guy, so is your sister-in-law, lovely Pat.

Here's a new anti-draft chant:

Rah Rah Rah Rud Resher
Let's all get that high blood pressure!

I love you very prodigiously. You are a colossal beauty and I dig the hell out of you.

I dig you in the morning
I dig you at night
I dig you in the afternoon
I dig you when we fight
I just can't stop digging you baby
OOO-WA

Love, affection, passion,
liking, fondness, attraction,
flames and rapture, John

(No Date)
Dearest Judy,

I've been thinking about where to go to school next semester, and I've just about made up my mind that if I'm accepted, I'll go to Circle.... We've gone through a lot of changes and separation, and we've made it through each time, loving each other more. If we can handle this *last* separation, we could rule the world with our love. It will be tough for both of us, but as long as we stay "both of us" we're all right. We live with other people around us, but for me there is no other person as important as you.

Lovingly yours, John

During the summer of 1970 John spent three weeks hitch-hiking around the West in search of America—and some friends who were draft dodgers, living in Spokane. He wanted

me to go with him, but the idea of telling my parents I was
leaving the summer job at my mother's office in order to
thumb around the country with my boyfriend was still beyond
me. We argued about it and John decided he "had to do it
anyway." The night before he left I gave him a pair of
aviator sunglasses as a going-away present.

Monday Night June 22
Dear Judy,

I'm in the most beautiful area of the world tonight. I'm
in Moorcroft, Wyoming. I'm staying with a *real* cowboy. I
may never leave this place—well, I will leave, but only
to return to you. . . . This is really more beautiful than
Colorado, if it's possible, and even more wild than the
field next to Dave and Ingrid's house. I've seen antelope
walking around wild sheep. The cowboy gave me a ride
from Cheyenne to Moorcroft, fed me and I got to take a
shower finally. . . . Tomorrow morning the cowboy (with
boots and a cowboy hat) told me I could go to a city about
ten miles from here and get a ride to Spokane on a U.S.
Mail truck. I've got $5.00 left and I haven't lost my
sunglasses yet, but I did lose 2 canteens in two days, or
else I'd have more money. I love you and miss you. I love
this beautiful country, too, but I love you more than all
the mountains and antelope in the world.

Love, John

June 23
Dear Jutes,

This is just too much. I'm riding in a bus now headed
for Spokane. It's called ELF (Earth Liberation Front).
They support alternate lifestyles. They have a lot of
these crossing the country, and a ranch in Washington.
It's hard to write. We're going to spend the night in
Yellowstone. Every time I see something new, I clap my
hands and say, "I do believe in Judy," then wait for you
to appear.

I was stopped twice by cops in Wyoming and they were
really good people. One state trooper outside Buffalo,
Wyoming, checked my I.D. (That's all they do, just in

case you get killed they want to know who you are) and talked to me for about 20 minutes. And hitchhiking's illegal as hell in that state.

I walk a lot in the 100 degree heat, it's not too bad but I would have gone blind without the sunglasses. . . . Write now, because I'll be in Spokane soon.

Miss you, John

(No Date)
Dearest Judy,

Well, I did it again . . . I forgot to call. I didn't really forget, only I remembered at 12:30 A.M. whereupon I immediately dashed to the nearest phone . . . but then I thought I might make your parents mad calling collect so late. Now I can't sleep until I talk to you. . . .

This trip is really getting me to see things in perspective, and how. I want to come home as soon as I can. . . . I got my official 1-Y classification, so I can't fool around any more. Haircut, job, school, living with you forever, the works.

We went to Canada Saturday and Sunday, where a girl from Wheaton and her husband live in a log cabin. The function of a mosquito is to keep people out of the woods. There were billions all over all the time. The water and air are clean and it's beautiful from the inside of mosquito netting. I'll tell you all about it when I get back, soon.

Love, A man called John

I was exhausted now, but didn't want the letters to end. I had been sitting on the floor reading for hours and my body was stiff and achy. I looked in my case for the next batch, but they weren't there. I knew there were more. I shuffled through some loose papers at the bottom, notes I had held on to. I pulled them out. The first was something John wrote during his Second City days, upon returning from a short road tour. At the time we had our first kitten, the first Whisper.

July 18 (1972)
Well I'm awake and happy, you are next to me. Close. There are so many things I want to say. Happiness is letting Whisper attack my toes so she won't wake you.

Now that I'm awake I can say, I love you, with a clear head, and say, Wow! Please God help me and Judy, I need her strength so often, sometimes I pull a muscle in my brain. I FEEL FREE and lucky. . . . Ready for a short poem?

> To be home again is warm
> Life and Fun on
> The run
> Play with me friend
> Feel with me

My thinking is still a little spaced, but coming in for a smooth landing.

I kissed you many times while you lay next to me. I wouldn't trade that for all the fame, money, or power in the world.

> I'm smiling a lot now. The feeling is you. . . .
> How much do I love you? A bushel and a boo.
> To sleep to live to die, can be summed up
> with a sigh. I'm home again.
> Love
> Smile when you think of me

And another note from "SNL" days. I recognized this from early 1979, when John first began to earnestly try to quit cocaine.

Judy, I'm afraid of myself because of what I'm capable of doing to you. If I was the kind of person I want to be, at least I say I want to be, then why do I hurt you? Is it because no one can *be* that person? Do I kid myself? When I fail, who am I? . . .

I want to take care of you, but I feel I'm not capable. The most difficult thing to deal with is disappointing you or finding myself unable to help you. When I'm sick, you help. When you are [sick], I freak. Is it because I feel helpless. What can I do? Hide in . . . drugs?

Please, Please, Please don't think I'm going back to my old pattern. I may have slipped a patch, but not a pattern. What I really want is forgiveness that may not be deserved.

I'm going to beat this thing, God damn it! I know I can now. I may cause you pain, but I love you. You are my soul, my heart, my eyes to this life. This may happen again. Whatever it is, I can only say I'll try with all my heart, which may not be enough. And if that is the case I respect your decision to live your life without the pain and confusion I bring to it. Don't worry about me if you decide it's not worth it and I won't worry about you. You're my *wife*. I'll do what I can to keep you.

I finally had had enough. Memories had flowed as easily as tears, and for a time, both felt good. The obsession took over, and I read with the insatiable curiosity of a madwoman on an emotional binge, caught up in an unfolding drama. But I already knew the end to this story, and it was uncomfortably close.

I realized how wasted I was. I was empty, tired, I could barely unfold my legs to stand up. I stood motionless for a moment. I needed fresh air. The sound room door's snug fit held for a second, then opened with a "whoosh" into early morning sunlight. Dispiritedly I took the few steps to the bathroom and stood in front of the mirror. I looked awful: my eyes were red and swollen with dark circles underneath, my skin pale. The image I saw reflected didn't even look like me; it was some other woman, someone older, who looked me sadly, steadily, in the eye. A short poem ran through my head: "All that was left from her lover who died/Were photos and letters and the pain inside." I silently dedicated it to the woman in the mirror.

Chapter 18

TRICK OR TREAT

LATE OCTOBER AND NOVEMBER

Woodward continued to pass along information on pretty much a weekly basis. He advised Pam that it was important we not tell anyone of his suspicions about the L.A. police because he didn't want them to be on their guard. One afternoon he told me, and later, Pam, that he had his "first solid piece of evidence" connecting Cathy Smith to the police; he had the phone record from the hotel where she'd stayed when she first left L.A. It showed several long conversations to a member of the narcotics department's home, which he said were "too long to be anything but suspicious." He also talked to Cathy Smith's lawyers about meeting with her, and they were amenable to early November in Canada.

Working on the music for the *West Heaven* video filled some of my time. Rhonda wanted to use a synthesizer to represent the wind, ocean, or stars, to add a sense of the unknown. Although we would hire a professional for the final track, I bought a small synthesizer so we could begin experimenting. With the help of two friends, we set up an old four-track tape deck and recorded our first multi-track version of Rhonda's song. Now the design of the video began to evolve more clearly in my mind.

A few days later, Steve and I cleaned and rearranged the sound room, and installed a newer, less complex four-track. Moving things around, he uncovered a box forgotten in a corner, a package for John that had arrived after his death. I'd never even opened it. Inside was a drum machine, which Steve incorporated into the music system and showed me how to operate. Once again, the music room—the vault—was fully ready for use.

The sound room quickly became the most active room in the house, between *West Heaven* rehearsals and jamming. With the synthesizer and drum machine, anyone could play, and we wailed away many nights with various friends. Steve often recorded us, then we'd play our music back and laugh. We accumulated several recordings, which we called the "vault tapes." One favorite was a song on which I sang "You can always get what you want, you just don't need it" in a modified rap style. We liked it because the music was so odd; it was very free-form, sometimes totally incongruous, then surprisingly coming back to a central theme. Steve contended it was an underground hit.

Steve was a joy to spend time with. We had a very child-like relationship, innocent and easygoing. We laughed a lot and enjoyed playing or listening to music, which I was finding to be a great escape. Steve often asked me to come to the Letterman show, but I was uncomfortable with the idea of going to 30 Rockefeller Plaza where he worked. It was the "SNL" building; I just didn't want to deal with it. But I kept telling myself I would go, soon.

I thought about asking Steve to work with us on the music for *West Heaven* but was leery of work (especially something about John) changing things between us. However, when Rhonda's first choice for co-producer fell through, I suggested him. She thought he'd be a good addition. When I asked Steve, he said yes without hesitation. We began to make plans to record our basic track (drums, bass, guitar, and keyboard) after Thanksgiving.

Work on my Ninth Street place was underway and I was scheduled to move in January. And I was vigilantly keeping diaries which I knew would become the basis for a book. On many levels it appeared I was going on with life. I was still bothered by a dark feeling, though, an underlying sense that I was not well. My thoughts were not constantly on John anymore; often several hours would pass with no conscious thought of him. Then I would suddenly remember, again, that John was gone, and find myself startled by the realization.

The Tenth Street house was still on the market and I wished someone would buy it. An image of the big, old, empty house struck me and, with Halloween in the air, it took on the aura of a haunted house. I remembered watching the West Village Halloween parade from Mitch and Wendie's place on Tenth; a great parade, with people in amazingly wild and fun costumes. A celebration took over the whole street. I decided that having a haunted house on Tenth Street was a party opportunity I couldn't pass up.

The house was decorated and readied for the festivities. Instruments were set up in the studio and a stereo system in the house. The idea of throwing a party seemed fun, but when Halloween arrived I was very nervous—I wasn't emotionally ready to be a hostess. I couldn't come up with a costume; I felt silly dressing up. My best idea was to wear my widow garb, which struck me as classic black humor, but not very funny.

I wasn't used to celebrating Halloween, even as a child I wasn't terribly successful with it. In kindergarten my mother and sisters dressed me up in an elaborate costume, gave me a globe to carry, and told me I was Christopher Columbus. I couldn't pronounce the name, and none of the kids knew who I was. Adults seemed to think my costume was great, but my class voted a little girl dressed as a bride the winner of the costume contest. In third grade, my sister Pat made me a great monkey outfit with a long tail. She was going to be an organ grinder and I'd be on a leash. Unfortunately I came down with measles, so the organ grinder went out with two bags, explaining there was a sick monkey at home. (She worked hard for her monkey.)

After grade school, I don't remember taking part in Halloween. John always shunned it, saying he wore costumes for a living, it was the last thing he wanted to do on a night off. So it was in keeping, perhaps, that I chose at the last moment to wear an oriental dress I had, and professed to be "turning Japanese."

The house was sufficiently spooky on its own, and with the decorations and weird music (largely vault tapes), it was a good atmosphere for Halloween. The sidewalks overflowed with celebrators, and typical of New York, there was a vast range of types about. I was concerned that the party would become an open house. The potential for it turning into a nightmare was real, so I asked a few friends to help with the door.

People arrived as the parade wound its way past the house. Laila was an Arab terrorist, Rhonda was Sheena, Queen of the Jungle, and Steve a professional boxer complete with trainer. Carol Klenfner, who was several months pregnant, was "Not-So-Little Bo-Peep" and Mark Lipsky came dressed as a woman, his wife dressed in a tux as his date. I have to admit I found it rather disconcerting to see my business manager dressed as a woman, and was so nonplussed that I decided to see *Mark* and ignore the costume. People looked pretty funny, especially when you scanned the group. Not everyone had costumes, but most at least wore masks. One person wore a bag over his head.

I opened the door to a man in a dirty old coat and ghoulish mask that covered his entire head, and asked who it was. I thought the muffled reply was Billy Murray, but wanted to be sure and asked some identifying questions he refused to answer. Then Laila came up and said in an Arab accent. "Let him in, he iz okay.... It's Billy," she whispered in my ear.

The man we thought was Billy proceeded to act in a very strange manner. He stood by himself a lot, or uncomfortably close to people, but never talked to anyone. He was mildly upsetting, and a couple of friends expressed concern over "the weirdo." To double check, I asked Bob Tischler, who had also known Billy for a number of years, who he thought it was. "It's Billy," he replied.

About ten minutes later, Tischler came to me and said excitedly, "That guy's not Billy! He just pulled me into a closet and I said, 'I know who you are,' and the guy said 'So what's the joke!' It wasn't Billy's voice!"

"Are you sure?" I asked, and Tischler said that when they were in the closet, he noticed that the guy was shorter than he. Billy is taller.

I found myself in a somewhat familiar situation, but with none of the familiar solutions. At the Blues Bar, John, Danny, or some other man usually handled the door, and if there was a real problem, Bill Wallace or Smokey were around to help. Now I wasn't sure what to do. If this fellow was making people uncomfortable, I thought he should either take off his mask or leave. But should I ask him? Not alone, I decided. Who would be my strongarm? Mark seemed most appropriate, and since I was ignoring the fact that he was dressed like a woman, I asked him.

Mark explained to the mystery man that he was causing some concern and it would be appreciated if he removed his mask. The fellow refused and Mark said he'd have to do so or leave. The phantom continued to give the man dressed as a bombshell a hard time as I stood by wondering what to do. "Isn't it kind of weird, you wearing a woman's dress and telling *me* to leave?" said the intruder, poking at Mark's chest.

What followed was a bit of a farce, with various people trying to kick our intruder out of the house, him gaining reentry and being kicked out again. I had a conversation with him at one point and became somewhat frightened. When I saw him the second time around, he was with a woman who claimed to be a friend of a friend, saying, "He is who you think." I blew up at her and kicked them both out.

The next day I phoned Billy to see if it had been him after all. He wasn't in, so I asked Mickey if Billy had come to the party. "No, he stayed here last night," she replied.

"He did?" I said, thinking, *I knew that guy was crazy.*

"No, he didn't," she blurted out. "I'm sorry, he told me not to tell you, but that was him. That was his idea of a Halloween trick . . ."

It had been a good trick, and after an initial reaction of feeling foolish, I realized how I'd overreacted. Of course it was Billy! And even if it had been someone from the streets, he didn't really do anything to scare me. I realized I was still not responding normally to situations.

On a plane to Chicago for a quick business trip, flipping through *Chicago Magazine,* I came across an article on Chicago actors, featuring John. At the Ambassador East, where I stayed, John's picture jumped out at me on the Pump Room wall, and at Second City, where I stopped to see friends, several photos of John were prominently displayed. At breakfast in a neighborhood restaurant, I was coincidentally seated at a table below a picture of the Blues Brothers. It was nice to see that John was still very much a Chicago celebrity.

The Blues Bar, now known as U.S. Blues, had moved down the street to a basement location. Steve Beshekas was still working on the place, but it looked great. All the original assets were there: the jukebox (the only one I know of with every Blues Brothers single), photos, Blues Brothers memorabilia, the pool table. My first night in town, Jimmy and I stopped by. There were some Second City cast members and a few others hanging out, drinking, and listening to music. Blues Brothers' songs played on the juke. It didn't seem odd that I felt John's presence in the room.

Absent mindedly I paced in the direction of the TV, my vision focused on the screen. Someone was switching channels and stopped on the news. A body in a body bag was being taken by medics through a crowd to an ambulance. For a moment I thought, This is it, this is John being removed from the Chateau. I'd never seen the news footage, but several people had made reference to how often they saw it. Then I remembered a bad joke about the clip which had filtered down to me. Michael O'Donoghue had made some flippant remark that John looked like a beached whale. Oh, this isn't it, the body's not round enough, I thought, and at that moment "March 5, 1982" was superimposed on the screen. I let out a groan, turned, and walked back toward the bar, my heart pounding madly.

It was difficult to assimilate that the image on TV was John, that underneath the canvas lay his body, that the people standing around had come to see him be removed from the Chateau. How strange that after all these months I would see this in the Blues Bar.

A few days after returning from Chicago I had a disturbing dream. John was in his casket, his hair was wrong, and he was too big for the box. The image faded and for a moment there was only darkness. Then suddenly John appeared as a ghost, but not the ethereal, spiritual type I'd fantasized in the past, this was a frightening decaying version, like Landis used in *An American Werewolf in London*. It startled me awake and I thought, why would that image appear to me now? I imagined John said I was holding him back from his next world and I had to release him. I was frightened and wrote in my diary to shake the feeling.

I had resolved that the next time someone I knew was a guest on "Letterman," I'd go up there. The opportunity presented itself a few days later when Hunter Thompson came into town to promote his new book. I felt awkward at the studio. I was glad to see Billy and Mickey Murray show up and was more comfortable sticking close to Mickey. After the show, as people gathered in the hall, I turned, and to my surprise, saw Robin Williams. My pulse raced and I had an urge to run, but wasn't sure if I wanted to run away or run at him. I felt nervous and confused, and angry that he affected me so strongly. I wanted him to say something to me, but wasn't even sure he would recognize me. I turned away and shortly there was a tap on my shoulder. "How are you doing?" Robin asked. I felt a warm concern from him which I hadn't expected.

"It's still pretty up and down," I answered coldly. "How have you been?" I responded automatically.

"It's been pretty crazy. You know I went to the grand jury last week."

"Yes, so I've heard." I knew he wasn't finished yet and was therefore unable to talk about it. "How did it go?" I asked anyway.

"It wasn't too bad," he said, staring at the floor. He mumbled something, then looked at me again. "I'm not allowed to discuss the hearing, yet, but I'd like to talk some time when I can. I'm sorry I haven't . . . I'd like to be able to clear up anything I could for you." I realized he felt bad about the situation, that perhaps he was, well, ashamed might be too strong a word, but he certainly gave the impression he felt guilty and wanted to make amends. This contact made the world of difference to me; for the first time, his folly became human.

"I'd like to talk, too," I said, making an effort to sound more up. "I'd like that very much."

Later, at the Odeon with Laila and Rhonda, I felt "out of it" as they conversed about men and relationships. It was difficult for me to join in because all my related experiences were with John, and I didn't want to keep bringing him up to make comparisons. All I could think to say was "Forget it and take advantage of the time you have together," but that seemed too obvious and perhaps a bit dismissive of their problems. It made me feel very distant, very different from my close friends.

A few days after Woodward's meeting with Cathy Smith he phoned to tell me about it. I was anxious to hear everything.

Bob said her lawyers were present for the interview, but they let her say whatever she wanted. She confirmed much of what I'd instinctively known: that (as far as she knew) John had only used heroin the last week, on what she considered a limited basis; that she and John got to know each other that last week (she'd met him at "SNL" once, but they didn't really know each other); that she was responsible for the injections. She elaborated that John was into cocaine, and only mixed heroin with it occasionally. She also insisted that the last shot she gave him was pure coke.

"I think Nelson is more involved than he's let on," Bob said. He seemed hesitant to say this, sensitive to my friendship with Nelson. Bob also questioned whether John had actually died of an overdose. "I think it's more likely that it was a combination of stress, work, and drugs," he said, then paused. When he spoke again his voice was less factual. "Smith said John was worried when he heard you were sick. She said he'd phoned and left several messages saying 'I love you.'" I was grateful she'd shared that with Bob.

Bob was at a point where he wanted to organize everything and go through it all with Pam and me together. There were a few more people to talk to in New York and he needed one more trip to Los Angeles. "There are some heavies in the drug world who are getting unhappy with my investigation," he told me, but he said he wasn't worried about it. It worried me, however.

"After I return from L.A., I may be ready for my first article, which I'm thinking will be on the police end." Bob said Cathy Smith had opened up a few more leads on that and confirmed other suspicions, agreeing to sign affidavits attesting to what she'd told him. "What are her lawyers thinking?" I wondered aloud. "Is it that they think she could turn states evidence?"

"I think so," Bob agreed.

I felt sad after talking with Bob. I kept thinking, if only I could have held on to John one more week. I wrote in my diary: "Last night as I was falling asleep, I imagined [John's] body next to mine, holding me from behind as he slept, his warm breath on my neck, his arms around my body, his knees nestled into the back of my knees. He was soft and warm and our bodies fitted together in an 'S'. . . . I know how much he loved me, and I don't think I'll ever be that sure of anything again. There is still much pain at knowing he is gone forever. . . . I'll never wish for anything more than to go back and relive that [last] week."

A few days later the Klenfners invited me to dinner. I was unaware that it was to be a party until I got there and found a roomful of people. Although my immediate reaction was to retreat, I was happy to see Danny and several other good friends. Still, I mostly stayed in the kitchen, helping Carol. After a short while, Danny came up to me and in a somewhat excited manner suggested, "Come on over and say hi to Robert DeNiro." Startled to learn DeNiro was there, I turned and saw him in a corner talking with some people. "He wants to talk to you but he's a shy guy." My heart was racing and I knew I couldn't approach him.

"I'm shy, too," I replied, feeling angry.

"Come on, make the first overture," Danny pleaded.

"I really think he should come to me," I said stubbornly.

"He didn't kill John," Danny said in frustration.

"That's not the point," I mumbled. I knew Danny only wanted to help, but he'd fueled my anger instead. Couldn't he understand that I felt DeNiro had been disrespectful of John?

Now I was really uncomfortable and busied myself in the kitchen. A while later, a quiet voice said, "Excuse me, Judy." I turned and found myself facing DeNiro. My heart sped up. "Ah, I don't think we've ever actually met . . ."

"Yes, John introduced us a number of times," I said. Normally I would let it go, aware that DiNiro meets a lot of people, but under the circumstances I felt it was important.

He was ill at ease and I realized this was not easy for him, either.

"Listen, I'm sorry I didn't contact you at the time of John's death, but at the time I was confused." He fidgeted with his jacket and hung his head as he spoke. "I didn't want to be part of a public spectacle."

"Neither did I."

"Yeah, I know, but I was angry with the way the press linked me to the death, which was not the truth."

"Well, I was hurt by what I judged at the time to be a lack of respect toward John."

"I know, I know," he agreed, nodding. "I should have contacted you. John was a good guy, I liked him."

I was relieved to have expressed my feelings and felt my anger lifting. Now that we were talking, I could finally see that DeNiro was only human, too.

Later that night it struck me as interesting that I'd run into both Robin Williams and Robert De Niro in the same week, and what a great release the conversations had been. Danny was right. They had not played a role in John's death. I could now accept that neither intended to insult John or hurt anyone. It felt so much better to forgive than to hold on to the anger.

Chapter 19

HAPPY HOLIDAYS

NOVEMBER–DECEMBER

*A*s the holiday season approached, I found myself feeling more and more exhausted. The pressures of Christmas and New Year's Eve were getting to me, and Thanksgiving's appearance signaled little time left to come up with an answer to the oft-repeated question, "What are you going to do for (fill in holiday here)?" One would have to live in a vacuum not to have heard that the holidays are especially difficult after losing someone, and my many invitations to dinners and gatherings were proof that my friends and family were certainly concerned. So I was relieved when my parents decided to spend Thanksgiving in New Jersey with Pat and her husband, John, because it provided an easy solution to step one of my dilemma.

Pat's house was filled with the aroma of the feast when I arrived. My parents and I sat and talked for a while, but I wasn't really with them. I was having unusually intense memories. I felt low, sad, and it was difficult to shake my preoccupation with the past.

Thanksgiving had been John's favorite holiday. It was an easygoing day, shared with friends or family. He would be in and out of the kitchen all morning, excited by the progress of the meal, occasionally helping with something, a ready taster of anything in the making. He loved a turkey dinner, and especially an oyster dressing I made. His expression showed total concentration as he carved the bird, his face beamed as he presented the platter. Time spent on a meal for John was duly rewarded. An interviewer once asked, "Do you cook for

John?" "Everyone cooks for John," I replied. He didn't even have to verbalize that he would like something. He told you with his eyes.

In an effort to bring myself into the present I decided to play with my nephew, Robbie, who was almost three now. I went downstairs and sat in a little chair beside him. He was setting up a board with roads and buildings on it. "Whad'ya got there, Rob?" I asked as he opened a box and dumped about forty miniature cars on the floor.

"Cars," he stated, haphazardly placing them in his toy city. I noticed his Bluesmobile, a toy replica of the car from *The Blues Brothers*; it seemed to shout at me from among his playthings. He held it up.

"Oh," I said, somewhat startled, "a police car."

"Uncle John's car," he said in his choppy, little boy way. My eyes filled with tears. I wondered what "Uncle John" meant to Robbie. A man in the movies, who had a little toy car just like Batman? He wouldn't remember the summer he visited the Vineyard and took over Uncle John's house as only a toddler can. I remembered John turning to my mother one day, pointing to Robbie, and saying with great admiration, "And you raised four of these!" I watched Robbie in a blur for a while, as if in a trance, before blinking away the tears.

Getting ready for bed, I felt worse by the minute. Every move was an effort, my body was excruciatingly heavy. In resignation I stood motionless, my arms hanging at my sides. I saw myself in the mirror and thought, Maybe I'm *not* going to make it after all! Maybe this will never be an old face. For the first time in a while, the sadness exploded from me; I just stood there and cried. I remembered a time when I considered writing John a letter, to be kept with our will, in case I died first. I wanted to say I loved him and that he should be strong and carry on. Now I couldn't grasp what it was I thought there was to "carry on" for. I could move into my "perfect" little coach house, I thought, but things would be far from right. It was just a facade I was building so I would appear okay. Perhaps it really would be my last home after all.

Before going to bed I wrote a short poem:

Maybe I'll die of a broken heart
Maybe it's true, I'm not so smart
But life is heavy on my mind
And though I'm not the quittin' kind
Been thinkin',
Maybe I'll make a new start
And see what's on the other side

Back in New York, we had several nights of rehearsals for *West Heaven,* working on the basic track and vocal Rhonda would lip-sync to when we filmed her. We planned to do a remote recording at Steve's loft, then go into the studio for overdubbing later. With Paul Shaffer on keyboards and Steve on drums, the music was really pulling together.

The recording itself went basically well; for a rough mix, the song sounded great. Rhonda was unhappy with her vocal, but we could redo it in the studio. At least we could use the "scratch vocal" for the syncing. Rhonda had lots of ideas for what needed to be done in the studio. Selecting photos for the montage section, I was happy to find my trips through them more uplifting than painful. The up mood of the project was beginning to influence me.

Meanwhile, Rob was still trying to help out with the gravestone. He spoke with another representative from the Chilmark Cemetery to be sure we were clear about what could and could not be done. A natural stone was very much encouraged —an idea I'd already accepted—and a new concern was expressed. John's visitors were leaving miscellaneous items (notes, calling cards, beer cans, etc.) which were blowing around the cemetery. This was upsetting the people who found debris on the graves of their deceased relatives. Would we be willing to surround John's plot with bushes?

John's plot was about ten by ten, and to surround it with bushes seemed awkward; would people stand outside this square of bushes and look in? The image was annoying, and lacking another solution I felt frustrated.

Early December

How unusual it is to be unafraid of death, and the freedom

it gives you to live. I'm sometimes a little afraid of losing that feeling. . . . .

Talked to Woodward today. Was thinking about what his article is—what it means. He's talked to [many of our close friends and] business associates. What does it mean that we have (as a whole) [talked to him] . . . about drugs, the drug scene? . . . I feel that it is a bold and admirable thing we do as a group—talking to Woodward. . . . We *must* talk to try to heal this wound.

Thinking about how things have progressed over the last few months' . . . I seem to have released a lot of the anxieties surrounding death, press, etc. I never read final version of *Penthouse,* although I may someday. Don't know. I think Woodward thing was helpful for me to release all the feelings that came with the info I had vs. lack of info. . . .

A while ago I resented Dr. C. for saying that "Someday this would all be just a part of my life." But now I wish I could look back and not feel the pain. At first it seemed I would never stop crying. Now it seems as tho I always will cry some, but it will just be more spread out all the time. One thought I can't shake is when John said, "Get out! Before I really hurt you!" I had no idea what he meant. Now I feel as if he knew. How could he have known? . . . Sometimes I wish I could get high and get away from myself. . . . But I know you can't escape with drugs. . . . My thoughts about life seem to be pretty mixed up. Sometimes I worry about whether I want to have kids or not, other times the image of myself as a fine old woman seems to be disappearing, slowly fading. . . . I must find something to live for—or something to die for. . . . I don't know. I'm not tired and I'm afraid to turn out the light, and so I just write nonsense. I think I'm not feeling so great because I need exercise. But I'm just not motivated. Maybe I always exercised for John. I think most of what I did revolved around John one way or another.

* * *

On December 7, I went to the Vineyard with Stelio (my line producer), Bob (the cameraman), his assistants, and Steve to shoot our first footage for *West Heaven.* Since this was to be a shot of me walking the beach at Chilmark, our main concern was the weather. I was hoping for a crisp, sunny day. However, the temperature had dropped considerably during the night, and although it seldom snows on the island, I worried that this would be one of those times.

We arrived earlier than expected, and decided to do a trial run. Stelio stood-in for me, walking the beach while Bob and I went over the shot, then I was filmed walking along the shore. It was freezing and a strong wind burned my cheeks. Ah, well, if it didn't change tomorrow, this look was okay. It was a stormy, unsettled look; maybe it was more appropriate anyway.

We woke up the next morning to find a beautiful snowfall had covered the island. Fortunately, we had the shot from the day before, which I felt was better than if I walked in snow. The crew headed home, but it was so lovely that Steve and I decided to stay another day. I made a note in my journal about our respite: "Sunday was beautiful, snow drifts up to 3 ft. Steve and I went down to beach. Gorgeous. Slid down cliff, falling into crevasses hidden by snow. On most accounts, romantic. Strange, though, because John and I so wanted to spend time there last year in the snow. And here I was, snowed into 'our dream house' with someone else, romping in the snow. Steve falling down on me, feeling that moment of warmth when you are surrounded by new snow on one side and a body on the other. A kiss which is both warm and cold."

Before we left, Steve and I went by the cemetery. The stones that marked John's grave had been removed and I was upset, thinking maybe this had been done so people wouldn't be able to find him. We marked the grave with some rocks we found in the field, then pulled the Jeep up to the grave and played the rough mix of "West Heaven" loud enough for all the neighboring deceased relatives to enjoy.

Dec. 21

Xmas Season, walking New York, uptown. Great stores, crisp feeling, not too cold. Can't stop image of John saying to me, "You'll see, it will be easier when I'm dead." I think he had said something like "I'm not going to live as long as you" first. I don't think he was high. I know I was crying, and I told him that was not true, that was all I could say, and now I hope he understood that my inability to say more was because the idea was so upsetting.

Dec. 22

As Christmas draws nearer, panic decreases. That's not what I thought I would write, but it's basically true. It is still more emotionally difficult, but the deadlines have been met. Plans are made and packages mailed. Steve is the only real case of late shopping.

Xmas is funny. I want to enjoy it, but it's hard. Had nice time tonight. Drove out to Conn. to place James and K. are renting. We sang Christmas carols. James played along. I even played a little guitar on a few songs, which I haven't done for anyone for a long time. It was fun. I can't explain my mood shifts. When I was running around today, shopping, I started to cry in the back of a cab. I have that feeling again of vulnerability.

Dec. 25, 11:45 A.M.

Christmas at last! Another deadline met. One week and it's New Year's, then, perhaps, the seasonal "joy" will cease and emotions will steady.

The other night I stayed in, alone, to relax and catch my breath from all this rushing, emotions, etc. I was thinking how much [various friends' kids look like their parents]. I imagined having a little boy, a part of me and John. Suddenly, the realization that I had let that possibility slip away hit me, almost as if I'd just lost the (imaginary) little boy, too. I cried hysterically for a while, feeling for the first time the absolute sadness and desire to have that child. Any part of John to live on (a girl, too, altho my thought was a boy, a little him, I guess). Up to now . . . I have sort of accepted that I don't [have a child], rationalizing . . . as if it was all for the better. But tonight I finally felt the sorrow of the loss, I finally felt my grief over this issue.

Dec. 26, Noon.

Christmas Eve at Pat's was nice. She does everything so perfectly. Robbie loved it, although he was disappointed that all presents weren't for him. Had a good Christmas morning, then came on home.

Interesting how solid you can feel one moment and how out of control the next. I drove home from Pat's, walked into the house, and found a present with a drum pedal just sitting on top. There was no card, but then, the pedal is a card, I guess. I opened the present and it was an electric guitar, about two-thirds normal size. It was so sweet, I burst out crying. I felt a rush of different emotions. Guilt for one. I had a lot of problems selecting a gift for Steve. Then I sort of left it till the last minute and got him a sweater and something he needed for his loft. As I wrapped them I wondered if I was having a problem buying a present for Steve, just because I didn't really get John anything particularly special last year. I think it made it impossible for me to feel good about getting anything special for Steve. He's been so lovable, and still I'm confused in terms of how I feel about him. . . . I felt so bad, was so upset, I wondered if I could handle going out for dinner. Finally I just laughed at myself—sitting there with this guitar in my lap, crying. Sometimes the hystericalness of myself makes me laugh.

Dec. 26, 2:00 A.M.

Stayed home tonight . . . packing (repacking) John's things for move. I can't believe how much I still have. It seemed like I gave away so much. Apparently I'd just had enough at some point and stuck a bunch of things in boxes. I forgot and thought I'd given them away. Actually, it's kinda nice to see some items I thought I'd gotten rid of. . . . It's nice to have some of these things that seem to be so much *him*.

Watched a rerun of "SNL." It seemed like a long time ago. . . .

After the show (had left TV on) caught end of promo for "Entertainment Tonight." "And we'll say good-bye to the greats who took their last bows in 1982." And they flashed a photo of John, singing as Jake. Then they said, "Stay tuned for *Love with the Proper Stranger,* starring Steve McQueen and Natalie Wood." How transient life is.

Sometimes when I think how weird it is [that I'm] alone, I realize, we were *together* a long time!

Dec. 27

Feeling low again today. End of the year blues. Went thru my clothes tonight. Almost done packing. Still have to tackle the sound room. Then someone else can move me.

Watched "Entertainment Tonight." Said John was volatile, talented, etc., good stuff. "Who at thirty-three seemed to have it all, then wasted it for a high of cocaine and heroin." Oh well, hard to hear, but true. Anyway, they showed a good selection of photos . . . and they said he made the transition to movies successfully. It was fine, really. In fact, it was very nice, it's just that I'm still thrown by certain things, like hearing something like, "he threw away his life." That sort of takes over my body and I can't think straight. I guess there is some good in seeing this stuff. Seeing his pix with others who died this year. Another reality dose.

Jan 1, 1983. Good-bye to L'Annee Noire.

The New Year is finally here and I welcome it! Steve and I drove to James and Kathryn's in Conn., arriving on a prayer and a generous reserve gas tank. Just as we were about to leave the city, Danny phoned. He was in town for a night, and was at Wise Maria's with his new girl, Donna. We went and had a drink with them. Danny seemed good. Donna seems really nice. . . . They came by the house before we left and I played the rough mix of "West Heaven," describing the video. They seemed to like it. That makes me feel more confident about the quality.

The next day we both phoned people to wish Happy New Year. I was glad we came, the day was good. I felt at peace and happy to be with Steve. Calling my family was hard. Dad was okay. "Hope this year will be better. Let me get your mother." Mom was sad, I could tell in her voice, although she tried not to sound it. She struggled a little with just what to say, wanting to come up with something to give hope to 1983. Then I called Rob, who was leaving so we didn't talk long. Just as well, that was the hardest. He was anxious to get the year over with, too. Also, he said, "I haven't forgotten what this day is to you" and that was really what I had been blocking all day, what everyone else was sidestepping. That this should have been our wedding anniversary. I thought to myself, how could it just suddenly *not* be my anniversary? And then I started remembering other anniversaries. I was so nervous the year the Blues Bros. played with the Grateful Dead in San Francisco. I told John it would be a madhouse, we'd have no time to ourselves. He promised it would be okay. I had my doubts, but since he really wanted the gig, I went along. And it did work out, it was great. After the BB finished playing, John and I went back to our room and listened to the rest of the concert on the radio. We took a long bath and made love. Then we met up with others at the party and were presented with a cake. It was one of our best anniversaries. Suddenly I wanted to remember every year. How many could I remember? Last year, oh last year started out bad. Oh, God, I could go crazy if I let myself. I cried when I got off the phone with Rob. I could hear Steve playing a drum machine in the basement, and was so glad he was with me. Earlier in the day we had been laughing and I did feel a certain hope for the new year. [Sometimes] I have pangs of guilt, because I'm here and able to laugh, and a part of me thinks that's not right. But, I know there's nothing to be done about what's happened. Nothing I do now negates anything I felt, still feel, for John.

This past month I have cried several times at the thought of "midnight"—and no John. But when midnight was counted down, Steve was there and this is my life now and it was fine. I'm lucky to have had someone as sweet at Steve "waiting" for me. It is as if he was always there from the time John died, waiting. And he is wonderful and he came to me in 1982. I was going to write, he's the only thing about 1982 that wasn't black! Hmmm.

Chapter 20

CALLING WEST HEAVEN

JANUARY–FEBRUARY, 1983

The first few days in January, I intended to call some old friends and say Happy New Year, since I hadn't sent Christmas cards. But each night I'd decide not to. I realized I couldn't bring myself to call for the same reason I hadn't sent cards; I didn't have anything "up" to say, not enough anyway. In fact, I was feeling unable to communicate in general, preferring to hide out alone in my apartment. I noted in my diary, "There must be a point where you just say, enough! At least I hope. But for now, I feel best being here and keeping busy. Something will come from it. After all, this is really something to experience, this grief. It's kind of, well, it's all I have, and so I want to get into it."

Jan. 5

While in the waiting room at my doctor's I came upon the *People* mag. from the week John died. I'd never seen it and felt a bit numb at first. Couldn't stop myself from flipping thru. Saw pix of John's mom leaving church, pallbearers carrying coffin, an old one of J. and me, Danny on motorcycle, some misc. J. pix, as well as helicopter shot from the grave-yard. Pretty strange. I've found myself unable to remember just who the pallbearers were lately, I mean, all eight of them. I kept getting six and then not being sure. I took the magazine with me. I stole it really, I couldn't ask and just had to have it. Will look at it again later. Jimmy's face is so sad in the photo, and Danny. . . . The article itself was annoying. Not a bad article, but some old wrong stories. J. demanding phone at the Pump Room, etc. etc. "But there was a softer side to Belushi. His marriage to his high school sweetheart was strong to the end. 'She loved him very much and he her. It was obvious to anyone who saw them together.'" What I know, and must keep foremost in my mind, is that we were true of heart. The other stuff is bullshit getting in the way of what's worth remembering.

Jan. 6

Met with Woodward. More strange assorted info. Dates, addresses, names. It's odd to still be finding out things that John did. It's not stuff I didn't know—he often phoned as he went from place to place—so I know how he moved around town. But it's pretty weird, as if I'm spying.

Technically it's my birthday. Happy Birthday to me. Thirty-two. Now I'm only a year younger than John. And then I'll be the same age, and then older. So far I'm having a very strange birthday. My mind is racing. My body is exhausted. My arm hurts [from blood test]. If I had a sleeping pill, I'd take one. Ah, ha! I'll try the opiate of the masses—TV!

Jan. 9

Backtrack—Fri. Had a nice birthday after all. Mark and Karen surprised me with a lunch party, invited several other friends. It was really sweet. Rhonda and Steve came back to my place after. At lunch I received a beautiful box of roses (three dozen or so) from John and Deborah Landis, Danny, and Eddie Murphy. As we were putting them in water at the house, more flowers arrived. One arrangement from Alba [cleaning lady] (I was surprised and touched), one from Anne and Deanne (knew they'd remember), Bernie, Mrs. B, and a plant from James and Kathryn. I was a bit overwhelmed. It got to a point where we'd just start laughing when the bell rang. Rhonda and I were admiring them all and I said, "Looks like someone died." Which, of course, was to the point. I also received a slew of cards. The attention was heartfelt, and just what I needed.

Jan. 10

Went with Kathryn (*her* birthday) to Bishop Moore's for dinner. Drank too much. I've been overdoing it a lot lately. Doesn't feel too good. It's pretty boring, actually. Guess I'm avoiding dealing with *life*.

At home, I noticed the *People* mag. again. I sat and looked through it like a child with her first storybook. And it's a disturbing story. At first I just stared at, reread, the headline: "JB, 1949–1982: A Life That Guaranteed Death At An Early Age." Was it really? Was it guaranteed? Did everyone always know? Each photo was a world of its own to me; *Animal House, Lemmings,* working out, meeting Mayor Byrne, our trip to Europe. Then I turned to the helicopter shot of the graveyard, and thought, And then he died and we had to go and bury him, and here we are putting John's body in its final resting place, and there's Danny leading the funeral procession. I still cry when I see Danny's face, and Jimmy's, carrying casket. Although it threw me into some childlike regression, I think it was a reality bomb. Suddenly I realized how long, how many times I had gone over the same pages, looking at the photos, trying to really grasp that this was what happened. Finally I closed the mag. and thought to myself: A life that guaranteed a full life—whenever death might come his way.

Jan. 15

The fact that there has been an end to John's life is becoming a part of my consciousness. Of course, I've *known* it all along, but now I'm really feeling it. Tom Schiller and I were talking about loss (his mother died when he was young), and he said there's a sense that becomes continually stronger, that that person never could have been any older; the life they lived was all that was intended. He said that it would eventually even feel right. I think that is beginning to make sense to me. It seems a rather profound thought, in fact. It's still hard to think of [me] being old, and that John would just be one part of my life.

Jan. 17

Pam spoke to Montagna [L.A.D.A.]. He said Nelson Lyon accepted immunity and testified before the grand jury. Phoned Nelson. I caught him off guard and he overcompensated with an enthusiastic, "Hello, hi, how are you?" I was direct and said, "Listen. I've known since August that you lied to me about your involvement with John, and now that you've finished with the grand jury, I'd like to talk to you about it." He sounded relieved. He said right away that the thing that bothered him most was having to lie to me. "I'm not apologizing for it," he kept saying, almost apologetically. He thought it was the best thing to do at the time. I asked if he'd go over what really happened. He said that that afternoon John had said, "Let's go in the back. I've got something I want to show you," or something vague like that, and they went to the back room and Cathy Smith pulled out the hardware, etc., and Nelson joined in. He confirmed that Smith did the injecting. "Didn't you ask him what it was, or didn't he say something about it?" "No, not really . . . " I've already forgotten what exactly he said, nothing new really. Basically it was what he'd told me before, only now he admitted that they were shooting up. He said he thought it was just coke. I asked if John had said anything about what his plans were and he said he talked mostly about Paramount and *Noble Rot,* that he said he was going back to New York as soon as he got things straightened out with that.

Nelson said he felt better, much better, for having told the truth. He felt stronger now, although it had been difficult between telling Vivian and going to the grand jury. I felt mixed emotions after our talk. I was disappointed that he didn't know more about what John was thinking in terms of the drug use. I'd hoped they'd had some big, heart-to-heart talk about it. I guess I'll just never know. I felt sorry for Nelson, because I know this has been difficult. Then I felt pissed off, thinking that he should have stopped John. Then I knew he couldn't have.

Jan. 19

Mitch and I were talking about Woodward. He had read somewhere that Bob was from Wheaton and asked me, "Did we know that?" And I said, "Of course, we knew that." He asked something else about how he goes about writing, and I said, "Well, actually, about *all* I know is that he's from Wheaton—in fact, I've never actually read anything he's written." Mitch started laughing, and I laughed and told him it was true, but I hadn't told anyone else that. I said I'm trusting John on this one, because he read his stuff, and was always fascinated by it. Actually, he read some aloud to me at the time, but that's really all I know of it. Mainly I know of his reputation. "Oh well, it's only a series of articles," I concluded, "in the Washington Fucking Post!"

Jan. 22

Had a headache a good part of the day, really bad. At one point I thought, this is the first headache I've had since John died. It's so odd how you categorize everything as a "first," as if it's different because a person is gone. I mean, some are different, but I had headaches when John was alive and not around, so it's not like I haven't gone thru this alone before. It's true I remember him being there when I had a bad headache, either giving me a neck rub or getting cold towels for my head, or freaking out because he didn't know what to do. But I can't believe how I think sometimes.

Jan. 23

Didn't film today because of scheduling problem, so now we will film on J.'s birthday. Oh well, must have been destined. Music session at studio tonight.

Jan. 24 Happy Birthday John.

Had to get up at ten-thirty (was in studio until four A.M.) to meet with Stelio. Yesterday house was turned upside down by crew. Later, when I described the house to Laila, she said, "Sounds like it was visited by John."

During first few takes I keep thinking, Why am I doing this? I don't know what I'm doing. It's probably stupid anyway. It's costing me a lot of money. I could have taken a trip around the world, or rented a villa somewhere, or done something *nice*. John often said he couldn't understand why anyone would work if they didn't have to.

We finish one take and I call a short break to touch up Rhonda's makeup (but really it's to break tension). After completing Rhonda, we still had two more setups around house. Finally finished about two in the morning, so I didn't go to the studio where they are right now, working on a final mix of the music. I came right to bed, while the crew continues to clear out under Stelio's direction. I'm exhausted and yet not sleepy. Well, I wasn't sleepy, that's why I wrote. Emotionally it wasn't too bad a day. I'm glad we filmed, because by keeping busy, it made the day easier.

* * *

Several days later, I realized I hadn't cried for at least one week, which made it the longest time I was aware of during which I hadn't. It was a funny accomplishment to note, but it gave me a sense of improvement. I also had a curious "daydream." I saw an image of myself as an old woman, sort of a fantasy jump to the future. A kid asked what my life with John had been like and I sort of scrunched up my wrinkled face as if trying to remember, and said, "That was a long time ago." My imaginary reaction startled me and I wondered if it could be possible that someday I would be so blasé about that time of my life.

February was very active, between working on the video and moving into the coach house. My Morton Street apartment was never put back together after the filming, which gave it an "unhomey" atmosphere—a good transition, however, so that I looked forward to getting out.

I toyed with the idea of giving up grass for a month to see how that would affect my dreams. In anticipation of February being demanding, and in deference to improving my health, I decided it was a good time for this private experiment. I threw in abstinence from hard liquor as well.

I had agreed to do an interview with *People* magazine, to talk about the video, but was uncertain it was a good idea; was I strong enough to handle it? What if they asked upsetting questions? We said I couldn't talk about Cathy Smith at all, for legal reasons. There was some truth to that, but regardless, I just didn't want to talk about her. What could I say, that I wasn't even sure how I felt? I wasn't so sure how I felt about anything, actually, that's what made me nervous. So I concentrated on the video, its symbolism and what was being said in that. And I thought about John in terms of what made me love him, hoping if I focused on those issues, it would work out.

Feb. 7

Still no smoke or hard liquor. Don't really find it hard. In some ways I'm becoming at peace with myself. I must maintain sincerity, honesty, and courage to face reality.

Feb. 9

It is getting easier to enjoy good memories. I think looking at these photos in the video over and over is helpful. *People* phoned all day long, checking facts, etc. Can't tell much by things they ask. I'm prepared to be embarrassed, but hope [the writer] got a positive attitude from me. Talking to Stelio and Rhonda about video last night was nice. Rhonda loves that it's so personal, done in simple, classical form, showing sides of J. she says should be shared. She always makes me feel like it's an important thing to do. Stelio told us he cried a little when he was syncing the video to the music. All in all, doing the video has been rewarding, but exhausting.

Feb. 10

Jimmy came to town tonight. Had good talk. Told him about Nelson. Talked about his family. He said an interesting thing about John. Woodward asked when he thought John was happiest, and Jimmy said John always seemed happy to him. It's an interesting viewpoint. Perhaps an obvious one for a younger brother—but indicative of something. The truth is J. was often happy. I can't get hung up and forget that. Whatever battles he had within, he was often at peace, a happy-go-lucky guy in general, happy more often than not, and maybe that in itself is something most people don't achieve. That was what was so appealing about him, his spirit.

Sat. looked over video several times. Am working on final changes in my mind. It's very close and I'm feeling good that it will come together.

When I was talking to the guy from *People,* I said something about wanting to share J.'s struggle because "John lost the fight to drugs and he was a strong man" and he said, "Well, a lot of people said that he wasn't very strong," gablah, gablah . . . whatever he said. I realized that I was thinking of the strong man who was forceful in his work and who I leaned on and who helped me and so many others. But I guess where J. wasn't strong was in helping himself.

Feb. 15

Not smoking grass has begun to effect my dreaming. I'm dreaming so much now and so clearly, that when I wake, I think I haven't slept. I forget the dreams fast, too, but seem to have several a night.

Feb. 21

Haven't written since last Weds. due to push to finish
video. Week kind of a blur. Trying to remember important
feelings. Move from Morton Street took place Fri. Thurs. I
had to get last of personal items together. Found letter I
wrote J. from airport when I left him in L.A., when he was
on binge which sent me to Dr. Cyborn: "John, my honey, I
think it is good to leave L.A. today because I love you too
much to watch what you sometimes go through in this business. You are not an 'investment' to me . . . you are my life
and I love you; good movies, bad movies, good press or bad, or
none at all. I feel too much in the middle of what's going
on, with thirty calls a day and everyone's opinions. Everyone has something they want me to 'make' you do, but all I
want is for you (us) to be happy. So when this is over,
whatever is decided (in terms of the work) we'll still have
each other. Remember, you are an artist and a genius and go
for your best shot. *But*—Hollywood is a *business* town, so
don't let it destroy you . . . please be strong. My heart is in
your hands."

I was so glad I'd found it because his keeping it meant it
must have been important to him; also I'd forgotten I wrote
him and it made me feel better to remember that I had
communicated these thoughts.

I was so busy there wasn't much time to think about move.
Didn't get too emotional, except when I checked out the
house for last time . . . a hundred memories flashed. . . . I
only cried for a moment, then pulled myself together.

Chronologically I've skipped a lot. Pam is in town and she
and Stelio accompanied me to the "Today Show." Went pretty
well, I think. Linda Ronstadt was on just before me, which
was good since I was concentrating all morning on what
I wanted to say and it was good to relax and just converse for
a few minutes before I went on. Jane Pauley was very nice
and I think I touched on most of the points I wanted to. I
emphasized that the video was meant to give an insight to
John and express my personal mourning, but more importantly, make a universal statement about loss and life and

death. The *People* magazine came out as well, and I guess it's okay, I can't really get too into it. Most of the broader things—about John or how I perceive what's happened since his death—would make me crazy if I really thought about what they said, but the brief comments on the video seemed fine. They said something I liked about "the sweet and tender *West Heaven*" and called John the "anarchic samurai comic she knew and loved."

Saturday Video on "SNL." Strange day. Spent my first night at 52 W. Ninth on the second floor of the main building (tenant just moved) so Mom and Dad who had just arrived could stay in coach house. (The fewer stairs the better for mom with her bad hip.) Didn't get up until about noon and spent a couple of hours with Pam taking care of various business—finalizing contract with NBC and Rhonda, going over legal affairs. The coach house was literally wall-to-wall boxes in the morning, and whenever I'd go over to see how the crew was doing—Mom, Dad, Rob, Pat, John, Jimmy, and Derek [Pam's godson]—they were working away. I was reminded of the Swiss Family Robinson, everyone pitching in, happily doing their chores. They rigged a laundry basket on a rope to pull things up to my bedroom from the window overlooking the living room. The music was blaring rock 'n' roll, and to my surprise Dad was not complaining. It really touched me to see them all doing so much to help.

Woodward came into town and went to "SNL" with my family. I couldn't handle going and watched at home with a small group of friends. Seeing video on TV was sort of anticlimactic. Hard to know what audience thought, felt. After the show I gave a party at the Blues Bar. Pretty nice group, everyone complimentary. Of course, who's going to come to my party and tell me my video was a bore? Anyway, as exhaustion set in, felt more distant. The bar got really crowded, lots of people I didn't know. . . . Fell out about six, awakened by Pam at three. She was at Woodward's hotel for our meeting. Sooo . . .

Feb. 24

Meeting with Bob. Thought we were going to go over all info, but he was more general. He's writing three sections: 1) John as a man, and his career. Showing him as the guy who worked hard, had family and friends, and an energy that created and planned and drank in life. 2) The last two mos. [through last] eighteen days of his life. This he says is sad, but hopes John is understood by this part, so he is seen in a social context. He read a little to Pam and she cried. I don't know if I should read this part. He said there are no surprises. 3) The drug scene in L.A. This part I'm not to talk about with anyone. He's not sure when he will be able to publish it because an investigation has begun and certain info may blow the possibility of busting some of these people. This, he says, is the biggest "good which could come from all this." He said none of the people are friends, just people who the trail from John led to. Bob didn't want to tell me any names, so that I would not "know anything" which certain people might like to squelch.

*   *   *

I received many letters about *West Heaven*. I was not so obsessed as with the letters after John's death, but I was thrilled by the response. I reread them, choosing ones that might help in our attempt to sell Rhonda's song to a record company. The following were some of my favorites:

Dear Judith,

   I saw, indeed was touched, by your tribute to the man you Love. . . . A lot of things were printed about the "details" concerning the events of a year ago. Your "video greeting card" was to the point, the *essence* of John the person, not John the media topic. In a word, Loving. That kind of Love is a safe harbor in a world that in reality is Zanier than John ever was.

Thank you for sharing that . . .

Sincerely,
Timothy Torbert

Dear Mrs. Belushi:

After seeing the wonderful tribute you aired on SNL, I tried to locate a copy of the song "West Heaven." I'm hoping you might help me. . . . I didn't know your husband, but like many people, I loved him in a different way. He brought a lot of joy and laughter to my family. When he died, just like when Lennon died, we were all very sad.

I thought I knew what you were going through and how you felt. I found out on Oct. 7th, when my brother died, just how painful it really is. I guess it's not the same, but I love my brother very much and it was so much easier to love him when he was alive. I don't know exactly what it is, if a good part of me died like the old cliché, or if something bad in me grew, but I do know that my life will never be the same. Young death is too sad, it makes your mind overwork and twist out of shape. And there is rarely anything I see, hear, or touch that makes me think of him with anything but pain. But when I heard that song, it made me smile instead of cry. I would love to hear it again . . .

> Thank you,
> Dorothy Newell

There were many lovely letters, but the one that meant the most to me came from Tino:

Dear Judy,

I wanted to write and tell you how wonderful the *West Heaven* video was. It was great to see John with his family, with his grandmother who was so important to him, sitting on the beach like a kid playing in the sand, and you two lovers, from high school to loving husband and wife. The effects were terrific and the music touching. You created a loving, warm, intimate tribute to a wonderful man. I was sad to see the Morton St. home so empty, but I have great memories that will last forever of times together there . . .

Both Atlantic and CBS Records considered Rhonda's song briefly, but the final word was the same from both: the song was too sad. It was curious. Here was a song which to those dealing with death, was a positive statement about life. But to those who weren't on that level, to think about loss and change and life and death was just too sad. It made me realize I had changed very much in the past year.

Chapter 21

VIKING FUNERAL

FEBRUARY 28–MARCH 5, 1983

Pam had a transcript of the interview Van Ness, the L.A. underground reporter, supposedly taped with Cathy Smith shortly after John died. It came from an unnamed source, and she had agreed not to copy it. Respecting her agreement, I didn't take notes when I read it. However, that night I couldn't get it out of my head. I decided to put the dialogue on paper, in hope of releasing it:

"Summary as best I recollect:

VN: First thing we've gotta do is get you away from *Penthouse*. What did you say to them?

CS: I don't know. Didn't talk long. Maybe they were wired. I don't know who that girl was. For all I know, maybe she was Judy's sister.

VN: They were wired. They have things on tape.

CS: Who knows what she had up there.

VN: They say you said you kept him alive for five days.

CS: I might have said that. Yeah, I probably said that. I did.

VN: I want to help you.

CS: You and (?) (name was crossed out) have been good friends.

VN: We want to get people off your back.

CS: Good, I'm tired of having to look over my shoulder all the time.

VN: We want to get you money.

CS: Good. I could use some money. God, I could use some money.

VN: You could pay back (?) then. Do you know how much (?) has laid out for you.

CS: Yeah, I know. I want to pay (?). You've both been good friends.

VN: I want you to know we're taping.

CS: Okay.

VN: Now tell me. J.'s friends keep saying he didn't shoot up. What's the story? Did you shoot him?

CS: Yeah. I shot him.

VN: Was he a junkie?

CS: No, he definitely wasn't a junkie. Maybe a hype, but no junkie.

VN: How many times? . . .

CS: I don't know. Maybe twenty. . . . You know, it's all my fault.

VN: Now, Cathy, don't do this to yourself. The man was a physical mess.

CS: Yeah, you don't have an enlarged heart . . .

VN: He was a walking time bomb. Let's get one thing straight. Did you have a sexual relationship with him?

CS: No.

VN: Okay, let's just get that out of the way. Who can hurt you?

(Talk about various people. Names are deleted, but I recognize Leslie—sometimes—and Nelson.)

CS: (Name deleted) is the only one who can hurt me. He was there.

VN: No, he's too scared.

CS: He was a friend of John's and that's why he was there. He said he wanted it "all over him."

VN: Don't worry about him. He's dropped totally out of sight.

CS: Good. . . . Ya know, John was a great guy. I really miss him. Guess I'll always miss him. I didn't know he was having marital problems. He was always phoning and saying he loved her. At the same time, he'd give you a pat on the arm and say, "Everything's okay." He was a really good friend.

(Something about last evening. She says she shot him up
last at three. They talked till about seven. She left at
ten.)
CS: He must have died about ten-fifteen."

After writing I still had trouble sleeping. One thing that
bothered me was the reference to "marital problems." Then I
realized Smith said "she didn't know we were having . . ."
That told me her impression was that things were okay. So,
in fact, she was able to console me. And for the first time I
had a glimpse of the real Cathy Smith: she was confused,
scared, and guilty; I felt sorry for her. It was an uncomfortable feeling. Her actions were directly related to my husband's death and she'd gone on to slander John, or at least
allow herself to be used in the telling of fabricated stories. It
was really simpler to hate Cathy Smith. Now that I saw her
as human, compassion stirred and my emotions were thrown
into turmoil.

March fifth was rapidly approaching and I knew I needed
a plan, something to help me get through the day. I decided
to have a symbolic Viking funeral. I called Huey Taylor on
the Vineyard to ask if he could help find an appropriate
vessel for the ceremony, and he graciously offered to take
care of it. A number of people made arrangements to join me.

Living in the coach house was already comfortable. There
were still a few unpacked boxes in the basement, but the
house itself was surprisingly together for the short time I'd
been there. It really was perfect for me.

One night after Rhonda and Laila had been over, I was
feeling rather complacent as I straightened up the kitchen. I
like my house, I thought. John and I would have been very
happy here. The realization startled me. Until that moment,
I thought of the coach house as a place for *me, my* place. I
guess in a way, I thought it would have been too small for
"us." But in that instant I felt how much John would have
loved it. It was a terribly sad thought, it was the saddest
thought I'd had for a long time. I later wrote, "I miss the
sharing, I miss his enthusiasm, happiness, and just only
John."

March 2

At this time last year I was in bed with a 103-degree temperature. Karen [my secretary] stayed overnight so Dr. Gould wouldn't put me in the hospital. I just barely made it to his office, I was so sick. After he did tests, I fell asleep on a bed in a back room until Karen came for me. Meanwhile, in Los Angeles, John was shooting up for the first time with Cathy Smith. Somehow I can't help but feel this is connected. I know Dr. Cyborn would say I'm looking for pat answers in things that have no meaning, but I think somehow my soul knew. I don't really understand, but have a strong sense that our psyches affected each other strongly. Time and space must be transcended. Life is so different for me today than one year ago. And how *not* to lose touch with having fun? Sometimes I feel so boring. But it's not parties, or going out, or more people contact that I miss. It's John. I wish he could be in this quiet, peaceful place with me. I can't help but want to cry out, "We almost made it! What went wrong?" I know "right and wrong" are not valid when it comes to death. I wish I believed in a traditional concept of God. Then I would have someone to pray to for guidance.

*   *   *

Laila and I flew to the Vineyard on the fourth and were up late. Before going to bed, I pulled out my diary to write and habitually glanced at my watch for the date. I was surprised to see that we had passed into the dreaded day. My heart sped up and I began to feel anxious. I found myself thinking about three things at once. I wrote, "It's just another day, but it's crazy to think it isn't any different. It's the day that changed everything."

That morning Huey brought over the boat, a bale of hay, and some kerosene. Rob and Walter Wlodyka, a local lobster fisherman—among other things—and friend, repaired the boat and rigged a sail out of an old blue sheet. Laila, Pat, and I helped with final touches. We taped a pink flamingo, one of the plastic garden variety, to the bow—my idea of a substitute mermaid. Laila had some little flags with which we also adorned our vessel: two Albanian flags crisscrossed in front of the flamingo, an American flag atop the mast, and a United Nations flag waving at the stern. Someone brought up the question of a name for the boat. Laila and I were quick to know what it should be and boldly painted "The Black Hole" across the stern. True to itself, the name soon disappeared, the paint absorbing totally into the wood.

The vessel completed, we loaded it into Walter's truck. The rest of us, including my nephew Robbie and the Klenfners, piled into the Jeep and Walter's wife Betty's van. The road to Huey's camp, where the winds were best, was underwater. It was exciting to plow on through, the water spraying past the car windows. Everything about the journey fit the occasion; we were a caravan with a purpose, we could not fail.

At Huey's, Walter put on hip boots and a navy-tested water suit, then he and the guys carried the Viking ship down the long path to the beach. They went back for an aluminum boat we needed for launching, only to return with two more friends, Kate Taylor-Witham and her husband, Charlie. Next the men put the bale of hay in the Viking ship and doused it with kerosene.

All was set, so I said a few words to the group to commence the ceremony. I told about the day John said he wanted a Viking funeral, and concluded, "Today we will symbolically carry out the Viking funeral. I've brought some personal items to place in the boat, as well as some things from others." I opened a brown suitcase. "First, I have some video tapes which should remain between John and myself." I placed them on the hay. "And this is another private something," I said, pulling out a scrapbook I'd made for John's birthday about four years before. On the front "Happy Birthday John" was embossed in gold. Inside was our "Polaroid porno." Taking a last look at the crooked lettering, I opened the book and put it face down on the hay. "Here's a garter belt for good measure and some items friends have asked to send off." I explained that the flamingo came from the Chilmark yard, a much treasured gift to John and me from my brother Rob, and that the flags were from Laila. I then added a pack of Merit cigarettes from the Klenfners, a cross from Rhonda, a guitar pick and a flower from Tino and Dana, a blues harp from Danny, and an IOU John owed Billy

Murray, who said he would light a fire in New York at six in the evening, about when we lit ours. A microphone represented James and Kathryn, and flowers were added from Pat and some friends. Kate took off a beautiful oyster shell bracelet she was wearing and, ignoring my protests, added it to the pyre. The kids added some stones and thought this was lots of fun. I christened the ship with Jack Daniels, took a swig, and passed the bottle. Rob and Pat each gave me a hug as Walter took the boat out. There were a few tears shed, nothing heavy. Robbie wanted to know where the Viking ship was going, then cried because he didn't want us to burn "the pretty boat."

The boat *was* pretty. She was old and the paint was chipping, but it was a warm, worn blue. The sail was well rigged in very much the shape of that on a Viking ship. She was tied to the rowboat and Walter hauled her out, rowing hard against the rough waves. We'd made a torch from a stick, tying one of John's nightsthirts, soaked in kerosene, to the top. Walter carefully lit that, then gracefully extended it to the bale of hay. The ship went up in flames immediately. Once Walter was sure the fire was going strong, he cut the vessel loose. Ablaze, she headed out to sea in all her bittersweet glory. We watched her for about twenty minutes, until the smoke was only a silhouette on the horizon.

Later I wrote, "The 'funeral' was very successful and made the day go very fast. Earlier, I'd been rushed to get flowers to J.'s grave. I just didn't feel right until something was there. Laila and Michael came with me to the florist, and we got several bouquets. While we were at the cemetery, Pat and Robbie came by. Pat showed Robbie which flowers were from them, but he couldn't understand how they were for Uncle John. He wanted to know where John was, and none of us seemed up to explaining properly. Later in the afternoon I went to the grave alone and took Polaroids of the flowers, which looked very nice. Then I sat there and cried. I spoke aloud, because I wanted to speak out to John. I said I missed him and was working on getting over being mad at him. 'Of course, I guess you counted on that. You know I always do.' I said I loved him and would forever, and then cried again, wishing none of this were true. I don't know how to feel any less sad, and I guess I shouldn't worry. It will just take time. But time is so unreliable. I remember a year ago as if it were yesterday. And yet the time between seems like forever."

Chapter 22

OB-LA-DI, OB-LA-DA

MARCH 6–APRIL

After the anniversary, Rob returned to New York with me. He had decided to learn to work with neon at a studio in Soho, and would stay in my studio apartment for a month. I was happy to have him there. The weather was rainy and gray, which fit my mood. I took to sleeping late, sometimes into the afternoon, then moping about until dinner. Rob was out most of the day, then returned about five-thirty, by which time I would have myself together. I'd phone Karen daily, but seldom went to the office. There were lots of things I could do around the house—I had yet to tackle the boxes in the basement and few pieces of art had been hung—but I didn't have the energy. My only daily interest was "All My Children," a soap opera that came on at one, my cue to wake up if I were still in bed. I couldn't put my finger on what was different. I had been feeling progressively better since Christmas, and the anniversary went well, but now I was going downhill again.

For James's birthday, I decided to throw a small party. I got off my butt long enough to get flowers and food, and Laila and I put up decorations. The place felt like a home, and everyone commented on how great it was, much better than Morton Street. The next day, I kept thinking that I must have let John down; Morton Street wasn't homey enough. I could talk myself through why that wasn't logical—we didn't own Morton Street, for instance, and it was, after all, quite nice. Logic didn't change how I felt; the coach house was special, everything had that personal touch, and I didn't

290

deserve it. John worked hard so we could have what we wanted, and now he wasn't here to share the rewards. With all the nice things in the house, it still felt empty.

About mid-March, the grand jury met again in Los Angeles to decide if they would charge Cathy Smith. Given Nelson's testimony, it was likely a charge of furnishing (injecting John) and supplying would be made. Although the D.A. asked for a murder charge, no one thought the prospects were good. The events around the death were too unclear and neither the *Enquirer* reporters nor Van Ness had testified; to prove a connection between the death and the drugs was difficult. This charge seemed hopeless.

A friend called to tell me "a leak" reported that Cathy Smith had been charged with second degree murder and extradition papers had been sent to Canada. My heart began to pound and I felt light-headed as I phoned Pam to relay the news. Pam said she would call the D.A.'s office and get right back to me.

I recognized from my reaction that I wanted Cathy Smith to be charged. I had been afraid to admit it, not wanting to be disappointed and feeling the authorities didn't care what had happened to John. He was doing drugs, he was *bad*, so it didn't matter. If John and Cathy had been drinking, and she drove them into a tree and John died, she would have been arrested immediately and quickly sent to prison. But when the offense involved drugs, no one wanted to know about it. For the first time, I felt that the law was responding as it should. "Justice moves slowly," Woodward said one day. Well, we would see. Finally Pam phoned back. The leak was premature. When a charge was made, someone from the D.A.'s office would let us know.

I came down with a cold the next day, just the excuse to stay in bed *all* the time, which I did for the next few days. Meanwhile, Pam and I worked out a statement for the press reacting to the grand jury. I wanted something simple, basically, that I hoped the focus on John's death would have some positive outcome. Pam suggested that if an indictment were made, we say, "the decision of the grand jury to indict . . . speaks for itself." And she added a line commending the "Los Angeles District Attorney's office for displaying strength of conscience and character by requesting a charge of murder in this difficult and controversial case." We ended by expressing a "hope that the tragedy of John's death would have broader social ramifications, from which we can learn, grow, and become a healthier society."

Two days later there was another leak—Cathy Smith would be charged the following day. The Toronto police announced receiving papers to arrest her. Pam called to say Smith was charged with several counts, including supplying, furnishing, and murder. I felt numb as we spoke, but when I hung up the phone, in an explosion of emotions, I cried.

That night and the next day my phone rang constantly. Family members wanted to know what would happen now. The extradition process was difficult and once again the prospects didn't look good, but at least the charge was made. My hope was that Cathy Smith would stay in Canada, protected by the complication of the laws, and the whole mess would go away. I refused some interviews, including *Time* magazine, which was tempting. The TV news wanted me to read my statement, otherwise it was of no interest to them. I chose not to. *People* magazine wanted to know if they could use some of my photos from *West Heaven* to run with a piece on the reopening of the case. The photos were too personal and precious to me to be in any way connected with the trial. On the day Cathy Smith was indicted a reporter from CBS news rang my bell, asking for an interview. I told him over the intercom that I'd sent out a statement and would make no further comment. He continued to ring until I had ignored him for some time.

Things settled down after a few days and I began to make an effort at completing my move. I pulled out some framed pictures and items from the basement and put them around the house. Many of these were from our trip to Asia in early 1981. We'd gone to Japan with Danny, his girlfriend, and Smokey to promote *The Blues Brothers*. Then John and I continued on our own to Thailand, Bali, and Hong Kong. A news clipping, misplaced in one of the boxes, reminded me of our excitement on arriving in Japan—and our surprise that the press was there to greet us. Another photo caught a moment when our interpreter had to get up from an interview because John and Danny made her laugh so hard. Unwrapping a statue of Buddha brought back a day John and I had strolled the busy, steamy streets of Bangkok, searching for treasures. A Balinese painting of village life reminded me of a hot day on Bali when we took out a boat and stopped at a remote island. How curious the people were about the hair on John's chest. Children asked if they could touch him.

Nestling into the big leather chair across from Dr. Cyborn, I was pleased to have a dream to recount. Sessions that started with a dream were usually good. I told him what I remembered: "I seemed to have gone to visit John somewhere, I don't know if he was working or what he was doing, but we hadn't seen each other for a fairly long time. We were happy to see each other and wanted to have sex, and decided to go to his room. Then I remember this image of driving a dilapidated old car up the stairs and into his room—as if this were normal—but some of his roommates and friends are there. So we go off to find a place to be alone, but in the middle of the search, the phone rang and woke me up."

"Let me get this straight, you drove the car up the steps?" Dr. Cyborn asked.

"Yeah. Right up to his room."

"What does that make you think of?"

"Well, it reminds me of a scene in *Animal House*, when one of the characters drives a motorcycle up the stairs."

"Um-hum. And you say there are other people in the room. Do you recognize any of them?"

I thought about this, but couldn't remember anyone. We talked a little more and then Dr. Cyborn collected his thoughts. "Well," he said, "the dream sounds like a college situation, and you mention the reference to *Animal House* which is about fraternities. I'd say this dream is a wish that you and John could go back to that innocent time when your biggest problem was finding a place to have sex. You know, Judy, when someone dies, we express our guilt in our dreams. You've come in with all sorts of dreams expressing your guilt for not being with John in Los Angeles or for not being able to stop him from doing drugs. Sometimes the anger is with yourself, and sometimes you've placed it on others. After the guilt and anger, in the grieving process, comes sadness. I think it is an important step for you to have had this sad, sweet dream. It means you are beginning to forgive yourself and John."

I continued to feel sad, preferring to be alone. One night, when I went out to dinner with friends, I debated whether or not to have a drink. One side of me said, "You're feeling okay, go on, loosen up," while another little voice said, "You feel low, what are you doing here? You should grab something to eat and go home." It suddenly struck me that I avoided fun because I felt guilty when I had fun; I realized that holding back was another way to avoid going on. A part of me was guilty for being alive, and therefore would not allow fun. At the same time, I felt a new responsibility for being alive, one that made me want to shape up and value every moment. I wanted to live up to that, but instead of being inspired by it, was paralyzed. The voice suggesting a drink won. In fact, it was such a good idea that I had several. I felt pretty good that night—might even say I had fun. The next morning, however, I woke not feeling so well. The night out hadn't done anything to boost my spirits, in fact, I felt even lower. For the first time I thought of myself dead, and lying in a grave in the cemetery next to John. I'd never visualized the two graves before. It felt okay.

The following day Laila came over and our conversation soon led to a discussion about life and death. Still depressed, I said I no longer believed suicide was necessarily wrong, or at least I could imagine a situation where someone might feel that suicide was the best alternative. Laila became very upset. "How can you say that?" she asked in disbelief, and went on to praise life and all there is "to live for." "We all have our own purpose, it isn't for us to make death decisions," she said with authority. "Suicide is bad karma, I don't want to hear you talking like this. It's especially bad for those you leave behind." There was an oddity to the conversation; I felt as if I'd awakened and realized some other voice had been speaking for me. It was sobering to hear Laila's reaction. I later wrote, "I needed to express my feelings about suicide to go beyond them. I've had the feeling shaken out of me, and it seems very distant from my reality now."

Bernie Brillstein and Second City had created a scholarship in John's name for students in the Chicago area. They were planning a benefit performance of the Second City show currently in L.A., of which Jimmy was a cast member. I was asked to write something about John for the program, which was needed right away.

I struggled with the piece, finding it more difficult than I'd imagined. Still, the project was good; it forced me to zero in on things in John's life that were important in his development as an actor. Everyone knew about his career after Second City, so I talked about how his talent and craft developed in the early years. It forced me to focus on the essence of John; something I hadn't been able to do for some time.

Anne and Deanne returned to New York, and *Titters 101* became a priority. It's always difficult to reorganize after a break, but we were soon into the swing of things.

I noticed a vast improvement in my concentration and attitude when working. We sat at the table and tossed around ideas with our customary lightheartedness, each trying to make the others laugh. Then we'd settle down, one of us at the typewriter, and work line by line.

We got right to work on a new piece, an Anaïs Nin parody in diary form about a young girl whose romantic interest is later revealed to be a horse. Reading over the Nin diaries for research made me self-conscious about my own diaries. It was interesting how *Titters* seemed to continually throw my life back in my face.

April 2

It makes me sad to think of times when J. was sad, so I'll just have to think more often about times when he was happy. Yesterday, I thought, "He had an infectious enthusiasm for things he wanted to do." He really did have a way of making things seem important and fun. It's odd, I refer to him as dead, but it is so contrary to everything I know about him. Then there are weird thoughts. Is his body just lying in

that coffin the same as he looked when I last saw him, or is
he decomposing? That's an awful thought, one I've been able
to avoid pretty much, but sometimes I wonder. I thought of
asking Dr. C., but I'm not sure I want to know.

The cemetery commission suggested it might be to everyone's advantage if John were moved to a new location. They
had a plot in mind which had no other graves around it, thus
solving their problems with debris blowing or visitors walking over other graves. It also had enough room to allow for
planting, which they thought I would like. Still, it's not an
easy decision. I wish the new spot was spectacular. It's amazing how difficult all decisions about the grave have become
for me.

*   *   *

April was shaping up to be a very busy month, filled with
anxieties. I was nervous about going to the John Belushi
Second City Scholarship Fund benefit in Los Angeles. John's
mother, father, and brother Billy would be there and I was
concerned about their feelings. And, of course, Jimmy had to
perform, perhaps even do one of John's scenes. The people
from Paramount, John's studio for *Noble Rot*, might be at the
show, and I was confused about how to deal with my anger
toward them. After all, I had my grudge and resented the
idea of having to bury my feelings if I saw them. Finally, I
decided to write Michael Eisner, the President of Paramount,
and express my hurt and anger at their lack of response to
John's death.

On April 17, I flew to Los Angeles and stayed with Tino
and Dana, who had a calming effect on me. Tino suggested
we go bowling to pass the day before that night's performance. It turned out to be a great way to shake the
nervousness.

We arrived early at the Huntington Hartford Theater and
went backstage. Jimmy was nervous about speaking after
the show, and about doing an old scene in which he based his
character on John. Once during "SNL" days when Jimmy
was visiting, the two of them went to the Whitehorse Tavern—
the bar where Dylan Thomas literally drank himself to death—
and John gave a dramatic accounting of the event. The scene
portrayed an older brother's romanticization of the tragedy

to his younger brother; Jimmy recreated John's storytelling. The scene was good, and I said it was well worth doing if he felt up to it. The irony only made it more powerful.

The lobby was full of people by the time I returned from seeing Jimmy. My in-laws, Bernie Brillstein and his wife, and many of the Second City people had arrived. Penny Marshall, Carrie Fisher, Bette Midler, Howard Hessman, Carl Reiner, and other famous faces were accosted by the press. I felt a little funny being so anonymous—not that I wanted attention since I was feeling pretty fragile. It just seemed odd that at this event which honored my late husband, the press didn't know who I was.

I sat in the center of the second row, and Jimmy often played to me, trying to make me laugh. The Dylan Thomas scene went perfectly; although it was funny, it was bittersweet. At times I was struck with how similar Jimmy's moves and expressions were to John's. And I was happy to see, again, how good he was, really good at what he does.

When the show ended, Jimmy got a warm hand. "I'd like to thank everyone for coming," he said. "One thing that stands out in my memory about John was his generosity. I think that's been matched by the generosity of the crowd here tonight in helping to raise fifty-two thousand dollars for the Scholarship Fund. Yesterday I was talking with John's manager, Bernie Brillstein, about the show tonight. I was telling him I felt kind of nervous. Suddenly I said to Bernie, 'What an asshole, huh?' 'Yeah,' Bernie agreed. 'But he was the most loveable asshole I ever met.'

"Last night, while I was lying in bed, I said into the dark, 'You asshole.' And to my surprise I heard, 'Nice mouth!' 'John! What are you doing here?' I asked, sitting up. 'I need some cigarettes, a hundred dollars, and the keys to the car,' he replied. So I gave these to him. Then I said, 'What about the benefit, John? We're doing this benefit tonight.' 'I don't do benefits,' he responded. 'Is there a party after?' 'Yeah.' 'Well, maybe I'll see you there.'"

There was a big laugh and the audience applauded wildly. Tears welled in my eyes as Jimmy twice attempted to say his final word, defeated by the cheers.

During the intermission some paper requested a photo of

Jimmy and me, and now all the press people knew who I was. "Judy, could I get a shot?" "Judy!" "Judy, over here . . ." followed me as I left the theater.

Shortly after returning to New York, I was on a plane to the Vineyard. I met James and Kathryn for dinner, then went to their cabin. James said he had written a song he wanted me to hear in which he mentioned John. He seemed a little nervous as he looked through his cassettes, explaining that each verse of the song was a vignette from a particular time in his life. He pulled out a tape and put it on. It was pretty, with an up tempo, which I liked. The first verse was about a friend telling James that he and his wife were splitting up. The friend asks to borrow his truck and the chorus follows, "That's why I'm here . . ." The next verse is John's:

> John's gone, found dead
> He dies high, brown bread
> Later said to have drowned in his bed
> After his laughter, the wave of dread
> Hits us like a ton of lead
>
> I mean to learn not to burn
> And to turn on a dime
> Walk on if I'm walkin'
> Even if it's an uphill climb
>
> Try an' remember that workin's no crime
> Just don't let 'em take and waste your time
>
> And that's why I'm here
> There'll be no more message tonight
> That's why I'm here . . .

It was difficult to react immediately. I was somewhat shocked by the abruptness of the beginning. I didn't know what "brown bread" was, but assumed it was heroin. I still found it difficult to accept that John had died from heroin. After listening again, I asked James about the brown bread reference and he explained that it was a Welsh colloquial expression for "found dead." "Oh," I said, "I thought it was heroin." This upset James and he said he would change it. "No," I suggested. "Let me sit with it a while. I really like the song." James gave me a copy to keep.

The next day I listened to the tape in my Jeep, over and over, feeling very emotional. I went to the cemetery and stood at the new spot the commission had suggested, then went to John's grave. It *did* feel better, but to move the grave! It was such a hard decision. I walked back to John's grave and began to pick things up: change, a beer can, old flowers, some notes. Suddenly I burst out crying. I was mad at John for dying for such a stupid thrill. I was angry that I had to spend so much time being sad and having to make decisions like what to do with his grave. "I just keep reliving the sadness," I said aloud. "God damn you, John!" I yelled, threw the items I'd picked up into the Jeep, and left.

Back in New York I wrote, "I'm in a weird mood. Lately I find myself thinking, 'I can't believe John did it, I can't believe he died young.' I'm pissed off at him, I feel like I'll never find anyone I could love so much. No one seems right. Just a thought—on *my* gravestone please put: 'Thank God it's over!' "

Rob finished his apprenticeship and was scheduled to leave in early May. Even though we kept different schedules, I felt sad that he was leaving. I would miss listening to his stereo filtering across the courtyard, hearing about his day, being able to just pop over to talk. And, of course, having Rob there meant I didn't really live alone.

Writing in my diary one night I noted that it suddenly felt like a long time since I had seen John. And it was clear that the last day I saw him was only getting farther away.

In early May I heard from Woodward. He had a few questions, and told me he had finished his piece and was editing. He said it really ran the gamut of emotions from funny to sad, and showed how many people tried to help John with his drug problem; it illustrated that his negative behavior wasn't simply accepted or ignored. Bob said it looked as if the piece would run in sections, every day for a week. I hung up feeling I would be glad when this was all over; it had taken

much longer than I thought, and much more energy than I
ever imagined.

That night, shuffling through some old papers, I found a
mailgram sent to John at "SNL" in 1977. It read:

> Saturday we watched your show with Marixa Lao. She
> had severe pain all day, but refused medication Sat.
> evening to be alert for your show. When you held up the
> cardboard M and threw her a kiss, she lit up like the sun
> and the entire hospital cheered with her. Your kind act
> helped overcome her pain and fear enough to permit her
> rapid improvement and discharge on Tuesday.
>
> Thank you for helping her. We're all fans now. We
> think you are super.
>
> > Night Nurses
> > Children's Hospital, Stanford, CA

I remembered Marixa. I never met her, but I knew about
her. I'm not sure how she and John met. Probably someone
asked John to give her a call in the hospital. One of the
difficult things that came with John's fame were requests
from friends to call people in hospitals. Usually, if someone
bothered to ask, it was something serious, and most often
people asked for kids. I didn't ever know him to refuse such a
call. John was wonderful, sweet, and charming, asking the
kids about themselves and telling them what he was doing.

Marixa somehow really entered his heart. I don't remember what her illness was, he didn't talk much about her, but
I knew he kept up with her. When he was a guest on a
Richard Pryor television special in L.A., he invited Marixa to
come by the set. I only knew about it because when I said I
thought I'd come by that afternoon, he said, "Would you
please come in the late afternoon, because Marixa is coming
today. She and her parents are driving a long way and I
want to give them all my attention." I remember feeling a
little jealous, and had to remind myself that this was a
young girl who was very ill.

Should I call Woodward and tell him this story? John was
private about things like that, he wanted to help on a personal level, he seldom talked about his "good deeds," so it

was unlikely Bob knew about her. Well, it was a story to illustrate that side of him, but Bob had a lot of good stories about John helping others. I should just relax and feel comfortable with what Bob said and trust that the articles would ultimately provide a well-rounded portrait. Besides, it was a little late. And how would he use this story? I didn't really know much, I didn't have any of the kind of details Bob was always looking for. I put the mailgram into an envelope marked "Letters to John," happy to still have it after all these years.

Chapter 23

REST IN PEACE

MAY–JUNE 3, 1983

Writing a Jack Kerouac parody for *Titters 101* inspired Anne, Deanne, and me to take a mini road trip to Montauk, Long Island, where we rented a cottage to finish the piece. After checking in, Deanne and I walked the beach while Anne made business calls. We were talking about *On the Road*, the model for our parody, and how Kerouac overused the word "sad" as an adjective—the sad night, the sad highway, the sad American dream, etc. "It's funny, but it seems easier to remember a sad time than a happy one," Deanne said. My first thought was that maybe people have more sad times. Then I remembered having a happy thought the other day; I couldn't recall what it was, but I could remember smiling and the way it felt.

"Well, happiness seems to flow out of you," I said, "while pain feels as though it attacks you. Maybe that has something to do with it; happiness is released, fleeting, whereas sadness can get stuck inside."

"Well, it's often difficult to stop reliving a sad moment," Deanne agreed, "so maybe that's true."

"I've been noticing how much clearer memories of unresolved issues seem, I mean, when I think about John. I can remember arguments word for word sometimes, but when I think about a great time, I seldom remember what was said. I'll remember where we were, how John looked, how I felt, and I might recall something that was said. But memories I'd just as soon forget keep repeating."

"Yeah, I know what you mean, I think I'm the same

302

way. The trick is to learn to let go of the pain, to release it."

"I'm trying to keep that basic idea in my consciousness, to focus on the positive now. I haven't been doing that well, really," I admitted, "but I'm aware of it at least." The sun was setting and the red of the sky was reflected in the water where it lapped the shore.

"I know it's not the same," Deanne said, "but when Rex and I split up, I went through a really down period."

We talked about the similarities and difficulties of coming to terms with the change. "Well, at least you don't have to worry about whether or not to move Rex," I concluded. We laughed and it felt good to be able to make light of my situation.

The cemetery commission suggested that if I were going to move John, I should do so before the summer. I realized my indecision was due to a specific dilemma—would John's spirit be affected by moving his body. I talked with Jimmy, admitting that although I didn't believe John's spirit and body were connected, it's the kind of thing you'd hate to be wrong about. And I was concerned with how his parents would view a move. Jimmy suggested he speak to an Albanian priest to make sure there wasn't any religious barrier. He was told that it was all right to move a body, but the new ground should be sanctified. Father Katre said he'd be happy to come to the Vineyard and perform another ceremony. After speaking with the rest of John's family, I decided to go ahead with the move.

Mark Lipsky contacted the funeral home and worked out the details. Jimmy suggested we have someone there to be certain everything was handled properly. I asked Walter Wlodyka and he was quick to agree.

On the Vineyard, a cemetery representative showed me the boundaries of the new plot. There were actually two plots because they figured people would walk over one to reach John's. After he left I walked around the cemetery looking at gravestones for ideas. I liked ones that gave information about the person. Captains were big on having a ship or fish symbol and I noticed "Mother" or "Wife of" was the most identified relationship. At the back of the old section was a reporter with a very moving eulogy from Franklin D. Roosevelt. I decided to go to the other island cemeteries to do more research. It struck me that this was a strange way for a young woman to spend her time.

Woodward wanted to look through my photos, and we sat at the dining-room table in the coach house, slowly flipping through photo books as I described the history of each picture. It was easy to become enthusiastic about sharing the memories they evoked. I realized this was a wonderful way to get a good feel for John, and wished we'd done it earlier. We finished the books and moved on to the piles of photos I had in suitcases and drawers. Bob was responsive to my stories, laughing and asking questions, and every so often requested to take this or that photo with him because it evoked a mood which would help him with his writing. "This is wonderful," he said many times. "These photos will be such a help, they offer such insight."

We counted up the photos Bob was taking and I wrote the number on a piece of paper which he signed, noting that he'd borrowed them, although I didn't ask him to. I was nervous about letting some of them out of my possession, since they were irreplaceable, but Bob said he would take good care of them and I trusted he would. And there were a few I would never want reproduced, like one of Landis and Mitch holding me upside down. I didn't worry about it, though, knowing he would need a signed release of each before he could reproduce them.

Jimmy met me in New York to go to the Vineyard ceremony to consecrate the new plot. The move was to take place early the following morning, and we would fly up the day after.

May 25 3:45 A.M.

Just took sleeping pill. J. is getting moved in two hrs, at six. I've had a lot of trouble sleeping tonight. Started having weird, ghostlike images, flying thru the air, sweeping down on me like in a horror house. Images that were in some stage of leaving the human body and becoming something else.

12:30 P.M. Woke up about eight-fifteen this morning to Walter's phone call. The move didn't happen because the vault and coffin are cracked. (I didn't even know what a vault was.) Now we'll need a new coffin and a court order. We phoned Father Katre. He was familiar with this problem and said it sounded like they could still do it before the weekend. I spoke with several people and it does look like they can do it by Sat. We set the ceremony for Sun. . . . Although Walter woke me from a dark sleep, I could tell right away that all had not gone well. I remember thinking, Wait a minute! This isn't what was supposed to happen. I thought I'd wake up and it would be all over. For a while I thought it meant we couldn't do the move. Maybe it's a sign, I thought. Maybe it's too disruptive. Maybe we *are* disturbing his rest. I had horrible images of what it would be like to move him to a new coffin. It was pretty awful and I doubted myself and my feelings about life and death for a while. But I finally told myself again that his body is nothing more than the remains of the house where his energy once dwelled. I think he would have liked his new gravesite better, and I just have to hold on a little longer to get him there.

* * *

Jimmy and I flew to the Vineyard later that day. We were both tired and cranky, and I was struck by how much like brother and sister we really were. The next day, feeling much better after a good night's rest, we went to the funeral home to select another coffin.

I didn't remember where the funeral home was located, although I knew the general vicinity. The outside wasn't recognizable either, but the interior was familiar. The gentleman who greeted us was solemn. He was heavyset, with a thick neck, and seemed uncomfortable in his suit. His shirt collar was too tight, and his deep, gruff voice seemed to confirm that he was being slowly choked. We spoke briefly in the hall before he asked us to follow him into the display room.

He opened the door to the room where John had been laid out and we entered without looking at each other. The room was set up altogether differently, now filled with various styles of coffins. We wanted one that wouldn't crack and he said several would fill that requirement. Much like a car salesman, he described the various models. Then Jimmy asked questions about the move and I asked that special care be taken of the ring John was holding. Suddenly Jimmy asserted, "I think I should be there when the move is made."

The undertaker spoke slowly and deliberately: "We find ... that it is better ... if family members are not present ... when we make moves."

"Well, I'm his brother and I feel it would be better if I were there," Jimmy insisted.

With classic Godfather-esque delivery, the undertaker informed us: "The funeral business ... is a very depressing business."

We were silent a moment, then Jimmy said to me, "Let's just go outside and talk about this a minute." We walked out front and sat on the stairs. Jimmy lit a cigarette and took a long drag. "Let's just cool out a minute," he said, exhaling. We sat quietly for a while. I looked down and noticed some tiny flowers at my feet, just beginning to bloom. Suddenly I started giggling, and Jimmy laughed, too.

"How did our lives get so absurd?" I asked.

"This is pretty strange," Jimmy agreed.

"The funeral business ... is a very depressing business," I imitated and we laughed again.

Jimmy finished his cigarette. "Do you know which one you want?" he asked.

"Yeah."

"Okay, let's go and order it."

On the way home we stopped at the cemetery and I showed Jimmy the new plot. He approved enthusiastically, saying it was worth the aggravation. "This spot *feels* good!" he boomed into the crisp, fresh air.

I spent Thursday searching the Chilmark property for a stone to use as John's marker. I liked the idea of a beach stone, and had a few in mind. Mr. Andrews (who contracted gravestones) came by and saw the stones I'd selected, which I hadn't realized were all soft stones and not appropriate for a gravestone. He offered to show me more on Sunday, and I stressed that I wanted something unusual or dramatic.

When I woke Friday morning I heard a gentle rain on the roof. My first thought was that the move must not have happened. I phoned the funeral home and to my relief, was told all went well. Jimmy and I picked up some lilacs and went to the cemetery. The grave looked fine; the work had been neatly done and the stones that marked John's head had been moved as requested. I was so glad it was over.

Father Katre arrived at the airport late Sunday afternoon. It seemed out of character to see him in a dark suit and aviator sunglasses. He took my hands in his and said he was very touched by what I was doing. Embarrassed, I said I was only doing what I thought I should. "But we all don't do what we think we should," he said softly.

At the cemetery, Jimmy and I stood by the new grave somewhat awkwardly, unsure what to do. Father Katre carried a small bag, from which he pulled out his ritual robe and other paraphernalia. Quickly he donned his vestments (not removing his sunglasses, which was another good look), lit some incense, set it in a container on the rocks, and without explanation began the service in Albanian. For a moment, I felt upset; I wasn't reliving the funeral, I simply felt sad. Jimmy put an arm around me and held my hand. Although most of the service was in Albanian, I recognized a blessing that had been said for Nena. Father Katre's robes flapped in the breeze as he circled the grave, swinging the incense container, chanting. I imagined how odd we might look to someone driving by; this would be the perfect time for a tour bus. The service was short and sweet.

Jimmy left the next day, and I met Mr. Andrews and Sidney Harris, who owns the mineral rights in Chilmark. Mr. Harris was a spry old guy with piercing blue eyes and a remarkable knowledge of the stones in Chilmark. I described what I had in mind and he said, "Okay, let me show you this one." We walked through the brush to a specific stone in a wall. I said, "Maybe a little more dramatic," and he said, "Okay, follow me." He was an interesting man and very nice. We went into some unusual areas with brush so thick I hadn't known you could drive through it. It was a beautiful day, a good day to be tromping about. Our last stop was the

beach near the old brick factory—closed in 1870—on the
north shore. There was a stone there which was beautiful
when wet, really striking, and very nice dry as well. It was
the kind of stone that would look best with only a name on
it, which I was begining to think was the way to go. I would
mark the plot with a name stone, then have a more traditional headstone made later.

That night I wrote about the day and concluded, "After we
finished, I felt confused by all the choices. I met with Matt
Tobin, a landscape architect, at the grave to talk about what
I wanted done. He can't really do anything until I know
about the stone. Vicious circle. Some people came while we
were there, looking for 'Belushi.' Then another car drove up
to the old spot. I felt terrible that they were looking at this
empty plot of dirt, thinking it was where John was buried.
And it pissed me off that they drove up instead of parking in
the lot and walking over. I guess a lot of people do that,
which is what cracked the coffin. I'm glad he's moved, so
people can't just drive up like he's fast food."

The following night I had dinner with Vineyard friends.
On my way home I had an urge to stop at the cemetery. I
parked in the lot and sat listening to the radio, wondering
what I was doing there. At home I wrote, "Maybe I just want
to be sure I haven't disturbed John and night is the time to
find out. At any rate, I knew I had to be there, so I was. It
certainly doesn't scare me. The moon threw shadows which
moved slightly in a cool breeze. I pulled up alongside John's
new plot, got out, and left the radio playing loud. I started
walking around the plot, wishing I could make contact, but
knowing better. I started walking down one of the roads into
the cemetery, crying, wishing, trying to understand. I started
to run and it felt good to feel my hair flowing and the speed
of my motion. I flashed on myself running in my house after
Danny told me John was dead and thought, as I had then,
'What am I doing?' I stopped and bent over to catch my
breath, then walked back and sat on top of the grave. 'Come
on spirits, c'mon ghosts,' I yelled out. 'Come an' get me!' My
heart was pounding from my run. After a while a real fear
came over me: Ticks! That's all that's gonna get me. So I
came home."

I went and looked at the beach stone again and decided it was the one. Moving it was the next task, so I spoke to several people about how to do that. Doug Campbell, a friend who was also James's caretaker, Huey Taylor, and Walter Wlodyka all agreed to help, and we planned to meet at eight the next morning to give it a try.

I was still in bed when I heard a car pull up at seven-thirty. I was up and dressed by the time Doug arrived at the door. At the beach, Doug pulled out two six-foot crowbars, a shovel, post digger, and sledge hammer. Upon seeing the rock, which he really liked, he ran around the beach, checking out distances, angles, and heights, and determined we would have to "move 'er" about fifty feet. He started right in, shoveling sand away from the base of the stone. "Shouldn't we wait for the others?" I said, hopefully scanning the cliff, where I expected them to appear. "Oh, let's just get going," Doug insisted, and although I had my doubts that the two of us could make progress, we began.

Doug is a great American character with the strength and appeal of a strong, good-looking farm boy. A quiet, deter-mined loner with a friendly smile. The ease with which he worked was amazing. Our first objective, my leader explained, was to "flip 'er over." Now, I'm talking about a twelve-to-fifteen-hundred-pound rock. Doug easily picked up a moder-ate size rock, and using that as a fulcrum, stabbed his crowbar into the sand with one mighty swoop, so that its end was well under our rock. Then he pushed down on the bar, using the fulcrum to raise our rock slightly. My job was to slide fist-sized rocks into the opening he created. In this manner, our rock was gradually raised. We built slowly and carefully and all went well.

It took over an hour to get the rock flipped, then we both scurried about the beach collecting flat rocks to make a path on which to slide our rock along the sand. It was a beautiful day and I soon stripped off my jacket and sweater. As we worked, my hands were repeatedly smashed and I was get-ting sand burns. My arms ached and my enthusiasm was waning. When we began, I'd put an "X" in the sand where Doug said we would need to move our rock, to get it within reach of the tow truck. It seemed ridiculously far. I suggested going for help, but Doug just smiled and said, "Oh, it's no problem. We'll have it in no time."

About eleven I needed a break, so I offered to go to Menemsha and get us something to eat. When I returned, I could really see how far "we'd" moved the rock. We lunched, sitting proudly upon our prize. By twelve-thirty our rock was on the X and I was really excited. Now for step two! I took Doug back to his car, and tried to locate Huey, since he had an idea about getting the stone up the cliff with a tow truck. Having no luck finding him, I gave up and headed for home.

In need of gas, I pulled into the Up-Island station. I was beginning to feel the day; I was hot and tired. About to leave, I heard a familiar whistle approaching. Huey Taylor is a great melodic whistler; just as you'd recognize someone's voice, you'd know Huey's whistle. "Looking for me?" he asked with a sweet smile. I could tell he'd been working all day; his bushy hair was tousled and he looked hot and tired, too. But he had the tow truck and was ready to go. We picked up Doug. "Ten minute job," Doug predicted.

At the cliff overlooking the beach, Doug and Huey hooked a chain to our rock and moved obstacles out of its path. My job was to sit in the driver's seat with my foot on the gas to keep the engine from stalling. This truck was a little the worse for wear; sitting there with it shuddering and shaking, I imagined the stone pulling it over the cliff. Good way to go, I thought. About ten minutes later, our rock was up the hill, almost on the truck. Two hours later, we finally had the rock aboard, hanging somewhat perilously off the back, but the experts weren't worried, so why should I be? Triumphantly we drove the stone through Chilmark, depositing it in my driveway, where it would await the engraver.

At dinner with friends, I told the tale of getting the stone. It was nice to have an audience. On the way home, I stopped briefly at the cemetery to leave a rose from the restaurant on John's grave. The night was calm and I could hear the surf on the south shore. I felt calm, too. "Rest in peace, John," I whispered into the night, and didn't linger.

Driving home I remembered how down I'd been the other night at the graveyard, when I'd been so upset. I had a mental dialogue about it with "Dr. Cyborn": "How did you feel at the cemetery?"

"Mixed up."

"What do you mean by that?"

"I was sad, confused about death, angry."

"Angry at what?"

"Angry at myself, I guess. Angry that life is so hard. Angry that I'm still in such pain."

"Why are you angry with yourself?"

"I'm angry that I can't let myself be happier about the good things in my life. I'm angry I can't let go of the bad in the past." At this point the "conversation" came to a stop. I didn't know what to tell myself, to have "Dr. Cyborn" tell me. I wanted "him" to tell me how to achieve inner peace. I flashed again on Danny telling me John was dead. I fought falling into depressing thoughts, somehow escaping the pain of that memory. Once home, I phoned Rhonda to tell her about the adventure of the rock. I made her laugh and it felt good.

Chapter 24

IF IT'S NOT ONE THING . . .

JUNE–JULY, 1983

B ack in New York, I went to the Lipsky office for a financial meeting. Mark was on the phone. "Guess who just walked in," he said into the receiver, then, "It's Danny," as he handed the phone to me.

"How are you, Judy," Danny said enthusiastically. We exchanged brief cordialities. "Ah, listen, you've probably heard that Donna and I got married and I just wanted to apologize for not telling you sooner." I did know. Larry had told me on the Vineyard, and although it was a small wedding—only six people—I was a little hurt that Danny hadn't told me about it. "I would have liked you to be there," he went on. "A few people should have been there, but I just didn't want people flying in and the press finding out and all that." Now that we were talking, I understood completely. Hadn't John and I done the same thing? We were married in Colorado with no one but my brother and his girlfriend in attendance. We didn't even tell our parents until after the fact.

I got off the phone feeling good about Danny's marriage. A part of me wondered what it would mean to our friendship, but that was already in transition, this just added a new element. In fact, I was excited by the prospect of finding a new friend in Donna. Danny said they would be on the Vineyard in a week or so. I decided to go up earlier than planned to have an opportunity to get to know her.

John and Deborah Landis were in New York, and asked me to join them and actor Griffin Dunne for dinner. We were an odd foursome in that we'd each suffered recent tragedies.

John and Deborah were reeling in the aftermath of the *Twilight Zone* helicopter accident, both emotionally and legally. And Griffin, still mourning the death of his younger sister, Dominique (also an actress, best known for her role as the oldest daughter in *Poltergeist*), was suffering through the trial of her accused murderer. Not surprisingly, we got into quite an emotional discussion about the judicial system. Griffin spoke about the difficulty of being in the courtroom while the defense attempted to prove that his sister provoked her attack. I projected to Cathy Smith's trial and how they would portray John. It wouldn't be pleasant. "It's simply unbelievable what goes on to protect the accused," Griffin stated. He said one of the things he learned was how important it is for members of the victim's family to be at a trial. Deborah mentioned that their lawyer had stressed the importance of her attending the court proceedings with John. This raised an issue I hadn't yet thought about; if Cathy Smith went to trial, would I attend?

The next day, I phoned Pam to say I was considering attending the trial if Cathy Smith were brought back. She was quiet an unusually long time. Finally she said in a gentle voice, "I guess I can't think of anything worse to have to sit through, given what they'll do to John." I said I hadn't made a decision, and wouldn't, until there was a need to. I just wanted her to know I was thinking about it.

I had a dream to relay to Dr. Cyborn from that morning: "I was at the beach, sitting on a big stone on the cliffs, watching Mitch and Wendie down at the water's edge. Suddenly a wave swept over them and they appeared to be washed away. I ran to help and the wave just missed me, then they pulled themselves out of the water and everything was fine, as if nothing had happened. We packed to leave and Wendie said she'd lost a ring. I told her I'd seen one on a table, but that wasn't it. I was chewing gum, and wanted to throw it out, but it stuck in my mouth. I kept pulling and it just kept stretching. I couldn't get rid of it. That's all I remember."

"What is your relationship with Mitch and Wendie?" Dr. Cyborn began. I said Mitch was a writer and an old friend, and that he and Wendie, an actress, were married shortly before John died. I hadn't known Wendie well until we spent some time together last summer; and since then we'd become close. They lived a block from me, on Tenth Street, so we often had breakfast together, or I dropped in. They had just decided to rent a place in Los Angeles for three months and I was a little upset about their leaving.

"What does the ring mean to you? The one on the table?"

"I don't know." I tried to remember how it looked. "It's not like mine," I said, fingering my wedding ring.

"Could it be the ring you put in John's coffin?"

"Well, it wasn't exactly that, but, I suppose . . ."

"What do you think the gum means?" Dr. Cyborn asked.

I felt uneasy and picked at the lint on my pants. "I don't know." I continued with my free association. "I don't chew gum very often. When I do I usually just chew it till the flavor's gone, then spit it out."

"But in the dream you can't get rid of the gum. What is it you can't get rid of?"

"Well, umm . . . ah . . ." My mind was blank.

"I think it's so hard to get rid of you can't even get it out of your mouth. It's guilt. Guilt about not going to L.A. with John. Wendie and Mitch, a couple not unlike you and John, going to L.A. to work, sets off memories that trigger the guilt. The waves are waves of grief you don't want to feel. The ring is the ring you put in John's coffin, and what do you think the stone is?" I was with him now and knew before he asked that it was the gravestone. "So," Dr. Cyborn concluded, "these friends going to L.A. have opened up feelings you have not yet come to terms with. You are still guilty and mad at John, and these feelings conflict with your feelings of love. That makes you feel depressed."

"Well, it's not that I'm unaware of these feelings. But how do I get rid of them?" I asked.

"You've got to feel them, you can't just shut them up inside. Look how busy you keep yourself," Dr. Cyborn noted. "You don't sit in one place long enough to really give yourself time to feel. You are furious with this guy! He ruined your life!"

I was angry at Dr. Cyborn's choice of words. John didn't ruin my life, I thought. John made my life! Yes, I was depressed, and Dr. Cyborn was right about the conflict. Whenever I got angry at John, another part of me felt guilty for feeling that way. I took a deep breath and loudly exhaled. "See, now you're turning it off," he accused me.

"I thought I was spitting it out," I said.

"The problem is, you'd rather hurt yourself than John. You've got to start putting yourself first."

I left Dr. Cyborn on the verge of tears. Walking down the street, I felt angry. Was I angry with Dr. Cyborn or John? I put on my sunglasses, sat on some steps, and cried.

I went to the Vineyard for the stonecutting, and made arrangements for placing the gravestone bench and beetlebung tree. The weather was beautiful and I made sure to get down to the beach for a walk at least once a day, if not more. There, I could forget myself and become absorbed in my surroundings.

The beach walks were wonderfully healing. I wrote in my diary: "There is something about the ocean and fresh air which makes you wake up and see things more clearly. I've been making a rock garden with beach stones, which is also soothing. I think I'm accepting John's death better. I thought, okay, J. is dead and that is sad. But I go on, and I'm going to make it, I'll be happy again. I can still enjoy things. I can still create. And maybe I'll even fall in love. I have a lot of things to be thankful for. Dr. Cyborn is right about putting myself first, but I don't think he realizes that a lot of things people think of as things I do 'for John' are ultimately for myself."

And another entry: "Saw a shooting star when I came home and made a wish—to find happiness and someone to share it with."

And yet another: "I was just trying to figure out the semantics of how I feel about the way things went for the last few weeks of J.'s life. It's not 'sorry' exactly, but I will always regret not having had more energy at that time to devote to J. I don't want to feel guilty about it any more, but I will always regret it."

Danny and Donna arrived in June. The weather was great and we spent a lot of time together on the beach. Donna was an excellent listener and I soon poured out my heart to her. She was sensitive to my situation, and interested in knowing more about John to better understand Danny's grief. I liked her sensibility and sense of humor. The three of us got on marvelously. It felt good to be with Danny again, and I was pleased they'd opened up to me as *their* friend.

I was determined to plant flowers at John's grave before returning to New York, and finally did so the day before I left. It was a sizzling summer day, very hot. I waited till late afternoon, hoping to avoid the worst of the heat and the tourists. I wasn't particularly successful on either point. While I planted, several visitors, mainly bicyclists and mopeders, stopped at the grave. People usually wandered the cemetery looking at markers, finally asking if I could direct them to John Belushi. Two teenage boys were especially respectful, sitting silently on the ground near the Belushi marker. Finally one of them spoke to me.

"I'd read that there was no stone, but we thought we'd try anyway," he began. "Do you know what this monument is?" He pointed to the mound of rocks.

"Those mark John's grave," I explained. After we talked a while he asked, "Are you the caretaker for John's grave?"

I smiled at the interesting choice of words. "You might say that," I replied.

"Did you know John?" he asked.

I hesitated. "Yes, I did. I'm his widow."

He seemed startled by this, perhaps embarrassed, and stood abruptly. "Well, thank you for answering my questions," he said.

"Thanks for stopping," I said awkwardly. I was sweaty and dirty and my face was probably beet red from the heat. They must think I'm crazy! I thought. I imagined myself an old woman, gray and bent over, hiding behind the bushes at John's grave, being friendly to some visitors, admonishing others, shaking a crooked stick in the air as if I might attack: "Hey! You! Pick up that beer can! Whadya think this is, anyway?"

The next morning, I rose early to catch the plane to New York for a business meeting, planning to return within a day or two. Looking in the mirror, I was shocked; my face was red and swollen. At first I thought it was a bad sunburn, but why was it swollen? It didn't hurt. I made an appointment with a skin doctor in the city.

By the time I got to the doctor's office, there was an itchy rash on my hands. The doctor said it was poison ivy, but he wasn't sure what was wrong with my face. He gave me some cream and said to return in a few days if the condition didn't improve.

The next day my face was better, but my hands were bad. The rash had spread and there were big, red splotches on my stomach. I had a meeting with Mark, but was so obviously uncomfortable that he sent me to his skin doctor. Dr. Ramsay agreed that the rash was poison ivy, but was unsure about my stomach. He gave me pills for the itching and said to come back in two days. I wanted to return to the Vineyard the following day, but he said that until he could diagnose everything, it would be best if I remained in town.

One good thing about staying was that I would see Jimmy. He was coming to meet with the producers of *True West*, a Sam Shepard play he'd agreed to do. And Anne was also in town, so we took advantage of this time to work on our book. Writing was difficult, however, since I itched like crazy. Baths were recommended and I tried them all: tea baths, herb baths, ginger baths. I went to the doctor every few days, each time begging him to let me return to the Vineyard. I had a fantasy about diving into the cold ocean and finding relief. But Dr. Ramsay convinced me to wait a few more days. Apparently the blotches on my stomach were cause for concern, and he felt it was important to run tests. I had hoped to spend the Fourth of July with Danny and Donna, but agreed to stay.

The Tenth Street house had been sold and the closing was scheduled to take place without me. However, since I was in town, I decided to go. As I was getting dressed for the meeting, Woodward phoned. He had some questions about the shooting of *The Blues Brothers* movie. The questions led me to pull out my 1979 diary, to read him an appropriate section. "Oh, that's great!" he said. "That's really helpful. I'm having such a hard time getting a feel of what your day-by-day life was like then." Bob had implied a few times that he would like to see my diaries, but I wasn't prepared to let him. The 1979 one was the only old one I had that was substantial. The others were very spotty and they were all too personal to just hand over. "Is there some more you could read me?" he asked. "Something that would help give me the feel of what was going on then?" Flipping through the book I thought, why not? I began with our move to Los Angeles and read the daily entries, skipping over details I considered personal and unrelated to what Bob needed. There was a lot of talk about John working out; he had begun karate for the first time and we were both swimming. Lots of notations about John filming or rehearsing and my work on the Blues Brothers' book. I read about our trip to visit John's parents for the first time after their move to Julian. Most of it wasn't all that descriptive, but I thought it was interesting.

Bob was very responsive. This was the time John began to successfully move away from drugs, and I felt this day-to-day account supported that. I now knew that the seemingly little indulgences were signs of trouble (I read each to Bob), but hindsight offers such insight. I hadn't read the diary for some time, so I was easily persuaded to read on, even though I was running late. I went back to the beginning and read quickly up to where I first began. Bob said it was invaluable for him to have heard the progression and repeated that it was important to get a feeling for how John and I related and lived on a daily basis. I rushed to my appointment, feeling good.

June 30

Woodward has been very complimentary to me as a writer since he read the program from the Scholarship benefit. Said ". . . I wish I had people working for me with your perception," etc. Of course, flattery will get you everywhere, so I can't really trust this until I see his final piece and know what of his "honesty," "integrity," and "flattery" is for real.

Shopping at Balducci's, I overheard one of the clerks make a samurai joke, obviously imitating J. It made me feel good to realize that J.'s work still enters people's daily life and makes it more amusing, more fun. I imagined him talking to Mamma Balducci about her food. I bet she would have taken him under her wing. The stupid thing is that now I'm sad for the things J. "would have enjoyed."

*   *   *

A few days later Jimmy called. On returning to Chicago, he had an offer to do "SNL." He didn't know what to think and neither did I. They worked it out so he could complete his contract with *True West* and begin "SNL" a few weeks late. That night I wrote: "Jimmy's been offered "SNL." That's a hard one. Everyone I've told reacts as if the follow up on J. is too much. It's funny, but I think that would be okay. He already went thru that at Second City. Hell, he's gone through that his whole life. It would be a nice full circle if Jimmy could get something from "SNL." But it's so *hard*. It's scary to think about someone close to me going through it again. I don't know what to say. It's going to have to be a decision he makes for himself."

About the tenth of July, Dr. Ramsay and the specialists I saw decided they had run enough tests to discount the various illnesses they'd suspected. And when a friend mentioned a terrible reaction after cutting large poison ivy plants, I realized I'd probably done the same thing; I had attacked a root while planting at the cemetery. I was finally free to return to my island. The following day, however, I came down with strep throat and was laid up for another week. I couldn't help but wonder why all this was happening, when I was just beginning to feel emotionally better.

Back on the Vineyard, I quickly regained good health. July was full of great beach days and stunning sunsets. Many friends were on hand. I wrote a few hours a day, pounding away at the typewriter. I was working on a parody combining *Robinson Crusoe* and *Gulliver's Travels*. My mood was improving, although occasionally I turned down invitations, feeling the need to be on my own. I was often introspective during these times, and cried some, but there was a change in the crying; it was not so much an outpouring, but more a gentle release.

On July 27, I spoke with Woodward. He was still editing, but he had convinced the editors that the piece must run as a whole. He said otherwise he was afraid only the more sensational parts would run. He seemed to feel good about that. Bob also said he was still looking for a title. He liked what I had said to him at one of our first meetings, that John was "an American artist," and that he might use that. He also said a friend had suggested he call it "John." I didn't think that was very good because I thought most people would probably think of Lennon. But I didn't say anything, since, with Bob, I usually kept my opinions on certain issues to myself, always careful to avoid trying to shape his story. At this point, I didn't care what he called it.

Pam kept up with the L.A. District Attorney and reported that Cathy Smith's lawyers were appealing everything they could. Montagna estimated it would take a year and a half to get her back to the States. That sounded a long way off. There were also suspicions that Smith was testing the quality of heroin for some American dealers. Now the Canadian government wanted her returned to the U.S. for trial.

I had mixed responses to this news. She's gonna screw up, I thought, and then realized that she herself could overdose. For a moment, I even thought that would be the best thing. As if an observer to my thoughts, I was shocked: Jesus, do I really think it would be best if she died? I had thought of her as a person with a fatal disease, as if the end, death, were inevitable. Well, it's as if she does have a disease, I realized, only her disease is curable. I saw Cathy Smith backed into a corner like a frightened animal; the Canadian government was after her, Montagna was after her, and I suddenly felt uncomfortable to be after her, too. Was prison the answer? That certainly wouldn't cure her disease. But then, she might hurt someone else . . . It was an endless circle of thoughts, one I couldn't break for some time.

One night I went to a party on the beach. People were going off to their cars every so often, obviously doing cocaine. I wasn't used to seeing coke on the Vineyard. I didn't like to see it anywhere, but especially on the island—it was the worst kind of pollution I could imagine. I felt distant from the festivities and went home.

The next afternoon, I had a call from Shirley Sargent, a

bookkeeper at the Lipsky firm. She had something "very important" to tell me. We arranged a meeting for the following day. Something about it all was very strange.

Shirley nervously clutched a large envelope and began by telling me that she was resigning from the Lipsky firm due to certain problems she saw Mark creating, and a lack on his part to heed her warnings. "You always treated me well," she said, "and I can't let Mark just continue on the course he's on without letting you know." She pulled out a stack of Xeroxes and explained various documents and transactions that painted a bleak portrait of my financial situation.

Once home, I phoned Pam and relayed everything I'd been told. Pam was obviously upset, but remained calm and was reassuring. I was to send the Xeroxes to her and she would check them over. If Shirley's concerns seemed genuine, we would then plan our strategy; undoubtedly, we would meet with Mark. In the meantime, I wasn't to say anything to anyone about my encounter with Shirley.

I very much wanted to pick up the phone and call Mark, I was sure he could clear up everything. Things couldn't be as they appeared.

Chapter 25

THE CRUNCH

AUGUST–DECEMBER 25, 1983

I returned to New York a few days before the meeting with Mark to attend Jimmy's opening in *True West*. It was nice to have someone living in the studio again, and it looked as though Jimmy would be there longer than originally planned. He'd decided to join the cast of "SNL," but not to move the family to New York. He would return to Chicago on the off weeks. Many of my friends seemed to think it unwise for Jimmy to live in the studio; I guess they thought he was so similiar to John it would be difficult. I'd known Jimmy since he was twelve and to me he was very much his own person. As I saw it, Jimmy was family, and if I could help by giving him a place to stay, I would.

The meeting at Lipsky's was not good; indeed, my affairs were not as I'd believed. Although Mark insisted things were under control, it was difficult to determine just what my position was. At this point, Pam felt it best to bring in another lawyer, George Galloway, to advise us. At our next meeting it became clear that it was going to take some time to ascertain exactly where I stood financially and what needed to be done. Another meeting was set for the end of the month, so I returned to the Vineyard.

While on the island I tried not to worry about my situation. Still, I found I was nervous about spending, debating every item I bought and getting only essentials.

I stopped at the cemetery one night on my way home from dinner at a friend's. The night was warm and the moon bright. An occasional cloud drifted across its face. The

"Belushi" stone, looking rather eloquent, was in place on John's plot. A lost Blues Brothers cassette had reappeared in the car that day, so I put it on the tape deck and sat on the fence next to John's grave, listening to the music. At home, I wrote about being at the cemetery: "I contemplated the reality of John being buried there and the fact that I could sit there and listen to him sing. I wondered if I was going to cry, but didn't, and it wasn't that I held it back. It just didn't come. I felt okay."

I flew to New York for the Lipsky meeting. My immediate financial outlook was disturbing; changes needed to be made, and right away, but my biggest costs were mortgages, and I couldn't just stop paying those. The only immediate change we could make was to get my car out of the garage where I kept it and take it to Pat's in New Jersey. That was like removing a sliver from my finger when my hand was in a vice. We contacted Phantom's landlord and gave him the obligatory three-month notice. We talked about the possibility of moving to a smaller, less expensive office, but it was impossible to determine if that were possible, because it was still unclear what my budget would be. It was clear, however, that major adjustments had to be made. That night I noted, "I'm very torn between my feelings for Mark and my anger over my financial situation. I just don't see a happy ending here."

I slept well my first night back at the Vineyard and awoke to a gentle rain tapdancing on the roof. The air was muggy, but the light sparkled off the water and the day was surprisingly warm. I walked the beach, my head spinning, thinking about the meetings in New York. I heard myself think, "I'm having financial problems," and laughed at the seriousness of the voice in my mind. I imagined telling this to Rhonda, then explaining, "So I'll be leaving Mark's firm." This thought startled me; I hadn't realized it was necessary before, and recognized it was true. I would have to leave Mark. Overwhelmed, I started to cry. I sat on a log and sobbed.

On returning to the house I wrote in my diary: "Still feeling torn. . . . I was too dependent on Mark. I expected him to make too many decisions for me. In fact, I depended on him for various 'husband' decisions more than I might have a husband. I would never have let a husband handle 'our' finances—budget, loans, etc.—basically on his own, and just accept, 'Don't worry, everything's fine.' "

I went over my finances repeatedly, looking for solutions. Support for the Belushis was my major concern, since I had continued to help them regularly since John's death. Mr. and Mrs. Belushi lived in homes I maintained. What if I lost them? What would they do?

As much as I didn't want to, I knew I had to cut back the cash support. I procrastinated a few days, then finally forced myself to make the calls. I reached John's father first. I felt foolish, unable to explain what had happened or how it would work out in the long run. I made it clear that the down side could mean having to sell the ranch. "I'll do what I can to keep it, Dad," I promised.

"Oh, honey," Adam said, "whatever happens, I'll be fine, don't worry about me. I just feel bad because I wanted you to have the place someday."

Marian and Agnes were great, too. Marian was really the most affected because she had been plagued with various physical problems that hampered her ability to work. But she had managed before and emphasized that she would make it on her own again if necessary. She was nothing but grateful for the help John and I had given over the years. I was relieved that everyone responded with empathy. I was feeling guilty; I'd taken on the responsibility of helping out and failed, I'd let everyone down. But no one fed into my guilt. In fact, Agnes rallied, "Look, we were poor a long time, we can handle anything. We'll see it through this time, too. You've been wonderful to us. Believe me, I appreciate everything you've done for my family."

Before returning to New York for the fall, I stopped at the cemetery to leave some wildflowers. Walking toward the grave I could see lots of new objects on both the name stone and the mound: little stones, shells, and lots of change. On closer examination I found that someone had left a short straw, as in "cocaine" straw, on the Belushi marker. Even in death he can't escape it, I thought as I shoved it in my pocket. It made me angry and I realized it was the same reaction I used to have when someone offered John coke when he was trying not to do it. I sat in the spot where a bench would eventually be, and watched the sun disappear behind the distant trees. I felt good there. It occurred to me that one of the things I liked about the plot was that it was mine. There was no mortgage, no monies due. No one could take it away.

Sept. 18

Have been wondering for the past few days, just *what* to do about my financial situation. Tonight I feel I've begun to get a grasp on it, at least I have a direction for the future. The main thing is, *I'm* going to have to decide what to do. I can't let anyone else—Pam included—do that for me. In fact, it's most important that I don't let Pam make the decision, so if I'm not pleased with it, I have only myself to blame. I'm going to have to pick a new accounting firm myself.

*   *   *

I was up bright and chipper the morning of a meeting with a new accounting firm which had been highly recommended from several good sources. I exercised, showered, made breakfast, and took a bus uptown to Fifth Avenue and Forty-third Street. Ed London was fiftyish, very businesslike, but friendly at the same time. After hearing my situation and looking over a few papers, he was direct. "You have a big problem, an immediate problem, and an expensive problem." He needed more time to go over documents before making suggestions, so we agreed to meet later in the week. Based on the firm's reputation, I knew I would go with them if they would have me.

A few days later, Pam and I met with Ed London. He agreed to take on my account, made several suggestions as to how we might proceed, and speculated about various outcomes. He suggested I sell the Ninth Street house, Chilmark, the ranch, and Agnes's condo. I felt numb, but agreed to put the Ninth Street house on the market, since it was my largest investment. I didn't want to make any other decisions until we could establish what my capital was.

At home, after the meeting, I soon found myself busily organizing the keys to the building. I spent at least an hour identifying, marking, and putting sets on individual chains. Rhonda came over later and I said, "I don't know why I've wasted time with all these keys today." "You weren't wasting time," she said. "It's symbolic of getting your life in order."

Sept. 23

Went uptown to Dr. C.'s. He said he felt I should just sell the house, get a job, and let the new business managers rebuild my capital. He said not to put pressure on myself to try and do something fantastic. I have trouble accepting this. Walked to work with Jimmy. Told him what Ed London said about selling houses. He kept saying, "There must be some other way." We stopped at Shopsin's for a soda, then sat outside and talked nonsense. Felt better.

Sept. 27

Got up about eleven. Got place ready for real estate woman to look at building. I showed her coach house and Karen took her through other apts. I felt very alone today. J. was the only real thing, the only important thing in my life. None of the financial stuff would really matter if I had John. It's bearable to move on without him, but it's so much *less*. It's so much harder. I need someone. I want someone I could care about, give to, the way I could John.

*   *   *

Somewhere about this time it became clear that Woodward's articles were going to be a book. I'm not sure he ever actually told me, I think he just started calling it a book. I felt good about it; I thought it would add to John's stature. Bob also said he was considering letting me read his work, because I had "such a good memory for dates and detail." He said he'd never let the subject of a report do that before. I felt a strong bond had grown between us over the year and looked forward to seeing his work. It was frustrating that the change to a book meant waiting even longer for the finished product. But from all our conversations and meetings, I thought I had a good sense of what he was doing. I was confident the book would show John in a new light. And I believed it would illustrate that drug taking is not indicative of good or bad, but of the failure of the individual to choose wisely, and the failure of society to be of much help with that decision.

Oct 3

Went out with Steve last night. Sometimes I feel funny about the fact that we see so little of each other now. But I don't really want any more. Until I'm ready to make a real commitment to someone, it makes no sense for me to worry about this stuff.

Oct. 6, Noon

Yesterday I told Anne and Laila that I was closing Phantom, and that I might have to sell Ninth Street. I had to say something about the office since it was figuring into our plans. I didn't explain any details, just said I had two problems: first, getting some money to make my immediate budget, and second, making serious cutbacks. I explained I'd been advised not to tell anyone anything specific. "Oh, come on, we're not going to tell anyone," Anne said, but I said I just couldn't. I told them it was legally complicated and ultimately best for me not to say anything. Anne was concerned with the fact that I was only talking to lawyers and accountants and pointed out that it was important to keep my house in New York, my base. She said it's important to protect my emotional state if I'm to meet my economic potential. Anne asked how much money I'd need if the worst happened; she said we could raise money from people who wouldn't want to see me lose my house, as a loan or something. Basically, her point was "You can do it!" She got me back on track with some ideas I had that I was letting slide.

So I wake up today thinking about all this, and I find I'm a little angry with Dr. C. I feel that he's made a bad call in telling me to sell both my houses, as if he didn't understand the emotional involvement and how difficult it would be to give up everything right now. I understand that ultimately I may have no choice, but as long as I do, I can't figure everything strictly by numbers. I like Anne's enthusiasm to at least try to find a way to make things work. She's right, the accountants figure what's best on paper. I can't live on a piece of paper.

8:00 P.M. I just caught myself thinking, "John should be here to take care of this." I think it's really him, not Dr. C., I felt angry with this morning.

Oct 7

I realize that my financial problems have been a sort of "blessing in disguise." I'm feeling more in touch with reality—I've let myself become too involved with my pain. I don't think, however, that this would have been a "blessing" say, six to eight months ago. I wasn't ready then.

*   *   *

By the end of October I very much wanted a trip to the Vineyard. I resisted for a while, not wanting to spend the money on the plane and knowing I would be going up in December to close the house. But the urge was intense. Finally I gave in.

Oct. 21

Took noon plane. Went for walk on beach. Pretty chilly, but I felt better from the moment I got off the plane. I felt as if I'd been getting lost in the city, and needed to come here and see what life is about: the ocean and the sun and the weather and the moon and the cliffs. I stood with the sun on my face and took a deep breath and thought, I got out just in time.

Went to cemetery. Looking out over the graveyard, I thought, Well, this is a nice spot. There's something special about being here, it's a good place to think about life. I was disappointed that the trees weren't planted yet and was thinking how it would look some day and thought, Gee, this is where I'll probably end up. I laughed at myself because I think such serious things in the most naïve way. I picked up the coins that had been left on the rock and the mound, a large handful, mainly small change. "I wish they'd leave dollars," I said aloud. I remembered Bernie once saying John got more gifts of T-shirts and promotional jackets than anyone he knew. I responded, if people really cared about him, they'd send underwear and socks. Now I thought, Money just came to John . . . here he is in his grave and people are still giving him money.

Oct. 26

Returned to New York last night. Met up with Jimmy after "SNL." On walk home, he said he'd like to stay in studio, if I have the place for a while, and pay full rent. Janie and Jimmy Buffett are interested in renting the second floor on a month-to-month. (Since the house is on the market, I'm not supposed to make any long-term leases.) That could help.

It struck me that J. would be thirty-five his next birthday. But thirty-five is an age that does not compute with J. I cannot imagine him at thirty-five. He is eternally anything up to thirty-three. I had a rush of tears, a tightness in my chest, the reality surprising me a moment. A thought which caught me off guard. But then I was okay. I still wish he could be with me, but it's more a wish than a burning desire.

Nov. 10

Weepy tonight. Found a note from J. to me. It was a short note, just to tell me how much I meant to him and that he loved me. I broke down. Later I fantasized getting married again. As we stood to say our vows, I said to my new husband, "I never thought I'd be this happy again." But he's a faceless man, it seems like a hopeless fantasy.

Nov. 23

Dr. C. asked if I could see myself at forty and to describe myself. I said it was hard because I saw all possibilities at once. I would still be thin and in pretty good shape, unless I had a drinking problem. I would either drink a lot or very seldom. I would either be heavily into my work as an artist, or I would be raising children, etc. Dr. C. said because I was with J. for so long, he naturally became my center, life revolved around his goals. So, although I'm in my thirties, I haven't put much focus on my own goals. He said my description of life at forty was like a kid trying to decide what she wants to be when she grows up. He said it's important to find a direction and things I feel are worthwhile, or I'll go through life a sad person.

I think I've already thought most of that about myself, except the last part, about the value of a direction.

Nov. 25, Thanksgiving

Drove out with James and Kathryn to new place they've rented in Conn. Had a fabulous meal, a nice day in general. Pat was disappointed I didn't come down there, but it was sort of symbolic for me to do something different. I guess I feel the same about Christmas. I was thinking about the different reasons I want to, or don't want to, do various things at Christmas. I still don't know what I'll do, but at least I'm considering "why" I'm selecting possibilities. Wonderful, waking up today to a lovely snowstorm. Still on the warm side for snow, but nonetheless, there it is. Not so wonderful to wake up to was my dream. I remember one image clearly. I had a limo and as I walked up to it, suddenly it was a hearse with flowers. I stopped, startled, and it drove away.

Nov. 28

Driving back to city with Kathryn and James, I had a thought that John is like an echo, an endless echo that keeps coming back, slightly softer each time.

Nov. 30

Anne and I went to look at office space at B'way Video. We decided to share one, it's three small rooms. Rent won't be too bad and she'll help cover Karen's salary.

Such a strange, long, tiring day. Sad packing up office. I guess I tried to block it, move out and move on. A few times, as I'd find a photo, or clipping, or various souvenirs, I'd space out into a memory. Chris Barnes was helping pack up, and came upon the "Best of B.B.'s" album. He looked at me, cocked his head, and said, "It seems to me this is what we should be listening to." I hesitated and then thought, Yeah! So we played Side 1 and it really livened things up. There was a moment before we left when I felt all that had gone on in these offices, the connection to the past. But it didn't make me sad, at least not like crying. I realized there aren't any photos of the office and felt bad about that. It was a really nice place.

Dec. 2

Bernie phoned yesterday, excited that a Blues Brothers' check came in for Australian record sales. Thank you, John.

Dec. 4, Fri.

Told Dr. C. my dream from Thanksgiving, the limo turning into a hearse with flowers. He said the dream was indicative of my acceptance of the fact that I'm not going to die with John. Accepting that *he* is dead.

Have been very reclusive again lately. Any little thing can set me off, I guess it's the season. Am fretting about New Year's Eve. Janie (Buffett) says I can use her place in St. Barts, and highly recommends that I go there. Don't want to spend the money, though.

Dec. 5

In M.V. Came to close house for winter. Driving down road from airport, I realized I was smiling. It always feels so good to get here. Brought some photos along to color for Christmas gifts. Worked on that for a while. Should put house in order, but couldn't get into it right away.

Dec. 11

Went to Edgartown Yacht Club Christmas party last night, then to someone's house. Fairly large amounts of cocaine were passed around, and snorted by all (it seemed) but me. I was about to leave when there was a knock and it was a policeman. He was only there because of a complaint about a car in the road, or something, but my stomach dropped. I thought, Oh, great, "BELUSHI WIDOW BUSTED FOR COCAINE" would make a nice headline. I left soon after, jumped in my Jeep, and took off. The road was long and bumpy, a sand road in the woods. I was barreling along and started to skid, coming very close to going head on into a tree. "BELUSHI WIDOW CRASHES, DRUNK" I would have deserved. I sat there a while, my heart pounding, realizing I was running from myself real well now.

Dec. 15

Returned to New York after closing house. I did most of the things I had planned to do, so felt good about that. Cooled out some last few days there.

Went to Dr. C. Told him I'd been drinking a lot. He asked if I thought it was a problem. I said, when you have a headache five days out of the last seven from drinking, you figure it is. He said that in Jan. or Feb. he'd like me to try and not drink for a month to see how it feels. I immediately took up the challenge and said I'd do that in Feb.

I'm thinking I might just go to St. Bart's after all. I had thought I would wait until I had a better idea of my finances, assuming my new, restrictive budget would dissuade me. But things still aren't straight, and I discovered that if certain things don't work out, I could actually go bankrupt. So, I figure I might as well have this last splurge.

Dec. 25

Laila and Rhonda are going to go to St. Bart's with me! All is set for an early departure on the twenty-ninth.

I had a dream the other night and all I remember is J. walking up a dark flight of stairs toward me. I was leaving for St. Bart's and he wanted to go along. I said, "You can't go, you're dead."

Chapter 26

ST. BARTHELEMY BOUND

DECEMBER 29–JANUARY 12, 1984

January 2, Monday night.

Arrived on St. Barth's Thurs. (Now I know how to spell it correctly, not to mention where it is.) This is the first chance I've had to write since we've been here, but let me try to recapture the past few days:

Landed on St. B.'s about 6:30 Thurs. evening. Janie's friend, Dave, met us, and drove us to the house, which sits atop one of the highest points on the island. We have a vista which is quite spectacular.

We selected our rooms, then changed and headed to town, David at the wheel, now joined by his girlfriend, Mayja. Our first stop was a bar, a local hangout called The Select. It's close to the main harbor, which brings in all different types. Interestingly, it's also the Swedish Embassy. The Ambassador, a tall, thin, distinguished-looking black man with a long white wispy beard, and his son, "Fast Eddie," run the bar. The Select is similar in feeling to the Blues Bars, funky and filled with photos and memorabilia. Good, loud music seems to be abundant on the island.

We went across the street to an open-air French restaurant and were joined by a fellow known as TR. He avoided any conversation about what he does, and may be a smuggler. After dinner, TR invited us to his sailboat in the harbor. We drank more wine, smoked some joints, and listened to music for about an hour before returning to shore. We were exhausted and wanted to go straight home, but were forced to take the circuitious route of our drivers.

Fri. we slept late and were visited shortly after rising by TR, David, and Mayja. They took us to a beach called Senora, which was splendid—warm and sandy. We lunched at a nearby restaurant, under a big shade tree, and from there went on a small tour. We were constantly amazed at the beauty of St. B.'s.

After a quick shopping, we went on to TR's boat. TR opened champagne and laid out some pâté, cheese, and bread. The music was up and the others were dancing in mad abandon. Although we wanted to leave, once again, we were captive to our chauffeurs. TR kept opening champagne. Somehow we agreed to have a New Year's party.

Sat. was New Year's Eve and Laila's birthday. TR invited us on a sail, but Rhonda stayed home to spend time alone. We motored out of the pretty harbor of Gustavia and sailed to a nearby cove with a gorgeous beach, surrounded by a hundred acres of Rockefeller land with a very large Frank Lloyd Wright house. Quite a spot.

We anchored for an hour or two, drifting, eating, swimming. Laila and I passed on wine. It was cloudy and rained briefly. While I lounged on deck the gentle rocking of the boat seemed to encourage memories. I thought of a day not unlike this, when John and I sailed from a large island in the Caymans to a small one nearby. Along the way we stopped and snorkeled while the mate caught fish with a spear gun. On the small island we sat in a grass hut bar, the only structure, while the captain cooked us a wonderful lunch. It was a pleasant memory, it felt warm, happy. We held hands across the table and talked, just two tourists passing a beautiful day in paradise. We had many nice days, I found myself thinking.

Later that evening, we went to The Select for dinner. Champagne flowed, and we were off to a roaring start. Came up to the house about ten. The night was a blur of new faces. I didn't think about J. too much, nor in a sad way. (Rhonda and I did slam dance in his honor.) Later Rhonda sat in the yard and sang. All in all, the evening passed fairly painlessly.

Sun.—Jan. 1, 1984! Happy New Year!—stayed home and

relaxed. About four Reid (one of the people we met New Year's) showed up and invited us to body surf at "Washing Machine Cove." We had to walk over a large cliff, along a goat path. Some of it was quite scary, close to the edge over a gorge filled with water. Reid was nearly running as we approached, and was in the water before we were even off the cliff. The waves were ten to fifteen feet high and too powerful for any of us to go in. We explored the beach, sat and watched. I couldn't help think that J. would have enjoyed this spot. He loved to body surf and was vitalized the way Reid was from the ocean. I wondered if I would always think of J. when I saw something new.

On the way home we stopped at the hotel and were finally able to rent a car!

Tues.

—Freedom! Our own wheels! We went to the beach, lunch, laundry, shopping . . .

At The Select we met Harrison Ford and his wife, Melissa (who wrote *E.T.*). We talked quite a while, they were very nice.

Weds.

John seems to have come along on my vacation after all. I think about him often. Floating in the water, I miss having him to hold on to. I remember a hopeless attempt to make love in the ocean, ending in laughter and a quick return to our cottage. I remember snorkeling, holding on to his shorts as he led the way.

Jan. 7, Sat.

Happy birthday to me. On my way to Harrison and Melissa's. Wanted to jot down a few thoughts first. Our routine here is pretty funny. Laila seems to be on the phone most of the time and I usually read or write. Whenever Rhonda can, she sits out back buck naked, writing songs. We usually nap in the late afternoon, then dress for dinner. It's very much a ritual. We shower in order of how we get up, the biggest battle is over towels. There are never enough. After dressing, which of course entails a lot of "What are you wearing?" —except we don't bother to ask Rhonda any more, since she always wears her native wrap—we all cluster around Laila's mirror to put on eye makeup. This female fancy seems to lead us to discussions on relationships. Rhonda is going out with Reid tonight, so we'll probably talk about that. Well, gotta shower!

Jan. 8

Had a pretty good birthday, considering I wanted to ignore it. Didn't want to go over, again, in my mind, my last birthday with J., his last b'day, etc., so I kept pushing it out of my mind.

About one, Melissa and Harrison came by and brought me a present. Laila and I went with them for lunch and ended up at a place on the beach in a funny little town named Corisol. Corisol is heavily populated by people we thought looked a little like potato-head people—small potatoes, not big ones. At a bar, the proprietor told us about a local dance later in the evening. We decided to check it out.

Later in the evening, we again met Harrison and Melissa. Harrison is a real man's man, very set in his ways, sure of himself, and a nice guy, too. The fact that he has a really terrific wife says a lot for him.

Dinner was good. Rhonda and Laila wrote a story for me, which I read aloud. It was funny and sweet. They bought me a native wrap, very pretty. On one of my gifts was a gold crown, which I wore most of the night, but of course. At the end of dinner, the restaurant played, totally coincidentally, the sound track of *The Blues Brothers* movie. It was interesting, because I hadn't thought of J. since we'd left the house. Then there he was, entertaining us at my birthday party.

We walked down to The Select where I was given a house T-shirt and a bottle of champagne. We had been joking with

Eddie to let Rhonda perform there, and Laila brought it up
again. We told him we were called "The Cows," a very well-
known group among a select few in New York (we didn't tell
him we were the select few). Eddie said sure, he would get
some instruments and we could rehearse tomorrow, play on
the 10th. From there we went to the dance, which was
indeed a local affair. The band alternated between good
rhumba and bad rock 'n roll. When a friend of Harrison's
asked me to dance, I noticed a few hopeful glances from Laila
and Melissa, as if they were saying, "Maybe she'll like him."

Harrison and Melissa decided to leave, so I figured it was a
good time to exit. We invited a few people up to the house
and headed out. Of course, in the St. B.'s tradition, someone
brought a few bottles of champagne. The refridge had a
birthday surprise—a cake! We retired somewhat early for
this crowd, as I was in bed by two.

Jan. 10

Went down to The Select about five-thirty. Everything was
all set up for our show. Rhonda fooled with the piano trying
to get the best sound while I rearranged the drums. We were
all in good spirits, although a little nervous. We warmed up,
then went to eat.

About seven-fifteen we were ready to go. The other drummer didn't want to play at all, so I did the whole set. It all
pulled together somehow. The place was packed, overflowing
into the courtyard. In fact, they said it was the biggest crowd
ever, which can't be attributed to us, but just the fact that
it's St. Barth's and we were "three girls" playing at The
Select. We billed ourselves as "Rhonda La Vache and the
Udder Delights," feeling the French moniker was more appropriate for this "frog" infested island.

It seemed like everyone we've met was there. Champagne
flowed, but of course. Above the bar hangs a stuffed toy bee,
and if you stand in the doorway and hit it with the cork as
you open a bottle of bubbly, you win a free bottle. Harrison
hit the bee three times! Everybody seemed to have a good
time—people were hoppin.' Our big hit was "Sheena." At the

end, Rhonda sings, "I'm Sheena, Queen of the jungle. I beat my chest and come ..." holding the last word for a really long time while she pounds her chest. It's quite an effect— drove the crowd wild. We were a smash!

Soon after we finished everyone headed off in different directions. I went with a group in a dinghy out to a boat in the harbor. There were a number of people I knew on board, and we sat on the deck with the captain and talked. Music blared from the cabin, and suddenly it was a Blues Bros. tape. God damn, I thought. John has most definitely come on this vacation!

Chapter 27

I'M STILL STANDIN'

JANUARY 12–FEBRUARY, 1984

Back in New York, Jimmy and I had a breakfast meeting. A lot had happened while I was gone: a theater in Chicago wanted to do a John Belushi Film Festival; another wanted to show *West Heaven*; there were several family matters. By the time we finished eating, Jimmy was late for work. We continued talking as he looked for a cab. "I saved this for last, Judy, because it's making me crazy," Jimmy said. "*People* magazine ran a blurb on Woodward. They said his book on John is called *Wired*." He drew out the word "wired," emphasizing his displeasure.

I was stunned; it couldn't be. Then I realized it was probably incorrect. "Let's not get upset about it until we talk to Bob," I suggested. "I'll call him when I get home."

I left a message for Bob that it was urgent we talk, but didn't hear from him that day. The next morning I woke thinking about the title. It made no sense. It was certainly a far cry from *An American Artist* or *John*. How could he spend all this time finding out about John and then sum his life up with the word "wired"? My mind ran in circles. Well, there was one thing I was sure of; I wasn't going to lend my photos for a book called *Wired*.

Later that day Woodward's assistant called to let me know that Bob was on assignment in the Middle East and wouldn't be home till the end of the month. He wondered if he could help me with anything. "Yes, you certainly can," I replied. "I'm wondering if it's true that *Wired* is the title of Bob's book?" He seemed a bit taken aback, but responded that it

340

was. "Well, this is very upsetting to me." My voice sounded like a school teacher scolding a child, struggling not to let her emotions take over. "It certainly doesn't reflect the book that Bob and I have been discussing all this time." The Woodward drone tried to placate me, explaining that the choice hadn't really been Bob's. He said they had thrown around a lot of ideas, but nothing seemed to click.

"The publishers suggested *Wired*, actually," he said. I responded that it was too sensational. If it was the title, Bob and I had a serious problem.

"When is this thing going to press?" I asked. "I don't want to wait for Bob to come back and then be told it's too late to make any changes." I was assured that this would not be the case. Bob would call as soon as he returned.

January flew by. It was exciting to see Phantom come together in a new space. Being in the same building as Broadway Video meant I often ran into people I knew and hadn't seen for some time. It was often awkward, but I was strong enough to deal with the unexpected now. One day when someone asked what I was doing, I said, among other things, that I was keeping diaries for a book about being widowed. My friend looked thoughtful, then said, "Wow . . . Widowed . . . What a heavy word." I laughed at his reaction. It was a moment I noted because I knew that had that happened a year ago, I would have wanted to run from the building.

January 24, John's birthday came and went without much apprehension. I wrote in my diary: "Happy Birthday, dear John. I'd like to think of this as a day of celebration, but I'm feeling a slight anxiousness—a telltale sign that I still have some things to work out. Basically the day was okay. Kind of down, sad, slow moving. I only cried a little, after talking to J.'s dad, he's very sad. Remembering first birthday I spent with J.—gave him tickets to *The Odd Couple,* and we had an evening out in Chicago. His birthday in L.A. during *Continental Divide* was the best. I got him the sixty-eight Volvo he wanted. Tied streamers from the hood running into the kitchen so he followed them out to the garage. He loved that car. Well, I'm glad the day is over."

At the end of the month, Anne, Deanne, and I began to

spend time on *Titters 101* again. We handed in our text and began commissioning art work.

In February I began my abstinence from alcohol as agreed with Dr. Cyborn. This time I told my friends that I was not going to drink, and made a pact with myself not to smoke grass.

Keeping busy and developing a daily regimen felt good. I was getting out more, largely because I was working at Phantom, and my time spent alone was less down; being more disciplined, I didn't dwell on things. I began to find joy in little pleasures again: drinking from a favorite old cup, the smell of clothes drying on laundry day, even the act of closing the curtains at night and opening them in the morning was enjoyable.

Friends began to comment on my changed behavior. One night at Anne's, we got into a conversation about grief and how it consumes you. Her father had died in November, and for the first time, we really talked about that. Our topic turned from relationships with our parents to relationships with men. She said that of all the women in our crowd, I was the only one who was "trying to make it on my own," that most of our friends continued to rely emotionally on men. "I don't mean to sound weird," she said, "but I really think you've grown a lot since John's death." I felt bolstered by her support.

One day when I came into the office, Karen said she needed to speak to me. Her tone told me it was important. With some difficulty, she said she was resigning to take another job. I was unpleasantly surprised. "It's nothing personal," Karen said, "I like and respect you and have enjoyed working for you, but I feel it's important for me to make a change." I knew this was not an easy decision, and could hardly blame Karen for wanting more security. "I hate to put this on you now, but I've gotten an offer which I think will work out well." We talked about the new job, and I asked when they wanted her to start. She told them she would need to give two weeks notice. I said I understood and was sorry she was leaving.

After our talk I felt low. Karen's leaving was a symbolic end to the life John and I had created in New York. How would I get along without her? Rather than getting caught up in that line of thought, I made an effort to see it in a different light: maybe it was good for me to have a change, too. It would certainly help my budget. Knowing Karen, her decision was probably to take pressure off me as much as herself. By the end of the day I was feeling grateful for all the years of help Karen had given, and nostalgic about her leaving. I also felt confident that I'd be fine with the change.

Abstinence was interesting. During the first week, I found the most difficult moment was at dinner. I'd have a brief debate with myself about how unnecessary this self-denial was. My conclusion was always the same—I'd made an agreement with myself and would honor it.

One night, Laila, Rhonda, and I were out for dinner at Central Falls with several people we'd met on St. Barth's. Once again, the champagne flowed. We talked about the show at The Select, and Bruce Goldstein, the owner of Central Falls, suggested we do a show at his place. It was an exciting idea, and we all started to talk about who would play, etc. The longer we were there, the drunker everyone got, and the less I felt a part of the group. I declined offers of one alcoholic beverage after another, while sipping on cranberry and orange juice. It was interesting to see how people who are drinking respond when you do not. Many take it as a judgment on themselves. "Come on, one drink's not gonna hurt ya," they insist, or "Just have one with us," which is said more like, "Be one of us." At one point, when I leaned forward to hear someone, my face went directly over a glass of cognac. The aromatic vapors attacked my nose with such intensity, I could taste it. That's enough, I said to myself and left abruptly.

A few days later, at breakfast, Laila and I had an argument. I had tried to avoid it, but suddenly we were arguing, and it was way out of proportion. This bothered me all morning, and I was glad I had an appointment with Dr. Cyborn that afternoon. After my description of the argument he asked if I'd been anxious in general. I said no, that I'd been feeling pretty good for the last few weeks. I thought a minute. "The day before, during a photo session, I felt pretty out of sorts."

"I can't say for sure," Dr. Cyborn interjected, "but remember I told you to watch for funny feelings seven to ten days after you quit drinking. The body goes through chemical changes which affect the way you react." He also pointed out that March fifth was coming up and that I should expect to be more emotional. "I'm glad you're not drinking for a while, Judy," he continued. "It will be good for you to feel your emotions unhindered again. You're afraid not to be in control, and alcohol allows you to lose control. I believe if we could get to the root of that, then you would begin to let go naturally."

I still hadn't heard from Woodward. I dialed his number at the POST. "Woodward" came the familiar voice.

"Bob," I said trying not to sound as annoyed as I felt, "this is Judy."

"Hi! I'm sorry I haven't had a chance to get back to you," he said. "Things have been very hectic since I've returned." Bob sounded like his usual self. I didn't sense he was trying to avoid me, as I'd begun to think.

Then I jumped right in. "Did your assistant tell you I'm not very happy with your title?"

"Yes, he did, and I'd like to talk to you about that." Bob explained that he seldom titled his books. "I didn't really think *All The President's Men* was that good," he said. I expressed my feeling that *Wired* put the emphasis on the negative, and that from the beginning I'd stressed the importance of a full portrait. I didn't think the title was fair to John, nor a good description of what I understood the book to be. Bob said the reason he liked *Wired* was because there were so many different meanings for the word. "On the Hill," he began, "if you say someone is 'wired,' it means they're 'wired into the system,' meaning their connections are set, they're 'wired into the deal.'"

"I don't feel that describes John very well," I said, becoming more annoyed. "John wasn't a person who had connections. He *was* the connection."

"Well, I don't think all connotations of wired are negative," Bob continued. "For instance, if someone has been studying a lot for an exam, and really knows his stuff, you might say he was 'wired' for the test. His energy is up."

"Bob," I said, choosing my words carefully. "Wired means fucked up. You might just as well call the book *Fucked Up!* What people are going to relate to about that title is drugs, they're not going to think about connections or energy. They're going to think about cocaine and speed." I paused and took a deep breath to calm myself. "I'm glad to know how you came to this choice," I continued, "but I can't ignore what 'wired' means to me. If this is what you are going to call your book, and if this is all I know about it, then I cannot be associated with the project any more. I've thought about it, and I want you to know I'm not making any assumptions about the book, and I'm not saying this because I'm angry, but it is just not in my heart to have my personal photos in a book about John that's going to be called *Wired*."

Bob was quiet for a good minute. I waited patiently, feeling better for having said what I felt without becoming emotional or angry. When he spoke again he said he understood my feelings, that he respected my opinion, and would consider other titles. He said he wasn't promising anything, and even if he did want to make a change, the publishers would have to be persuaded. He then went on to say that people who had read the book seemed to feel it explained John in a way that made sense. He said he felt the book accomplished our goal of making an anti-drug statement. Then he threw out three other titles he said he'd considered: *On Sunset Strip, A Casualty Along the Way* (which was something someone said of John in an interview), and *Death of a Star*. All in all, I was reassured by Bob's attitude, and felt that the possibility still existed for a different title. We planned to meet in New York later in the month.

A friend invited me to an Al-Anon meeting. She said it was a wonderful program, helpful in ways I couldn't imagine, totally applicable for people who dealt with all substance abuse problems. I had declined her invitation for some time, but finally accepted.

During the meeting, I was put off by the frequent references to God and the emphasis on prayer. Frankly, I was bored and found it difficult to listen. At the break I picked up several pamphlets on the program and began to read. The literature defined Al-Anon as a fellowship of "relatives and friends of alcoholics who share their experience, strength, and hope in order to solve their common problems," and stated it was "not allied with any sect or denomination." All references to God were intended to mean "A Higher Power as you understand Him." That I could handle. And I was very interested in the emphasis on a need for spiritual growth to help yourself.

The literature sparked my curiosity enough to go to a few more meetings. One of the first new ideas I picked up was that alcoholism, or drug addiction, is a disease. At first I found it difficult to accept this idea literally. However, I had felt that perhaps John had a physical problem which made drugs affect him differently than they affected others, and the idea that his reaction could have been a disease—akin to an allergy—made sense. One of the things someone said to a newcomer at a meeting was, "Don't think, just listen." So I tried not to debate this idea with myself, but just to be open to it.

The more I read on the disease concept, the more sense it made. I learned that alcoholism or drug addiction is not curable; like diabetes, it can be arrested but never cured. Once abstinence is practiced, however, then *recovery* is possible. But abstinence alone is not enough. The compulsive behavior, which is inherent in all addicts, does not go away on its own, nor will the desire disappear overnight. The program itself—AA for drinkers and NA (Narcotics Anonymous) for druggers—is statistically the most successful for long-term recovery.

"One day at a time" also made sense to me. It was perhaps the only slogan I was familiar with, but I never had any real concept of its power. I learned from the meetings the value of addressing a problem, any problem, one day at a time. For instance, instead of saying, I'm never going to drink again in my life, you say, I'm not going to drink today. Then if you fail, you haven't made a failure of your whole life. You were simply not successful that day and you can try again tomorrow. Because the possibility for success within one day is good, this boosts your self-esteem and gives conviction to the idea that you can make progress.

The "one day at a time" philosophy was a good way to approach my own problems. Each day I attempted to put my focus on some single improvement, and each night I would evaluate how I'd done. If I didn't accomplish my goal, I could try again. "Keep it simple" was another slogan, so I wasn't trying to make grand changes. At a meeting I found a book entitled *One Day at a Time in Al-Anon*, which provided a one-page message for each day of the year, about dealing with an alcoholic or with your own peace of mind in a broader sense. I decided to use these messages to give myself focus, reading the day's message in the morning before I got up, and again at night before going to sleep.

Feb. 12

I went up to "SNL" for the show last night. (Robin Williams was the host.) The show was fun. The energy was up, it was exciting to be on the floor again, waiting for the show to begin. The theme music put a chill up my spine, just like it always had. I've avoided going because I was afraid it would be too emotional. But it was good. After the show, Jimmy said he felt down and didn't want to go to the party. He's trying not to drink, too, and didn't want to be tempted. We walked for a while and talked and I shared with him the "one day at a time" philosophy. Then we stopped at a bar and ordered two Virgin Marys. We walked home, which helped Jimmy finish winding down. It's the first time he hasn't gotten drunk after a show. He felt pretty good! I felt pretty good! It's a little as if I'm coming out of hibernation.

Feb. 17, 1:30 A.M.

What a day! Too much information ... Woodward and Pam came to town today. Talked about title *Wired* ... We tried to convince him that it focused on drugs too much, was misrepresentational of the overall book. He didn't really seem to agree with that, but he was concerned that I didn't like the title. Moved on and talked about the book in general, and when we should read it. He is concerned with several issues. One is idea that we'll read something someone is quoted as saying, call that person and ask if that's what they said, then get that person to phone him and say they didn't say that. Also concerned about us not having to take responsibility for anything. He said he will make it clear in his articles that what is reported is his responsibility . . .

Bob said . . . in all confidentiality, that it looks as if Cathy Smith will return to the States (in several months) and plead guilty. The best part is—no trial. She gets two or so years and it's over. That would be a great relief. Woodward said it had been curious to him as to why her lawyers let him talk to her so freely. He said to one, "What are you doing? She's clearly guilty." "I know," said the lawyer, "I want her to figure that out." The idea that she is going to plea bargain makes me feel that I've made many correct choices.

[After this meeting Pam and I went over my financial situation.] To be brief and to the point, I have *no* cash left, in fact, I'm in the red. This is a serious problem, I say to myself, but I'm not going to let it make me crazy. I'm going to take out a loan, which should get me through until things work out.

I found some old notebooks the other day, and just skimmed through them a little while ago. I found two poems I'd written about John. The first one was a very simple rhyme: "Independent and Free/And sweet is my honey/He keeps me laughin'/'Cause he is real funny . . ." etc. I vaguely remember writing it. I was surprised by my reaction, that it didn't make me sad. Then a few minutes later I found another: "You numbed me with your cocaine/You filled me with your lies/You were so into yourself/You couldn't hear my cries," etc. etc. A horse of a different color. Quite a bit of hostility. I remember writing the last one. It was actually a song for *Titters*, so it wasn't exactly about John, but obviously the heart of the anger was mine.

Tonight I felt very good about myself. I well could have been hysterical after all that went on today, but at this point, I'm doing okay. I feel vulnerable, but not alone. I have my family, but most important, I have myself. And lately, I'm my best friend.

*   *   *

The following day, Jimmy, Pam, and I met with Woodward and his editor. I was concerned that Jimmy might get angry, but he was very calm, very articulate and convincing. Nonetheless, I didn't feel we persuaded them to use a different title. My diary entry for that evening indicated my disappointment: "I feel a little sad that the title will probably be *Wired: The Short Life and Fast Times of John Belushi*, as if I've lost one of the elements of the reconstruction of J.'s good name, so to speak. Various goals were—finding out what happened in L.A. (successful as possible); receiving justice in terms of the law, i.e. C.S. (which has a promising outlook); and giving J. the man some dignity. The last one will be in part successful . . . if I can believe what Woodward [has said about the attitude of the book]. But having the title be so connected to drugs is not respectful of J."

Before we parted ways, Woodward said he would weigh our concerns and get back to us quickly. He thought it best if we didn't read the manuscript until closer to the publishing date (which was going to correspond with a series in the paper), and we asked to be given at least a month to digest it. Since Pam had vacation plans for early May, we needed it by April. Bob agreed. As we hugged good-bye, Bob said to me, "You might be mad at me, but I think you're going to agree it's a good book." His words threw me totally, my heart raced. I had retained some hope that the book would be okay, but now Woodward seemed to be telling me it wouldn't. I would be mad at him! I said nothing to Pam or Jimmy about the ominous remark, immediately deciding to ignore it, since there was nothing more we could do at this point.

Feb. 24

Thinking about drinking, or *not* drinking, as the case may be. It seems to me that what you're after is that first rush, the physical tingle, the floating feeling that pulses through your body. More stimulant is never as good as that first moment. I'm considering the idea of a straight lifestyle. And when I say "straight," I mean *straight*. No drink, smoke, or pills of any kind. (Even birth control, eventually.) It's kind of a new high in its own way. That old "high on life" concept. Life is a state of mind. Get rid of the fog and look it straight in the eye. (Does life have one or two eyes?) Who knows. Maybe at my twentieth high-school reunion, the people who will be out in the driveway—the ones who were out there drinking in high school, snorting at the tenth reunion—will be the ones who are straight. Why, maybe it would be more than a fad! Perhaps it could become a way of life!! And that way of life could grow and eventually become a world consciousness! Naaaaaaaaa!

Jimmy (in an interview) said, "People from Chicago are starting to make their mark here [New York] . . . my brother, Bill Murray, guys like that started it when they went on 'SNL.' They opened up the holes so other people from Chicago could go through . . ." That's right, I thought, and the proposed title, *A Casualty Along the Way* came to mind. J. was a warrior of sorts, a samurai. I (currently) am a survivor— the samurai's widow. "I'm Still Standing," an Elton John song, keeps going through my mind today.

Chapter 28

THE BEST MEDICINE

FEBRUARY 26–MAY 12, 1984

My disposition was more and more inclined toward working, as I was anxious to complete *Titters 101*, for which I had to make a dummy layout. I had also agreed to play bass with Rhonda in a performance at Central Falls, billed as The Cows. This meant I had to learn to play bass parts to five songs. The date had not yet been set, but it looked like it would be the first week in March. My only request was it not conflict with my plans to go to the Vineyard on the fifth.

While at a birthday dinner party for Anne, I found myself thinking a lot about my work. Things were just begining to come together with something I was writing, and I was excited about getting back to it. I had planned to meet Steve later, but it didn't work out. I was a little surprised to note that I didn't mind; I was more interested in going home and working.

Feb. 27

Steve and I are drifting apart, mainly, I think, because I can't commit myself. We don't talk about it (that's another big reason), but I think I'm still too involved with John to be fully with someone else. As I was coming downtown from Anne's party, it occurred to me that not so long ago I probably would have gotten drunk and been one of the last to leave. Now here I was with the book on my mind, rushing back to work at midnight on a Sat. night. And another thing, I must be putting all my sexual energies into writing. It's the only explanation for why I write in these diaries so much. I almost *need* to write before I go to sleep, to help clear my head, run down. Then I usually watch *Mary Tyler Moore*, which comes on for two shows in a row. I like the working-woman-on-her-own theme. (Mary doesn't seem to have much of a sex life, either!)

Feb. 28

Went to meeting with Ed London. Some good news, some bad. Even though we've concluded dealings with Lipskys and some things are worked out (I don't have to take out a loan!)—still my problems are not over. Some will go on for years . . . probably work out in the long run, but my budget must be drastically reduced. Still unsure how I can make it work, although I know I can.

March 1

One month *no* alcohol! Not one drop passed through these lips. Now I think I'll continue to stay alcohol-free for an-other week.

March 5, 10:00 A.M.

Well, here it is, the second anniversary of J.'s death. I'm certainly doing better than I was last year. And, of course, two yrs. ago was the saddest day of my life. I'm on a plane to M.V. right now, making my pilgrimage. I had serious hesitations this morning when I woke to find it snowing. My first thought was that it was too crummy to fly, the plane might not even go. And even if I got to the Vineyard, it would be raining or snowing and the cemetery wouldn't really be visitable. I called the Vineyard airport and they were still open, but not very confident they would remain open. I thought about what I'd do if I didn't go and realized I needed to do something in connection with J. today. So I decided at least to try. After all, what kind of a pilgrim would I be if I stayed home just because the weather was bad?

Last night we had our first performance of The Cows, at a little bar downtown, sort of a rehearsal for the Central Falls show. We were uncertain about a lot of things, like endings, but it was an impressive debut, if I must say so myself. The audience seemed to really enjoy Rhonda's music. We didn't start playing until midnight, which means, technically, that the Cows were born on Mar. 5. We ended the show (our encore!) with "West Heaven."

I couldn't have planned this time around the fifth better if I'd tried. Well, actually, I did try—I kept trying to keep us from playing this week—shows what I know. But it's great to feel life moving on, growing. It was good that I had so much to do, new things to learn, and creative endeavors to pursue.

After I came home I watched a bad sci-fi movie on TV, about a scientist who died (I guess) and his colleague who saved his brain and made him into a giant monster. At any rate, he was a monster, I don't know how he got that way, but he was angry he had such a yukky body. So anyway, the monster says, "Do you know what day this is? It's the anniversary of my death. I think I'll make a pilgrimage to my grave." Talk about synchronicity. (I hope he's not going to the Chilmark cemetery.)

Midnight (On the Vineyard)

To complete my pilgrimage story . . . When I pulled up alongside the grave, I saw three bouquets and started crying, as if someone had pushed a button. I took the rose I'd brought from New York, pulled on my rain hat, and went to read the cards on the flowers. My nose was running, so I went back to the car for a tissue. How stupid of me not to bring any! Luckily I found a paper towel. It was cold, so I sat in the car with the heat on. I didn't know what to do. Did I want the radio on or off? On. I sat, listened, and thought. The slush turned to snow. I was reminded of J.'s wish to be on M.V. for a snowstorm and that it had snowed the day of the funeral. Suddenly I had an anxiety flash. Was I wrong to move him? I got out and walked to where he was first buried, wondering if it would feel better, as if he belonged there, but it seemed too small, or something, too tight. I remembered the crowd gathered around the open hole in the ground. Funny, I didn't know the cemetery at all that day. Now I know it so well.

I returned to J.'s grave. "Why did you have to die, J.?" I said aloud, not for the first time. I don't believe he hears me, but it seems to be something I ask myself when I'm at the grave. Standing at the new plot, I felt safer, more protected. It is a better spot, at least it's better for me. I got back in the car to warm up, and laughed. I am really wacky. Moving J.'s grave! But it was right. The first spot was too much like a new subdivision. J. wouldn't have wanted that. His new spot is the new frontier, things will build up around him—that's the way his life was. I felt better, glad I'd come. "I Want a New Drug" came on the radio. It's a song that basically says, I want a drug that doesn't do bad things—like make you stay up late, talk too much nonsense, feel shitty the next day, spend your money, etc. The only thing they neglected to say was one that wouldn't kill you. Anyway, it's a funny way to do an anti-drug song. I rolled down the window and turned up the radio. I always feel good playing music there.

I had planned to take a late afternoon plane home, which gave me a few extra hours. I decided to check out my house. This time of year in the Vinyard is bleak. But there is a peacefulness.

The wind ripping off the ocean made it very cold at the house, but I went to the cliffs—I'd come all the way to the edge of the world, might as well take a look! It was freezing, but what a sight. I wished I were dressed to go on the beach, but didn't want to chance getting sick. I drove to Oak Bluffs to see Larry Bilzerian, but his store was closed and he wasn't home. I thought he might be at Danny's—Danny doesn't like his house to be empty, so Larry often stays there. Decided I had time to see. We both pulled up at the same time. Went in and talked for a while. The weather was dismal and I really didn't feel like getting back on a plane, so it was easy for Larry to talk me into staying. I lay on the couch to watch TV and fell asleep. When I woke, I was pleasantly surprised to find that Larry had made dinner. Afterward, I watched a video while he slept on the couch and the fire blazed. All in all, it really wasn't a bad day.

March 7

Cows at Central Falls last night. Went well, place was packed. Too crowded, actually. Anyway, it was fun . . . nice to see so many friends turn out. Danny came with Larry, which surprised me. James and Kathryn came, and I know James is into an early schedule now. Anyway, I felt a lot of support from people, a little as if it were a "coming out" party.

March 18

Talked to Rob last night. Said he was at his "girlfriend" Sandy's. He sounded pretty good. Said he "lucked out" meeting Sandy, she's terrific and he wants to tell me more about her later. He also said he was really broke—the worst he's been since high school. He only has thirty dollars to last this month. If Rob can live week to week and laugh about it, I can find a way to make my budget work without getting bent out of shape.

March 19

Anne, Deanne, and I worked until nine, then Deanne left. D. keeps reasonable work hours, always having an "end time" predetermined so she can meet her boyfriend. It is a pet peeve of Anne's. "You mean you're leaving before we finish?" "I told you I had to leave at nine," Deanne says, unaffected by A.'s attempts at making her stay. It's not a bad plan, really. If I had another life, I'd do the same. Anne and I worked for another two hours.

March 29

Someone from the *Village Voice* asked if I wanted to do an interview with the guy doing coverage of "the Woodward book." Said I'm not going to do interviews around it.

*   *   *

Sandi and Robert were visiting Jimmy and we made plans to have dinner at Ninth Street with my sister Pat and Robbie. I made stew the night before, so I could work right up to dinnertime. Of course, I worked longer than I should have and got home a little late. Everyone was already there and it was a pleasant change to walk into the house and find it active. My nephews were playing in the living room, their toys spread out over the floor, and Pat and Sandi were heating up the stew and getting the rest of the meal together. The boys were happy to see me and wanted to play. I invented a game with some oversized pillows, standing them upright to create a "house." They'd both go inside and I'd reach in and tickle them. We play fought, rolling in the pillows. It was so wonderful to be able to pick them up and safely toss them on the cushions, or crawl after one while the other clung to my neck, riding on my back. Naturally, I tired of this much more quickly than they, but was able to divert their attention to a videotape for kids. They lay on the pillows together, wrapped in a blanket. It looked so cozy. After we ate, Jimmy watched TV with the kids while we gals talked. It was a nice evening. The two boys had a lot of fun and were so cute together. At the end of the night they were walking around with their arms around each other.

After everyone left, I settled into bed to write: "The house is perfect for an evening like tonight. I haven't had enough time when it was together and I was together. As soon as I was moved in—well, frankly, I can't remember much about last Mar. right now. Let's see Apr., May, ahh, May. I went to the Vineyard a lot to deal with the grave. Oh boy, I just shot off into a trance spurred by gravestone thoughts. Asked myself for the umpteenth time, 'Why can't I get J.'s headstone?' And it occurred to me that it felt a bit like putting a sign up. I like the mound of stones the way they are. Maybe

I'll put a flat marker. I've got it! It could be like a Hollywood Boulevard Walk of Fame star! Yeah, now I'm thinking . . ."

April 2, Mon.

Tim Mayer told me he talked with Katharine Graham [publisher, *Wash. Post*]. She read *Wired* and said it was heavy on drugs. Oh, well, I guess there's no getting away from it. My only hope now is that it's clear about the struggle. Tim asked how I came off and she said, "She sounds like a very patient lady," to which Tim went off on a rant extolling my virtues as he sees them. Dear Tim.

April 20

Just recalled a conversation with Mom the other day. We were talking about the Woodward book. I said the book was going to talk very specifically about drugs, and J.'s last days in particular. She said she often felt badly for not saying anything the time she thought things were amiss. (When she copy edited *Blues Brothers: Private* for me, she thought J. was either drinking too much or maybe doing drugs.) I said, "Well, that's everyone's regret who dealt with J." And she said, "I don't suppose I could have been any help to J., but I might have been some help to you."

April 26

The death of Robert Kennedy's son David has upset me. He was found dead in a hotel, "cause unknown" as yet. But he had a drug problem, so the drug checks are on and the press is all about his problems. It's painful to watch the public spectacle of scrutinizing our "royal family." "THE CURSE OF THE KENNEDYS," etc. Makes good press. . . . Had an odd altercation with Laila at dinner over something she said about David K. It wasn't what she said as much as my reaction which is of interest. She was just repeating some info she'd read, and I was annoyed; she made it sound as if "this is what he was like" when, to me, it was just gossip. I came down on her pretty hard, seemingly from out of no-where. Interestingly, I'd been to an Al-Anon meeting earlier where we talked about how we often react in nonrational ways during a time of recovery. And that's just what I did—I wasn't reacting to L.'s story, but to an association I feel between David K.'s death and J.'s. It made me realize, once again, that I'm *not* a recovered widow yet. I apologized to L. later, explaining what I had felt and she apologized, too. I feel better for it all coming out.

* * *

As spring bloomed I found myself getting into an earlier work schedule. I had nearly completed my design for *Titters 101*, and felt good about it. And I was begining to look forward to returning to the Vineyard for the summer. At the back of my mind, however, was the fact that Woodward's book would be released soon. Pam got a copy of the manu-script and we decided that she would read it first. That week I threw myself into my work with a passion.

Chapter 29

BELUSHI BABYLON

MAY 15–JUNE 30, 1984

"Well, I can't say that our highest hopes have been met . . ." Pam's voice trailed off. I sensed she was stalling; she was working to put aside her emotions, to separate the lawyer from the big sister. It was obvious she wasn't going to say what I wanted to hear. Pam cleared her throat and began in a soft voice: "I think the book is a strong anti-drug statement, but not in the way I'd hoped. Bob captures events well, but he doesn't capture any sense of the people. I suspect it was a failure on our part not to recognize the difference between a great writer and a journalist." She paused. "It strikes me now that it was a mistake to give Bob so much access to John, such honesty on the ups and downs. The downs dominate his portrait. I felt no sense of the good that was there, which explains why the bad was worth going through. It's a very sad picture. I felt very little of your essence, either. One has a vision of a man who loves you very much, but wanders. There is little shown of your relationship but frustration. I think one wants to cry for you."

I was sitting on my bed and fell back. The life seemed to drain out of my body and a numbness set in. The book was a travesty—it was clear now—but I can't say I was surprised. I had refused to lose hope that *Wired* might meet some of my expectations, but I'd known since the title issue that it would be a letdown. I sat up, grabbed a pen and paper, and began making notes.

"There's not much about the police," Pam continued, "in

terms of the issues with which we approached him, or the kind of information he has implied to us. Nothing about Smith being an informant, nor her association with Gates." Pam's voice was showing signs of distress. She wasn't her crisp, encouraging self, but instead spoke as if she were trying to sound hopeful. "I felt Jimmy came off well. He seems more real than most of the people I know in the book.

"In terms of John's career, I didn't feel any of the greatness . . . the greatness did not come through. One gets a feeling of a spoiled brat who goes for the easy laugh. After *Animal House* it doesn't sound like anything John did was successful. For example, *The Blues Brothers* is only discussed in the most negative manner. It just sounds like a disaster. There's no mention of the tremendous audience reaction, for instance, not any of the positive or rave reviews, just some negative ones." I felt a rush of anger. A movie that brought in over a hundred million dollars should not sound like a disaster!

"A good portion, about a quarter of the book, is on the last week of John's life. It's very negative and takes on a heavier emphasis in the way you're left feeling about John's life than I think is fair."

Pam paused, seeming to search for just the right words. "I can't say how my perspective is colored, being so close and all." She took a deep breath. "If the morality lesson is there, then I don't want to say it's no good. But I don't know if it's there. I am concerned about your reading it. I especially feel you shouldn't read the final section."

Pam gave me a general outline, sometimes pointing out key items where she had problems. The use of quotes from my diaries worried her; she felt giving permission for excerpts might conflict with my own book contract, in which the use of my diaries was exclusively promised. "I never gave permission," I said, and told about the day I read Bob sections over the phone. "It never dawned on me he would excerpt them, I mean, I knew he'd use information from them . . . I don't see how he could be very accurate. I read them quite fast." I felt betrayed. Bob knew all along that I was doing a book, with material from diaries. He never said anything about quoting from them, never checked to make sure what he used was correct. My worst fear was confirmed;

my sense of trust in Bob had been foolish. A chill shot through my body. How many people had said never to trust a reporter? "Can he do that, I mean, legally? Don't I own my diaries? Doesn't he need permission?"

"I'll have to check the law pertaining to diaries," Pam responded. "I'm not sure." I was racing now, my heart pounded and my face was hot. My head felt as if it were stuffed with cotton. He can't get away with that, I thought. He needed permission. They'll have to take them out.

"Another thing I found disturbing," Pam continued, "was the disclosure of expenditures." There was a full page footnote detailing a month's expenditures, she explained. Pam felt it was out of line and off the point. She had mentioned this to Bob (she had gone over some of her problems with him the day before) and he responded that he felt it demonstrated John's generosity. It had never occurred to me that Bob would be so crass as to list our expenditures. I let him look at the books to see contracts, trace John's steps through receipts, check out phone calls, and the like. If it showed John's generosity, I wouldn't mind. But I wasn't so sure I liked the sense of "John's generosity" as a footnote.

Pam concluded and we decided she should send both Jimmy and me a manuscript. I appreciated her concern about my reading it, but I'd gone through too much with Bob to ignore the final product. Pam said Bob was anxious for my reaction.

I was surprised by the style of *Wired*. I had expected the book to be in the first person, but the voice was that of an omnipresent third person. *Wired* purports "John did this and then he did that," as if the reporter had been there as events unfolded. Trudging through the pages, being led by Woodward, was like watching a bad play with a heartless double playing John. It was a grim and insensitive performance, with an occasional bright moment when something would be right on the money. Still, I felt no compassion for John's character. There was no reason to care about what happened to him. A few scenes were told well, and a few brought out good qualities, but they were far too few, and were ultimately lost in an overload of drug information. Woodward often said this was a cautionary tale, but the reader had no empathy with the protagonist, a much needed element for

the morality lesson to be effective. There was little of the
sense of joy or wonder that were as much John as his dark
side. This imitator lacked John's warmth, gentleness, perception, dignity, persuasiveness, intelligence, sense of humor,
and deep sense of love. Woodward captured his alienation,
anger, and explosiveness, and he portrayed every character
defect in detail. But without the heart, it didn't reflect the
man. This was mostly what Pam had noticed, but what she
couldn't know was when the information was distorted, out
of context, or simply inaccurate.

I also felt bad about John's not being given credit for
attempts to pull himself together. Times when he was straight
were glossed over, and his efforts to quit cocaine sounded
insincere at best. However ill-conceived some of the attempts
may have been, John did, I think, make some good choices.
Smokey is a prime example. Bob made it sound as if Smokey
had been forced upon John as a watchdog, when hiring Smokey
was his own idea. The stories Bob chose to tell about Smokey
were basically true. But because they were all that was told
of him, the book left the distinct impression that Smokey did
nothing but wrestle drugs away from John.

Wired closed with me saying, "He talked about Brando a
lot. . . . Maybe he related to the characters he did, that's
what I assumed . . . the guy who is fucking up, but doesn't
mean to." THE END. Nice. But I had also said, "the guy who is
learning to deal with his conscience, like Brando's character
in *On The Waterfront*. The guy who is struggling with, 'What
is the right thing to do?' "

After reading the manuscript I went over with Pam the
major inaccuracies and items I thought were slanderous. It
was the same old story: my only recourse was to ask for
factual corrections. Since the whole book gave a slanted
erroneous portrait, Pam felt it could be damaging to force
corrections of factual mistakes, as if that were all that were
wrong with the book. Resignedly, I had to agree.

A few days later I received a package and a note from
Woodward:

Dear Judy:
    Enclosed are five more pictures of yours that you loaned
me. Unfortunately they were used in the book. I realize

this was contrary to your desire. I explained to the photo editor at Simon and Schuster who did the layout. In the confusion and duplication of some shots, those five got used. I'm sorry. It is my fault that I did not make sure all of them were returned.

Cordially,
Bob

Until this letter, I hadn't known some of my photos were in the book, since I read a manuscript only. I was furious. Pam was already on vacation so I called George Galloway at her office and read him the letter. "Do you think I have a good case against Woodward for unauthorized use of photos?" I asked. "You have a very good case," George assured me. "Then let's sue his ass," I decided immediately.

As soon as I handed in my work on *Titters 101*, I went to the Vineyard. Jimmy (who had completed the "SNL" season about a week earlier), Sandi, and Robert were already there and we shared our anger and frustration. Excerpts would be syndicated in newspapers nationally starting the following week, so we felt we needed to prepare the family members for the onslaught. We decided to talk with everyone and explain that it wasn't what we had hoped, that it was an ugly, one-sided portrait and we didn't recommend reading it.

The series began on Sunday, May 27, and ran for a week. After the second day I didn't even look at it because it was too upsetting. The selections were all the most sensational, so now the portrait was totally black.

The phone started to ring on Sunday and didn't stop for several days. At one point I sat cross-legged on my bed, phone in my lap, talking for several hours straight. Every time I hung up I just stared at the phone until it rang again, usually within seconds. I was beseiged with calls from friends expressing their sorrow or anger over what they read, and wondering how I was holding up. Many people who were interviewed by Woodward said they'd been misquoted. Another common complaint was that they felt used; after talking about how John influenced them in some good way, or sharing funny and warm stories about their friendship, all that was quoted was something they'd said about drugs, which was most often in response to a question.

I, in turn, was trying to reach family and friends to see how they were doing. Mrs. Belushi was nearly hysterical after the first article. She had ignored our suggestion and read it. "This is pretty bad, Judy," she said. "John sounds like an animal." She brought up some specific references, things I knew to be untrue and told her so.

"Who is this Bob Woodward, anyway?" she asked. I never heard anyone sound so desperately angry. "What gives him the right to say these things? Can't you sue him, isn't there something we can do?" We talked a long time. I felt responsible for her distress, and powerless to do anything about it. "Does he have children?" Mrs. Belushi suddenly wanted to know. Yes, I replied, Woodward has a daughter. "Good. Because someday I hope something like this happens to her so he can know how it feels."

My mother could barely speak. "I . . . just don't know what to say . . . I'm so sorry, honey. It seems so many people let you down . . ." I could tell she was fighting back tears.

My father was very agitated. "I'll tell you what," he raved, "Bob Woodward said he was going to stop by here the next time he was in town. Well, I hope he does! I've got my shotgun ready in the closet. I hope he does stop! It will be the last stop he ever makes! He can't talk that way about my son-in-law and daughter—" His threats ended abruptly as he began to cry.

John's sister Marian, his brother Billy, and his father were faring slightly better. They decided not to read anything after Jimmy and I had spoken with them. Marian said she took her phone off the hook the first couple of days and cried a lot, but she was feeling better. "You know, Judy," she said, "it doesn't matter what other people say about John. I grew up with John. I don't need someone else to tell me about him. I know who John was." I was concerned about my nephew, Adam, who was fourteen now. "Adam's doing fine. Sometimes kids say mean things, but I told him to ignore them, so he just walks away. I'm just glad he's old enough to remember his own times with John. You know, John was so nice to Adam when he went to the set of *Continental Divide* that time, and I have those cute pictures of them." Marian began to cry. "I'm sorry, I don't mean to cry, I mean, I feel okay, it's just that he was my brother and I miss him."

"Don't apologize, Marian. I understand. You have every right to cry."

"You know," Marian added, "whenever people find out that I'm John's sister, they're always so nice to me. They're so respectful and say nice things about what John meant to them. People loved John. Don't worry about it, honey, this isn't going to change that."

Pam's office and Bernie's were swamped with requests from newspeople wanting to do interviews with me. I was also hearing from friends who were getting calls from journalists. At one point, I was on the phone and had an emergency interruption. "This is the unlisted numbers operator," a woman said. What on earth could she want, I wondered. "Your line has been busy so long, I had to interrupt. I have a message for you from the producer of the 'Phil Donahue Show.'" She proceeded to give me a name and number. "They want to interview you." I thanked her and hung up, amused for the first time since the *Wired* insanity began. "The power of television," I said aloud. It was the third time I'd gotten the message that day.

I called Bernie's office to go over messages. The "Donahue Show" wanted to have both Woodward and me on together, I learned, as did "Nightline." I pictured the two of us in a television studio, Bob in a suit, looking calm and confident. Me sitting quietly, well composed. The interviewer asks a question and Bob replies. Everything is very civilized. A typical American controversy, each side presenting its viewpoint. Suddenly I snap. I jump him. My hands grasp his neck and we tumble to the floor. He is red-faced, choking, helpless. I'm kneeling over him, pounding his head against the floor . . .

"I don't think I'm emotionally ready to be in a room with Bob right now," I said. In fact, I wasn't ready to do interviews in general, but I had to do something, just to make a public statement that I didn't support Woodward's book. I decided to limit my comments to the network morning shows, a statement to *Newsweek* and interviews with *People* magazine and both daily Chicago newspapers.

A few days after I'd received Bob's letter about the photos, Simon and Schuster, along with Woodward, were slapped with a lawsuit in the District of Columbia for unauthorized use of personal photos. George said we should make a petition to stop distribution of *Wired* as our next step; we wouldn't expect to win this drastic an action for a photograph dispute, but it was good for our legal position to show how serious we were. He also relayed a conversation with the Simon and Schuster lawyers. They were taking a rather amused view of it all at this point, saying the publishers were pleased to have a lawsuit, since, in their minds, it meant more publicity and more sales. They, of course, contended that in no way had the photos been used intentionally and that this was only a minor infraction which certainly could be settled quickly. They suggested they could probably scrape up five hundred dollars or so to cover the use of my photos. Since I've bought photos for books, I knew that even as a fee, if I sold them up front, that wouldn't be enough. And, I told George, I had a figure in mind to cover my distress over the fact that I didn't want to be associated with *Wired* in this way. I was thinking more along the line of a hundred thousand dollars, which I would give to the John Belushi Memorial Foundation.

I had to pull myself together before the interviews and think through what I wanted to say. I needed to get myself to the beach, take a walk, and relax. In the week since the syndication began, I had become so anxious and overwrought that I looked frazzled and was beginning to lose weight.

As soon as I set foot on the beach and took a deep breath, I felt a release from the stress. I walked briskly at first, still feeling the speeding effects of my anxieties. Then I consciously began to slow my pace and let my senses take in what was all around me. I saw a good rock to add to the rock garden and picked it up. Damn, if I'd been thinking I would have brought along my basket and collected rocks! Oh well, I could pile them at the foot of the cliff. Ah, ha! What's this? A beautiful old weathered gray oar, washed ashore. Perfect for my display of treasures from the sea. The sun glittered on the waves and a cool breeze blew off the ocean. Okay, I thought, *Wired* is what it is and I'm disappointed. So what's the up side?

The interviews went fairly well. My emphasis was that the book failed most painfully as a portrait of John the man, as the concentration was almost obsessively on the dark side. But I did not argue that the focus on drugs and the confusion they can bring was a truthful picture.

June 26

Flew to New York yesterday for a meeting about doing a documentary on John, or a project from "SNL" work. I feel that in the wake of *Wired* I should put something out there that would more directly and humanly represent John. Returned home to quite a bit of mail, several notes and letters of support about *Wired*. One friend said she bought the book, started to read it, then threw it out. She said she was "very saddened by it."

There was an odd letter from a woman I couldn't place at first. Said, "We've had our differences in the past . . . let's call a truce to clear John's name. . . . Seems to me there are many inaccuracies. . . . Anyway, my thoughts are with you." Finally placed the name as the woman writer who was involved with the *Penthouse* article. Another letter from a fan said she and her family love John so, they rushed out and bought the book only to feel heartsick. She thanked me for "speaking out and setting the record straight" and "for giving back to me the John Belushi whom I felt I knew and loved."

Also got a letter from [a young fan of John's with whom I have a kind of pen-pal friendship]. She said she heard I was having a "rough go of it" and wanted to tell me not to let it get me down, and to "keep my chin up. . . . I know that's easier said then done, but I've been thinking about you and you've got my support. Believe me I really do know where you're coming from on this. Everything will turn out right, hopefully. Remember, angels are watching." It's just too sweet for words.

Chapter 30

DARE TO COMMUNICATE

JULY 3–NOVEMBER 15, 1984

On the second anniversary of Liz's death, Rob sounded pretty good. He and Sandy were in love and work was going well. He admitted that a part of him felt guilty that he was involved in a relationship and life was going on. He planned to spend the afternoon at a quiet spot on the beach at Tennessee Cove. Sandy understood. "All in all," he concluded, "life is looking up."

July 8

I have a strong feeling of John today. I miss him in many ways, but was thinking of him physically. I loved his strength, his massiveness, his grace, even his clumsiness. His energy just tingled sometimes. And when he was in a quiet mood, everything seemed so peaceful. I visualized him lying beside me, reading. I have so many questions. "Do you want to die from drugs?" I imagined asking. Not as a warning or a plea, just curiosity. I remember the day he got the letter that Tom Long had died. (His friend from summer stock, a terminal illness.) He'd just crumbled, literally, fell to the floor crying. He should have phoned, but I guess he just couldn't—not knowing he was dying. It seems he just hated to deal with death, perhaps feared it, so that he had to laugh in its face somehow. I wonder if drugs helped do that, let him appear to be unafraid?

* * *

368

Mid-July I received a letter from Jann Wenner, publisher of *Rolling Stone*. "We are writing a story that will examine in detail how *Wired* was researched and written, trying to ascertain whether there are inaccuracies, omissions, or misrepresentations." I declined without much thought. I was trying not to think about it any more.

July 18

Heading toward an extremely busy time. Looks as if "The Best of J.B.," a collection of his "SNL" work, is a go. I'll probably do that at the end of the year. I'm glad. I think it's important to continue to get John's work out there, so that part of him, the part he created, will live on.

I've agreed to five college lectures in the fall, during the same period I'm promoting *Titters*. I told the agency I couldn't do a prepared lecture right now, but was willing to talk briefly about myself, then field questions from the audience. The agent said that would be fine. I thought it might be interesting to see what college kids think about John and how they react to *Wired* ... might even be good for me. It may be a little schizoid, since with *Titters* interviews I'm saying up front that I won't talk about *Wired* or drugs, and then, at the colleges, I'm sure that's mainly what we'll talk about. But when I do publicity, my focus should be on my own work. The lectures are to communicate on a more personal level.

* * *

At the end of the month, Lynn Hirschberg, the writer doing the *Rolling Stone* article on *Wired*, contacted Pam and tried to convince her I should talk with her. I declined again. An interview was too risky and I was just begining to feel better.

A few days later Lynn called me at home. "I'm calling to beg you to talk to me," she began. "I just spent two days with Woodward, and he's such a strong voice. I really need you in the piece and you're not there at all." I said I wanted to stick by my decision and felt good about it. She said something like, "Wouldn't you talk to me for just one hour?" I said I'd think about it.

July 30

3:00 A.M. Woke up about an hour ago. Got Woodward on the brain again. Spoke with Pam today and Lynn (*Rolling Stone* writer) has—had—convinced her that I was hurting myself by not talking with her. I think she appealed to how organized Woodward was, how solid he appeared. ("All his notes were so organized and impressive.") I know how Pam feels, she wants to stand up and fight back. She wasn't here when I did my interviews. I'd had that feeling then, maybe still do some. . . . Lynn said Bob claims he never had any record of C.S. talking with the police officer from the narcotics division. Since Bob told Pam about the phone bill, too, that's what got her going. But ultimately, even if I talked to *RS*, it's not going to change what Bob says, or how organized he appears to be, or his impressive background. It's just me pitted against him. Even if I make a few good points, or come off well, it's not going to alter the junk he puts out. It's times like these that I feel angry with Woodward.

July 31

Jann (Wenner) phoned. Said he thought it was to my benefit to speak with them. He pretty much convinced me, but I said I needed to think about it. He said he'd go over my quotes with me before publication.

*   *   *

The next day I agreed to the interview and within days Lynn came to the Vineyard. We talked a little over an hour and communicated a couple of times during the next week or so. During our last conversation, as Lynn talked about Bob, I realized she was quite in awe of him; I had the uneasy suspicion she was convinced he could do no wrong. In fact, it sounded a little as if she had a crush on him. Her voice had an odd, unreal quality when she said, "This is really important to him, you know. After all, it's his career."

"I know," I responded. "It's just my life . . ." As if she hadn't heard me, she agreed.

After that exchange, I felt I'd gotten in over my head again. I could not do battle with Bob Woodward on his own turf and expect to win. I decided to get my focus back on my work and try not to worry about the *Rolling Stone* piece. There were one or two more calls from Lynn. She told me the title of her article was "John Belushi's Troubled Sleep," and that the cover art was "Great!" It was a really beautiful portrait of John, she was sure I'd like it.

The last week of August a package arrived from *Rolling Stone*. Hesitantly I pulled out the magazine. The cover was a nightmare. It looked as if the art notes came from a description of John in *Wired*. He had messy hair and bleary, half-opened eyes. His shirt, a dirty white, was disheveled. It was awful. I felt terrible. How could anyone think this was great? His face wasn't even proportionate, the forehead was about half his face. I read the article and was upset. For one, I had to confront some more unattractive descriptions of myself: "nervous," "hysterical," "obsessive," and (as "one friend said") a "professional widow." I didn't feel the slant was necessarily kinder to Woodward, although I did think it was sympathetic to him. But it was the same old shit: I said this, and Bob said that. There was no in-depth reporting to get to the bottom of anything. Nothing of value was revealed.

Sept. 6

Was just getting ready for bed and found the *Rolling Stone* issue on J. in my room. Made mistake of taking a look at the index to see what else was in issue. See cover story caption, something about me wanting *Wired* to have a "sympathetic" view.... My first reaction was that I didn't want it to be sympathetic. I actually looked up the word, and one meaning is compassionate. Yes, I think the story of *Wired* should have had a bit of compassion. I was watching TV the other night and saw an interview with actor Terry Thomas. He was asked about his notorious dislike of the press and journalists. He said he'd come to terms with it: "Never expect more than a grunt from a pig." Bless you, Terry Thomas.

Actually, I think what I've really learned from all this is

about Bob Woodward. In interviews, he keeps referring to John's story as being about the "failure of success." I think that's Bob's own story. I think he's terrified he's a fluke and feels he doesn't deserve what he has.

A few days later, I found myself feeling bad about the "professional widow" comment. As an attempt to turn around my feelings, I decided to pull all the unpleasant descriptions of me from the press items I had and see if I could write a humorous poem with them. When I finished, I did feel surprisingly better. The power of the words had been diffused and seemed silly. And I no longer felt silly, but strong. It was interesting. I fittingly titled my poem, "Me!"

> I'm muddle-headed, weak-willed
> Naïve and obsessed
> I never knew my husband
> And my life is a mess
>
> Nervous, confused
> I am more than absurd
> Whining, hysterical
> I'm emotionally disturbed!
>
> I am a professional widow
> I have no time for fun
> So don't invite me to your party
> 'Cause I just might come

The *Titters 101* publicity tour was booked so that Anne, Deanne, and I would do some cities alone and a few together. I wanted it to be clear that I was promoting our book; I would not talk about *Wired* or Cathy Smith, and preferred not to talk about John unless it was in a context of work. Some declined upon hearing this, especially television shows.

This wasn't the first time I had restrictions for interviews. When I did publicity for *Blues Brothers: Private*, people were told up front that I was promoting my book, not providing an interview on John. Most of the interviewers at the time respected that, but it did mean passing up a lot of good outlets. I made one exception with "Good Morning America" and agreed to answer a few questions on John. It was at the end of the band's tour, and the first time John was able to watch me give an interview, which made me more nervous than the interview itself. The interview was early and when I returned home, John had gone back to sleep. Smokey was awake, however. I asked him what they thought.

"Oh, I thought it went very well and John seemed to really enjoy it," he replied. "He really laughed when you answered the question about what he was like around the house. What was it you said?"

"I said he liked to lock himself in the library and read the classics."

"That's it." Smokey chuckled. Later, when John got up, he told me he thought I'd handled myself well.

"You were real good, honey," he said planting a kiss on my head. "From now on, I think you should do all *my* interviews."

It was annoying that *Titters 101* was released right on the heels of *Wired*. What lousy timing. Feeling gun-shy about the press, I considered leaving the promotion to Anne and Deanne. But I was tired of feeling isolated, I wanted to be part of our team.

My book tour began September 17 in Pittsburgh. I had a lecture the next night at West Liberty State, a school in West Virginia. Rhonda came along, and, neither of us ever having been to Pittsburgh, we were pleasantly surprised to find it a pretty city. We laughed a lot about my situation; I wasn't at all sure the interviewers would respect my requests, and had no idea what to expect from the students. "This is torture," I kept saying in my gruffest Lee J. Cobb imitation.

As we waited for the first interview, I played my bass guitar, which I'd brought in the hope that Rhonda and I might perform "West Heaven" at the end of the lecture. It depended on the facility. Now I was glad to have it along for diversion.

The interview itself went fine. The reporter, a gentleman from the *Pittsburgh Press*, was well prepared with questions about my book as well as some about working at Lampoon. He was interested to learn I was working on a book about being widowed and we talked about that at length. Finally, as his last question, he apologized and said he had to ask me one about John, or *Wired*. I don't actually remember what it was. Then he rushed off to finish his piece for the morning edition.

Rhonda and I picked up a paper as we headed out the next day. It was a very nice article in terms of me, and not bad in terms of promotion for *Titters*. The beginning was rather prophetic: "Judy Jacklin will be hearing the questions about John Belushi for the rest of her life. . . ."

It was cool and sunny in Pittsburgh, a nice day to be driven around the city. Most people I spoke with didn't really respect my request and asked at least one question about *Wired*, and several about John. But they weren't hostile and everyone did ask about my book as well. A cable show shot me in a comics store and focused on *Titters 101* and what it was like to be a woman in the humor biz. It was refreshing. My last interview of the day was a live television show. Watching the green room monitors, I couldn't help but notice that the audience was predominantly white-haired women. "Somehow I don't think this is a *Titters* audience," I said to Rhonda. A production assistant requested I sign a release. On a sudden impulse I signed "Janis Joplin."

By the time Rhonda and I were at dinner, we were giddy over various situations of the day. All in all, it had gone all right. The attention wasn't on the book as much as I'd have liked, but it was enough to be worthwhile. And there were some good exchanges. Rhonda assured me I was coming across well and was often funny, which she pointed out would help promote the book in its own way.

The next morning I had to be up early for another session, then at midday a student arrived and drove us to West Liberty. It was customary for lecturers to have a "press conference" and so before my lecture I was escorted to a room to face "the press." This consisted of a student, a local paper's reporter, a local TV station, and, I think, a local radio show. The TV camera was very old, and needed extremely bright and hot lights. The questions were exclusively about John, *Wired*, and drugs. I tried to be open and direct in my responses. One fellow seemed to have some grudge against me (or probably John, which he was directing at me) as he hostilely asked questions and thrust his microphone at my face with a "take that" attitude. I tried not to react to his antagonism, but he was overbearing, attempting to take over the interview. I decided to physically alter my position, turning my chair slightly after every question until I faced away from him. By the time he was repositioned I called an end to the interview.

I went back to my room to shake off the odd experience. Rhonda told me to forget it, I'd come to speak to the students and I shouldn't let it get me down.

It had been nine years, when the first *Titters* was published, since I last spoke to a large crowd. I was nervous, but confident I was well prepared. If someone threw out a question for which I had no answer, I would simply say so. I had nothing to lose.

During the questions I was able to work in most of my main points and was pleased that there were some about my own work and many about John's. The audience was warm and receptive and especially seemed to enjoy the personal stories I shared. The hour and a half passed quickly; I was surprised to see the sponsor signaling "time." I took one last question.

"Do you intend to marry again?" a student asked. The question embarrassed me, but I tried to answer honestly. "I liked being married. I think I'd like to marry again, but"—I shrugged—"it takes two to tango." I had not expected the audience to find that a funny response, but it got a big laugh. It was nice to end on an up note.

Later, Rhonda and I laughed at how exhausting our two days on the road had been. I pleaded with her to accompany me again, but to no avail. "I can't take the emotional drain of having to be with you when you do this," she admitted.

My next lecture was at Clemson University in South Carolina. I hired a personal assistant, Tamara Weiss, to go along for the rest of my lectures. Tamara also worked for James and Kathryn, who were touring not far from Clemson, so Kathryn decided to join us for that one.

Two young students, very much the southern gentlemen, picked us up at the airport. On the drive we asked about the university and discovered it was a big football school. In honor of the team's mascot, tiger paws painted on the highway indicated the Clemson exit.

As we pulled up to the school the boys said I should hurry and get ready for my press conference. "Press conference?" I asked with trepidation, since after my first lecture I told the lecture bureau I didn't want to do any press in conjunction with the speeches.

"Yeah, they've been waitin' for over an hour now," one said, flashing a perfect smile. I gritted my teeth as I was directed to a room to change. It was warm, so I put on a sleeveless T-shirt and a light jacket. We were ushered into a small banquet room.

Kathryn and Tamara didn't have any idea what to expect, but I thought I did. Boy, was I surprised. Twenty-some people crowded the room, most of them facing a table strewn with an array of microphones. Two or three television cameras were also set up. Kathryn and Tamara were seated at the back of the room and I sat alone at the table. I felt small behind all the microphones and altogether unprepared. "You're probably wondering why I've asked you all here," I tried. Kathryn and Tamara were the only ones to laugh.

A woman asked a question about *Wired* and the questions were serious. Once we got going I felt fairly at ease. I was asked some questions about drugs (Had I said "Drugs are fun?") and one man started attacking John in an angry manner. I forget how the conversation developed, but I remember him saying something about "all the money John spent on drugs was a crime," and I think he was debating my interpretation of John's struggle to straighten up. I stayed calm and tried to understand his points and respond genuinely. Somehow this exchange seemed to turn the tide and a friendlier mood took over. They asked what I was doing now, several questions about being widowed, and some more questions about John—What did I miss? etc. I was amazingly composed considering the session was intense and the room hot. "What are your plans when you finish your book?" someone asked.

"Well, sometimes I think I might like to start a band, and

other times I think maybe I'll open a microwave store." Once again, the humorous note signaled the end.

Afterward I felt a mixture of excitement and relief. I could hardly believe what I'd been through; it was like an interrogation. I felt good that I had maintained a calm presence of mind. It was draining, however, and I had a long night ahead.

The lecture committee (which included about five committee members, their dates, and a mother) took us to dinner. We chatted amicably and the young women in the group pored over my copies of *Titters*, laughing.

Once the lecture was underway, it sailed by. I felt the students asked more knowledgeable questions than those at my first lecture, and I was more concise with the now standard questions on *Wired*. One student gave me a hard time about drugs and another yelled at him to shut up. I said, "It's all right," and tried to answer his concerns. In general I thought everything went well.

We were not excited to learn that our hotel was an hour away. However, our two young women drivers were excited by the chance to talk to us alone. "It's so great to have a professional woman come and speak," the driver said in her ladylike drawl. They were quite ingenuous and sweet, asking us all questions about our work. One spoke of her desire to become a graphic designer. "Most of the girls here are just after their MRS," one said and they both giggled. By the time we got to our room we were beat. I soaked in a hot tub for a long while.

"Welcome to the Torture Tour," I warned Tamara.

The next day I flew to Chicago by myself. I had looked forward to going "home" and imagined that this would be the easiest, most fun leg of the tour. The first day I had only one interview, with the *Tribune*. A woman met me in the lobby and led me to a very small, windowless cubicle. She began with a question about how John and I met and continued along that line for a while. I felt uncomfortable and annoyed. She asked about something I'd said regarding John's struggle to give up drugs and I snapped. "We're getting into an awful lot of this other stuff now. Didn't they tell you I don't want to talk about *Wired*?" The interviewer looked at me for

what seemed a long time and then said the question was not
meant as a reference to *Wired* but to John as a person. There
was another uncomfortable silence. I began to ask and answer my own questions, talking about *Titters*, working with
Anne and Deanne, whatever. She picked up again, asking
about what I was doing now and we talked about my book a
while before I shifted the subject again to women and humor.

Walking back to the hotel, I wondered why I'd been so
agitated with the reporter. She wasn't really offensive or out
of line. I realized I'd been down before going to talk to her,
and it had to do with feeling disappointed and unimportant.
John was always treated like the Mayor of Chicago, and
everyone was gracious to both of us. Earlier that afternoon,
after waiting an hour to check in, I'd lugged my bags to my
room because I was running late, only to discover that all
but one of the TV shows had cancelled because I didn't want
to talk about John. Thanks for the support, Chicago. In the
room, I noted the absence of a welcoming note from the
manager, or a complimentary basket of fruit or wine. Not
that I'd expected anything—I was being silly to even think
twice about it—but I'd thought, maybe ... I guess I felt a
little as if I were invisible without John. My self-esteem was
low and that's why I was defensive with the interviewer.

The next morning, an agent picked me up for my rounds.
The radio people were great, and the day wasn't bad. My last
interview was with Irv Kupsinet, a local columnist with a
syndicated TV show. Both Kup and his wife, who produces
the show, were very friendly and said kind things about
John and how Chicago missed him.

The interview began and Kup's abruptness took me by
surprise. "Now, I know you don't want to talk about *Wired*,
but ..." Later he asked, "A lot of people have said that if
you'd been in Los Angeles with John he wouldn't have died.
What do you think of that?" I said I'd thought that for
awhile, and felt guilty about it, but had realized that I
couldn't predict what would have happened—or not have
happened—if I'd been with John. And more important, I
realized I didn't cause John's disease and I couldn't cure it.
And, ultimately, we're each responsible for our own lives.

This was my last interview in Chicago, and I was glad to

head out to my parent's house. The Kup show was on later that night and my parents wanted to see it. As always, I was uncomfortable watching myself. My mother was upset about the responsibility question, saying it was out of line, but both my parents said I'd done very well. I wasn't so sure. Later, in my room, I thought about the interviews and felt confused. What was I doing? Why did I dare attempt to communicate? What was the point?

The next day I was still feeling a little down when Juanita and Dan Payne (John's high school mentor) called. "I thought you might be there," Juanita said. They'd seen the Kup show. "We just wanted to say how proud we are of you. You're doing so well and being so strong. Those were hard questions and you sounded together and made a lot of sense. I think it's good for a lot of us that you've stood up to all this, that you're saying what you think." It was just what I needed to get me out of my doldrums and back on track.

My mother came with me to Detroit. The hotel had a copy of my *Chicago Tribune* interview. I was prepared for an unfavorable portrait, but actually the writer was very fair. It began, "She is interested in talking about the present, Judy Jacklin, John Belushi's widow, will tell you firmly. Not about *Wired*, not about Bob Woodward, not about drugs. Almost any reference to John Belushi as a person or a husband is greeted as an attempt to talk about the controversy around *Wired*. Even when she opens the door to talk about John herself, she quickly shuts it . . ." She also put a lot in about *Titters*, and up front at that. It was a long interview and covered most of what we discussed. I was pleasantly surprised.

The morning TV shows were very John-oriented and one was about drugs exclusively. At midday I did a radio show and the disc jockey concentrated on *Titters*. When it was over, my mother shook his hand and complimented him on a good job. The last interviewer was a friendly woman from the *Detroit Free Press* who included my mother in her article: "Jacklin's mother, Jean Jacklin, a lively woman who sells rare books, has joined her for the tour's Chicago-Detroit jaunt. 'I wanted to get a look at the glamorous life,' Jean Jacklin says during afternoon tea at the Caucus Club. The

Jacklins laugh and sweeten their tea—Jacklin with honey, her mother with white sugar—and Jean Jacklin sighs faintly. 'I'm glad I came. But, boy, never again.' She has misplaced her purse for the umpteenth time probably at the last stop, and their driver has gone to look for it. . . ."

My day's work completed in Detroit, I left my mother at the airport for her return to Chicago while I went on to meet Deanne in Philadelphia. It was a relief to have another person to take some of the pressure, and it helped keep the focus on our book. From there, we went to Boston and New York where we met up with Anne.

While in New York, I discovered that Clemson University had complained about my lecture; they'd believed I would speak on ethics in journalism and drug abuse. You can imagine my surprise. I called the three remaining schools and found that they, too, expected a formal speech.

I rewrote and extended the prepared section of my lecture, basically tying together all my subjects into a cohesive whole. I realized the theme that was of most importance to me was communication. Whether I was doing my books or talking to Bob Woodward, or even answering questions about John, it was a desire to share ideas. I renamed the lecture, "Dare to Communicate."

Personal influences prompted me to make the San Francisco leg of my trip; my brother had asked Sandy to marry him and I really wanted to meet her. I arranged my schedule so I could be there a few days before my last three lectures.

It was good to see Rob doing so well and to meet Sandy. Although she was very different from Liz, there was a subtle similarity I couldn't place at first. She was physically about my size, with golden brown hair, and pretty in a delicate way. Not to say Sandy was fragile; she ran five miles every morning and seemed very self-reliant. I thought she had a peaceful energy and liked her silent support of Rob; a hug or kiss after an emotional discussion, or just a touch that said "I love you." It was clear they enjoyed being together. I realized it was Sandy's love for Rob that reminded me of Liz.

Rob and I talked a great deal about our emotional states. He'd been concerned that it was too soon to marry, but had carefully considered. He would always love Liz, and Sandy understood and respected this. But he loved Sandy and felt lucky that she loved him; he was ready to move on.

We also talked about *Wired*. Rob called it "an opportunity missed," which he thought a shame. And he felt bad for all it was putting me through. "But I do envy you, in that you can do things like *West Heaven* and the video of John's 'SNL' work. It's a way to express your love, which I think is great."

Later, on the bus to the airport, I wondered if Rob weren't doing better than I. Here he was, in love and engaged, and I didn't even have a man in my life. Or, maybe worse, I had a very active relationship with a man who was dead.

By the time I met Tamara at the Nashville airport, the depression of leaving my brother had passed. I realized I couldn't compare our progress in terms of things like love and marriage. We each had our own paths to follow. In my own way, I was making a new life; that it did not include a man was unimportant. I was, for the first time in my life, really focusing on myself. As for John, he would be with me all my life, whether I married again or not.

It was essential to me that the Vanderbilt students respond favorably to my lecture; I didn't want another college to feel let down. I was nervous, fearful I was out of my league, afraid I would fail. If this doesn't work, I thought, I'll never give another speech.

Shortly before I began, one of the students showed me an article in the school paper entitled, "Oxfam or Belushi?" Unfortunately, an Oxfam rally was scheduled at the same time, and a faculty member was encouraging the kids to go to it, emphasizing (rightly so) that world hunger is an important responsibility. My turnout was no doubt affected, but still the room was two-thirds full. I began, "I was sorry to learn that my lecture tonight conflicts with the Oxfam rally," and surveyed the room. "I guess that makes you the students with no sense of the values which are truly important to human existence." The audience recognized the reference and laughed. I was off to a good start.

I spoke for about forty-five minutes, the body of my speech coming from questions that were asked most often in my earlier lectures. I talked about *Wired* and the press, saying I was proud to have made the attempt to talk publicly about a serious problem. I stated, "I always considered journalists to be an integral part of democracy as protectors of the truth. But it has been my experience that most reporters aren't as interested in relaying what you have to communicate, as they are in using what you say to fit into the story they want to tell. . . . We like to think of ourselves as an 'informed public,' but it strikes me that news stories are chosen for their mass appeal. The fact is, we are not an informed public, we are consumers."

I then read my poem, "Me," which got a good laugh and segued nicely into talking about work. I said I'd learned an invaluable lesson watching John work on stage at Second City: to respect the value of failure. Not only could you learn from an attempt that fails, but risking failure was an essential ingredient of success. "In order to try for the exceptional in your work, you have to take risks. And when you take risks, you have to understand that some will fall short. It's in the progress of keeping at it, overcoming the failures and recognizing the successes, that we reach our potential. I think this is true whatever you do."

When I asked for questions, I found I'd explained *Wired* well enough to make it less of an issue. Drugs were still a top concern, and someone was a little heated that I was talking about alcohol as if it were a drug. I remained calm and said, "Yes, that is exactly what I'm saying," and referred him to AA if he wanted to better understand that concept. My continuing to talk the matter through diffused his anger. I closed saying, "I'd like to leave you with this thought: There is one thing that everyone in this room has in common; we are all dying. This life, as we know it, goes very fast, so I urge you to take the time to get to know yourself. I believe we are fortunate to live in a country where anything is possible. I suggest you determine what you want and communicate it with those you love. And don't let anyone else's idea of who you are get in the way of what you want to do with your life. Good luck to you, and good night."

The student committee was very pleased with the evening. On the way back to my room my escorts spoke about my lecture and I saw I had made them think in a different way about some important issues. One of the students said I'd been the best lecturer that year. I asked who else had been good. "Well, William F. Buckley drew the biggest crowd," he said. "But personally, I thought you were much more interesting." The others agreed. Well, all-fucking-right! I thought. My risk had paid off.

I returned home from the lectures feeling I'd earned my money. It had been good to get away from my closed world and have some direct communication with people. I had been so focused on the details of *Wired* that I had lost any real sense of the situation. John's sister was right; people loved John and a book wasn't going to change that.

Chapter 31

LETTING GO

Dear Mrs. Belushi,
Because of the timing of this letter, it is probably obvious that it's a response to the book *Wired.* . . . Forgive me if . . . I offend you in any way. . . .

I bought the book out of curiosity . . . to see how Bob Woodward would present [John's story]. You see, I stopped drinking and using other drugs in January of 1982—I was sixteen—and over the past three years I haven't read one book about addiction that hasn't disgusted me with its lack of understanding. I was hoping *Wired* would be an exception—it really wasn't—but nonetheless it had a profound impact on my life—a very positive one. . . .

After "being sober" . . . for three years, I've never related to a person's story as thoroughly as I did to John's. I know [it] was not all accurate, and was clearly out of proportion—but I think I might have read it differently than most . . . [because] I focused on, however little there was in the book, the good things.

. . . I honestly believe that the overall image of the John Belushi in Bob Woodward's book is *not* the man you knew—just like the overall image of the "deeply disturbed child" the alcoholism counselors gave my parents was not the person they knew. And my parents were right and the counselors were wrong. Just like Bob Woodward did in his book, the counselors in treatment were looking at the surface, the drug and its effects, rather than the person behind the drug—the real person that only those close to me knew and argued for.... I know how frustrating this can be and how much it hurts. I find myself defending John to people who have read the book and seen only the black and white on the pages (mostly the black) and missed the gray. I think I saw the gray because it's exactly where I fit in on the spectrum.

[What I wanted to tell you is] the book has changed my life. My abuse of drugs (alcohol) never got bad enough to really hurt. So it always left me questioning if I ... needed to stop at all. I didn't really want to stop when I did. I was fortunate enough that circumstances led me to treatment even though I didn't think I needed help. I related so much to the gray of John's story—his early use of drugs almost perfectly paralleled my own—that I know it would continue along the same course if I ever tried them again. At one point in the book you are quoted as saying something to the effect of, you hope that some good can come out of John's death. It has shown me my possible future, which I could never see before, and possibly saved my life. I am very grateful to you for that....

Although I had a strong feeling that my involvement with Woodward had been a necessary step, almost as if I had no choice in the matter, I could easily lose any sense of why it was necessary. This letter firmly fixed the answer for me.

I was anxious to get to work on "The Best of John Belushi," but between the holidays and another benefit in Chicago at Second City, the year came quickly to an end. I went through minor mood swings and again debated what to do for Christmas and New Year's. After some indecision, I decided I wanted to be home, with my friends. Indeed, 1985 came to me much more gently than the preceding few years. I toasted auld lang syne and looked forward to the year to come.

The new year did not begin on a great note. After a meeting with my business managers, I decided to close the Phantom office. It was a convenience I could no longer afford since I could work at home. The Ninth Street house was still for sale, but the market was slow and I was advised that a sale could easily take a year. Meanwhile, I couldn't even consider having a balanced budget until after the sale. Interestingly, the meeting didn't get me down; I was confident about my resources and options. If the Ninth St. sale didn't set things right, maybe one of my projects would do well.

The lawsuit with Woodward over photos was proceeding slowly. I was forced to spend days going through my diaries, pulling entries on Bob. We requested documentation as well, including a copy of Woodward's contract with Simon and Schuster, which his lawyers kept neglecting to hand over. When we finally received it, I was upset to discover that Bob's contract was dated less than two months after our first interview. I no longer had to wonder, I knew; from the outset Bob calculatingly took advantage of the situation. His lawyers relayed a message that he hoped I didn't misunderstand the contract. It was a deal for "a book with photos," he contended, there was no reference to who it would be about. It became a book on John at a later date, he said. Yeah, right.

The fact that Bob was still concerned about what I thought of him told me something. I had felt he was an honorable man, with real, not feigned, integrity. But his code of ethics was different from mine. I'm sure he felt that by not having John's name on the contract, he could "honestly" tell me he wasn't doing a book on John. For Bob to continue to try to convince me that there had been no deception, after I'd seen his contract, told me how sincerely convicted he was to his half-truth.

Another attempt was made to settle the photo suit; I think the offer was upped to fifteen thousand dollars. It was tempting. I had acted in anger, and now the negative energy was zapping me. I was scheduled for a deposition on January 17, which made me uneasy. I wanted to settle, but my legal fees were already fifteen thousand and I wanted to get something for John's Foundation. Weighing all this, I decided my minimum settlement figure would be thirty-five thousand.

The morning of January 17 I woke early and found a beautiful snow-covered courtyard. My lawyer, George Galloway, was to fly up from Washington, D.C., but he phoned to say the airport was a mess due to the storm. He would call the lawyers and work out a later date. Woodward's lawyers did not reschedule, however. They offered thirty-five thousand.

For a moment I was hesitant to let the issue end. It would

mean letting Woodward off the hook. But the settlement
would give me a little over fifteen thousand to give away.
That would certainly bring some good energy to a bad experience. I had wanted revenge on Woodward when I sued and
settling would symbolize letting go of that. It was time, I
decided. It was time to move on.

Cathy Smith's court date was approaching and the D.A.
was confident she would enter a guilty plea. However, since
returning to the states she'd had new counsel. Howard
Weitzman, who gained notoriety as John DeLorean's de-
fender, was pushing the D.A. to agree to no jail sentence.
Mantagna held firm, since the charges for furnishing and
supplying alone carried a worse penalty than what he offered. Montagna was asking for three years, while the other
charges carried eight to twenty. And since there were two
witnesses confirming her guilt, her most sensible choice was
to plea bargain. But Smith entered a plea of innocent. Pam
spoke with Montagna and said it was the first time she'd
noticed tension in his voice. The preliminary hearing (or
pre-trial, which determines if the evidence warrants a trial)
was set for February 11.

I realized I'd counted on a guilty plea. Cathy Smith was
supposed to return and plead guilty! I blamed Weitzman,
suspecting him of wanting publicity.

The wheels of justice in motion, I had to decide whether or
not to attend the proceedings. The D.A.'s office felt my presence would benefit their goal. They did not believe Weitzman
would actually let her stand trial—if the prosecution won in
pre-trial, everyone was sure Cathy Smith would then plead
guilty—so this was it. John's mother lamented it would look
"as if no one cared" if no family attended and I agreed. I
decided to go.

I asked Smokey to accompany me to the pre-trial and he
accepted. Pam would attend at first, but she most likely
would not be there the entire time.

The arrangements set, I talked little about my concerns
over the upcoming trial as most of my friends thought I
shouldn't go. But I was determined; it was my responsibility.
I tried not to think about it, but did. I found myself conflicted
over the use of the word "innocent" in terms of Cathy Smith.
It seemed a contradiction in terms to see headlines stating,

"CATHY SMITH PLEADS INNOCENT." Finally, I sat down one afternoon and wrote a poem. I thought I was going to write something about her not being innocent in the legal sense, but the theme took an unexpected twist.

INNOCENT

You said you are innocent, when you know it's a lie
Life is not fair, so you kick and scream and cry
You believe you're a victim, and so long as you do
That is all you can be, your suffering comes from you

Innocence is a freedom that you've never known
You keep your feelings locked-up
You keep your ego stoned

But the power is within you
To heal the pain, to make you whole
Understand you rule your life
Forgive yourself and take control

Innocence is a plea you utter in your sleep
Believe the Lord can hear you
And know your soul He'll keep

I was surprised with the outcome, embarrassed by its, well, innocence. It was especially curious that I ignored the social context I had intended to address.

The month before the hearing, I began to edit "The Best of John Belushi." It was nice to have a creative project as an excuse to examine John's work. It was good to laugh, to appreciate the sense John had of himself when working, to discover just how infectious his humor remains.

About this time I tried a simple form of meditation, focusing on a peaceful image or idea. At first it was very difficult, my mind wandered nearly uncontrollably. But when I'd become aware of wandering, I'd just bring my focus back. My ability to stay with my meditation improved slowly, and I felt renewed by the process.

My hair had been annoying me for some time. I was torn

between growing it long and cutting it very short. Now I wanted a drastic change. Fearlessly I entered the bathroom with a pair of scissors and, with the flair of a sculptor, created a very short, geometric cut. I liked it, it was a combination of sixties mod and punk. It was stylish, chic! The change was good, too; it was a cleansing.

Shortly before the pre-trial, the hearing date was rescheduled for March 19. The following day, I came down with strep throat.

Rob and Sandy were married on February 23. The entire family attended, as well as friends from Chicago, Aspen, and New York. The day was gloriously beautiful, as was the bride. Vows were exchanged in a flower-laden courtyard with Robbie as ring bearer. Afterward, when Rob and I hugged, he said, "I really hope you'll be this happy with someone one day." His happiness was infectious.

March 5

I woke today with a very pleasant feeling. I was comfy and warm and a heavy rain beat against the roof. Where am I? It's somewhere nice—not San Francisco, not the Vineyard . . . Ah, yes, I am at the Vineyard, but not at my house. I'm at the Charlotte Inn. It's the third anniversary of John's death. Even last year, I could not have imagined I would have come so far, be feeling as—I hesitate to say "good" and consider saying "okay." But I'm feeling pretty good in general. At least I see a decent and worthwhile life in front of me. The lack of a love in my life makes a dramatic difference. But these past ten months or so have been a remarkable change from the previous two years. And I feel more, and better, changes coming within the next few months, the next year. Perhaps today will be a step back, a day to remember the sadness. Or maybe the sadness is always with me and this is a day to let more out?

After I remembered why I was here, I knew there was no sense in trying to go back to sleep. The Cathy Smith situation came to mind. When will that happen? What will go on? Am I really going? A line from the *National Lampoon* editorial about John's death went through my mind, something like "But most of all we feel bad for Judy, because now she will have to go through the [messy details]." Well, that sure was right. The nightmare is over, but the pain is still in me. The loss is still frustrating. I try to think of today as John's re-birth-day, and look to some of the more positive things about our life together. To think of John as reborn into another life requires faith—which I partially have. Sometimes I feel a tremendous sense of everything being interrelated. That "all is one." But that consciousness is hard to hold on to.

In a way, I think of John's passing as a new adventure for him, one we all are part of, and he's just begun ahead of me. He is like an astronaut whose destination is so far away that he will not return in my lifetime. I want to be happy for him, and I'm pissed off at the same time. But I will take the voyage one day, and he will have made my trip less frightening by his pioneering. I don't put much on the idea that I will ever figure it out, but I do have moments of feeling it is true. Trusting in those feelings is where the faith comes in. The universe is so magnificent, why not just have faith in it?

April 24

I'm beginning to feel a rebirth of my own. My interests are changing. I'm fascinated with trying to understand things like life, death, health, world problems. I've been walking in circles around those issues the last few years, but now I'm facing them, delving into them. I realize how little I know and am eager to listen to others, even those I disagree with, because they provide new insights. The only negative is trying to write a book at the same time I'm learning how little I know.

*   *   *

In late April another pre-trial date came and went, the defense requesting another extension. The new date was set for August. At this point, I realized I couldn't keep rearranging my life around these dates; it was too draining. I cancelled my plans to attend. I felt such relief with this decision that I knew it was right.

The more time passed, the more uncertain I was about how I felt about the trial. Did I really want Cathy Smith to go to jail? Would I go to the sentencing? I put these things out of my mind. No sense worrying about it yet.

By the end of May I'd finished assembling the master of "The Best of J.B." and in July I was on the Vineyard again, writing. I'd rented out the Chilmark house, to help it pay for itself, and got a little cottage for myself on the North Shore. I became very disciplined in my daily routine of meditation, exercise, and work. Mitch and Wendie and James and Kathryn were also on the island, so I would often catch up with them or other Vineyard friends for fun. Barbecues were big in the evening, and I was often home and reading in bed by eleven. It was a very productive, quiet summer.

In August, I returned to New York. I was back about a week when my mother called to say that my father needed open heart surgery at the end of the month. He'd had chest pains and finally went to a doctor. Tests led to the decision for a quadruple bypass within the year. He had not been feeling well for some time and the doctor promised the surgery would relieve his symptoms. Dad decided the sooner the better.

My sisters and brother and I talked, and agreed that at least one of us should be there for the operation. The timing was difficult for all of us, but it was easiest for me to re-arrange my schedule. I wanted to be there anyway.

The day of the operation my mother and I were at the hospital early. The surgery took several hours and went basically well, although there were some difficulties. The surgeon explained that they would observe my father a few more hours before sending him to intensive care. We decided to wait there.

During the day, looking around the hospital, I found a chapel. As a kid I had been to the hospital a number of times, but didn't remember it. It was nice; cozy and tranquil. During the operation, I retreated to this room several times, whenever I felt frightened about the possibility of losing my father. I would sit in a chair up front, close my eyes, and visualize him in the operating room. Then I'd send him love, which I felt and visualized as waves of energy. I would imagine him coming out of a successful surgery, making his recovery, and, finally, being in wonderful health. I also prayed that he would feel protected. And that I would not lose sight of my own inner strength, whatever the outcome. I felt better after my visits to the chapel, even if I only sat briefly.

About seven o'clock my father was moved to intensive care. We were warned that he would be gray and bloated, but it was still upsetting to see him. He opened his eyes and seemed to recognize us, then fell back to sleep. Exhausted ourselves, we went home.

My mother and I sat in the kitchen and reported to family and friends by phone. We were finally on our way upstairs when the phone rang again. "You get it, will you?" my mother asked. "I'm just too tired to talk any more." It was the hospital; my father had begun bleeding again and was going back into surgery. My heart dropped. I was numb, afraid to think or to feel. This is it, I told myself. He's not going to make it after all. As we wound our way back to the hospital I was racing inside: It's going to be all right, it's going to be all right ... But another inner voice advised that I find a doctor to give me some Valium. The night was very dark and lonely. My mother sat next to me, puffing at her cigarette. "I'm really scared," she said in a quiet but distinct voice.

"I am, too," I said, and we continued in silence.

At the hospital, I visited the chapel and was able to collect myself in the now familiar room. I never did attempt to find some Valium; I realized I would be all right—whatever happened—without it.

My father pulled through the surgery again, although his recovery was very slow. He was doing okay at first, then on the third day he slipped into a semi-coma, although every once in a while he would respond. Even when he seemed unconscious I talked to him, saying how much we loved and needed him, telling him about my nephew's first days at school or whatever else was going on. And I talked through positive visualizations about getting better. It was a difficult time, but I felt surprisingly okay.

My dad finally regained consciousness, but was disoriented and had no memory of the operation or where he was. He believed he was in some kind of jail and kept asking me to hire a good lawyer to get him out. Still, during this time, as I fed and helped nurse him, we had a couple of wonderful conversations. I asked about his childhood, which he had no trouble remembering. And he shared with me on an emotional level, talking about his feelings and hopes for the future. At one point, when he was confusing a dream with reality, I realized he might be in and out of touch for the rest of his life. How would we cope? I sat with that idea for a minute. A warmth within nearly overwhelmed me, seemed to shine through me. I knew we would be okay; love would see us through. I held my father's hand and listened to his fantasy, appreciating the joy of our having that moment together.

During this ordeal, I realized that for the first time in my adult life I was dealing with a difficult situation without feeling that I wanted to run off to have a drink or smoke some grass. If this was what "growing up" was about, then I liked it. Even though the situation wasn't ideal, I had found that by keeping a strong focus on the love in me, and by trying to share it, everything could be okay.

When I returned to New York, it was time to plan for the release of "The Best of Belushi." Coincidentally, the pre-trial for Cathy Smith finally began. I busied myself with preparations for the publicity party and paid little attention to the news coverage, although every once in a while I would come across something on TV or see a headline. Information I had known for up to three years was now "news." It was odd to know so many of the characters in this unfolding drama, hard to believe that all these people assembled daily to discuss John's death and this woman's responsibility in it; a woman I'd never met, but who was undeniably in my life.

A party for the release of John's video was set for October 6 at the New York Hard Rock Café. The Letterman Band, headed by Paul Shaffer, with Steve on drums, agreed to play. Rhonda, Paul Jacobs, and I would join them on three of Rhonda's songs, including "West Heaven." Then Danny and Billy Murray, along with three of the Blues Brothers' horn players, would perform. It was a hot ticket.

I had agreed to do promotion for the video. Then, of all things, it was announced that the verdict in the Cathy Smith trial would be handed down on the same day the video was scheduled to hit the stores. When I first learned this I balked at the idea of doing any interviews, then agreed to a limited amount. This time I had only one precondition: I would not talk about Cathy Smith.

The party itself was a smash. People were there from every phase of my life with John, and new friends as well. Some flew in from L.A. and Chicago, and, just as amazing, people who never left downtown came up! It was a happy show of support for the project, for John, and for me. The place was packed, but this only added to the excitement. The energy was up, and when the band played, I felt great. The party was exactly what I had wanted it to be. It was that old, good-time feeling of the parties John and I used to throw when we felt as if we owned the city.

In November the court ruled that the evidence against Cathy Smith was sufficient to warrant a trial on charges of murder. In December she appeared before the court and pleaded not guilty. Once again the family was put on hold as to what would happen. For myself, the idea of "one day at a time" was becoming important in all aspects of my life. There was still the likelihood that Smith would plea bargain before a trial ever took place. Still, I knew not to count on it.

After the "Best of . . ." publicity, I took a two-day break on the Vineyard. It was cool and the fall colors were splendid. In the spirit of Halloween, I bought a little pumpkin, forgetting that I was leaving the next day. Driving home, I remembered the last fall that John and I had spent together, much of it on the island. I was commuting to New York three days a week to see Dr. Cyborn, while John stayed in Chilmark, hanging out with Larry. I remembered how proud they were to have spiced up the house with pumpkins, flowers, and dried corn for my return. I had a warm feeling as I saw John in my mind, happy I'd returned from the city. "Do you like this here?" he asked, adjusting the corn hung by the door. In the evening he and Larry played checkers, yelling and pounding the table as if they were playing for their lives. The winner would laugh and chide the other, the loser sulking and planning his revenge in the next game. I saw a checker table in an antique store and bought it for them. John's face lit up when he saw it; a whole table designed for checkers!

I decided to leave the pumpkin at John's grave and pulled into the cemetery. Climbing out of the Jeep, I heard a loud rustling coming from John's plot on the other side of a bush. The sound triggered an image of wind blowing in a forest on a fall day, the dry leaves almost rumbling. What could that be? I felt drawn toward the sound. Once around the bush, I saw the tree in the corner of the plot bending and swaying, with leaves flying from it, as if a giant, mythical bear were shaking it. I stood there stupefied, wondering what was happening. Suddenly, I noticed the swirling leaves in the tree were the shape of a funnel. *John!* I thought, and then my rational mind took over: a small tornado. I watched it twist and bob as it caught in the branches, until, finally, it sort of "hopped" out of the tree and headed toward me. I thought that perhaps I should run, but felt no fear and just stood there watching it kick up dust and debris as it moved closer. It came within a few feet, crossed the road in front of me, and hopped into another bush. In an instant, it shot straight up and disappeared.

I turned and took a quick look around. There was no one else in sight; I was the only one to have seen the "tornado." The tree was still swaying, leaves continued to fall. Wondering if some unusual wind had cut through the cemetery, I sat on the bench beneath the tree. Leaves fell for some time, but fewer and fewer until all was at peace again. I sat long after everything was quiet. It was a clear, still day. I saw nothing else unusual.

Later, at dinner, I told some friends about my experience and asked if they'd ever heard of such a thing. They looked at each other in a funny way, and said it was interesting that they had commented earlier about what a calm day it was. One fellow, a sailor, said it was possible for an isolated whirlwind to develop when a low pressure and high pressure wind met, or some such explanation. "I guess that's what it was," I said. But I don't think any of us believed it.

I visited my parents before Christmas. Dad was doing well; other than a little shuffle in his walk he was recovering beautifully. He enjoyed his therapy class and was proud of his accomplishments. I was so grateful to find his spirits up that I decided to stay at my parents through New Year's.

I was invited to some parties in Chicago for New Year's Eve, but felt like staying low key. My friend Sue Stitt Keller was interested in a quiet time, too, so we met up in Chicago, visited with some friends in the early evening, had dinner, and left for the suburbs about ten-thirty. We stopped at my parents to wish them a Happy New Year, then headed out to Sue's parents, expecting to get there by midnight, but they'd just moved and we ended up lost. Sue and I couldn't help but laugh at ourselves as we drove up and down the quiet streets of Wheaton, trying to find our way, remembering that some fifteen years before we might have been doing basically the same thing, except that we would have been drinking and looking for a party. I told Sue that I'd wanted to do something different this year, and I had. This was the first year since I was sixteen that I'd been completely straight—not even a toast of champagne—for New Year's Eve. I felt good about my life and expected 1986 to be a year of continued growth.

Chapter 32

ANGELS ARE WATCHING

1986

*I*n January I rented a house on the Vineyard to experience winter there. I found a place in Vineyard Haven, close to town with a view of the harbor, and moved in at the end of the month. I originally planned to stay one month but it quickly expanded to three.

I was worried about feeling isolated living alone on the Vineyard, but I found I kept very busy and saw enough of friends not to be lonely. A book entitled *A Course in Miracles* provided daily lessons which I began in earnest. The preface stated that the *Course*'s only purpose "is to provide a way in which some people will be able to find their own Internal Teacher." I soon believed I would be such a student.

My business manager called to tell me about an offer to buy Ninth street. I had recently taken it off the market, after deciding to co-op the building and sell the apartments. That way I could get most of my money out while retaining the coach house. Now a young couple wanted to buy the entire property. They made a very good offer, and would let me rent the coach house and studio for another eighteen months. Looking out on Vineyard Haven harbor, I took in what my manager was saying and observed how peaceful I felt. I wasn't the least bit eager to get back to New York; in fact, I had begun to think I didn't want to return at all. This arrangement was a perfect way to ease into a move. Without hesitation, I agreed to sell.

In the late spring, Cathy Smith entered a plea of no contest to the charges brought against her by the State of California. I was relieved that the drama was finally coming to an end and decided to attend the sentencing if I could. The first court date conflicted with a family gathering, so it was out of the question. That was cancelled and rescheduled for August. The D.A. told Pam he felt this date was firm. I needed to make a West Coast trip, so I made arrangements to be in L.A. at that time.

Another consideration was my option to make a statement to the court. One of the things the *Course* taught was the value of not judging. At first this was confusing and I thought it meant I should say nothing. Then I read in the text: "Teach only love, for that is what you are. Only by teaching it can you learn it." It seemed that somehow I should be able to offer love through my recommendation to the court. Through my lessons I was learning to go within to listen to my Internal Teacher. I needed to listen very hard to discover how to deal with this situation.

As I had the year before, in July I rented out the Chilmark house and got another for myself, a one-bedroom with a small guest house where I set up my office. My first week there, Jimmy visited with Robert.

There was a long wooden walkway from the main house to the guest house (where I slept during Jimmy and Robert's stay) and every morning about six I would hear Robert's footsteps as he ran down to see if I were awake. We had nice talks, the two of us, during those early mornings. Robert was five and half now, a little boy with ideas and observations and questions, questions, questions. It was really the first time we'd spent any significant time together and I enjoyed it very much. One day we fell into a conversation about the Belushi family and just how everyone was related. He wanted to count up all the family members, so we made a list. Robert insisted that we add John because "Uncle John was a Belushi!" he said with certainty.

"That's right, Robert, and I'm a Belushi because I married Uncle John."

"We're all very sad that Uncle John died," he stated, then twirled around on my swivel chair. I wondered how much a child could understand of these things. But then who's to say that adults understand any better?

"Yes, Robert, when Uncle John died, we were all very sad, but as time goes on, the sadness goes away and we remember how lucky we were to have had Uncle John in our lives."

Robert considered this idea. "But we're still sad," he said somewhat determinedly.

"We'll always be sad that Uncle John died so young," I said, "but we aren't always sad. And you know why I'm not sad?" I asked. Robert shook his head. "Because I love Uncle John and always will and that's a good feeling." Robert looked thoughtful for a moment. Suddenly his face lit up.

"My dad is taking me fishing today."

Sentencing day for Cathy Smith rapidly approached. As I considered how to deal with a recommendation to the court, I was especially influenced by the *Course*'s emphasis on the need of forgiveness for healing in one's life. I often repeated lessons that dealt specifically with forgiving, concentrating particularly on Cathy Smith. It wasn't long before I had let go of my vengeful feelings concerning her. And the more I thought about what to say to the court, the more I knew that my main concern was that Cathy Smith needed help with her addiction. And it was society's duty to offer that to her. At the same time, I saw the Belushis in need of what they saw as justice, and a jail term seemed to offer them some satisfaction. I meditated on the issue quite a bit, and kept coming up with the thought "Be true to yourself." It came to me one day that perhaps Pam could write a letter representing all of us. We discussed at length my views and those of the others, and then she went to work.

The first draft arrived, and although it was a good letter, I didn't think my position was clear. I asked Pam to send copies to the family for their suggestions. Several phone calls later, we had a handle on how to represent everyone. Pam reworked it and we had our letter:

Dear Judge Horowitz:

I write on behalf of John Belushi's family: his widow, Judy Jacklin Belushi; his parents, Adam and Agnes Belushi; his sister, Marian; his brothers, Jim and Bill; and my family—his in-laws—the Jacklins. The Court has asked for our views on the proper penalty for Catherine Evelyn Smith, given her plea of no contest to charges of involuntary manslaughter and furnishing illegal narcotics in connection with the death of my brother-in-law.

I was told that it would also be appropriate to share a sense of the loss John's family suffered when he died. I will attempt the first task but can tell you bluntly that I am inadequate to the second. My powers of explanation and expression are insufficient to describe John's importance to his family and the pain of his loss. My sister tried to write you personally. She is an artist and writer by profession; yet she found she could not . . . condense her feelings in a letter. . . . Perhaps we can offer instead, her personal view of John, a five-minute videotape entitled *West Heaven*. . . . The video captures, better than words, the man she loved for 15 years and lost.

With regard to sentencing, the majority of the family supports the imposition of a jail term. Indeed, the maximum allowable penalty seems light. It is difficult to explain to most how probation could even be an option. . . . My sister Judy . . . is concerned, however, that Cathy Smith is in need of rehabilitation, given her past drug dependency, and believes it should be the interest of the Court to see that an attempt is made to help her. While it is reported that Cathy Smith is not now using drugs, Judy knows from experience that abstinence does not heal the problems that lead to drug use. John himself abstained for [the better part of] a year and a half before the involvement that led to his death. For these reasons, Judy believes the cornerstone of Cathy Smith's sentencing should be an effective residential treatment program, whether in prison or otherwise.

As a whole, the family believes it's important to set an example in every drug case. Cathy Smith should not be treated more harshly because her victim was a celebrity; nor, however, should she be treated more leniently because John had a drug problem. John has paid with his life. John's family continues to pay through their suffering. Cathy Smith should pay with a measure of her freedom, just as others have in similar cases. . . .

One possible injustice looms large in our minds. . . . Cathy Smith sold her "confession" to the *National Enquirer*. . . . We do not know whether she has otherwise sold her "story". . . . It would seem to us most improper if Cathy Smith were to profit from John's death. . . . The message our society should send to those who inject heroin and cocaine in others is simple—"No. This is wrong. You will not profit." The Court should use its power to the utmost to support this message.

. . . Thank you for considering our views.

A few days before I was to leave for L.A., Weitzman asked to change the sentencing date. During Cathy Smith's physical (necessary for court proceedings) it was discovered that she was injecting heroin again; it appeared they wanted the extra time for her to straighten out before sentencing. The new D.A. assigned to the case, Eldon Fox, tried to fight the change, but lost. Sentencing was set for September 2.

When I first heard about the change, I was surprised. Maybe I'm not meant to go, after all, I thought. Or maybe Jimmy's not meant to go? He had planned to attend with Pam and me, but he'd be out of the country that week on a publicity tour for his latest film, *About Last Night*. Should I change my plans to accomodate the new date? I thought of all the meetings I would have to cancel and rearrange. My stomach tightened and I felt uncomfortable. I should just have faith this plan is right, and not worry about it. I could extend my stay with Rob and Sandy, then return to L.A. if the sentencing remained on the second. That felt right.

I had a great time on my trip up and down the West Coast. I flew into San Diego and spent two days at Billy Belushi's, then we drove to his father's in Julian. My nephew Adam was visiting and Jimmy came down from L.A. with Robert. One day we all went horseback riding, Jimmy trailing behind, leading Robert's pony. He looked like some old Mexican painting; an hombre slumped in his saddle, straw cowboy hat cocked on his head, a long lead gently pulling along the little boy who was the same proportion to the pony he rode as his father was to his horse.

In L.A. I saw some old friends and had a business meeting.

It felt good to be back without memories haunting me. One day there was a message from Nelson Lyon; he asked me to come by his house. I felt nervous for a moment, but it quickly passed. Deep down I knew it would be good for us to see each other.

I was pleased to see that Nelson looked healthy. He was friendly and gracious and we chatted before he got to the point. He said that after John's death he'd gone through a terrible time. He began drinking again until finally he hit bottom and, fortunately, recognized it. He was thankful he'd pulled himself together, was working at his sobriety and feeling good about life again. Nelson hesitated a moment, gathering his thoughts. He looked me in the eye and said, "I want to apologize for lying to you." I accepted his apology and said I understood. We talked more, sharing stories of recovery. Before leaving I told Nelson I was so happy to see him doing well. He felt the same of me. In our hug I felt a warmth—the power of forgiveness.

In Portland, I spent time with Pam, seeing her new house and hiking up Mt. Hood. I also finally signed a new will. It was something I should have done a long time ago, since John was still the beneficiary on my old will, which would have held things up in the event of my death. For a long time I just didn't care, but now I was again ready to face the responsibility. It felt good knowing everything was in order.

In San Francisco I visited with Rob and Sandy and stayed five days at the Green Gulch Zen Center. There I learned new techniques of meditation and prepared for court. I focused on remaining calm and trusting in the outcome. One of my biggest concerns was how I would react when I saw Cathy Smith in person. Not so long ago, she frightened me or made me angry. I visualized being in the room with her and feeling at peace.

A few days before the court date, I became concerned that Pam wasn't flying in until the morning of the sentencing. What if something went wrong with her flight? I couldn't see myself going alone. It will be all right, I reminded myself. Have faith! The next day Billy called and asked if I'd like him to go with me. I was thrilled.

Billy and I both stayed at Jimmy's house the night before

sentencing. I woke early, did my lesson, and meditated. One of the unknowns of the day was whether I would be able to talk to Cathy alone. Pam told the D.A. I would like to, if he could arrange it. I very much wanted to, although I never thought through what I would say. I knew that if I had the chance, it would come.

Billy looked handsome in his suit and helped me decide what to wear. I made a light breakfast and we joked about our concern with dressing for court. An officer picked us up at the house and we went to the airport for Pam. We arrived at the courthouse a half hour before the proceedings began.

Billy was edgy and paced the halls smoking. When it was time to go to the courtroom, he held my hand, drew a deep breath, and stood tall. Once seated, he, Pam, and I sat close, touching, reassuring one another. Pam was going to make a statement, and I was a little nervous for her. Most of the others in the court were press. They realized we must be family and moved to sit behind us. Suddenly Pam put her hand on my knee and said, "Judy, there's Cathy," motioning with her head toward the defense table. Weitzman, Smith's lawyer turned and looked at us, Cathy did not. I didn't feel any hostility or anxiety when I saw her. She was just a woman; an unhappy-looking woman.

The players in place, the judge entered and got things underway immediately. There was a certain amount of legalese, then Pam was the first to speak. She began by introducing Billy and me and said that Jimmy had wanted to be with us, but due to other commitments, could not. She mentioned that my beliefs led me to abstain from making judgments, and said that "the rest of the family did not feel so limited." I remember smiling and thinking that it seemed to me people were more limited by believing they must make judgments. I felt a little like an observer from another world. Could any of these people understand that had Cathy Smith, or Joe Blow, walked up and shot John, I would still react the same way today? I would still focus on the fact that the attacker was in need of forgiveness and healing.

Pam made an impressive family spokesperson. Billy had his arm around me and whispered that she was good. When she came back to her seat I took her hand.

One thing that stood out was the contrast of Cathy Smith's situation. It appeared as if no one were there with her, except her lawyer. I felt a deep sense of compassion for Cathy. There was no anger, no conflict, only sympathy.

Both lawyers gave their speeches, and I thought both made good points. Weitzman read from our letter that I had recommended rehabilitation, making a dramatic, sweeping turn, pointing, and putting the focus on me as he did so. Billy was edgy when Weitzman spoke. When he read from *Wired*, specifically quoting Jimmy, I whispered in Billy's ear, "It's just as well Jimmy isn't here," and we held back a laugh, knowing how hard it would have been for Jimmy to have remained silent at that moment.

When a recess was called, Weitzman introduced himself, saying he understood I wanted to talk with Cathy. He spoke to her, she nodded her head, and stepped into an outer room. I got up and went over to where he was standing. "I just need approval from the officer," he told me, trying to get the policeman's attention. While we waited, Weitzman spoke to me briefly. I sensed he was sincerely trying to help Cathy, and not just grandstanding as I had once thought. Suddenly it seemed as if everything were set and Weitzman began to open a gate for me to go in. My God, I thought. "I'm going to talk to her ... I wonder what I'm going to say! ... Just then, the D.A. appeared and said he didn't think I should talk to Cathy until the sentencing was over. He stood between me and the door, and I could see he was determined that I wait.

The entire procedure took about two hours. The seats were uncomfortable and I wondered how people did this day after day. Finally the judge gave his sentence. His statement was somewhat long and began with something about John being responsible for his own death. This made Billy angry and I put my hand on his leg. "That fact, however, does not absolve you of responsibility," the judge continued, addressing Cathy. "You provided drugs for several people and you injected those drugs into several people. You did so on a continuing basis and for a substantial period of time. And every time you stuck a needle into someone's arm, you were putting their life at risk. As a result of your actions, John Belushi is dead. That behavior to me is totally unacceptable. And to make it clear to you how unacceptable it is, I believe a prison term is necessary . . ."

The judge ruled that Cathy Smith serve three years in the state prison and she was swiftly ushered from the room like a bad act pulled off the stage with a cane. A few minutes later, the D.A. told me that Cathy did not wish to talk to me now. I wasn't surprised. It didn't seem appropriate to me right then, either.

As we left the courtroom, the usual swarm of press people followed us and yelled questions. We had said inside that we would make no comment, but they need their footage for TV. I remember someone yelling above the confusion, "Judy, do you feel better now that justice has been served?"

Afterward, Pam left directly for the airport and Billy and I went to get something to eat. At first I felt relieved that it was over, than I caught myself feeling sad. I was overwhelmed with what a tragedy John's death was, how it affected so many of us and now a person was going to prison. How odd it was that we sat in a comfortable restaurant while Cathy Smith was probably sitting in a jail cell, waiting to be taken to her new residence. I became concerned that prison was going to lead her deeper into drugs, that she might die there. Then I remembered my commitment not to judge. Just as I could not judge what *should* happen to Cathy Smith, I could not judge what *had* happened to Cathy Smith. She was on her path and I was on mine. Perhaps prison would be good for her. I certainly could not know.

The sentencing completed an important chapter: it was important for me to be in that room, to see the conclusion, and, most important, to see Cathy Smith. And I made my attempt to speak with her, even though it was unsuccessful. At least I tried, and I knew she'd been willing to see me. That felt good. Yes, I thought, everything had fallen into place nicely. But then, angels are watching, after all.

Chapter 33

FULL CIRCLE

JANUARY 1987 . . .

*I*n January 1987, I became a resident of Martha's Vineyard. On the day we closed the sale of Ninth Street, I decided not to rent as planned; I was ready to leave the city. It was time. In just over two months I bought a house, was packed and ready to move.

My last night in New York I went out with Rhonda. I didn't worry that I'd miss the city; I wasn't drawn to it any more and had spent little of the past year there. But I was feeling sad about the distance the move would put between myself and my good friends. All the same, I sensed the change was right. It was finally my adventure, my choice for a new direction for my life. Hey, if I didn't like living there, I could always move back!

It had never occurred to me I might some day live in-town on the island. The Vineyard had always meant solitude and beaches. But there I was, in a big old Americana family home in the historic district, just above the town of Vineyard Haven. I felt the house was right the moment I walked in; it was a "happy" house. I knew just where my furniture would go, how I would use the nine rooms, where I would work. I debated briefly between it and a small, cozy place near Lake Tashmoo that was more embracing and protective—like the coach house. But I realized this was a time for me to be more open. In the bigger house I could visualize family gatherings, friends on retreat, activity! But at the same time, the house did not feel big; the rooms were modest-sized and warm. There wasn't the sense that when alone I would feel lost there.

With the help of my parents and an enthusiastic crew from the Haunted House Cleaning Co., we unpacked the two hundred and some boxes within two weeks. My father spent days at the kitchen sink, washing everything that didn't fit in the dishwasher; New York soot was suddenly more visible in the cleaner environment.

I had room now to hang some items from the Phantom office, which had remained in boxes in the Ninth Street basement the last few years. I wasn't sure how much of "John" to put around. Would it make others uncomfortable? I decided not to worry about others and to put up whatever felt comfortable to me. I filled a shelf in my bookcase with family photos, both Jacklins and Belushis, and put several framed pictures of John, as well as of my close friends, around the house. I hung the gold records, John's framed magazine covers and other awards in the hallway to my office. The office was filled with my own design awards, publicity photos, and some Blues Brothers memorabilia: a Blues Brothers clock from France, one of Jake's hats, the first pair of handcuffs Danny used in the act to attach his briefcase to his wrist. It was nice to have these mementos back, and somehow it all worked in an old seafaring house.

Sixty-five was the average age of the other homeowners in my neighborhood, but I found my neighbors to be interesting and young at heart; true Old Yankee free spirits. Take Hamilton Benz, for example, a widower two houses down. Although a retired stage manager of operatic productions in his late seventies, he continues to teach voice lessons and often treks to Boston for voiceover work. I was honored to receive an invitation for cocktails at his home. His penchant for classic gin martinis was mythical among his young friends on the island, and although I had never tried one, I looked forward to taking part in his ritual. We quickly became good neighbors and friends.

By March, I was ready to get to work on a rewrite of my book. The house and my office were in order, but my creativity was not. For a week I sat in front of my new word processor, trying to remember what it was I had thought to do. This grew tiring and I soon found myself in front of the television. The heat in my den was not working and would not be fixed until spring. So I kept fires going—ah ha, an activity—and spent much of my day in pajamas, wrapped in a blanket, watching TV. At first this concerned me; I felt guilty, I worried I was spending too much time alone, that this was how I would spend the rest of my life—a New Yorker in the wilderness! In my meditations, however, I found a sense of peace with the idea of not working for a while; I gave myself permission to enjoy doing nothing. After two weeks, I suddenly felt clear as to what I needed to do. From then on the work flowed, and I wrote an average of six hours a day, five days a week.

My days were busy and nights were often quiet. I continued to enjoy solitary walks along the beach and the beauty of the island. I tried to finish work in time to watch the sunset, then often swung by Larry's, where I was always welcomed. I met new people and expanded old island friendships. Anne Beatts, Rhonda, my sister Pam, and Jimmy B. all visited that winter. Each visitor sensed my happiness in my new island home.

One evening in mid-May Hamilton called. "My friend, Victor Pisano, who wrote and produced the PBS miniseries I acted in last year, is coming over to make pasta vongole for dinner Friday. He'd like to meet you." Hamilton, who enjoys being provocative, warned, "You must remember to watch out for Victor. He's recently divorced and quite the ladies man. He's Italian, you know . . ." He drew out "Itaaaalian" for emphasis. "You can't trust Italians," he chortled.

Hamilton's house was uncharacteristically active when I arrived—opera was blaring and Victor, or at least I assumed it was Victor, was busily cooking. There was also a woman sitting at the kitchen table. Victor, lean with classic Roman features and dark eyes, had a mass of curly dark hair. I guessed he was in his late thirties. He wore khaki deck shorts—tight and contoured—a look I was never wild about on men, although he did have nice legs. I suddenly felt rather masculine, with my short cropped hair, baggy pants, and impulsive salacious thoughts. Ladies man, I reminded myself . . . Not my type, I immediately concluded.

Hamilton introduced us all. Victor, it was clear, was not

born in Italy. I later learned he was third-generation Italian American, born in the Boston area. The woman, Christina, was a business partner of his from Great Britain, who was putting together a package for a film he'd written about an Irish revolutionary woman. When they talked about it he used a convincing Irish brogue, which was pretty funny. There was a strange mixture of modesty and arrogance about Victor. His words weren't bragging, but I felt his body language was. He didn't pay me much attention and I imagined he had also concluded I was not *his* type. Later in the evening, Hamilton played piano and he and Victor sang grand opera arias. It was an engaging moment, they were both so wrapped up in the music, each trying to out-sing the other.

Before we parted, Victor said he would like to have me to his place for dinner one night. I was surprised he'd asked, and not really sure he would call. Nor was I sure I wanted to go. I decided there was nothing to lose by spending some time with him; he seemed nice enough, and it wouldn't hurt to have a date. One thing's for sure, I thought, I'm not going to sleep with this guy.

Victor picked me up and we drove down a long, wooded road to Lake Tashmoo, where I'd almost rented a cute little house. Arriving at Victor's, I recognized it immediately as the same place. "How odd!" I said. "You know, at sunset I often go to the pier on the other side of the lake, and I've noticed the same light is always on over here. I could place it as this house because of the long pier. I thought maybe no one had rented it and it had been left on by mistake."

"No, I've been writing. I put in a lot of nights. I sit at that table over there." Victor pointed out his setup.

We talked about writing while he put some finishing touches to dinner. A wonderful aroma filled the cottage. I noticed how neat and orderly everything was. We had a cocktail, but I barely drank mine and only had one glass of wine at dinner, not wanting the liquor to affect my judgment. I also observed Victor's drinking, which was minimal.

We had an enjoyable evening. As all good writers should be, Victor was a great storyteller, and he entertained me with colorful tales about his family history. He was very proud of his heritage, as he was of his three children, all girls, ages ten, seven, and four. He showed me photos; all different, each was a beauty in her own right. They lived with their mother outside Boston and he saw them at least every other week. When he spoke about his children it was easy to sense his great love for them, and perhaps a bit of his sadness about the separation of the family. I also saw Victor as handsome for the first time.

I asked how long he'd been divorced and discovered he wasn't; he and his wife had been separated for three years and were making legal moves toward a divorce. He spoke highly of her, but said it had been over between them for some time before they finally split. He prided himself on having been faithfully married for sixteen years, and regretted that it hadn't worked out. His talk was open and honest, without pretense.

Victor had made reference to a car accident that had changed his life, so I asked about it. In England, in the spring of 1985, he'd had a head-on collision. "I was on the wrong side of the road—the left," he quipped. He was pronounced dead at the scene, and gave the paramedics quite a start when he came to in the ambulance. "Ever since then, I've been a different person," Victor said. "Several things changed. For one, I lost thirty pounds almost immediately and never gained it back—sort of a crash diet. I used to have anxieties and concerns, but after the accident I knew something was controlling my life that I had no power over. And I knew, whatever happened, that I was taken care of, so there was nothing to be afraid of anymore, not even death. Now I can't wait to get up every morning."

"Are you afraid of ghosts?" I asked.

He smiled. "I'm not afraid of anything."

When Victor took me home he didn't even attempt a kiss. Curious, I thought, but just as well. I liked him, but couldn't see past becoming friends; we were really very different. Either he was looking to me for friendship, too, or perhaps I wouldn't hear from him again.

A few days later, Victor called. He was at Hamilton's and wondered if he might stop over. It was a warm spring day so I made some tea and we sat on the front porch. I talked more openly about myself this time; I felt comfortable with Victor now. Through our conversation I discovered he was unfamiliar with John's work. He wasn't much of an "SNL" fan; he didn't care for put-down humor, which he thought much of the show was. But he did think John had stood out and, after first seeing him, had predicted John's success. He hadn't seen any of John's films, except for bits and pieces on TV. All the same, Victor said he clearly remembered his thoughts on hearing of John's death. "I was pissed," he said. "I thought it was a waste that such a talented guy was lost, but my heart went out to his wife. I didn't know who you were, but it was you I felt for." Victor didn't understand why people got caught up in drugs. He'd lost his best high-school friend to drugs and never even once tried them, not even grass. "There were times when people put me down for it," said Victor, "but I would just smile. Arrogance, I guess."

I found Victor to be an interesting man with varied experiences, many very different from mine. A noticeable difference was our involvement in sixties culture; his was as a folkie, he'd played acoustic guitar, sung in coffee houses, taught at a free school in Marblehead. He joked that the movement went on without him when Dylan went electric. I was a hippie, into rock 'n' roll and protest; an antiestablishment sensibility that hadn't really left me until recently.

There was a sweetness, an innocence about Victor that I liked. He was sensitive and yet very manly. Although he often spoke in pronouncements, and was quick to defend his position vigorously if he disagreed with you, I admired the fact that he knew who he was and felt good about himself.

On his next visit, Victor gave me a video of *Three Sovereigns for Sarah* starring Vanessa Redgrave the miniseries he'd written and produced about the Salem Witch Trials. It was a powerful tale; I was impressed by both the writing and the quality of the production. Victor also told me he'd be leaving the island for a while, at least until the summer crowds had gone. He wasn't yet sure if he'd return in the fall.

Just before leaving, he asked me out for dinner and dancing. Reluctantly, I turned him down. The sexual tension was growing between us, and I didn't want to get more intimately involved if it couldn't lead to something more.

Over the summer Victor called from time to time. Between
writing and the influx of summer friends on the island I was
very busy. The farther away we got from our last meeting,
the less I felt the closeness that had begun to develop between us; I felt awkward on the phone. But he continued to
call.

Kathryn and James arrived toward the end of August.
Kathryn asked about my book and I said I was near the end
and finding a new strength to share: that a woman could find
happiness on her own, that life could be fulfilling without a
man. Kathryn agreed that this was an important message,
and true. Still, she admitted, being in love could be wonderful. Hadn't I met anyone interesting? I mentioned Victor,
but described him as a momentary flirtation. And anyway,
he'd left the island and probably wasn't coming back to
live. Besides, until I finished my book, I wasn't likely
to find anyone who could put up with me. I needed to put
the book behind me first, to symbolically be done with
the past it represented. Romance somehow didn't seem to
fit in.

In late August, Victor returned for a weekend and was
staying at Hamilton's. I joined them for cocktails—I wore
something more flattering and a little makeup this time—
and found I was surprisingly pleased to see Victor again. He
was all smiles, too. He looked great, in fact, I had to admit he
was one good-looking man! He'd just bought a new Jeep, and
wanted to take me for a drive, so we cruised the island at
sunset, talking away like long-lost friends. When we returned, we went to my house. I was attracted to Victor and
decided to let down my defenses. I can't say exactly what
changed my outlook, it just felt right. I resolved to go with
the moment and forget about having everything figured out.
At first, neither of us took the initiative—a curious, nonag-
gressive standoff took place. Then, all hell broke loose. Victor only returned to Hamilton's for clean clothes that long
weekend.

Victor began making regular weekend visits. At first, I would
feel a bit bewildered upon seeing him—although I knew he
was coming—as if I were afraid he wasn't real, or thought he

might not return. Then there he was, and I'd find myself smiling. We spent a lot of time alone. He often made dinner; he is a fabulous cook and enjoys the process as much as the result. We took long walks on the beach or drove to some secluded spot to watch the sunset, and although we occasionally went dancing, or to a movie, we preferred to spend the evening cuddling in front of the fire.

Early in November, Victor gave me a copy of *Constance*, the screenplay he'd written about the Irish revolutionary. I liked it very much; his sensitivity and sense of the visual and powerful came forth in his work. He seemed to have a special understanding for strong, compassionate, headstrong women.

Shortly after that, Victor asked if he could read some of the book I was working on. I hesitated briefly. My writing was so personal, so telling, it seemed a little as if we should have our time to grow together before he learned about me from my book. I was afraid he would think it was a sign of mistrust, or guardedness on my part if I didn't let him read some. "Well, how about if I give you the first three chapters right now, since they're the most together?" I suggested. While I worked in my office, Victor settled in on the cozy front porch to read.

At the end of the day, I was surprised to find him with the chapters on his lap and a disturbed look on his face. I sat next to him and he gave me a hug and some compliments about my writing. But he was distant and needed to take a walk by himself for a while. It took him a little time after he returned to talk. "I didn't quite finish the chapters," he said. "I don't think I should read anymore. I can't imagine *you* when I read this, Judy, it just seems like someone else to me . . . some other person. And it makes me angry with John for hurting you." Later he told me something else bothered him: there were so many parallels to his own life and to John's family. "The descriptions of John's parents could be of mine. And Nena sounds so much like my grandmother, not exactly, but the energy, the spirit, the love John had for her . . . And although John and I are very different in a lot of ways, I realize we had a lot in common."

We talked for quite a while about Victor's family, John's

family, my family, growing up, pain, love. I was touched by the depth of our conversation.

Victor was bothered by a few odd coincidences he had learned about from his reading. He hadn't realized, for instance, that I was good friends with Kathryn and James. He was currently in the middle of negotiations to produce a PBS music special of James in concert. When Victor had first mentioned this to me, I told him I knew James but didn't go into detail. He now felt awkward, realizing the closeness of our friendship. There were other coincidences that just made him shake his head. It was especially odd to realize that the four Belushi kids and the four Pisano kids were all born within weeks of one another.

We talked late into the night. Victor admitted he felt a little like running away, as if there were something bigger than us going on, and this was the last chance to avoid it. I had similiar feelings, as if I had to choose between two paths, and the one with Victor would dramatically change my life. But we seemed more right for each other every day; we inspired, helped, and challenged each other. Even our arguments brought good results. Our passion was all-embracing.

It didn't take long before I began to notice a change in myself. My mood was decidedly silly when I was alone; I'd find myself lost in thought about Victor, smiling, or dancing around the kitchen as I prepared dinner. I was especially fond of any love song on the radio and began to worry about what to do with my hair—I had to grow it out—and what to wear when I saw *him*. I was seeing myself anew through Victor's eyes; he made me feel pretty and sexy and feminine. And I felt needed—he needed to spend time with me, I could tell—and *I* needed him in my life. I realized that if anything came between us now, I would fight to keep him. One day I realized I had never felt so intensely about anyone but John. It was finally clear; I was in *love*.

Once aware of this new state of existence, I decided to do the unadvisable: tell him. Every woman knows the fastest way to scare off a man is to say the "L" word. But I was sure he loved me, I could see it in his eyes. Of course, I'd heard that before, from many a sorry girlfriend just before she found out she'd been wrong. Well, if I were wrong, then I might as well scare him off now, before I fell any deeper. I softened it a little. "I think I'm falling in love with you," I told him. He was quiet and didn't respond right away. Then he looked me in the eye and said, "I love you, Judy." It sounded right.

Rhonda came to visit for a week in October, and Victor came down that weekend to meet my good friend. He was noticeably nervous at first, I suppose I was, too, but the two of them were quick to hit it off. We sat up late playing music and singing. The next night at dinner, I could tell Victor was pleased to be accepted by Rhonda. I was thrilled that they liked each other.

Victor's mother sensed something different in her son and wanted to meet me, so I was invited to Thanksgiving at his parents in Nahant. Victor's kids, grandmother, his two sisters and their families would also be there. We would spend the night, ". . . but in separate rooms." He shrugged apologetically.

Needless to say, I was nervous. I wondered if Victor's daughters would be upset that a girlfriend was coming to a family gathering, but Victor said they would be fine. "Maybe they'll think I'm getting in the way of your getting back together with their mom," I suggested. Victor assured me they were adjusted to the separation. "My kids look through the Sears catalogue and select women they think would be good for me. They're very excited about meeting you."

I drove to Nahant Thanksgiving morning, and easily found the Pisano home, a large coach house, of all things. Victor, his father, and his three children all greeted me at the door. His father, who looked nothing like Adam Belushi nor spoke with an accent, was reminiscent of him all the same—in carriage and natural dignity. Mrs. Pisano would have been easy to pick out of a crowd; Victor looks very much like her. She is very attractive and looks much younger than her years. She was friendly, full of energy, and clearly loved having her home filled with family. It struck me that she and Agnes would get on like sisters.

Victor introduced me to everyone while his youngest daughter, Vanessa, peered at me with big hazel eyes from behind Victor's leg. Her shoulder-length, blond curls were worthy of an angel. "How old are you, Vanessa?" I asked, although I knew the answer. She hesitated a minute, not sure she wanted to speak to me yet. "Three," she replied. Suddenly her expression brightened. "But I be four soon!" She looked up at Victor. "When I be four, Daddy?"

"In six days, Nessie!" Daddy said emphatically.

"Six days," she repeated. "That not long," she stated with a look which said she knew this for a fact. By the end of the evening Vanessa was on my lap, hugging me tenderly. Shirley Temple had nothin' on this kid.

The older girls were more reserved at first. Rebecca, or "Becca," stared at me a lot and smiled. She was seven with long, straight, chestnut hair and cute as a button. She had an unusual grace, an ease with people, and a quick mind; clearly a leader. Becca spoke to me freely, and often, and soon was taking my hand when she did so.

Jessie was not unfriendly, but kept her distance. She was blond, tall, and lanky; a young Donna Dixon and at ten she no longer had that innocence which allowed the younger two to accept me immediately. She was shy, often looking away when we talked, or gazing at me with her head slightly bowed, her expressive eyes curious.

I enjoyed the day with Victor's family. I felt welcomed by everyone, and especially by his grandmother Votano. "Ma" is in her nineties, small and frail but full of spunk. She is one of those rare people whose spirit grabs you the first time you meet. As soon as she saw me, she opened her arms to embrace me and said, "Oh, Judee, I lova you," in a sweet, high-pitched voice. Later she came to me in the kitchen and said, shaking a finger at me, "You staya witha Vickie. Vickie's a gooda man, he lova you, I aska him. He's a gooda for you. Ya," she nodded determinedly, a knowing gesture, "you be gooda together." She held my face in her hands and gave me a kiss. "I lova you, Judee!"

The James Taylor Special was set to be shot in December. I felt a little nervous, having my lover produce a show for a friend. And since from the time I knew Victor he was already negotiating with James, I hadn't felt it was appropriate to tell James and Kathryn how involved we were; they simply knew we'd dated.

Victor's production office for James' Special was a Boston hotel where we stayed the week before the concert. I was impressed with the preproduction work; Victor's crews seemed good and on the ball, the theater he selected was beautiful and every seat in the house was good. Things seemed well in place for James to work his magic. During the week, I also enjoyed getting to know Boston, sometimes with Victor as tour guide, sometimes on my own.

Kathryn and James arrived, and while the men worked Kathryn and I went for lunch. I finally felt free to tell her I was in love; it wasn't just "an affair," but a wonderful romance. She looked at me as if trying to read my soul; could it really be true? Perhaps a moment of skepticism . . . then happiness. "At last, Jude!"

The concert was fun. Victor's daughter Jessie sat with me; she was excited because it was her first rock 'n roll show. It was good for us to spend time together, to begin to be at ease with each other. James was magnificent and it was an honor to see him perform in such an intimate house; a jewel box, he called it. Afterward, I was relieved to know that Victor had done a good job—a great job—and that James would have a terrific special. I was also pleased that James went out of his way to spend some time with Victor after the concert. Kathryn had obviously told him my news.

My parents came for Christmas, but of course they were mainly interested in meeting Victor. They couldn't have been more pleased; they thought he was great and were so happy that there was a good man in my life again. I know my mom went home with dreams of wedding bells.

Victor and I spent a quiet, romantic New Year together, ushering in 1988 with hopes for continued happiness. Around that first week of January he began talking about renting another place on the island; we wanted to be together as much as possible and all this traveling back and forth was getting to us. But it seemed an unnecessary expense to get another place; I suggested that perhaps he should consider moving in with me. Victor was adamant: he would not move in with me. Until we could get a place together, we would not live together. What would people think of a man moving in with me? He wouldn't have it!

Our decision took a month of "discussions." Victor didn't like the idea, but clearly it would take us a few years before we could make a move that would be suitable for both our needs, and we both wanted to be together, now. But he wouldn't move in until his divorce papers were signed, which he expected to happen in February. Allowing for delays, and working around a few other scheduling problems, we decided he would officially move in on April 9.

The first of March, I went to Nahant to be with Victor. I was returning to the island for the weekend, and when he realized the fifth was the anniversary of John's death, he changed his plans to return home with me on the fourth.

March 6, 1988, Sunday

Victor and I drove back together Fri. We must have gone to sleep about eleven, and I woke up, wide awake, at two-thirty. There was a brilliant full moon—I felt as if its pull had shaken me awake. I got up and went to my office, turned on the TV, and put things away. I decided to look for some documents I need to find for a lawsuit with the Commonwealth over John's residency at time of death. Before I knew it, I was shuffling through copies of police and coroner's reports, searching for a form an officer filled out the day John died. I thought it probably had his residency. It was odd that I would be doing that on this date, I knew, and yet it was interesting. I didn't get hung up reading details, I simply flipped through the papers looking only at forms.

Perhaps it was some kind of test of how far I've come since those papers first entered my life. Going through them didn't get me down. Some are familiar to me now, like pages from a book that I remember, not only the contents, but the emotional turmoil they caused. Looking at these papers I remembered, but did not react, did not relive the emotions.

After I finished going through all the files, I read for a while. The sun was rising when I finally began to feel drowsy. I watched the big red ball of sun slowly peek over the horizon. It was a beautiful day, this March fifth.

I slept till almost ten and had a leisurely morning. Victor said he would make breakfast for me, "since this is an important day to you." He was very sweet. I knew the fridge was bare, since we'd been gone a few days, but he said he'd find something. Shortly, he carried a pretty tray of food, juice, and coffee to the den. "I heated up this quiche you had in the freezer," he said. It was the peta John's mother had made when she last visited. I'd forgotten I had any left. "I don't even think about these coincidences any more," Victor said. "Obviously we were meant to have this peta today."

In the afternoon we went out to the cemetery, stopping at a friend's to see some new spring lambs. They were adorable. The flowers at the grave looked nice, and once again I found a bouquet from my family. I recalled how that had once made me burst out crying. Victor and I sat a while on the bench. I talked some about the gravesite. It was nervous talk, I felt I had to say something. "Let's have a moment of silence," Victor said, taking my hand. In the silence, I prayed. Then he and I took a walk around the cemetery before we headed home.

Anne sent flowers and a few people called. About four I meditated, a very joyous meditation. We made a nice dinner and went to a movie with a friend. It was a good day.

Victor needed to go home Sunday and took the last ferry. I drove him to the boat and we stopped at the store. Waiting in the car, I suddenly looked up and saw him standing outside, looking at me. I was surprised to see him and reacted, smiling and giving a quick little wave. I immediately recognized it as the same reaction I'd had the last time I saw John alive. I'd turned and looked out the cab window and was surprised to see John watching me. I smiled and waved. It felt exactly the same, that wave, the way I did it, the way it had surprised me to see John looking at me and how it made me smile. I had a momentary fear that this was a bad omen. Perhaps I would never see Victor again. I pushed that idea from my mind and replaced it with a happy one. Later, at home, I thought about it again briefly. No, the energy is good in my life now. I will not live in fear, but in the Light. What will become of Victor and me is based on hope and faith. He may not be with me always, but his love will, and that is enough. Day by day I can only try to enjoy all that has been given me, to share what I can, and to be who I am.

*   *   *

Mid-March I made a quick trip to L.A. on business. I stayed with Jimmy and was able to see several friends including Mitch and Wendie who were out there working, Tino and Dana, Laraine Newman, Deanne, and the Landises. It was great to see people and have them remark that I was looking well. I felt good; there was nothing but freshness to our laughter. I sensed that my friends knew I was truly happy, that my happiness was infectious.

Jimmy asked about my finances, was I secure? I told him things were good; I was still dealing with a few repercussions of my problems, my budget was tight compared to what it had once been, but I had no complaints. Jimmy was also doing well. He finally felt confident about his career and was making good money. As he spoke, I felt a sense of pride in him; he was successful and working hard. With a very serious look he suddenly announced, "I think it's time I take on all the financial responsibilities of the Belushi family that you've been carrying. You've been wonderful, you've made it easier for me to reach financial stability, and I can handle it now."

My conversation with Jimmy stirred up unfinished personal business. Mark Lipsky was now living in L.A. and although I'd forgiven him in my heart, we still had not spoken since I left his firm. I phoned, feeling a little nervous, but Mark sounded sincerely happy to hear from me; it was nice to hear his voice again, to hear he was doing well. "One thing I want to say, Mark, is that even though some things went amiss, everything has worked out. And there were a lot of good things you did for me." It felt good to clear the air with my old friend, to put our dispute behind us. We were friends again.

I also saw Billy Murray on the set of *Scrooged*. It was fun to be there, Billy looked good and was in a great, playful mood. Sitting in his trailer, I told him that I had fallen in love, and was going to live with Victor. His face suddenly took on the expression of "the honker," a character I first saw him develop in New York, when he would stand in the street and direct traffic like a bum. His jaw jutted out to one side and he looked me square in the eye. In an almost cartoon voice, talking out of the side of his mouth, he said, "You would desecrate John's memory in such a manner."

Only Billy could make that funny. I laughed heartily, knowing it was another sign of my good health. My trip was a success, but still, I couldn't wait to get back to my little island and Victor. Home.

I awoke on April ninth excited at the thought that Victor would arrive with his vanload of possessions at the end of the day. I had been preparing the house for his arrival, emptying one room that would become his office, ordering another dresser, clearing out half my bedroom closet. Anne Beatts had visited over the weekend and helped me with the closet. It was a good purge, one that called for help from someone not afflicted by the emotional attachment you can feel for your old clothes. And I only snuck one or two items into another closet when she wasn't looking.

A decision I alone could make was to put away many of John's photos. I had bought a book for widows and widowers called *Starting Over* and it contended that, when remarried, you should "get rid of the ghosts." I didn't agree altogether, but it was inappropriate to have so many photos of John around now that I would share the house with another love. I knew having some remembrances of John placed about wouldn't bother Victor—that was one of the reasons I loved him. I left a photo out as well as the awards and magazine covers hanging in the hallway to my office.

The integrating of Victor's things into the house went fairly well. It was uncanny how well our possessions meshed, and how Victor had exactly the items I was missing. For instance, I had a dining table and chairs, and a few small pieces to hold dishes, but no credenza or substantial piece for the dining room. Victor had two matching pieces with shelves which fit in perfectly, finishing off the room. The most symbolic example was a deck table for which I had no umbrella. Wouldn't you know, Victor had an umbrella to match, but no table.

As Victor began to set out his personal items—knickknacks, mementos, bowls and cups he wanted out—I felt a little uncomfortable. He was sensitive, asking "How about this here?" or "What do you think?" But I had lived alone some time now, and for a moment every change seemed monumental. I decided it was a good idea to let him put things as he liked, then live with them a while before reacting. Within days, most everything began to blend. It was nice to combine our lives.

Overall, I think Victor and I adjusted to living together quite well very quickly. I had forgotten how much give and take there must be, but when you love your partner, it's worth it. I enjoyed Victor's spirit, his energy in the morning, the joy with which he woke, his singing in the shower. I liked to hear the music he played on the stereo filter through the house. Some mornings he would enthusiastically sing for a while before he'd begin to write, or play along to Irish songs on his pennywhistle. One morning I heard a rousing orchestration of The Star Spangled Banner blare forth, then over the house intercom, "Ladies and Gentlemen, the President of the United States," followed by a long, enthusiastic, wolflike howl.

Interestingly, that first month I found myself thinking of John more than I had for quite a while. Victor's antics often reminded me of him: the way John used to enjoy running in to give me bulletins about the day, the way he danced around when he was excited about something. Old memories kept surfacing unexpectedly. I remembered John's discovery of Mozart and his decision to be a conductor—if only in front of the stereo. I recalled how he came home one Valentine's Day, led me by the hand into the sound room, put a record on, got down on one knee, and sang along with Elvis Costello to "My Funny Valentine." The memories were nice, not sad—not even a little. I realized that although I would always love John, it was very different than the love we shared when he was alive. He would always hold a special place in my heart, but the man who held my heart now—the man who filled my mind, sparked my passion and shared my dreams—was very definitely Victor.

Once we were settled, it was Victor's turn to be subjected to the stress of meeting a stream of family members. Jimmy was the first to come. His visit was important, sort of a bestowing of blessings. We were all nervous, but Victor paid Jim the respect of being my "brother" and Jimmy paid Victor the respect of being the man in my life. My sisters both came to visit within a few months. I felt they had accepted Victor from the minute they heard about him, knowing that I loved him. Billy Belushi's visit was the first marked with some tension. He took Victor to task some, testing. Victor stood his ground and they slowly began to get a sense of each other; perhaps, ultimately, becoming all the closer for it.

Victor contended through all this that he didn't really care what anyone thought of him except me and my parents. Regardless, he tried very hard to understand everyone's protective feelings and to be as giving as he could, knowing that people wanted to see just who he was. He made wonderful meals for everyone and cut short his writing to spend more time with our various guests.

Just when he thought he was done with the pressure, Danny and Donna came to the island. We invited them for an early dinner and, as with my family, Victor was very concerned to have everything just right. Donna later told me that Danny had been nervous and flustered all day. He was quiet throughout the meal, sitting close to Donna with his arm around her. She and Victor did most of the talking, largely about art and music. Donna kept giving me a knowing smile, sensing the intensity of my feelings for Victor. Later we heard from several people that Danny told them what a wonderful guy Victor was, saying he was perfect for me.

We had fewer guests over the summer, as we rented out the Chilmark house and had Victor's kids with us much of the time. Each visit became more relaxed as the kids began to feel comfortable in the house and neighborhood.

During the fall we were visited by Agnes and then Marian Belushi, and each got on famously with Victor. I felt good that my late husband's family was so supportive. Aggie expressed her desire to still be "Mom." I assured her she was Mom in my heart, nothing could ever change that. She took to Victor immediately; and he to her. Agnes was very happy for me.

The approaching Thanksgiving holiday was happily anticipated. My mom and dad would be with us, as would Victor's girls. We were excited about their meeting each other and Victor had been telling the girls to be on their best behavior for weeks. I had no doubt my parents would love them. It was not so long ago that the meaning of Thanksgiving had escaped me. This year I knew how truly blessed I was.

We had to adjust our usual sleeping arrangements to accommodate everyone. The two older girls turned over their customary room to my parents and we made a makeshift bedroom out of my office. Everyone was settled in a few days before Thanksgiving.

We took care of various dinner preparations the night before, and got up early Thanksgiving day to get the turkey in the oven. My mother and I were in the kitchen, pulling breakfast together, when I heard Becca and Jessie giggling behind me. "Judy," one of them said, "we need your keys." I turned to see the two, shoulder to shoulder, their adjoining wrists in the air. They were handcuffed together! They had found the old Blues Brothers prop. Unfortunately, I had long since lost the key. In fact, these cuffs had quickly been replaced, for show use, by a set that could not lock, to avoid just such an occurrence. "I don't have a key," I told the two little trusting faces. They didn't believe me. My mother knew from my expression that I was telling the truth. We both found the situation unbearably funny. Victor entered to hear the bad news.

"Oh, sure, this is real funny," Victor said. The girls were beginning to realize their situation. "I didn't put them on, Jessie did!" Becca informed us.

"What are we going to do?" Jessie asked. "What if I have to go to the bathroom?"

"This will be a good lesson in cooperation," my mother offered.

"Well, I'm going to have to help them brush their hair," Victor said. He took one by the hand and the chain gang started out of the room.

"What shall we do?" I asked.

Victor stopped and looked at me seriously. "Just set two places *real* close together . . ." As they headed up the stairs, Becca was heard to say, "I hate you, Jessie!"

Locksmiths, like many other folk on the island, do not work on Thanksgiving. In fact, the only one listed in the yellow pages seemed to have gone away for the holiday. We had no recourse but to call the police.

Now, consider the conclusions an officer might draw when you say you have children in handcuffs. I introduced myself to the dispatcher and carefully explained. "Well, you see, we have quite a houseful here for the holiday, so we've put Victor's two older girls in my office, and . . . well, I don't know if you remember, but when John and Danny used to perform as the Blues Brothers, Danny would attach his briefcase to his wrist with handcuffs . . . Um, well, I had the cuffs displayed in my office and this morning the girls spied them, and, well, being curious, slipped them on. Unfortunately, I have no key . . ."

The dispatcher, who had patiently listened to my rambling explanation, burst out laughing. Once she had laughed herself out, she said someone would be right over.

Two police officers arrived promptly and entered looking very official. The girls had become very quiet, afraid that perhaps they'd done something illegal. At a glance, the officers knew their key would not work. In a valiant effort to avoid ruining the keepsake cuffs, one of the officers requested a bobby pin. He struggled with the first lock for nearly fifteen minutes. Suddenly Becca jumped up, her wrist raised in triumph, shouting, "I'm free!" Jessie was out in a matter of minutes.

We were fortunate to have the girls again at Christmas. The handcuffs were hidden away and the presents were purchased. Victor had promised me the best Christmas ever and I was probably as excited as any of the kids.

After hours of opening presents, all that was left were some things for Victor and me from friends, so we told the kids they could go ahead and play with their gifts. They gleefully ran off to do so. When we got to the last present, Victor said, "Oh, this one's from me." I opened the package and found a replica of the Old State House in Boston, one of the landmarks he'd shown me when we first walked the city together. The tower came off—the replica was also a box. I admired the detailed work while Victor sat quietly. Finally, I lifted the roof. Inside was another gift, obviously earrings or a ring. I opened it and was surprised to find a beautiful gold band ringed with sapphires and diamonds. It looked like a wedding ring. I just stared at it.

"You know what it is, don't you?" Victor asked.

"What is it?"

"Don't you know?"

"No, what is it?" I asked again.

"Well," he cleared his throat, "it's sort of an engagement ring."

"What do you mean, sort of?"

"Well, it's an engagement ring."

I blushed and hugged him. This was so totally unexpected. We laughed. Victor kissed my neck. "So what do you say?"

"Well, I'd like to be engaged," I said. It still seemed so unexpected—well, not unexpected, but sudden. I mean, wasn't this the kind of thing you planned? We did say before we started living together that it was a step toward marriage, but, to commit myself? Was I ready?

"Listen, I know we need more time—we can take all the time we want," Victor said, "but I told you, you mean the world to me. I love you and when you're ready, I want us to marry." I held on to him. I did love him. I wanted to be his wife. "Maybe I should get down on my knee," he said, doing so. "Judy, will you accept my engagement?" We both laughed at the choice of words.

I looked into his eyes and said, "I accept your proposal of engagement." We sealed it with a kiss.

Becca came back into the room. Victor and I were beaming; she knew something was up. "Look at what your dad just gave me," I said, extending my hand. "We're engaged."

Becca let out a whoop and ran off to tell the other girls. I knew that saying yes to Victor was not only a commitment to him, but to his three daughters as well. They could retire the Sears catalogue.

As the shock wore off, I was very happy about Victor's proposal. "I've never been a fiancée before," I pointed out. "This is something new." Later, Jessie said to me, "When you and Dad get married, Becca and I want to give you 'something old, something new, something borrowed . . .' " I imagined the girls in the wedding procession. I saw Victor, handsome and smiling, take my hand for the vows. I recalled an old dream, with a faceless groom. Gone now are the nightmares. I imagined telling my brother, "I never thought I'd be this happy again."